Chinese Naval Shipbuilding

Titles in the Series

China's Future Nuclear Submarine Force

China's Energy Strategy: The Impact on Beijing's Maritime Policies

*China Goes to Sea: Maritime Transformation in
Comparative Historical Perspective*

*China, the United States and 21st-Century Sea Power:
Defining a Maritime Security Partnership*

Chinese Aerospace Power: Evolving Maritime Roles

Studies in Chinese Maritime Development

Andrew S. Erickson, editor

POWERED BY THE WORLD'S second largest economy and defense budget, China is going to sea with a scale and sophistication that no continental power ever before sustained in the modern era. Its three sea forces are all leaders in their own right: the world's second-largest blue water navy, the world's largest blue water coast guard, and the world's largest (and virtually only) maritime militia.

While paramount leader Xi Jinping is working to transform his nation further into a "great maritime power," at a minimum today's Middle Kingdom is already a hybrid land-sea power. Amid European decline and American fiscal and strategic challenges, this historic transformation has the potential to end six centuries of largely Western dominance of the world's oceans. To properly inform its strategy and policy, the U.S. Navy and nation must understand this momentous sea change.

Since its establishment in 2006 the China Maritime Studies Institute has been conducting research and holding conferences covering the broad waterfront of Chinese oceanic efforts in order to advise U.S. Navy leadership and support the Naval War College in its core mission area of helping to define the future Navy. The Studies in Chinese Maritime Development series assembles the resulting proceedings into edited volumes focusing on specific topics of importance to further understand the dynamics of these changes.

Chinese Naval Shipbuilding

An Ambitious and Uncertain Course

Edited by Andrew S. Erickson

NAVAL INSTITUTE PRESS
Annapolis, Maryland

This book was made possible through the dedication of the U.S. Naval Academy Class of 1945.

Naval Institute Press
291 Wood Road
Annapolis, MD 21402

First Naval Institute Press paperback edition published in 2023.
ISBN: 978-1-68247-900-1 (paperback)

The Library of Congress has cataloged the hardcover edition as follows:
Names: Erickson, Andrew S., editor of compilation.
Title: Chinese naval shipbuilding : an ambitious and uncertain course / edited by Andrew S. Erickson.
Description: Annapolis, Maryland : Naval Institute Press, [2016] | Series: Studies in Chinese maritime development | Includes bibliographical references and index.
Identifiers: LCCN 2016043787 (print) | LCCN 2016044864 (ebook) | ISBN 9781682470817 (hardcover : alk. paper) | ISBN 9781682470824 (ePDF) | ISBN 9781682470824 (epub) | ISBN 9781682470824 (mobi)
Subjects: LCSH: Shipbuilding industry--China. | China. Zhongguo ren min jie fang jun. Hai jun. | Warships--China.
Classification: LCC VM299.7.C6 C55 2016 (print) | LCC VM299.7.C6 (ebook) | DDC 338.4/76238250951--dc23
LC record available at https://lccn.loc.gov/2016043787

♾ Print editions meet the requirements of ANSI/NISO z39.48-1992 (Permanence of Paper).
Printed in the United States of America.

31 30 29 28 27 26 25 24 23   9 8 7 6 5 4 3 2 1
First printing

Contents

List of Exhibits   xi

Acknowledgments   xiii

Introduction. China's Military Shipbuilding Industry   1
Steams Ahead, On What Course?
Andrew S. Erickson

Part I. FOUNDATION AND RESOURCES

Warfare Drivers: Mission Needs and the Impact   19
on Ship Design
Christopher P. Carlson and Jack Bianchi

Status, Goals, Prospects: Party-State Strategic Requirements   41
for China's Shipbuilding Industry
Morgan Clemens and Ian Easton

Resources for China's State Shipbuilders: 62
Now Including Global Capital Markets
Gabe Collins and Eric Anderson

Part II. SHIPYARD INFRASTRUCTURE

Key Factors in Chinese Shipyards' Development and   75
Performance: Commercial-Military Synergy and Divergence
Sue Hall and Audrye Wong

China's Naval Strength: Current and Future   107
Alex Pape and Tate Nurkin

Monitoring Chinese Shipbuilding Facilities   134
with Satellite Imagery
Sean O'Connor and Jordan Wilson

Civil-Military Integration Potential in Chinese Shipbuilding   144
Daniel Alderman and Rush Doshi

Part III. NAVAL ARCHITECTURE AND DESIGN

PLAN Warship Construction and Standardization   167
Mark Metcalf

China's Military Shipbuilding Research, Development, and   177
Acquisition System
Kevin Pollpeter and Mark Stokes

China's Civilian Shipbuilding in Competitive Context: 189
An Asian Industrial Perspective
Julian Snelder

Part IV. REMAINING SHIPBUILDING CHALLENGES

PLA Shipboard Electronics: Impeding China's   221
Naval Modernization
Leigh Ann Ragland-Luce and John Costello

Underpowered: Chinese Conventional and   238
Nuclear Naval Power and Propulsion
Andrew S. Erickson, Jonathan Ray, and Robert T. Forte

China's Aircraft Carrier Program: Drivers, Developments,   249
Implications
*Andrew Scobell, Michael E. McMahon, Cortez A. Cooper III,
and Arthur Chan*

Part V. CONCLUSIONS AND ALTERNATIVE FUTURES

Maximal Scenario: Expansive Naval Trajectory to   261
"China's Naval Dream"
James E. Fanell and Scott Cheney-Peters

Medium Scenario: World's Second "Far Seas" Navy by 2020   274
Michael McDevitt

Technological "Wild Cards" and Twenty-First-Century   296
Naval Warfare
Paul Scharre and Tyler Jost

How China's Shipbuilding Output Might Affect   317
Requirements for U.S. Navy Capabilities
Ronald O'Rourke

List of Acronyms   333
About the Contributors   337
Index   341

Exhibits

Exhibit 0-1. Significant Chinese Naval Shipyards   xv

Exhibit 0-2. China's Primary Naval Order of Battle   xvi
              (Major Combatants), 1985–2030

Exhibit 1-1. Evolution of China's Naval Strategy—Impact on PLAN   28
              Warfare Area Capabilities

Exhibit 4-1. Shipbuilding Production Trends since 1990   76
              (in millions of compensated gross tons)

Exhibit 4-2. Historical Shipbuilding Production   78
              (in millions of gross tons)

Exhibit 4-3. Trends in Production, Ordering, and Forward   80
              Orderbook for World Shipbuilding (in millions
              of compensated gross tons)

Exhibit 4-4. World Historical Production and Orderbook Phasing   82
              (in millions of compensated gross tons)

Exhibit 4-5. China's Historical Production and Orderbook Phasing   83

Exhibit 4-6. Top 20 Chinese Shipbuilders from *China's Shipyards*   86
              Report 2003

Exhibit 4-7. Top 20 Chinese Shipbuilders, 2012   88

Exhibit 4-8. Shipbuilding Throughput Comparison   93
              of Major Shipbuilders

Exhibit 4-9. Shipbuilding Throughput Changes for   95
              Chinese Shipbuilders

Exhibit 4-10. New Ship Price Volatility   96

Exhibit 4-11. Complexity Ranking of Ships According to Average   100
Compensated Gross Ton (CGT) Coefficient

Exhibit 4-12. Composition of Chinese Shipbuilding Production   102
by Size and Complexity

Exhibit 5-1. Estimated Chinese Investment in Naval Ship Construction   108
by Type, 2010–24

Exhibit 5-2. Bohai (Huludao) Shipyard Military Output, 2006–30   123

Exhibit 5-3. Wuchang (Wuhan) Shipyard Military Output, 2006–30   124

Exhibit 5-4. Jiangnan (Shanghai) Shipyard Military Output, 2006–30   126

Exhibit 5-5. Hudong (Shanghai) Shipyard Military Output, 2006–30   128

Exhibit 5-6. Huangpu (Guangzhou) Shipyard Military Output, 2006–30   131

Exhibit 6-1. Configuration and Growth of China's Huludao Shipyard   139

Exhibit 7-1. China's White-Listed Shipyards   151

Exhibit 8-1. Types of GJBs (*Guojia Junyong Biaozhun*, PRC National   168
Military Standards)

Exhibit 8-2. Electromagnetic Compatibility—GJBs and MIL-STDs   169

Exhibit 8-3. GJB 4000-2000 Subject Areas   171

Exhibit 9-1. China's IDAR Technology Innovation Process   178

Exhibit 9-2. First Five Stages in Military Shipbuilding Research and   181
Development Process

Exhibit 9-3. Primary Organizations Involved in China's   183
Military Shipbuilding

Exhibit 10-1. Experts' Assessment of China Capability Gap   204
versus Class Leader

Exhibit 11-1. Key Shipbuilding Organizations Specializing in   228
Shipboard Electronics

Exhibit 14-1. PLAN—Platform Inventory in 2015   269

Exhibit 14-2. PLAN 2030—Forecast Platform Inventory   270

Exhibit 15-1. Far Seas Navies' Major Ships, circa 2020   288

Exhibit 15-2. Major Far Seas Ships, PLAN versus U.S. Navy, circa 2020   289

Acknowledgments

ON BEHALF OF THE China Maritime Studies Institute (CMSI), the editor thanks the Naval War College (NWC) Foundation for its important contributions in support of CMSI's 2015 annual conference and this resulting volume. The foundation's generosity has long played a crucial role in ensuring that such events and the publications that flow from them are of the highest caliber, and this past year has offered a particularly important example of that invaluable partnership.

As with all CMSI events and conference volumes, countless individuals have made vital contributions. While it is not possible to list them individually, the editor extends his sincere gratitude to all concerned. The support of the leadership of NWC, and of the U.S. Navy more broadly, has been crucial to our efforts. Finally, the Naval Institute Press is to be commended for its professionalism and dedication to the Studies in Chinese Maritime Development series in which this sixth volume appears. That series is the product of nearly a decade of constructive collaboration between two vital historic centers of American thinking on sea power: Annapolis and Newport.

ANDREW SVEN ERICKSON
NEWPORT, RHODE ISLAND
DECEMBER 2015

Exhibit 0-1. Significant Chinese Naval Shipyards

Map ID	Name	Latitude	Longitude
A	Huludao	40.717326 N	120.991750 E
B	Tianjin	38.994199 N	117.719167 E
C	Liaonan	38.801336 N	121.262866 E
D	Dalian	38.933534 N	121.640857 E
E	Jiangnan Changxing	31.347424 N	121.745001 E
F	Shanghai Zhonghua	31.258106 N	121.549125 E
F	Hudong Zhonghua	31.277320 N	121.569153 E
F	Shanghai	31.282742 N	121.560389 E
G	Wuhu	31.347728 N	118.352072 E
H	Wuchang	30.532536 N	114.286921 E
I	Liuzhou-Xijiang	24.305967 N	109.459692 E
J	Wuzhou-Guijiang	23.503942 N	111.320142 E
K	Guangzhou	23.073052 N	113.250160 E
K	Guangzhou-Huangpu	23.087421 N	113.415596 E
L	Guangzhou-Longxue	22.700191 N	113.650256 E
M	Zhanjiang	21.234871 N	110.420401 E

Exhibit 0-2. China's Primary Naval Order of Battle (Major Combatants), 1985–2030

Year	Ballistic Missile Submarines (SSBNs)	Nuclear-powered Attack Submarines (SSNs)	Diesel Attack Submarines (SSs)	TOTAL SUBMARINES	Aircraft Carriers	Destroyers	Frigates	Corvettes	Larger Amphibious Ships: LSTs & LPDs	Smaller Amphibious Ships: LSMs	Missile Patrol Craft	TOTAL SURFACE SHIPS	TOTAL NAVAL VESSELS
1985	1	2 <0%>	100 <0%>	103	0	14 <0%>	22 <0%>	0	N/A		333 (28 Hainan Type 037, 305 Shanghai III/Type 072/I)	369	472
1990	(1)	(4) <0%>	(88) <0%>	(93)	(0)	(19) <0%>	(37) <0%>	(0)	(58)		(215)	(329)	(422)
1995	(1)	(5) <0%>	(43) <0%>	(49)	(0)	(18) <5%>	(37) <8%>	(0)	N/A	N/A	(217)	(272)	(312)
2000	(1)	5 (5) <0%>	~60 (60) <7%>	~65 (66)	0 (0)	~20 (21) <20%>	~40 (37) <25%>	(0)	Almost 50 (60)		(100)	~110 (218)	~175 (284)
2002	N/A	5	~60	~65	0	>60	~60	N/A	>40	~40	~50	~150	~215
2003	N/A	~60	N/A	~60	0			N/A			~50	~150+	~210+
2005	(2)	6 (6) <33%>	51 (51) <40%>	57 (59)	0 (0)	21 (21) <40%>	43 (43) <35%>	(0)	20 (43)	23 (43)	51 (51)	158 (158)	215 (217)
2006	N/A	5	50	55	0	25	45	N/A	25	25	45	165	220
2007	N/A	5	53	58	0	25	47	N/A	25	25	41	163	221
2008	N/A	5	54	59	0	29	45	N/A	26	28	45	173	232
2009	N/A	6	54	60	0	27	48	N/A	27	28	70	200	260
2010	(3)	6 (6) <33%>	54 (54) <50%>	60 (63)	0 (0)	25 (25) <50%>	49 (49) <45%>	(0)	27 (43)	28	85 (85)	214 (214)	274 (277)
2011	1	5	49	54	0	26	53	N/A	27	28	86	220	274
2012	2	5	48	53	1	26	53	N/A	28	23	86	217	270
2013	3	5	49	54	1	23	52	N/A	29	26	85	216	270
2014	3 (3) [4]	5	51 [56]	59 (60+)	1	24 (27) [28]	49 (48) {54-58}	8 (10)	29 {30}	28 {33-34}	85 (~85)	224 (226)	283 (286+)
2015	4 (3-5) [4]	5 (6-8) [5]	53 (57-62) [59]	62 (66-75) [68]	1 (1) [1]	21 (28-32) [26] [81%]	52 (52-56) [52] [67%]	15 (20-25) [20] ["new" ~100%]	29	28 — {57} [53-55] [56]	86 (85) [85] [100%]	232 (239-254) [240]	294 (305-329) [308]
2016	4	5	57	66	1	23	52	23	30	22 — 52	86	237	303
2020	(4-5)	(6-9) <100%>	(59-64) <75%>	69-78 (69-78)	(1-2)	(30-34) <85%>	(54-58) <85%>	(24-30)	(50-55)	(50-55)	(85)	(244-264)	(313-342)
2030	*12*	*12*	*75*	*99*	*4*	*34*	*68*	*26*	*73*		*111*	*316*	*415*

Note: Smaller and/or auxiliary (e.g., mine warfare) vessels not itemized. 1985 only: IISS *Military Balance*, 1985, and IHS *Jane's*, op. cit. Anthony H. Cordesman, *Chinese Military Modernization and Force Development: Chinese and Outside Perspectives* (Washington, DC: Center for Strategic and International Studies, July 2, 2014), http://csis.org/files/publication/140702_Chinese_MilBal.pdf. Otherwise, default figure from that year's Department of Defense (DoD) annual report to Congress on China's military, available at http://www.andrewerickson.com/2016/05/u-s-department-of-defense-annual-reports-to-congress-on-chinas-military-power-2002-16-download-complete-set-here/. Figure in () from U.S. Office of Naval Intelligence (ONI), "PLA Navy Orders of Battle 2000–2020," written response to request for information provided to the U.S.-China Economic and Security Review Commission, Suitland, MD, June 24, 2013; op. cit. Craig Murray, Andrew Berglund, and Kimberly Hsu, "China's Naval Modernization and Implications for the United States," U.S.-China Economic and Security Review Commission Staff Research Backgrounder, August 26, 2013, http://origin.www.uscc.gov/sites/default/files/Research/Backgrounder_China's%20Naval%20Modernization%20and%20Implications%20for%20the%20United%20States.pdf. Figure in <%> indicates "approximate percentage modern" as assessed by ONI (ibid): "Modern submarines are those able to employ submarine-launched intercontinental ballistic missiles or antiship cruise missiles," while "Modern surface ships are those able to conduct multiple missions or that have been extensively upgraded since 1992." For 2014, §} indicates editor's estimate, which may use different metrics than DoD since DoD does not publicize its methodology. Where totals based on DoD and ONI's figures diverge sharply, the ONI-based total should be used, as DoD figures in these cases do not reflect one or more PLAN vessel categories. 2015 numbers and % in [] figures, only: ONI, *The PLA Navy: New Capabilities and Missions for the 21st Century* (Suitland, MD: Office of Naval Intelligence, April 2015), 14–15, http://www.oni.navy.mil/Intelligence_Community/china_media/2015_PLA_NAVY_PUB_Interactive.pdf. 2030 *highest-end* estimate assuming *maximally favorable* conditions for Chinese shipbuilding only: James Fanell and Scott Cheney-Peters, paper and presentation, "China's Naval Shipbuilding: Progress and Challenges" Conference, China Maritime Studies Institute, Naval War College, May 20, 2015. For further details on China's naval and maritime order of battle, see ONI, "China People's Liberation Army Navy (PLA[N]) and Maritime Law Enforcement (MLE) 2015 Recognition and Identification Guide," current as of February 2015, http://www.oni.navy.mil/Intelligence_Community/china_media/posters/PLA_Navy_Identification_Guide.pdf; ONI, "China Equipment," current as of February 2015, http://www.oni.navy.mil/Intelligence_Community/china_media/posters/China_Equipment.pdf; and Ronald O'Rourke, *China Naval Modernization: Implications for U.S. Navy Capabilities—Background and Issues for Congress* (Washington, DC: Congressional Research Service, June 17, 2016). The last of these, updated periodically, is available at http://www.fas.org/sgp/crs/row/RL33153.pdf.

Andrew S. Erickson

Introduction

China's Military Shipbuilding Industry Steams Ahead, On What Course?

"IN RECENT YEARS, China's navy has been launching new ships like dumping dumplings [into soup broth]."[1] This phrase has circulated widely via Chinese media sources and websites. Accompanying it are increasingly impressive analyses and photographs, most recently of China's first indigenous aircraft carrier, now under construction in Dalian. The driving force behind all this, China's shipbuilding industry (SBI), has grown more rapidly than any other in modern history.

One of this century's most significant events, China's maritime transformation is already making waves. Yet China's course and its implications, including at sea, remain highly uncertain—triggering intense speculation and concern from many quarters and in many directions. Beijing has largely met its goal of becoming the world's largest shipbuilder. But progress is uneven. Military shipbuilding leads overall, but military and civilian applications alike suffer from significant weakness in propulsion and electronics. It has thus never been more important to assess the quality and quantity of ships with which China is and will be able to supply its navy and other maritime forces, today and in the future. Yet until now, no book had focused on this topic and addressed it from a U.S. Navy perspective.

To bridge that gap, a diverse group of some of the world's leading sailors, scholars, analysts, industry experts, and other professionals convened at the Naval War College (NWC) on May 19–20, 2015, for a two-day conference on "China's Naval Shipbuilding: Progress and Challenges." Hosted by NWC's China Maritime Studies Institute (CMSI), it was cosponsored by the U.S. Naval Institute (USNI). This resulting book is the sixth volume in the CMSI–USNI series, Studies in Chinese Maritime Development.

CMSI was formally established on October 1, 2006. Its research and analysis of China's maritime capabilities help to inform U.S. Navy leadership and support NWC in its core mission of helping to define the future Navy. The annual CMSI conference is a principal function of the institute, supporting focused examination of the full range of Chinese maritime developments.

This conference, the tenth in a series, focused on a topic of great interest to Navy leaders: China's naval SBI. "Shipbuilding" includes construction of new vessels, the repair and modification of existing ones, and the production and repair of shipboard and associated equipment.[2] Paper presenters, discussants, and other attendees analyzed China's shipbuilding capacity in order to deepen understanding of the relative trajectories of Chinese and U.S. naval shipbuilding and the possible corresponding challenges and responses for the U.S. Navy. The overarching questions, of paramount importance to the Navy and other observers, included:

- What are China's prospects for success in key areas of naval shipbuilding?
- What are the likely results for China's navy?
- What are the implications for the U.S. Navy?

As the self-designated target year for China to become the world's largest shipbuilder, 2015 was a particularly appropriate time for the conference.[3] In some respects, China has already accomplished its goal, yet major problems and uncertainties remain as we look forward over the next thirteen years through 2030—the rough time frame for this volume's analysis.

This is an exciting time to observe the fruits of Chinese naval shipbuilding, perhaps even a significant inflection point. As part of its unprecedented overall emphasis on maritime issues, China's 2015 Defense White Paper states: "The traditional mentality that land outweighs sea must be abandoned. . . . [G]reat importance has to be attached to managing the seas and oceans and protecting maritime rights and interests."[4] The U.S. Office of Naval Intelligence's 2015 report concludes:

China is only in the middle of its military modernization, with continued improvements planned over the following decades. As we view
the past 20 years of [People's Liberation Army Navy/PLAN] modernization, the results have been impressive, but at its core the force has
remained essentially the same . . . built around destroyers, frigates and
conventional submarines. As we look ahead to the coming decade,
the introduction of aircraft carriers, ballistic missile submarines, and
potentially a large-deck amphibious ship will fundamentally alter how
the PLA(N) operates and is viewed by the world.[5]

Over 150 attendees participated in CMSI's conference. They hailed from
such institutions as Harvard, Yale, Princeton, Massachusetts Institute of
Technology, Johns Hopkins, University of California, and Virginia Tech, such
organizations as the RAND Corporation, National Bureau of Asian Research,
and IHS *Jane's*, such commercial enterprises and consultancies as *China
SignPost*™, as well as such U.S. Navy entities as the staffs of the Chief of Naval
Operations, U.S. Pacific Command and Pacific Fleet, and the Office of Naval
Research. There were also distinguished attendees from the navies and governments of such important U.S. allies as Japan, South Korea, Canada, France, and
the United Kingdom.

The resulting volume thus assembles insights from some of the world's
leading experts and analysts concerning one of the most important global
dynamics today. China's military data disclosure continues to fall short in
important respects, but CMSI's well-established investigative approach brings
transparency for Asia-Pacific policymakers tasked with responding to China's
rising naval presence. Given the complex, interdisciplinary nature of the subject at hand, CMSI sought to pair technical and industry specialists with
Chinese-language–capable subject matter experts. Chapter authors have com-
manded ships at sea, led shipbuilding programs ashore, toured Chinese vessels and production facilities, invested in Chinese shipyards and advised others
in their investments, and produced and presented important assessments to
top-level decisionmakers during critical events. In synthesizing their collective
insights with those of the other conference participants, this book fills a key
gap in our understanding of China, its shipbuilding, its navy, and what it all
means. As with all CMSI conferences and related volumes, all views expressed
by the contributors are theirs alone.

Volume Structure and Contents

This book addresses the impact of Beijing's substantial economic resources, growing maritime focus, and uneven but improving defense industrial base on its prospects for success in key areas of naval shipbuilding; the likely results for China's maritime forces, particularly its navy; and the implications for the U.S. Navy. It is divided into five thematic parts.

The first part surveys the foundation and resources for Chinese naval shipbuilding. Christopher P. Carlson and Jack Bianchi examine how evolving ways of war and missions have shaped over time the design, development, outfitting, and deployment of PLAN ships—the literal embodiment of Beijing's naval strategy. Morgan Clemens and Ian Easton then survey the role and requirements assigned to China's SBI by its civilian and military masters: the Chinese Communist Party (CCP), the Chinese state, and the People's Liberation Army (PLA). They include a case study on amphibious vessel development and production. Gabe Collins and Eric Anderson follow with an analysis of the diversifying sources and increasing extent of financial resources available to China's state shipbuilders. They highlight Chinese shipyards' dynamism, innovation, and mounting incentives to seek naval contracts to compensate for depressed civilian demand. This provides a broad context and framework for the next three parts, which examine specialized subsets of China's SBI: infrastructure, architecture and design, and remaining impediments.

Part two, on shipyard infrastructure, surveys China's vessel construction facilities and their production and evolution. Sue Hall and Audrye Wong provide important context by outlining SBI dynamics and global production trends. Drawing on Hall's years of experience as an international consultant on SBI issues, they trace Chinese facilities and activities over the past decade-plus boom and recent consolidation. They conclude by outlining challenges facing China's SBI and metrics for measuring its progress. Next, Alex Pape and Tate Nurkin survey in detail China's extant and projected military SBI production from the early 2000s through 2030, offering overviews of specific vessel classes and estimates concerning funding and order of battle. Sean O'Connor and Jordan Wilson then employ satellite imagery analysis to elucidate specific developments at three major naval shipyards: Shanghai Jiangnan Changxing Shipbuilding Company Ltd. (hereafter Jiangnan Changxing); Dalian shipyard, with its growing aircraft carrier experience; and Huludao, China's only yard that currently produces nuclear-powered vessels. Daniel Alderman and Rush Doshi conclude this part by examining ongoing two-way civil-military integration (CMI) efforts in China's SBI. While many Western experts remain skeptical of the extent and efficacy of such approaches, CMI enjoys long-standing, growing emphasis in China. One must understand implications of the apparently ongoing merger of China's two major state shipbuilders, China Shipbuilding Industry Corporation (CSIC) and China State Shipbuilding Corporation (CSSC), as well as of broader efforts to consolidate the SBI into fewer facilities of greater quality and capability.

The third part covers Chinese naval architecture and design, from standards to production processes to civil-military disparities, and China's prospects for narrowing them through its preferred centralized approach. Mark Metcalf begins by offering path-breaking analysis of a vital but obscure topic: national, military, and industrial technical standards for China's SBI. These standards, which Metcalf outlines systematically, quite literally inform each Chinese warship's course from conception to delivery. Kevin Pollpeter and Mark Stokes follow with in-depth analysis of that course, formally known as the research, development, and acquisition (RDA) process. They examine China's RDA system and the key organizations involved by tracing the Chinese concept of "integrated innovation" as practiced by CSIC, to date the primary builder of surface ships and submarines for the PLAN. Julian Snelder subsequently draws on personal commercial experience, together with industry interviews and data typically unavailable to scholars, to examine the civilian industrial underpinnings of Beijing's effort to become a great maritime power. Because privately owned Chinese shipyards remain weak compared to their Korean and Japanese counterparts, Snelder predicts that large state-owned enterprises will lead Beijing's maritime strategic-industrial transformation. If China succeeds in enhancing market-oriented performance while strengthening centralized oversight, Snelder judges, it will have the wherewithal to deploy a formidable navy indeed.

Part four addresses remaining shipbuilding challenges for China. These are substantial, particularly concerning information technology, propulsion, and aviation and other complex systems. Common to these bottlenecks is the centrality of sensitive, high-performance components that must work together as a sophisticated system-of-systems. This makes it particularly difficult for China to successfully pursue its preferred hybrid approach: obtaining critical foreign technologies and other inputs,[6] developing indigenously those unavailable from abroad, and integrating the results on a "good enough" basis. Leigh Ann Ragland-Luce and John Costello establish the importance of shipboard electronics to the PLAN's desired upward trajectory in sophistication, scope, and scale of operations. In part through in-depth examination of the Type 054A *Jiangkai II* frigate's electronics suite, they find that—despite

increasing prioritization—organizational parochialism, insufficient coordination, and other inefficiencies continue to impede Chinese progress in this
vital area. Andrew S. Erickson, Jonathan Ray, and Robert T. Forte next examine power and propulsion for China's conventional and nuclear naval vessels.
These capabilities quite literally determine how fast and far Chinese warships
can go, and what they can accomplish in many respects, yet they remain one
of the PLAN's key weaknesses. It is, in every sense of the word, underpowered. Erickson, Ray, and Forte find that China is working hard to master relevant technologies, and they highlight the most important determinants
of progress (such as the degree of Russian assistance) but emphasize that
improvements will be slow, difficult, and expensive. Andrew Scobell, Michael
E. McMahon, Cortez A. Cooper III, and Arthur Chan conclude the part by
examining China's aircraft carrier program and the motivations and choices
informing it. Citing the difficulties inherent in upgrading propulsion, power,
and launch technologies, their analysis suggests an evolutionary design path
for Chinese deck aviation.

The final part returns to the strategic level by weighing alternative futures,
offering overall conclusions, and suggesting key takeaways. Charged by the
editor with exploring what maximally favorable peacetime SBI conditions and
production might yield the PLAN by 2030, James E. Fanell and Scott Cheney-
Peters outline a possible path to a much larger, more capable navy with a much
greater mission set. Such a realization of the "China Dream" at sea would entail
a global presence characterized by a credible sea-based nuclear deterrent, multiple carrier strike groups, and an ever-present network of ships at sea. Asked
by the editor to consider what more moderate assumptions might mean for the
PLAN between now and 2030, Michael McDevitt notes that strong strategic
demand signals and guidance from civilian authorities, combined with solid
SBI capability, are already driving rapid progress. He projects that by 2020,
China will have impressive far seas–relevant naval forces second only to those
of the United States. This growing Chinese distant waters fleet will increasingly
resemble a smaller version of the U.S. Navy. Paul Scharre and Tyler Jost next
examine technologies that might change naval warfare dramatically and consider related Chinese thinking. Future outcomes, they contend, will be affected
by four key competitions susceptible to disruptive technology advances—hiding versus finding, understanding versus confusion, network resilience versus
degradation, and hitting versus intercepting. Advances in China's technology
base, shipbuilding, and design will have an impact on all four areas. Ronald
O'Rourke concludes with specific policy implications and recommendations
for the U.S. Navy and the civilian authorities who oversee it. For over a decade,

he explains, China's military maritime modernization effort (including its shipbuilding output) has affected requirements for U.S. Navy capabilities, particularly by renewing focus on high-end warfare. He traces resulting ongoing debates concerning strategy, budgets, and force architecture.

Summary of Conference Discussion

While the aforementioned chapters contain specific insights and nuances that merit readers' attention, in the editor's personal view the conference yielded the following key findings overall—none of which may be attributed in any way to a specific participant or organization:

- The growth of China's SBI is more rapid than any other in modern history, with a thirteen-fold increase in commercial shipbuilding output from 2002 to 2012. Although advancements in recent years are substantial in aggregate, they vary significantly by subfield.

- Through a process of "imitative innovation," China has been able to leapfrog some naval development, engineering, and production steps and achieve tremendous cost and time savings by leveraging work done by the United States and other countries.

- Fleet design and quality improvement efforts are driven by two factors. PLAN shipbuilding choices are informed by a combination of technological and strategic analysis produced by the PLAN's two main research organizations. Ship construction is increasingly subject to a detailed set of national and navy military standards.

- China's SBI is poised to make the PLAN the second largest navy in the world by 2020, and—if current trends continue—a combat fleet that in overall order of battle (i.e., hardware-specific terms) is quantitatively and even perhaps qualitatively on a par with that of the U.S. Navy by 2030.

- By 2030, the PLAN would still be in the early stages of increasing operational proficiency and its ability to engage in high-intensity operations in distant waters, but could nevertheless—together with other PLA forces—develop tremendous ability to actively oppose U.S. Navy operations in a zone of contestation for sea control in the near seas (Yellow, East China, and South China seas), while extending layers of influence and reach far beyond.

- By 2020, China is on course to build ships that will be able to deploy greater quantities of antiship cruise missiles (ASCMs) with greater ranges than those systems used by the U.S. Navy.

Additional Findings

In the editor's judgment, the conference also yielded the following specific insights.

Chinese Shipyards

The CCP has assigned the SBI a key role in China's development as a great power, including support for China's geostrategic endeavors. The state-owned shipyards also offer a major job and skills development program serving larger CCP economic objectives. Simultaneously, however, China's spate of recent construction necessitates the rapid development of the supporting and main-tenance infrastructure for in-service vessels—a difficult task even for the far more experienced U.S. Navy. When maintenance, repair, and overhaul are fac-tored in, a navy ends up paying a warship's initial purchase price at least two more times over its lifecycle. (As naval engineering specialists say, "You buy the boat [roughly] three times.") Mid-life maintenance will be a big "shoe to drop" for the PLAN, particularly as it increases its operational tempo and wears out its ships more rapidly. Thus far, China's approach has been similar to that of the Soviet Union: building new vessels hastily without adequately consider-ing upkeep costs or related personnel and infrastructure requirements (e.g., the need for sufficient numbers of specialized workers and dry docks). Beijing may thus "reap the whirlwind" as programs initiated in flush fiscal times enter a costlier phase, yet command less robust discretionary funding.

State-owned versus Private Shipyards

In aggregate, and increasingly together, CSIC and CSSC possess great resources and capacity but retain tremendous inefficiencies. Their institu-tional culture is still influenced by legacy values, norms, and incentives. Their monopoly structure remains one of the central impediments to improving effi-ciency and innovation. On the other hand, private yards are oriented toward short-term, profit-minded thinking and are not funded to engage in long-term research and development (R&D)–intensive projects. While CSIC and CSSC have increasingly undertaken naval and para-naval business to absorb excess yard capacity after commercial "Peak Ship" construction occurred around 2012, private yards have largely been left to fend for themselves. Throughout the industry, bureaucratic barriers to efficiency and effectiveness remain a problem, especially for propulsion and shipboard electronics systems and their integration into ships.

Chinese Shipbuilding Standards

Specific Chinese shipbuilding plans and military standards are derived from the Weapons and Armament Development Strategy, a highly classified document drafted by the General Armament Department and approved by the Central Military Commission. It includes sections assessing the international security environment, military equipment requirements, analysis of the strengths and weakness of Chinese armaments in relation to naval objectives, and assessments of science and technology development. One of China's most important national military shipbuilding standards is the 国家军用标准 (*Guojia Junyong Biaozhun*/GJB) 4000–2000 publication series, *General Specifications for Naval Ships*, a massive compendium focused on new and planned construction. It represents a major advance from China's copycat assimilation of thousands of U.S. standards during the 1980s and 1990s.

Programmatic Decisionmaking

To drive requirements, PLAN leadership integrates the analysis of its two main research entities—the technically focused Naval Armament Research Institute, and the strategically focused Naval Research Institute—to rationalize ship and weapons system design with naval strategy. The increasing diversity of PLAN mission areas (e.g., massive expansion of area air defense) is having a significant effect on Chinese naval ship design. Increasing capabilities demand increased processing power and sensor load. Greater payloads and supporting systems drive increases in ship size.

Naval Ship Design

New design and production technologies—as previously with computer-aided design and manufacturing software from Japan and Europe—are being imported into China, adapted, and deployed for military use. Advances in ship design are achieved through "imitative innovation," an official technology transfer policy based on a process of introduce/digest/absorb/re-innovate. This process takes existing technology and adds value to it by making it cheaper, better suited to Chinese needs, or otherwise improving it. Modular construction is expanding for both commercial and military ships. Modularity improves production efficiency—by enabling standard modules to be constructed and stored to better accommodate shipbuilding schedules—and also reduces uncertainties by employing common systems and subcomponents.

Military-Civil Disconnect

The greatest variation across China's uneven but improving SBI stems from its military-civil bifurcation. While subject to the aforementioned inefficiencies, the naval side appears to have by far the better funding, infrastructure, research institutes, designers, and workers. State-owned shipyards on the Ministry of Industry and Information Technology's favored "white list"—the ones building most of China's warships—receive not only preferential treatment, but also preferential support. The advantages enjoyed by military shipbuilding may be further enhanced as state shipbuilders seek to compensate for recent declines in commercial orders by securing contracts for naval and coast guard ships, the latter of which are being built even more swiftly and numerously. Learning is occurring rapidly. It typically takes ten to twenty repeats to double labor efficiency, and the PLAN is ordering longer production runs of fewer series, facilitating advancements in shipbuilding knowledge and competence. That said, China's military SBI still faces challenges in subcomponents (especially propulsion/power) and some sensors (e.g., antisubmarine warfare versions). On the commercial side, in marked contrast, many private shipyards risk bankruptcy and closure. The civilian shipbuilding workforce remains undereducated. Worker quality, lower than in South Korea and Japan, remains a major drag on productivity and high-end achievement. With regard to commercial shipbuilding, therefore, China has a massive capacity to build small, less complex ships and large, noncomplex ships but has demonstrated less capacity to build large, complex ships. However, even the commercial side is improving over time. For instance, partnerships between shipyards and "feeder" technical schools are being created to help enhance workforce capacity, in part by offering guaranteed jobs for graduates.

Particular Propulsion Weakness

Compared to the United States, China retains pronounced shipbuilding limitations in propulsion, some electronics, and certain advanced weapons systems. Propulsion is the single biggest shortcoming and is unlikely to progress until China's precision manufacturing capability improves. Conventional propulsion in submarines is moving toward advanced lithium-ion batteries, possibly as an alternative to air-independent power systems. Nuclear propulsion advances—especially in power density and acoustic quieting—remain difficult to ascertain, but a key variable affecting future progress will be the degree of Russian assistance.

Points of Contention

To be sure, in keeping with CMSI's rigorous academic approach, the conference generated significant debate. In the editor's assessment, the most important areas of disagreement included:

- Will Chinese state-owned shipyards merge again in a *substantive* fashion? CSIC and CSSC were unified until 1999 and then were divided along geographic and functional lines so as not to compete directly (CSIC controls the majority of R&D centers, for instance). Some believe true reintegration will occur—as widely reported in Chinese and foreign media before this volume went to press—to increase efficiency and available resources and to reach a State Council–mandated reduction in the number of commercial shipyards from several hundred to sixty. Those doubting that meaningful mergers will occur observed that most unions to date aimed to maximize geographical efficiencies and have been completed. They also note that CSIC and CSSC naval yards have already been reduced to only seven major facilities between them.

- What are China's prospects for reducing organizational barriers and increasing technological diffusion and absorption? Beijing is responding to organizational and technological impediments by emphasizing integration of commercial and naval shipbuilding processes, which some industry experts believe could improve quality and efficiency. Others maintain that this will actually reduce efficiency and increase challenges because of the fundamentally different natures of naval and commercial shipbuilding.

- Are Chinese shipbuilding standards effective design and construction tools, given cultural barriers to standardization and regulation? Some highly knowledgeable experts believe that overall, they "offer a workable road" to improved future construction. Others believe they are "hopelessly convoluted," outdated, and probably used selectively. Of note, in China's space industry it took top-level leadership intervention before program managers actually started to follow standards consistently. Several observers well versed in naval affairs emphasized that whatever the specifics, China is clearly putting sophisticated, capable warships to sea. Developments causing concern for U.S. and regional observers have been accomplished in spite of the limitations on Chinese shipbuilding raised by presenters, primarily those focusing on commercial issues (where Chinese shipbuilding is weaker than on the military side). To the extent that China can reduce or overcome these limitations, its accomplishments will be even greater.

Subsequent Developments

Between the conference and this volume's publication, new details emerged that inform the aforementioned debates but in no way resolve them.

With regard to organization, while there was no conclusive evidence of an imminent CSIC-CSSC merger, internal consolidation of each conglomerate was already well under way.[7] In May 2016, CSIC announced a plan to amalgamate key shipbuilding activities, including in leading naval shipyards. Three pairs of major shipbuilding subsidiaries, with military-related responsibilities as noted, are slated for mergers:

- Dalian Shipbuilding Industry Company (first indigenous aircraft carrier) with Tianjin Xingang Shipbuilding (fast attack craft)
- Bohai Shipbuilding Heavy Industry (nuclear submarines) with Shanhaiguan Shipbuilding Industry (repair)
- Qingdao Wuchuan Heavy Industry with Qingdao Beihai Shipbuilding Heavy Industries (unmanned surface vessels).[8]

In doing so, CSIC is attempting to clean up its internal operations and eliminate overlap and internal competition. This administrative measure does not change competition, capacity, or capability writ large, but rather is an incremental move in an ongoing consolidation process overseen by a Xi Jinping administration that firmly believes in the power of mergers and super-monopolies to serve key bureaucratic-economic functions.

As for technical specifications, in June 2015, a new joint PLA-China Classification Society standard (GJB) levied certain requirements on new construction of commercial ships in support of military mobilization needs. These requirements are strongly advocated by national security stakeholders but have subsequently triggered pushback from ship builders and owners, complicating their implementation.[9]

Implications for the U.S. Navy

CMSI conferences are designed to offer insights and policy recommendations specifically useful to the U.S. Navy. From the editor's perspective, the conference yielded the following takeaways:

- Chinese ship design and building advances are helping the PLAN to contest sea control in a widening arc of the western Pacific.

- Experts generally agreed that by 2020, the PLAN will be the world's second most powerful navy, with assets dedicated to far seas missions greater in capability than those of the United Kingdom, France, Japan, or India. Given the likelihood of continued government investment, cost advantage, and pursuit of integrated innovation, China's SBI appears to be on a trajectory to build a combat fleet that could be, *in hardware terms*, quantitatively and qualitatively on a par with that of the U.S. Navy by 2030.

- Whether China can stay on this build-out trajectory, given downside risks to its economy and the mounting costs of maintaining the existing fleet, is another question. Indeed, Beijing may face a looming inflection point, after which it is confronted with tradeoffs and difficult choices concerning resource allocation unprecedented in China's post-1978 era of economic and military expansion.

- Regardless of China's precise economic future, the PLAN—together with other PLA forces—will be increasingly capable of contesting U.S. sea control within growing range rings extending beyond Beijing's unresolved feature and maritime claims in the near seas. Experts generally agreed that by 2020, China is on course to deploy greater quantities of missiles with greater ranges than those systems potentially employed by the U.S. Navy against them. China is on track to have quantitative parity or better in surface-to-air missiles and ASCMs, parity in missile launch cells, and quantitative inferiority only in multi-mission land-attack cruise missiles. Retention of U.S. naval superiority hinges on next-generation long-range ASCMs (the Long-Range Antiship Missile [LRASM] and the vertical launch system–compatible Naval Strike Missile variant)—which are still "paper missiles" not yet fielded on U.S. Navy surface combatants. Additionally, new U.S. ASCMs may be unable to target effectively under contested anti-access/area denial conditions. Failing to fill this gap would further imperil U.S. ability to generate and maintain sea control in the western Pacific.

The Way Forward

At the CMSI conference and beyond, the aforementioned dimensions of China's maritime rise have rightly attracted growing attention. Directed by civilian authorities, the U.S. Navy, Marine Corps, and Coast Guard have taken notice. The current U.S. Maritime Strategy, issued in 2015, states: "China's naval expansion into the Indian and Pacific Oceans presents both opportunities and challenges." It adds: "The U.S. Sea Services, through our continued forward presence and constructive interaction with Chinese maritime forces, reduce the potential for misunderstanding, discourage aggression, and preserve our commitment to peace and stability in the region."[10]

Like its five predecessors, this volume continues the CMSI tradition of both addressing challenges from and pursuing opportunities with China. Increasingly, the U.S. and Chinese navies are meeting at sea and ashore. While the two sides will not always agree, to ensure avoidance of worse outcomes than the current peacetime mix of cooperation and competition, they must always understand each other clearly. It was in that spirit that NWC welcomed PLAN Commander Admiral Wu Shengli to represent his navy for the first time ever at the Twenty-First International Seapower Symposium in September 2014. Admiral Wu is clearly focused on enhancing professional military education for his service.[11] In February 2015, twenty-nine "fast-track" Chinese naval officers participated in a six-day exchange program with U.S. counterparts, including visits in Newport, Rhode Island, to NWC, with which the editor assisted, and the Surface Warfare Officers School. In July 2015, the editor was honored to accompany a delegation of twelve NWC students and NWC's deans of international programs and domestic and foreign student programs to reciprocate with visits to the PLAN Headquarters in Beijing and to China's Naval Command College in Nanjing.

On a subsequent visit to Nanjing, the editor visited the Zheng He Memorial Shipyard. Here, in the central Gulou district of what was once the Ming Dynasty's capital along the Yangzi (Yangtze) River, lie the Treasure Boat Factory Ruins. A world-leading shipyard six centuries ago, the facility produced many vessels for the maiden fleet of Zheng He, a Chinese Columbus who made seven Indian Ocean voyages from 1405 to 1433, reaching as far as Mombasa, Mogadishu, and Mecca. In a testament to the scale of the enterprise, this included Zheng's flagship vessel, which may have been as long as 136 meters (448 feet).[12] A smaller replica welcomes visitors today. Walking its expansive (if creaky) decks one sunny afternoon, the editor could not avoid the questions that lie at the heart of this volume: To what extent, and to what end, is China going to sea? Is China once again poised to engage in world-class shipbuilding? And if so, what use will Beijing make of this historic opportunity?

Whatever the ultimate answers, the U.S. Navy must understand its Chinese counterpart and where it is heading. Assessing what ships China can supply its navy and other maritime forces with, today and in the future, can help to point the way.

Notes

1. Widely circulated quotation published by *Duowei*, a New York City Chinese-language newspaper owned by a Hong Kong media businessman. "美国备战南海 中国海军急召退伍士官复役" ["U.S. Preparing for War in the South China Sea, Chinese Navy Recalls Retired NCOs for Service"], 多维新闻 [*Duowei News*], June 17, 2015, http://global.dwnews.com/news/2015-06-17/59661331.html.

2. For useful background in one of the very few books to address the subject, see Sarah Kirchberger, *Assessing China's Naval Power: Technological Innovation, Economic Constraints, and Strategic Implications* (New York: Springer, 2015).

3. Qun Shan, "Getting Ship-Shape," *China Daily*, December 31, 2003, 1, http://www.chinadaily.com.cn/en/doc/2003-12/31/content_294778.htm; Cai Shun, "Full Steam Ahead," *Beijing Review* 48, no. 10 (March 10, 2005): 36–37, http://beijingreview.sinoperi.com/en200510/693800.jhtml.

4. 中国的军事战略 [*China's Military Strategy*], http://www.81.cn/dblj/2015-05/26/content_6507373.htm.

5. Office of Naval Intelligence, *The PLA Navy: New Capabilities and Missions for the 21st Century* (Suitland, MD: Office of Naval Intelligence, 2015), 43, http://www.oni.navy.mil/Intelligence_Community/china_media/2015_PLA_NAVY_PUB_Interactive.pdf.

6. William C. Hannas, James Mulvenon, and Anna B. Puglisi, *Chinese Industrial Espionage: Technology Acquisition and Military Modernisation* (New York: Routledge, 2013).

7. Zhong Nan, "Shipbuilder Plans to Integrate Civilian, Military Businesses," *China Daily*, April 28, 2016, http://europe.chinadaily.com.cn/business/2016-04/28/content_24916473.htm; 包志明 [Bao Zhiming], "国有船厂大规模整合 北方主要企业6合3" ["Large-Scale Integration of State-Owned Shipyards—Main Northern Enterprises Consolidating from 6 to 3"], 财新网 [*Caixin Net*], May 22, 2016, http://companies.caixin.com/2016-05-22/100946282.html.

8. Jon Grevatt, "China Consolidates Aero-Engine and Naval Shipbuilding Sectors," *Jane's Defence Industry*, June 14, 2016; Jon Grevatt, "China Shipbuilding Industry Merges Key Subsidiaries," *Jane's Defence Weekly*, May 25, 2016.

9. 黄浩 [Huang Hao], 李胜财 [Li Shengcai], and 程荣 [Chen Rong], "军地专家解读新造民船贯彻国防要求相关问题" ["Military Experts Interpret Problems Concerning the Implementation of Defense Requirements for New-Construction Commercial Ships"], 中国国防报 [*China Defense News*], December 8, 2015, http://www.legaldaily.com.cn/Civil-military-integration/content/2015-12/08/content_6391029.htm.

10. *A Cooperative Strategy for 21st-Century Seapower: Forward, Engaged, Ready* (Washington, DC: U.S. Sea Services, March 2015), 4, http://www.navy.mil/local/maritime/150227-CS21R-Final.pdf.

11. Andrew S. Erickson, "China's Naval Modernization: The Implications of Seapower," *World Politics Review*, September 23, 2014, http://www.worldpoliticsreview.com/articles/14083/chinas-naval-modernization-the-implications-of-seapower.

12. International Zheng He Society, "Zheng He Memorial Shipyard in Nanjing," November 10, 2005, http://www.chengho.org/news/news8.2.php; Andrew Wilson, "The Maritime Transformation of Ming China," in *China Goes to Sea: Maritime Transformation in Comparative Historical Perspective*, ed. Andrew S. Erickson, Lyle Goldstein, and Carnes Lord (Annapolis, MD: Naval Institute Press, July 2009), 250–55.

PART I

Foundation and Resources

Christopher P. Carlson and Jack Bianchi

Warfare Drivers
Mission Needs and the Impact on Ship Design

A NAVY IS NEITHER built nor operated in a vacuum. National interests and goals inform the nation's military strategy, which flows down to inform the naval or maritime strategy. Since strategy is about ends and means, ships are the essential element of the "means" by which the "ends" of a maritime strategy are achieved. From the Chinese perspective, this idea is best captured in a simple, succinct observation: "Ships are the physical embodiment of maritime strategy."[1] And while this comment is in the context of civilian ship design and development, it is equally applicable to warships. When combined with the Chinese concept of strategy, which is based on the Soviet-era theory that emphasizes the scientific nature of strategy and the role of centralized decisionmaking, it is logical to conclude that China's naval strategy will directly influence the design, development, construction, and employment of its naval vessels.

This chapter describes how transformations in the strategy of the People's Liberation Army (PLA) in general, and the PLA Navy (PLAN) in particular, have led to related changes in ship design and equipment. The PLAN has progressed through three historic developmental phases in its naval strategy— "near coast defense," "near seas active defense," and "near seas defense, far seas protection"—since its founding in 1949, with each change resulting in an

expansion of PLAN geographic areas of responsibility and operational requirements. With each new phase in China's naval strategy, existing responsibilities
and requirements were complemented by additional ones, which drove development of larger, more capable naval vessels that could deploy at increasingly
greater distances from China's shores.

The PLAN's shift to a near seas active defense strategy drove China to
expand its expertise in a number of warfare areas, moving beyond its core
competency of antisurface warfare (ASuW) to effect significant improvements
in anti-air warfare (AAW) and antisubmarine warfare (ASW) capabilities that
had not progressed beyond those demonstrated at the end of World War II.
The more recent shift to a far seas protection phase has pushed the PLAN to
expand its warfighting horizons yet again, especially in the areas of deep-water
ASW, precision strike, and aircraft carrier operations. Understanding how past
changes in PLAN naval strategy affected the development of operational capabilities may help illuminate the direction and nature of PLAN modernization
efforts in the future.

PLAN Strategy: Historical Evolution

Near Coast Defense

From its founding in 1949 until the late 1970s, the PLAN maintained solely
a "near coast defense" strategy. Although the security challenges China faced
over these three decades changed drastically, the PLAN's strategy remained
limited to coastal areas. PLA strategy was focused predominantly on land-
based threats; thus, the naval strategy was of secondary importance to China's
overall national security goals.

At the navy's outset, its strategic focus was on protecting China's coastal
and river areas, in accordance with a Chinese Communist Party (CCP) central
committee decision in January 1949.[2] This focus reflected the fact that, in the
1950s and 1960s, the CCP was primarily concerned about coastal incursions
by "imperialist forces," particularly Nationalist Party (Kuomintang, or KMT)
forces in Taiwan.[3]

By the late 1960s, the KMT threat was eclipsed by the Soviet Union as
Chinese and Soviet forces engaged in border skirmishes. A Soviet land invasion from the north was now regarded as a greater threat than an invasion
from the sea, which rendered PLAN forces "almost irrelevant."[4] By the end
of the 1970s, PLAN forces were preparing for a potential Soviet amphibious invasion from the east, which would theoretically open a second front to

complement invading Soviet forces from the north. PLA strategy was then purely defensive and focused on national survival, rather than on capturing territory, resources, or defending sea lines of communication (SLOCs).[5]

Throughout this phase, the PLA Navy lacked the capacity for independent strategic missions and required coordination with the PLA and PLA Air Force (PLAAF). According to *Science of Military Strategy* (2013), "'near coast defense' was in essence the limited extension of land-based military battles to coastal areas."[6] Given this narrow emphasis, the PLAN focused exclusively on ASuW to repel any attempt at an amphibious landing. Anti-air and antisubmarine warfare were severely limited to a minimum self-defense capability with World War II–era weapons and sensors.

Near Seas Active Defense

From the late 1970s and into the mid-1980s, as China's geostrategic challenges changed, PLAN strategy began to shift from "near coast defense" to "near seas active defense." Implemented around 1985, this first official PLAN strategy would be the driving developmental force until the early 2000s. This strategy transformation shifted the PLAN's operational area outward from coastal areas to the "near seas," which encompass the waters within the first island chain (the Yellow Sea, East China Sea, and South China Sea) and their immediate approaches.[7]

Under this strategy, the PLAN was, for the first time, responsible for conducting independent, strategic-level operations.[8] If Chinese decisionmakers determine that China is actively defending its vital interests from foreign predation at the *strategic* level, "active" defense allows for proactive, even preemptive, actions at the *operational* and *tactical* levels—actions that an opponent might consider fully "offensive."

The goals of this strategy were "to uphold China's national unity, territorial integrity and maritime interests; handle local naval wars; contain and defend against sea-based invasion by hegemonic and imperialist forces; and safeguard Pacific peace."[9] Under these goals, likely operational objectives would be to reunify with Taiwan, defend or recover disputed maritime territory, protect SLOCs, and engage in nuclear counterstrikes.[10] After the 1995–96 Taiwan Strait crisis, PLAN analysts were especially focused on Taiwan-related contingencies, specifically establishing "local and temporary sea-control for sea-crossing and amphibious landing operations."[11]

The primary drivers behind this new naval strategy phase were Admiral Liu Huaqing (PLAN commander, 1982–88), civilian political support, the decreasing Soviet threat, and the PLAN's demonstrated potential. First,

Admiral Liu had a close relationship with China's paramount leader Deng Xiaoping and played a major role in crafting and proposing the near seas defense strategy.[12] Second, the need to modernize and expand the PLAN enjoyed CCP leaders'—most importantly Deng's—support. Such support was embodied in the Central Military Commission's (CMC's) 1985 decision to shift China's strategy from preparing for "total" war to "local" war. This CMC decision enabled Liu to formally propose the near seas active defense strategy that December.[13] Meanwhile, the Soviet threat was ebbing, especially as Soviet Premier Mikhail Gorbachev's foreign policies reduced tensions. Finally, the PLAN's Type 051 *Luda*-class destroyers (DDs) and Type 091 *Han*-class nuclear-powered submarines (SSNs) were well into series production by the mid-1980s; these platforms "may have enhanced Liu's confidence in endorsing the new naval strategy."[14]

The Cold War's end heralded nearly a decade of wars, crises, and incidents that fundamentally reshaped PLA thinking about ways of war and spurred Chinese leaders to accelerate military modernization. A further enabler was the resumption of access to Russian technology, systems, and expertise.

The U.S. ability to wage new forms of high-tech "informatized" warfare in Operation Desert Storm in 1991 shocked and awed the PLA. The 1995–96 Taiwan Strait crisis, the culmination of Beijing's reaction to increasing "separatist" activities by Taiwanese politicians, laid bare the PLAN's inability to thwart U.S. military intervention into a sensitive issue of core importance to Beijing. PLA leaders even mention Operation Desert Fox in 1998 as further evidence of the need to rapidly improve in response to U.S. superior capabilities. The North Atlantic Treaty Organization's routing of Yugoslav forces in the 1999 Kosovo war and the bombing of the Chinese embassy in Belgrade made China's leadership feel extremely vulnerable. This convinced President Jiang Zemin to launch megaprojects to produce advanced asymmetric systems, such as the antiship ballistic missile and other "assassin's mace" weapons.

Largely concerned with deterring Taiwan from formally declaring independence, Jiang oversaw the purchase of Project 956E *Sovremenny*-class destroyers and Project 877E/636E *Kilo*-class submarines from Russia, as well as accelerating the construction and commissioning of new classes of indigenous warships and submarines. He opposed proposals to develop an aircraft carrier, which he believed would be ineffective vis-à-vis Taiwan. At the operational level, Jiang pursued a service-based "informatization" approach to bring "network-centric warfare with Chinese characteristics" to the PLA.

Jiang also finally managed to wean the PLA from the private enterprises Deng had allowed the military to run to compensate for budgetary shortfalls.

Building on nearly a decade of demonstrated budget growth, Jiang convinced the PLA that it would be more lucrative for the armed forces to focus on developing within their official missions, rather than being distracted with nonmilitary business. Since 1989, the PLA has enjoyed rapid budget growth.

These external shocks and related factors significantly shaped Chinese national military strategy—and subsequently maritime strategy—and gradually the capabilities to execute it. While it can be difficult to connect these changes in capabilities to changes in PLAN strategy, examination of more detailed doctrinal writings and inductive analysis of acquisition programs and systems deployments clearly reveal their impact. In short, the events of the 1990s convinced Beijing's leaders that China's near seas interests were vulnerable to superior potential adversaries (namely the United States) and that warfare had become more sophisticated and demanding than they had previously thought. Accordingly, they increased funding for, and emphasis on, programs to increase the PLAN's ability to *actively* conduct near seas defense.

By shifting operations away from the coast, the PLAN addressed its inability to defend ships from air attacks. Initially, short-range point defense systems, based on European missiles, were introduced, but these systems only protected the ship fitted with the missile. After the 1995–96 Taiwan crisis, China reacted quickly by purchasing the Russian Project 956E *Sovremenny*-class guided-missile destroyers (DDGs) fitted with the Shtil (SA-N-7A Gadfly) surface-to-air missile (SAM) system. This system, and the S-300PMU (SA-10B Grumble) purchased in 1993, would provide the technological underpinnings for the new indigenous HHQ-9 and HHQ-16 and broader area air defense.

Near Seas Defense, Far Seas Operations

Since the early 2000s, China's growing overseas economic interests, as well as its increasing dependence on foreign raw materials, convinced the CCP leadership that Beijing needed to enhance its military capabilities to influence events abroad and to defend its overseas interests alone if necessary. Reassured by cross-strait quiescence and by China's newly developed deterrence capabilities to undergird it, President Hu Jintao became increasingly concerned with SLOC security for China's energy and resource imports. This requirement was codified in his "New Historic Missions" in 2004. Of the four missions, two were unprecedented: safeguard China's overseas interests and development, and contribute to international security (in order to further the former objective while bolstering China's international image and influence).

As the PLA's most externally oriented service, the PLAN benefited the most from this strategic reorientation. The Project 048 aircraft carrier program commenced in August 2004. In December 2005, Hu introduced the new operational-level concept of "information systems–based system-of-systems operations." This U.S.-style joint networked approach is intended to support both near and far seas operations comprehensively. Achieving it in practice will require enduring Chinese weaknesses to be addressed.

In recent years, PLAN strategy has begun to shift from an almost exclusive focus on "near seas active defense" to adding "far seas protection."[15] Further strengthening of near seas active defense remains the top priority, but a new outer layer has been added. This new approach requires PLAN "blue-water" operations in the "far seas," defined expansively as all waters beyond the first island chain.[16] CCP leaders have championed far seas defense and operations in some form since the late 1990s, though near seas active defense continued to be the primary PLAN naval strategy into the 2000s.[17]

PLAN goals under a far seas operations strategy include pushing China's "strategic front-line" outward to gain strategic depth and better protect China's survival and development interests. In short, this revised strategy simultaneously pursues "continuous improvement in near seas comprehensive operational capabilities" and "progressive transformation toward far seas protection and improvement of far seas operational maneuver capabilities."[18]

The drivers for this evolution are primarily China's growing economy, expanding international interests (including access to raw materials), overseas investments, and safety of Chinese nationals. From a homeland security perspective, China recognizes the importance, and vulnerability, of the economically rich and densely populated coastal areas; prominence of sea-based security concerns over land-based ones; and requirements to counter long-range sea-based threats.

China's three decades of rapid economic growth have resulted in increased dependence on foreign trade, especially imported oil. This dependence has increased China's vulnerability to potential sea-based threats, including piracy, such as in the Gulf of Aden, or military operations that block the flow of goods along SLOCs, especially at chokepoints such as the Malacca and Lombok straits, and the narrow passageways along the first island chain.[19] A flourishing "blue economy" generated a greater need to defend maritime resources, including fisheries, hydrocarbons, and minerals that would fuel continued growth.[20] Furthermore, the coastal areas are politically, economically, and culturally important, encompassing large portions of China's overall population and economic production. China has also boosted its overseas investments, largely in response to the "going global" investment strategy, and the number of Chinese nationals abroad has increased correspondingly. The PLAN is the military service most capable of reaching and protecting overseas investments and citizens in peacetime.[21]

These changes have triggered a fundamental shift in the threat axes, with sea-based security concerns becoming more prominent than land-based ones. China's continental threats have considerably diminished with the Cold War's end and the resolution of significant land border disputes with its neighbors, primarily Russia. But even as landward threats have decreased, Chinese analysts perceived a rapid growth in the sea-based threats to the country's maritime interests, especially concerning resources, territorial conflicts, and overall U.S. "containment."[22] As a researcher at the PLA Naval Research Institute explains, Chinese military analysts generally agree on the need to expand China's sea power; the debate is over how much to do so.[23] Finally, to counter long-range sea-based threats, China ultimately seeks to develop a far seas operational capability in order to launch operations along exterior lines.[24] Such capabilities will also provide strategic depth by pushing China's strategic front line far enough away from coastal areas to protect against adversaries' medium- to long-range precision strike capabilities.[25]

This new strategy increased PLAN responsibilities, but it did not lessen the priority of near seas active defense. Rather, Hu charged the PLAN with continuing to "enhance its inner and near-seas comprehensive operations capabilities" while "mak[ing] the transformation to far-seas protection (operations) step by step, and enhance far-seas mobile operations capabilities."[26] Integrating these new strategic requirements into its mission set has pushed the PLAN toward developing blue-water ASW capabilities, ship-based precision strike, and aircraft carrier operations. China's 2015 Defense White Paper underscores these, and other, requirements: to "build a combined, multi-functional and efficient maritime combat force structure," China's navy "will enhance its capabilities for strategic deterrence and counterattack, maritime maneuvers, joint operations at sea, comprehensive defense and comprehensive support."[27]

While the conceptual aspirations of far seas operations are nearly a decade old, the PLAN has only begun to develop the capabilities cited above. Some remain in development and testing or have only recently been fielded. Years remain before ships and crews reach a credible level of proficiency. Yet the CMC has levied these new requirements on the PLAN, and the navy leadership is doing everything in its power to meet them.

Naval Strategy: Just the Beginning

Official changes in strategy represent but the first step in warships' design evolution. While necessary articulations of national intent, they are insufficient by themselves. To implement them effectively, a nation must have the financial resources and technological base to design, develop, and build the platforms and associated military systems. Since the 1990s, the CCP has steadily increased the PLAN's budget, funding research and development, testing, and construction. There has also been a dedicated push to expand China's shipbuilding capability, which has seen explosive growth. China now has the world's largest shipbuilding industry and is one of the top two producers.

However, China overachieved badly and is now in the process of a painful shipbuilding sector consolidation to decrease the gross overcapacity and make the remaining yards more profitable. This problem will have minimal effect on state-run shipyards where PLAN ships and submarines are built. The bottom line is that China has provided adequate funding and possesses sufficient industrial capability to manufacture the weapons, sensors, and ships required by this change in naval strategy.

Strategy changes have driven required modifications to PLAN ships' mission capabilities. These are usually described in terms of warfare areas, with improvements themselves defined by functional requirements—what new platforms/systems must do to achieve the desired tasks. The mission is then divided further into performance requirements: measurable results the system must demonstrate in order to meet a specified goal. In the case of warships, this generally translates into the performance of their weapons and sensors.

Weapons, sensors, and fire control systems are a warship's raison d'être. Yet these systems constitute a small fraction of the ship's overall displacement. For modern frigates and destroyers, the payload weight fraction is generally between 5 and 10 percent of full load displacement.[28] This value is somewhat deceptive, however, as payload impact is not restricted to the systems themselves.

The U.S. Navy weight classification system divides a ship's weight into seven general groups: Group 1, Hull Structure; Group 2, Main Propulsion; Group 3, Electrical; Group 4, Command and Surveillance; Group 5, Auxiliaries; Group 6, Outfit and Furnishings; and Group 7, Armament. The Chinese national military standards document, *Ships Work Breakdown Structure* (GJB 2258-94), uses the same categories. This structure is also used in organizing the overarching series in the *General Specifications for Naval Ships* (GJB 4000-2000).[29]

A ship's payload falls into Group 4 (the ship's sensors and combat systems) and Group 7 (its weapons systems). However, weapons, sensors, and combat systems all require electrical power; thus, they will impact the size of Group 3. In addition, these same systems may require cooling water, high-pressure air, and hydraulic and/or lubricating oil, all auxiliary machinery within Group 5. Auxiliary systems will also need electrical power, placing further demands on the electric plant. Finally, payload systems require crews to operate and maintain them. Accommodations, galley space, food storage, potable water, lighting, heating, and air conditioning all fall into Group 6, along with yet another increase in electrical power requirements.

If a change in strategy demands an increase in the payload to meet a specific requirement—the addition of an area defense SAM system, for example—the total impact on the ship design leaves the naval architect with few options other than increasing hull size to accommodate new systems and personnel. Unsurprisingly, PLAN ship size has grown with the evolved naval strategy. This trend appears to be continuing as the land-based mockup for the future Type 055 guided-missile cruiser suggests it will be considerably larger than the Type 052D *Luyang III*-class guided-missile destroyers currently under construction.

Naval Strategy Impact on Warfare Areas

As China's naval strategy evolved, the mission capabilities deemed necessary to achieve new tasks drove significant changes in PLAN warship design and payload. Exploring even a handful of these changes thoroughly would be arduous and time-consuming and yet still would fail to portray adequately the PLAN's progression over its sixty-seven years of service. Given these realities, we broadly map changes in individual warfare areas to changes in naval strategy.

Exhibit 1-1 surveys China's naval strategy development, paired with timelines marking key changes in capability for major warfare areas.[30] At the very bottom is an indicator of the main source of foreign influence over time. The countries listed were the primary providers of systems and technical assistance that supported development of indigenous Chinese weapons, sensors, and combat systems responsible for enhancements within individual warfare areas.

Antisurface Warfare

Antisurface warfare is the PLAN's core competency. Recognizing its vulnerability to amphibious landings, China was an early adopter of the antiship cruise missile (ASCM). Lacking larger warships with heavy firepower,

Exhibit 1-1. Evolution of China's Naval Strategy—Impact on PLAN Warfare Area Capabilities

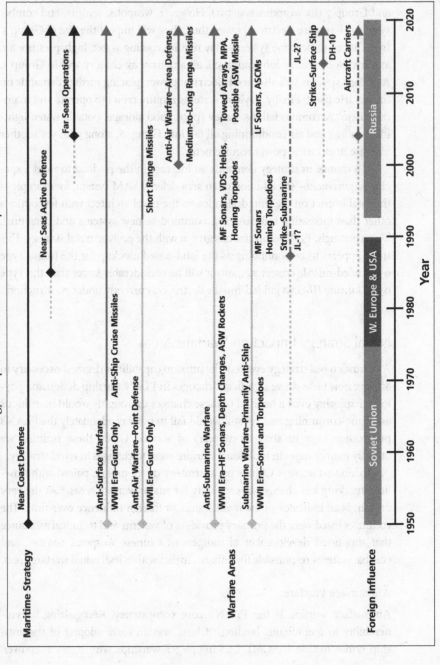

the young PLAN had to find ways to seriously damage approaching invading forces before it could land troops. Influenced by Soviet navy thinking that large surface ships were overly vulnerable to missiles and nuclear weapons, China was encouraged to develop a coastal defense fleet of missile-armed fast attack craft and submarines.[31]

Soon after signing the February 1959 agreement on technological aid to China's naval equipment, the Soviet Union transferred Type 542 (S-2/SS-C-2B Samlet) shore-to-ship missiles and Type 544 (P-15/SS-N-2A Styx) ship-to-ship missiles. Also transferred were several Project 183R (Komar) and Project 205 (Osa I) missile armed patrol craft and components for Project 633 (Romeo) submarines.[32]

Despite the departure of Soviet advisers in September 1960, China continued developing the Shangyou-1 (SY-1), a direct copy of the Soviet P-15/SS-N-2A Styx, and began the initial research of a longer-ranged variant, Haiying-1 (HY-1).[33] Notwithstanding Cultural Revolution delays, the SY-1 was accepted into service in late 1967 and fitted on Chinese missile patrol boats, converted Soviet-design destroyers and frigates, and ultimately the Type 053 *Jianghu*-class frigate. The HY-1J would enter service in 1975 on the Type 051 *Luda*-class destroyer.[34]

While the SY-1 and HY-1J were perceived as an effective defense against an invading amphibious attack, by the mid-1970s there were growing concerns about their vulnerability to new U.S.-deployed air defense systems. To help reduce this vulnerability, China introduced the lower-flight-profile SY-1A and HY-1A. But this was only a stopgap. Research commenced on small sea-skimming and supersonic missiles. The supersonic Yingji-1 (YJ-1) and HY-3 missiles' initial designs would prove flawed, and although later designs would successfully fly supersonically, their operational ranges were unsatisfactory and the missiles were canceled.[35]

As the near seas active defense concept was debated, the PLAN saw the need for a smaller but longer-range ASCM. During the coastal defense phase, SY-1- and HY-1J-armed ships were to be supported by coastal defense missile batteries. This would not be the case as the PLAN ventured farther from China's coast. This encouraged the PLAN to adopt smaller missiles, allowing more ship-based weapons. Engagement ranges longer than 40 to 70 kilometers (km) were also greatly desired, but this would be a long-term problem. The YJ-8 solid fuel missile program was started in 1976 and would reach initial operating capability (IOC) eleven years later.[36] A slightly modified variant, the folding wing YJ-8A, would become the main PLAN ASCM from the 1990s through the early 2000s. With smaller, stacked canister launchers, modified older ships enjoyed a 150 to 250 percent ASCM load-out increase.

As the YJ-8 was being fielded, China had already reached out to a French company, Microturbo SA, about buying small turbojets.[37] After purchasing approximately 150 TRI 60-2 turbojets, China began a crash reverse-engineering program to produce the engine indigenously. This would ultimately by accomplished by the mid-1990s; in 1998–99, the YJ-83 was accepted into service. The PLAN now had a medium-range missile that was difficult to counter due to its sea-skimming flight profile. The YJ-83, with a range of 180 km, would quickly become the PLAN's main antisurface weapon system, with the exception of the larger YJ-62 on the Type 052C *Luyang II* DDGs. But China's senior naval leadership remained dissatisfied—greater speed was still needed.[38]

Within several years after the Soviet collapse, China, still under a Western arms embargo, started reaching out to Russia to purchase advanced weaponry. In reaction to the 1995–96 Taiwan Strait incident, there was a dramatic increase in the purchase of naval, land, and air systems with the intent of deterring Taiwan from declaring its independence, and the United States from getting involved in "internal Chinese affairs." This purchase included the 3M80E/3M80MVE (SS-N-22 Sunburn), 3M54E (SS-N-27B Sizzler), and Kh-31P (AS-17 Krypton) supersonic missiles.

Since the early 2000s, Chinese engineers have worked with their Russian and Ukrainian counterparts to reverse-engineer the propulsion systems of these missiles. The PLAN is finally close to getting the ASCMs it has so long desired. The YJ-12, based on the Kh-31P (AS-17 Krypton) ramjet, likely entered service in late 2013 or early 2014 on PLAN H-6G bombers. The YJ-18, based on the 3M54E (SS-N-27B Sizzler), is undergoing land- and sea-based testing and could be deployed within the next two years on the PLAN's modern submarines—Type 039G *Song*, Type 039A/B *Yuan*, and Type 093 *Shang* classes—and the Type 052D *Luyang III*-class DDG.[39]

Despite the fact that the YJ-12 and YJ-18 are just now entering service, the evolution of the PLAN's ASCMs over the last sixty years was driven by the near coast defense and near seas active defense phases of its strategy. It will likely be some time before we start to see ASCMs whose designs will be directly impacted by the far seas operations phase. However, given historical development and demonstrated Chinese priorities, it can be inferred that higher speeds, longer range, and improved targeting are likely avenues for improvements. Given the few credible open source articles available, it can be argued that ranges out to 500 kilometers and hypersonic speeds (Mach 5 and greater) are performance characteristics that are possibly being discussed. This requires significantly greater targeting abilities than those possessed by current PLAN ships. Possible avenues include ship-launched stealthy unmanned aerial vehicles and direct satellite to ship data links—à la the Soviet radar ocean reconnaissance satellite.

Anti-Air Warfare

If ASuW was the PLAN's forte, AAW was one of its flaws. For most of the PLAN's operational history, air defense was based on short-range gun systems. Initially, these were manually aimed, unstabilized mounts that offered little hope of any real protection. The 1967 attack on Israeli destroyer *Eilat* by Egyptian Project 183R *Komar*-class missile-armed patrol boats with P-15/SS-N-2A Styx missiles showed the world the folly of attempting to use a World War II–era defense against a modern ASCM threat. When the PLAN looked at its ships' air defenses, they looked very similar to those of *Eilat*.

The PLAN was interested in fielding a missile-based air defense system but lacked one that would fit on its ships. The Soviet-supplied S-75 Dvina (SA-2A Guideline) SAM, produced in China as the Hongqi-1 (HQ-1), was simply too large. Even the Soviets had to put this system on a light cruiser to get it to sea; the PLAN lacked that option. The requirement for a low- to medium-altitude missile was first levied in 1965, but it would take two decades before the system started shooting down targets.[40] The HQ-61 SAM finally went to sea on the lead Type 053H2G *Jiangwei I*-class frigate in 1991.

Given the HQ-61's extended, tumultuous development, the PLAN hedged its bets, purchasing the French Crotale system in the mid-1980s.[41] Development and at-sea testing were largely finished before the Tiananmen Square arms embargo. This missile was first deployed as the HQ-7 on the Type 052 *Luhu*-class DD, *Harbin*, in 1994. Subsequently, the HQ-7 was the predominant short-range SAM on PLAN warships until the fielding of the HQ-10, a copy of the U.S. rolling airframe missile, in 2012.

While the HQ-61 and HQ-7 represented major PLAN improvements, both SAMs were short-range, point-defense systems—designed to provide protection only to the ship fitted with the SAM. An area defense SAM (missiles with a range exceeding approximately 15 nautical miles) would not be seriously considered until after the Central Military Commission was rudely surprised by Beijing's lack of palatable military options in the 1995–96 Taiwan Strait crisis.

Immediately after the cross-strait crisis, Chinese leaders realized that any attempt by the PLAN to prevent U.S. aircraft carriers from intervening was bound to fail as PLAN ships had to operate away from land-based air defenses. Lacking an organic ship-based area defense system left PLAN ships vulnerable to attack by U.S. carrier aviation. This put the near seas active defense strategy at risk, as the United States could stymie any operations in the near seas by dispatching a carrier group. This critical deficiency had to be dealt with, and quickly. Accordingly, China turned to Russia.

By purchasing the Project 956E *Sovremenny*-class DDGs, not only did the PLAN acquire a supersonic ASCM, it also received its first area defense SAM with the Shtil (SA-N-7A Gadfly). While Chinese experts recognized the Shtil exceeded anything they had, it was still a relatively short-ranged system (32 km). To rectify this, Beijing also purchased two ship sets of the Rif-M (SA-N-20 Gargoyle) long-range SAM and built the Type 051C *Luzhou*-class ships to put it to sea. This last purchase was likely insurance against any potential development problems with the HQ-9, China's indigenous long-range SAM based on the Russian S-300PMU (SA-10B Grumble). By the end of 2010, fifteen years after the Taiwan Strait crisis, the PLAN went from having no area air defense–capable ships at sea to sixteen, including four with an advanced long-range capability (Rif-M and HQ-9).

Today, the PLAN boasts over thirty area AAW platforms, including twenty Type 054A *Jiangkai II*-class guided-missile frigates (FFGs) with the HQ-16 vertically launched modified Shtil-type missile, and six Type 052C *Luyang II*-class DDGs with the HQ-9. China continues to build Type 054A frigates and has commissioned the lead hull of the Type 052D *Luyang III*-class DDG, which will reportedly be fitted with the extended-range (150 km) active homing HQ-9A.[42]

As with ASuW, these remarkable changes in the PLAN's AAW capabilities were driven by an urgent need to support Beijing's near seas active defense strategy. Future far seas operations–inspired improvements could include SAMs with engagement ranges out to 300–400 km and likely a ballistic missile defense capability.

Antisubmarine Warfare

Antisubmarine warfare is another significant PLAN weakness. But unlike AAW, the most telling system improvements are very recent, and Chinese crews are far from proficient with their new equipment. From 1950 through the mid-1980s, the PLAN operated with essentially a World War II ASW system based on high-frequency active sonars, depth charges, and ahead-thrown rockets. The early sonars (SJD-1, 3, and 5) were based on the Soviet Tamir 5 and 11 systems, improved copies of the British Type 128 sonar first produced in 1937.[43] Depth charge rails and throwers could lay a moderate size pattern, and China's copy of the Soviet RBU-1200 could deliver six unguided ASW rockets to approximately 2 km. Against a nuclear-powered submarine, or even a modern conventional submarine, such capabilities are virtually useless in deeper water. Still, as long as the PLAN was only concerned with executing near coast defense, they provided baseline self-defense capability.

As PLAN leaders considered the requirements for a near seas active defense, improvements in ASW capabilities were likely viewed as essential, as ships would now be venturing beyond the shallows. Fortunately for the PLAN, warming relations with Europe and the United States beginning in the mid-1970s allowed access to more modern sensors, weapons, and ASW helicopters.

By the late 1980s, the PLAN had begun experimenting with helicopter operations on a modified Type 053H *Jianghu II*-class frigate, and since then every medium-to-large PLAN surface combatant has at least a helicopter landing deck, if not a hangar. China's purchase of French helicopters, the Super Frelon (Chinese Z-8) and Panther (Chinese Z-9), fitted with the French HS-12 dipping sonar and Italian A244s ASW homing torpedoes, yielded major gains. The PLAN also purchased several sets of Raytheon's DE-1160 series sonar suite from an authorized Italian producer. Three such systems were installed on Type 051 *Luda*-class destroyer trials ship *Zhuhai* and on China's two Type 052 *Luhu*-class destroyers. The DE-1160 system is an integrated hull and variable depth sonar (VDS) that operates at medium frequency and has a considerably improved detection. The DE-1160 would become the basis for the Chinese H/SJD-7 integrated, medium frequency sonar that is on many PLAN warships.

Renewed relations with Russia gave China access to the MGK-335EM sonar suite on the Project 956E *Sovremenny*-class destroyers, Ka-28 Helix ASW helicopters, APR-2E ASW rocket torpedoes, and probably assistance with the propulsion system in the Chinese Yu-7 lightweight ASW torpedo— a U.S. MK 46 Mod 2 copy. These systems greatly enhanced capabilities, particularly against conventional submarines in shallower near seas waters. But against a quiet nuclear submarine, PLAN surface ships remained extremely vulnerable, especially in deep water.

Within the last decade, PLAN surface combatants have exhibited significant improvements in ASW capabilities to support far seas operations. During construction and sea trials, both Type 052C *Luyang II*-class destroyers and the Type 054A *Jiangkai II*-class frigates were seen with towed array deployment ports on their transoms. In March 2012, a CCTV-7 video showed the Type 054A FFG *Zhoushan* (Hull 529) streaming a passive towed array.[44] Shortly thereafter, the designations H/SJG-206 and SJG-208 began appearing on Chinese websites. The H/SJG-206 was described as a tactical system, like the U.S. SQR-19, while the SJG-208 was described as a surveillance towed array, similar to the U.S. Surveillance Towed Array Sensor System.[45]

Subsequently, both Type 052 *Luhu*-class destroyers underwent modernization overhauls in 2012 in which the H/SJD-7/DE-1160 VDS was removed and a towed array system installed in its place. In addition, several Type 056 *Jiangdao*-class corvettes on the building ways started showing indications of towed array systems fitting. Then in 2014, a large access door suddenly appeared on late-model Type 054A frigates and Type 056 corvettes, with a similar door on Type 052D destroyers. Later Internet photography would show this was a deployment door for a new VDS system, often described as an active towed array comparable to Thales's CAPTAS 2 system. If this most recent assessment proves correct—available photographic evidence is compelling—then the PLAN has leapt to technological levels consistent with current European systems.

Deployment of passive and active towed arrays, and the Y-8Q maritime patrol aircraft's recently reported IOC, strongly suggest that China is in the process of deploying deep-water ASW capabilities to support far seas operations. Should the active towed array prove similarly capable to Western European systems, it would also be very useful in shallower waters and enhance the near seas active defense capability. But although the PLAN is deploying some very sophisticated sensor systems, it will take years of training before crews become proficient in fully exploiting their capabilities.

Submarine Warfare

The PLAN has historically valued submarines highly, largely based on its exposure to early Soviet naval thought and understanding of what the U.S. submarine force accomplished against Japan during World War II. Currently, China has the world's largest submarine force with approximately 65—10 to 12 nuclear-powered, and approximately 53 conventional, including several test submarines, and so on.[46] However, despite the lofty reputation and high numbers, the PLAN submarine force has the same mission focus as it did in the 1950s: an antisurface force with very limited self-defense ASW capabilities. Even the new Type 093 *Shang*-class SSN would be horribly overmatched were it to face a modern, very quiet Western nuclear attack submarine.

During the 1960s through the early 1980s, China produced numerous Type 033 *Romeo*-class submarines. These boats had very limited sensors and torpedoes and could do little more than defend China's coast. As the PLAN adopted near seas active defense, submarines with better sensors and weapons would be needed to patrol waters farther away. Interestingly, the first Type 035

Ming-class submarine was produced in 1971, but production halted after three hulls in 1979 and did not resume until 1987. It was then, the late 1970s through the mid-1980s, that near seas active defense concepts were debated and finally approved. Perhaps transforming naval strategy forced reassessment of the Type 035 *Ming*-class design to enable it to fulfill expanded mission requirements.

Type 039/039G *Song*-class submarines, which started entering the fleet in 1999, are more capable with an improved sonar system, homing torpedoes, and likely designed from inception to use YJ-82 submerged launch ASCMs. This suggests the influence of near seas active defense strategic concepts. While the YJ-82's range is minimal, less than a standard YJ-8/8A's 42 km range, a submerged launch capability was a significant step forward. The soon-to-be-fielded YJ-18 will considerably enhance the Type 039G's ability to attack surface ships.

Even purchase of eight improved Project 636 *Kilo*-class with the 3M54E Club (SS-N-27B Sizzler) in the mid-2000s, and introduction of the Type 039A/B *Yuan*-class diesel attack submarine (SSP) in 2006 with a Stirling engine air-independent power (AIP) system all point to an antiship mission bias.[47]

Save for the Type 094 *Jin*-class ballistic missile submarine (SSBN), no PLAN submarine is fitted with a passive towed array—the Type 094 appears to have a Russian-style towed array deployment tube on the upper rudder. The most capable sensor currently fielded on the Type 039A/B *Yuan*-class SSP, and likely the Type 093 *Shang*-class SSN, is the SQG-207 low-frequency passive linear flank array. Neither this sonar nor the hull arrays are even remotely adequate for detecting a very quiet submarine, but they will work well against noisier surface ships.

One of the more vexing issues with China's submarine force is trying to fit nuclear-powered attack submarines into their naval strategic concepts. Some Chinese naval analysts have argued that "the new SSN [Type 093] fits in well with the PLAN's offshore defense strategy."[48] The fit is forced at best; it is hard to justify investing the resources to develop nuclear propulsion by near coast defense and near seas active defense requirements. Submarines are less vulnerable to air attack than surface ships, but this benefit applies to any submarine. Furthermore, the Type 091 *Han*-class SSN is very noisy and can easily be detected and tracked by modern passive systems, particularly submarine towed arrays. The Office of Naval Intelligence's 2009 report suggests that the first two Type 093 *Shang*-class SSN hulls are nearly as noisy.[49] And even if the later units are somewhat quieter, they will still be quite vulnerable.

So why build SSNs when an AIP-equipped Type 039A/B *Yuan*-class likely has the necessary endurance requirement demanded by a near seas active defense and is fitted with the same sensors and weapons as a Type 093, but is immensely quieter? The answer most consistent with our understanding of China's evolving naval strategy and historical SSN development is that national pride, not naval strategy, drove the decision.

Mao Zedong is quoted as saying that China would build a nuclear powered submarine "if it took 10,000 years."[50] For the naval strategist, this is hardly an encouraging comment. But if the initial goal was for China to develop the *ability* to produce nuclear-powered naval vessels, then construction of the Type 091 *Han*-class SSN starts to make some sense—one learns by doing. That the Type 093 SSN is still under construction, despite its limitations, demonstrates that preserving and nurturing the ability to produce nuclear submarines continue to resonate strongly within the PLAN. Interestingly, far seas operations requirements—primarily endurance and speed—best justify nuclear-powered submarines. The recent deployment of Type 091 and 093 SSNs to the Indian Ocean demonstrates the advantages of mobility that nuclear power provides.[51]

However, if PLAN SSNs are to survive while conducting far seas operations in the future, they must become considerably quieter and more adept at deep-water ASW; this includes towed array sonars. Both are high hurdles that must be cleared, a time-consuming process. The starkness of this dichotomy between the PLAN's surface and submarine forces is ironic; the former has embraced ASW, the latter has yet to do so. Perhaps the Type 095 SSN reportedly will incorporate these features and become the PLAN's first true blue-water nuclear-powered attack submarine.

Strike Warfare

The requirement for the PLAN to conduct strike warfare is fairly recent, likely driven by far seas operations strategic needs. Within the context of near coast defense and near seas active defense phases of the naval strategy, the Second Artillery Corps had adequate firepower to conduct attacks against land-based targets within the near seas area. The same can be said for strategic strike. So where does that leave the PLAN?

Some analysts stress the PLAN's long-standing desire for an SSBN dating to the late 1960s. However, the lone Type 092 *Xia*-class SSBN, like its SSN counterparts, was an object of national pride.[52] Despite the outlay of significant resources, however, there is no evidence the Julang-1 (JL-1) submarine-launched ballistic missile was ever accepted into service.[53] There is also no evidence the Type 092 SSBN ever conducted a deterrent patrol. One Chinese analysis states, "The *Xia*-class actually is not a genuine deterrent capability"—the vessel's true worth was more symbolic.[54]

Within the context of far seas operations, an SSBN force is far more justifiable and very likely drove demand for multiple submarines in the follow-on

Type 094 *Jin*-class. The Type 094's missile, the JL-2, also makes considerably more sense as it greatly outranges the JL-1 (about 8,000 km versus 1,600 km).[55] The JL-2 reportedly completed testing in 2012 and reached IOC in 2013.[56] To date there is no evidence a Type 094 *Jin*-class SSBN has made a deterrent patrol, although DoD expects them to commence in 2016.[57]

Long-range precision strike from surface ships is very new and definitely reflects the influence of far seas operations. The Type 052D *Luyang III*-class destroyer with the universal vertical launching system (VLS) will be the first PLAN platform capable of firing the Donghai-10 (DH-10) land-attack cruise missile (LACM), although it is rumored that the next generation Type 095 SSN will also be equipped with a DH-10–capable VLS.

The U.S. Navy has long charged carriers with strike warfare as a primary mission. From World War II through operations against the Islamic State, U.S. carriers have conducted strikes against targets deep inside another nation's shoreline. Most carriers in foreign navies, particularly those of Russian origin, lack this capability. Soviet/Russian aircraft carriers are more closely associated with extending air defense boundaries by providing fighter cover for naval vessels and to protect the motherland from LACM attacks. The PLAN's first aircraft carrier, *Liaoning*, is restricted by its Soviet heritage to largely providing air cover for formations beyond land-based fighter range. And while the J-15 Flankers may be able to carry some ground attack ordnance, the load-out will be limited by ski jump restrictions. These limitations are not unrealistic for a vessel the PLAN designates a trials platform. Future aircraft carrier designs will likely be fitted with catapults that transcend this constraint, but these ships remain well in the distance. Regardless, desire to expand PLAN fighter air defense, early warning aircraft/helicopters, and ground strike potential was driven by far seas operations considerations.

Conclusion

China's naval strategy has evolved through three distinct phases over the last sixty-six years from near coast defense to near seas active defense to near and far seas operations. With each new phase, the PLAN's area of responsibility and mission set grew. But while China is currently extending its field of view to far seas operations, the priority of conducting near seas active defense remains. As each new strategic phase was adopted and implemented, the changes drove the need for more capable naval vessels that could deploy, operate, and survive at ever-greater distances from China's shores.

The demonstrated improvements in warfare area capabilities tracked across decades correlate strongly with the changes in naval strategy. This reflects the scientific nature and centralized decisionmaking inherent in Chinese strategic thought processes. From 1950 through today, PLAN platform technical capabilities have evolved considerably, reaching parity with Western navies in some warfare areas but still lacking in others. The more recent shift to far seas operations has caused the PLAN to expand its warfighting horizons once again, especially in the areas of deep-water ASW, precision strike, and aircraft carrier operations.

With time the PLAN will gain more experience as it deploys farther and more frequently. This will enhance its proficiency in the various warfare areas and strengthen its confidence—reason enough to monitor its progress closely.

Notes

1. Xie Wei and Lu Chao, "浅析我国海洋发展战略及未来船舶发展趋势" ["An Analysis of China's Maritime Development Strategy and Trends in Ship Development"], 船海工程 [*Ship and Ocean Engineering*] 42, no. 3 (June 2013): 128.

2. Shou Xiaosong, ed., 战略学 [*Science of Military Strategy*] (Beijing: 军事科学出版社 [Military Science Press], 2013), 207 (hereafter, SMS).

3. Nan Li, "The Evolution of China's Naval Strategy and Capabilities: From 'Near Coast' and 'Near Seas' to 'Far Seas,'" in *The Chinese Navy: Expanding Capabilities, Evolving Roles*, ed. Phillip C. Saunders and Christopher Yung (Washington, DC: National Defense University Press, 2011), 111. See also Peng Kehui, "略论新中国海洋战略的历史演进" ["A Discussion on the Evolution of the Maritime Strategy of the People's Republic of China"], 社会科学论坛 [*Tribune of Social Sciences*], October 2012, 2.

4. Li, "The Evolution of China's Naval Strategy and Capabilities," 111–12.

5. Ibid., 113.

6. SMS, 207.

7. Ibid., 208.

8. Ibid.

9. Ibid.

10. Ibid.

11. Li, "The Evolution of China's Naval Strategy and Capabilities," 118.

12. Ibid., 155.

13. Ibid., 124.

14. Ibid.

15. 中国的军事战略 [*China's Military Strategy*] (Beijing: 中华人民共和国国务院新闻办公室 [State Council Information Office, PRC], May 2015), http://www.81.cn/dblj/2015-05/26/content_6507373.htm.

16. Liu Huaqing, 刘华清回忆录 [*Liu Huaqing's Memoirs*] (Beijing: 解放军出版社 [PLA Press], 2004), 434, as cited in Li, "The Evolution of China's Naval Strategy and Capabilities," 129.

17. Ibid.

18. SMS, 209.

19. Liu Dexi, "创建现代新型海洋大国的战略思考" ["Strategic Considerations for Becoming a Modern, New-Type Maritime Power"], 新远见 [*New Thinking*], November 2012, 20. See also Zhang Wei, "中国特色海权理论发展历程综述" ["A General Review of the History of China's Sea-Power Theory Development"], 学术前沿 [*Frontiers*] (July 2012): 10–11.

20. Liu, "Strategic Considerations," 15–16. See also Xie and Lu, 128.

21. 方晓志 [Fang Xiaozhi], "加强中国画远洋海军建设的必要性与可行性" ["An Analysis of the Necessity and Feasibility of Strengthening Construction of a Far Seas Navy"], 中国与国际关系学刊 [*Journal of China and International Relations*] 2.2 (2014): 106–14.

22. Wu Shengli, "深刻吸取甲午战争历史教训坚定不移走经略海洋维护海泉发展海军之路" ["Learn Profound Historical Lessons from the Sino-Japanese War of 1894–95 and Unswervingly Take the Path of Planning and Managing Maritime Affairs, Safeguarding Maritime Rights and Interests, and Building a Powerful Navy"], 中国军事科学 [*China Military Science*], no. 4 (August 2014): 3.

23. Zhang, "General Review," 32.

24. Wu, "Learn Profound Historical Lessons," 3.

25. SMS, 209.

26. Nan Li, "China's Evolving Naval Strategy and Capabilities in the Hu Jintao Era," in *Assessing the People's Liberation Army in the Hu Jintao Era*, ed. Roy Kamphausen, David Lai, and Travis Tanner (Carlisle, PA: U.S. Army War College Press, 2014), 262.

27. *China's Military Strategy.*

28. Full load displacement is the displacement of a warship that is ready for service and includes its crew, general stores, consumables, ammunition load, aircraft and aviation stores, fuel, lubricating oil, and other variable loads. In the U.S. Navy, it is not the maximum displacement of the ship.

29. 国防科学技术工业委员会 [Commission of Science, Technology, and Industry for National Defense], GJB 2258-94 舰船工作分解结构 [*Ships Work Breakdown Structure*]; GJB 4000-2000 舰船通用规范 总册 [*General Specifications for Naval Ships—Parts 0-9*].

30. Initial operating capability year information used in diagram is based on commissioning dates of PLAN platforms with those capabilities, taken from multiple years of *Jane's Fighting Ships*, *Combat Fleets of the World* (U.S. Naval Institute), and *Weyer's Warships of the World*.

31. S. G. Gorshkov, *The Sea Power of the State* (Elmsford, NY: Pergamon, 1980), 196.

32. A. S. Pavlov, *Warships of the USSR and Russia 1945-1995* (Annapolis, MD: Naval Institute Press, 1997), 70–71, 157.

33. "浅析中国反舰导弹" ["A Preliminary Analysis of China's Anti-Ship Missiles"], *Shipborne Weapons* [舰载武器] (May 2008): 35–47.

34. Ibid.

35. "蓝天碧海献丹心 刘兴洲院士与同事们研制冲压发动机的轶事" ["Blue Sky and Sea Offer Loyalty: Anecdotes on Scramjet Development by Academician Liu Xingzhou and His Colleagues"], 中国航天科工集团公司 [China Aerospace Science and Industry Corporation], November 11, 2011, http://www.casic.com.cn/n103/n135/c545513/content.html.

36. Christopher P. Carlson, "China's Eagle Strike-Eight Anti-Ship Cruise Missiles, Parts 1, 2, and 3" (Washington, DC: Defense Media Network, February 4, 2013), http://www.defensemedianetwork.com/stories/chinas-eagle-strike-eight-anti-ship-cruise-missiles-designation-confusion-and-the-family-members-from-yj-8-to-yj-8a/.

37. Ibid.

38. For details, see Andrew S. Erickson and Christopher P. Carlson, "The Need for Speed: China's Pursuit of Supersonic Anti-Ship Cruise Missiles," *Naval War College Review* (forthcoming).

39. Office of Naval Intelligence (ONI), *The PLA Navy: New Capabilities and Missions for the 21st Century* (Suitland, MD: ONI, 2015), 16, 19.

40. Norman Friedman, *World Naval Weapon Systems,* fifth ed. (Annapolis, MD: Naval Institute Press, 2006), 571.

41. Ibid., 572.

42. ONI, *The PLA Navy,*15–16.

43. Friedman, *World Naval Weapon Systems,* 571.

44. "CCTV Exposure 054A Frigate with Towed Array!" March 2, 2012, http://www.jeixun.com/article/201203/7710.html.

45. "H/SJG-206 Type Line Array Towed Sonar," March 2, 2012, http://blog.sina.com.cn/s/blog_5976c16801011u8u.html.

46. Office of the Secretary of Defense (OSD), *Military and Security Developments Involving the People's Republic of China 2015* (Washington, DC: OSD, 2015), 26.

47. ONI, *The PLA Navy,* 19.

48. Andrew Erickson et al., ed., *China's Future Nuclear Submarine Force* (Annapolis, MD: Naval Institute Press, 2007), 55.

49. ONI, *The People's Liberation Army Navy: A Modern Navy with Chinese Characteristics* (Suitland, MD: ONI, 2009), 22.

50. Erickson et al., ed., *China's Future Nuclear Submarine Force,* 69.

51. OSD, *Military and Security Developments Involving the People's Republic of China 2015,* 19; OSD, *Military and Security Developments Involving the People's Republic of China 2016* (Washington, DC: OSD, 2016), 22.

52. Erickson et al., ed., *China's Future Nuclear Submarine Force,* 186.

53. National Air and Space Intelligence Center (NASIC), *Ballistic and Cruise Missile Threat* (Wright-Patterson Air Force Base, OH: NASIC, 2013), 22.

54. Erickson et al., ed., *China's Future Nuclear Submarine Force,* 186.

55. Friedman, *World Naval Weapon Systems,* 503.

56. ONI, *The PLA Navy,* 19.

57. OSD, *Military and Security Developments Involving the People's Republic of China 2016,* 26.

Morgan Clemens and Ian Easton

Status, Goals, Prospects

Party-State Strategic Requirements for China's Shipbuilding Industry

THIS CHAPTER EXAMINES the requirements imposed upon China's shipbuilding industry (SBI) by the Chinese Communist Party, the People's Liberation Army (PLA), and the Chinese state. Existing as it does within a Leninist system, the industry plainly acknowledges the leading role that the party-state must play as guide to the industry's structural and product optimization.[1] The chapter thus probes strategic roles the state expects the industry to fulfill, both commercial and military, to better serve its own strategic goals. In doing so, it highlights basic challenges currently facing the industry that may inhibit its fulfilling those roles and seeks to identify how industry and state are collaborating to overcome these obstacles. It particularly focuses on the basic guidance the state directs toward the industry and the impact of resulting policies. It is a consideration, then, of how the state's intentions for the industry interact with the industry's present conditions to produce policy directives and guidance. It concludes that the state has assigned the industry a key role in supporting China's continued development as a great power, and that the state has equally determined to carry out a series of far-reaching reforms within the industry so as to enable it to fulfill its role.

To reach this conclusion, the chapter progressively surveys the industry's historical background before considering the expectations imposed upon the industry and the explicit policy guidance provided that is intended to meet these expectations. The chapter then identifies and examines several key issue areas within the industry that have received particular attention from the state or that hold out serious prospects of retarding the industry's progress. It is upon evaluation of the industry's progress in addressing these issues that the state's future policymaking will be based. Finally, several of these issue areas are given more concrete illustration by a brief examination of one aspect of the industry military shipbuilding, namely vessels intended for amphibious operations. The ultimate objective is to gain a clearer understanding of the top-level policy pressures and fundamental problems that define the course of China's modern shipbuilding industry.

Historical Background[2]

Since 1978, China's SBI has undergone enormous transformation and progress. The industry was one of the first to begin the process of corporatization, as the Sixth Ministry of Machine Building was abolished in May 1982 and its assets reconfigured into the China State Shipbuilding Corporation (CSSC/中国船舶工业集团公司). Ensuing years saw rapid growth in both the industry's output and its global market share as it leveraged China's vast reserves of low-cost labor and benefited from the demand created by China's burgeoning export economy.[3] The large, world-beating shipbuilding sectors in Japan and South Korea were explicitly looked to as models for successful development paths (but with tight state control of the Chinese sector remaining a given). The result was rapid development and perhaps the single most successful attempt at commercialization and entry into the international market on the part of a Chinese defense sector. Beyond CSSC, the larger industry benefited from its close geographic proximity to the earliest centers of China's post-reform economic development along the southern and eastern coasts, especially Shanghai, Shenzhen, and Dalian.[4] By the 1990s the industry was producing more than one million tons of commercial shipping per year, half going to export orders.

In 1999 there came a major reorganization of the industry when CSSC's shipyards and other assets in northern China (north of the Yangzi River) were split into a second conglomerate known as the China Shipbuilding Industry Corporation (CSIC/中国船舶重工集团公司). This was undertaken as part of an effort to introduce competition and impose greater efficiencies. They were deliberately accorded similar resources and industrial capabilities to foster active and sustained competition for both state and commercial orders. Nonetheless, China's two single largest shipbuilding firms, CSSC and CSIC, are directly owned and controlled by the state through the state-owned Assets Supervision and Administration Commission. As two of the ten conglomerates that comprise the defense industry, they are integral components.[5]

Despite their size and importance, however, CSSC and CSIC did not (and do not) comprise the whole story of China's SBI. At their division, the two conglomerates accounted for nearly three-quarters of China's shipbuilding output, but barely a tenth of the total number of shipyards and shipbuilding facilities in China. The balance was made up of hundreds (if not thousands) of small yards and other facilities, either privately owned or managed by local or provincial governments, engaged in both ship construction and repair. These yards continue to vary widely in size, stability, and competence, ranging from large integrated manufacturing groups competing alongside CSSC and CSIC for international orders, to small "beach yards" supporting the coastal trade and local fishing industries. These local shipbuilders' output grew at much the same pace of the big conglomerates and by the 2000s formed a significant component of the broader SBI in China, accounting more than 10 percent of total construction from 1999 to 2008.[6] Indeed, the industry's rapid growth— from a negligible share of the world's total production in 1980 to nearly 20 percent by 2008—vaulted China into the shipbuilding forefront.

It was at this high-water mark that China's SBI encountered its first serious, systemic crisis, when the financial crisis of 2008 sent much of the world outside East Asia into recession, undercutting exports (and by extension general trade) and depressing new shipping demand. Chinese shipyards' orders quickly plummeted as international debt and monetary worries made effective financing increasingly difficult. These troubles (and the sharp competition for orders they induced) quickly revealed the serious, industry-wide problems that low labor costs and burgeoning demand for shipping had previously ameliorated or even obscured. Among those problems were low product quality, obsolete equipment, outdated construction methods, and an often poorly trained and equipped workforce. Together, these problems imperiled many shipbuilding enterprises' viability and even the long-term sustainability of the industry itself. These concerns prompted direct, energetic state response, with many active measures intended to bolster the industry and enable it to fulfill its planned economic and strategic role.

Present Situation

Despite having seen the SBI reach unprecedented heights only to falter amid global vicissitudes, China's objectives and expectations for the industry, at least in the broadest terms, remain largely unchanged and are indeed focused on restoring its economic and financial foundations to sound condition. In particular, China still intends to become a "shipbuilding power" to rival any other. This hinges on several factors: development scale, product quality and production efficiency, structural optimization, and development sustainability. "It is on the basis of these factors that China's shipbuilding industry as a whole will rise or fall, and will meet or fail to meet the objectives set out for it by the party-state, whose ministries and other organs are the only institutions qualified to quantify and judge the industry's progress."[7] The political importance of the industry's success or failure in making China a shipbuilding power is magnified by the industry's critical role in the broader economy, with 113 of the country's 135 major industrial sectors highly dependent upon or otherwise strongly connected to shipbuilding.[8] As Xi Jinping and China's current leadership attempt the arduous task of transforming China into a middle-class society, it will be critical for them to ensure that the industry acts as an economic engine rather than dead weight.

The industry is also critical to China's development beyond the simple economic context in that the industry (especially the state-owned conglomerates) is critical to naval development. Xi Jinping has stated that "China's effort to build a middle-class society is entering a decisive stage under new historical conditions," during which external conditions represent a serious potential threat to achieving internal development objectives.[9] It will, of course, fall in large part upon the navy (with its inherent mobility, versatility, and long reach) to counter and neutralize these threats.[10] Indeed, the party's guidance to the PLA identifies the primary threat direction as from the sea, necessitating a military capable of answering a principal "threat of high-end war" emanating from the sea, encompassing both territorial disputes (e.g., Taiwan, the Senkaku/Diaoyu and Spratly islands) and the possibility of containment in the western Pacific and the northern Indian Ocean.[11] All threaten China's ultimate socioeconomic development objective.[12]

The People's Liberation Army Navy (PLAN) must therefore undertake increasingly varied advanced missions ever farther from shore while facing progressively greater threats (especially from missiles). These will include joint force coordination, long-range precision strikes, and many other types of complex operations. The ultimate result will be that PLAN technological requirements will inexorably increase, especially in terms of advanced, multirole vessels.[13] Such vessels can only come from China's SBI, which will be called on to support development of carrier groups and amphibious forces, civil-military force integration, and the fusion of naval, coastal, air, and space forces into an integrated security system.[14] Indeed, when confronting the military market, the primary issues facing the industry are proliferation of digitization and increasing numbers of intelligent systems, in terms of both components and systems integration.[15] Most importantly, the industry will be charged with integrating (within vessels) precision strike systems, electronic warfare equipment, network warfare equipment, and information systems.[16] It must supply these to the PLAN at reasonable, sustainable costs, which will necessitate an efficient and self-sustaining industry.

The state of the industry thus assumes deep political and strategic significance for China's leadership, for larger economic development, and for critical military modernization. Correcting the industry's weaknesses and inefficiencies, all too apparent since the global financial crisis, assumes paramount importance in achieving the leadership's larger strategic goals for industry and country alike. Execution, however, is proving difficult. As Chinese analysts have noted, China's economy is entering a "new normal," with growth abating, development refocusing on quality and efficiency, and "new industrial sectors" arising.[17] China's SBI must adapt. This requires continued institutional reforms: methods of operation, resource allocation, and ownership structure, and continued efforts to bolster innovation, research, and development.[18]

To address common problems facing international shipbuilding, China once again utilizes Japan and South Korea as models. Zhang Guangqin, China Association of the National Shipbuilding Industry's (CANSI's) former head, contends that China's industry must be reformed and improved to the extent necessary to make the "China shipbuilding brand" equal to those of Japan and Korea. According to Zhang, this would particularly entail achieving comparable physical concentration of production facilities.[19] Similarly, the State Administration for Science, Technology, and Industry for National Defense (SASTIND) has emphasized the degree to which Korean shipbuilders have responded to market changes by consolidating and integrating vertically with systems and components manufacturers, while also noting that Japan's response has been to increase its vessels' technological edge, especially in efficiency and environmental protection.[20] Indeed, even the structural reforms evident in the Korean industry are seen as products of increasing technical advantages, with SASTIND contending that Korean shipbuilders recognized early on that their own technological and engineering capabilities were not entirely sufficient to produce the sort of energy-efficient, environmentally sound vessels needed to remain competitive on the international market. Their response was to engage in "symbiotic development," establishing formal relationships (or even merging) with enterprises capable of producing systems and equipment needed. Though not necessarily representing vertical integration in the most literal sense, these sorts of "long-term win-win cooperation mechanisms" are presented as important means of achieving and maintaining "shipbuilding power" status.[21]

The 2009 State Council–issued Shipbuilding Industry Restructuring and Revitalization Plan describes the more specific "contradictions that were daily being made more apparent" by plummeting orders and skyrocketing financing problems resulting from the global recession. Among them were weak independent innovation capability, overly expansive growth patterns, redundant investments, serious excess capacity, lagging shipboard equipment development, and little marine engineering equipment development progress.[22] Enumerated in 2009, these problems still constitute the industry's primary obstacles.

Solutions

The question, then, is how China intends to overcome these problems in order to develop and maintain an internationally competitive shipbuilding sector befitting a rising great power. The party-state has by no means failed the industry in terms of providing guidance and direction. The aforementioned 2009 State Council plan lists nine principal tasks for restructuring and revitalizing the industry:[23]

- stabilizing production
- expanding demand
- developing marine engineering equipment
- supporting corporate mergers and acquisitions
- improving independent innovation capabilities
- transforming enterprises technologically
- actively developing the ship repair business
- opening up the international market
- strengthening enterprise management.

Thus, the focus is on stabilizing and expanding shipbuilding enterprises' income streams in the near term and sustaining them in the longer term by promoting structural adjustments: integrating shipbuilding resources, ship repair, and marine engineering equipment production resources, and fostering the joint shipbuilding and supporting industry development.[24] The 2009 plan outlines policy measures to help execute these tasks, including increasing operating credit available to producers and foreign purchasers, accelerating replacement of obsolete ships and single-hulled tankers to foster demand, and strictly controlling investment in new production capacity.[25] While the 2009 State Council plan was to some degree an emergency measure and technically covered only 2009 to 2011, the directives and policy prescriptions it provides are of such a long-term, fundamental nature that they still generally represent the party-state's guidance to the industry. This is emphasized by the fact that the State Council's 2013 Implementation Plan for Accelerating Structural Adjustment and Advancing Transformation in the Ship Building Industry offers a basically identical analysis of the problems afflicting the industry and what measures must be taken to rectify them.[26] Though these are prescriptions from the state to industry, it is clear that both sides are expected to play an active part. Chinese analysts point to a definite delineation in roles, with the state concentrating on large-scale integration and restructuring, expanding financing channels (bonds, banking, insurance, capital markets, etc.) especially for nonstate enterprises, and providing direct financial support and preferential tax policies, while individual enterprises seek to improve personnel quality, build their technological innovation capabilities, develop higher-value-added products and services, and begin to determine their greatest strengths as a basis for future specialization. Moreover, enterprises must also pay closer attention to market demands and develop more collaborative relationships with their customers.[27]

It is clear, then, that the Chinese state and SBI face complex tasks to make China into a first-class shipbuilding power. Since space considerations preclude detailed consideration of each task, the following section will instead attempt to examine these tasks in terms of several critical issues facing the industry. These include organizational restructuring, resource integration and reduction of excess capacity, accelerating demand and increasing exports, expanding production beyond simple shipbuilding, promoting civil-military integration, improving financial arrangements, and improving personnel quality. By briefly examining these admittedly broad issue areas, it is hoped that some of the vital tasks facing the shipbuilding industry will be brought into sharper focus.

Critical Issues

According to Xi Jinping, in the context of China's SBI, there is no task more important than comprehensive transformation or restructuring.[28] Particularly problematic is the industry's excessive bloating: Chinese analysts note that in 2013 China had more than eight hundred shipbuilding enterprises, compared with only twenty in Korea, and that as a result capacity utilization was at only 75 percent, due also to the aftereffects of the financial crisis.[29] It was largely with this specific problem in mind that the State Council issued its 2013 Implementation Plan.[30] A major problem with both private and state-owned shipbuilders (and especially enterprises owned by local and provincial governments) has been persistent focus on infrastructure investment and simple expansion of production capacity. Even after the financial crisis created underutilization of existing facilities, many enterprises remain fixated on building more and larger docks, slipways, and other production facilities because of inertia, fixed planning, and institutional logrolling. Moreover, many such new facilities were not cutting-edge and would do nothing to make the yards more competitive in the future.[31] Obviously, such blind expansion does little to make China a sustainable "shipbuilding power." Thus, according to the 2013 Implementation Plan, infrastructure investment should be focused on establishing modern shipbuilding methods, accelerating the development of informatization within production, promoting "lean shipbuilding" utilizing energy- and material-efficient processes, and otherwise reducing costs and increasing efficiency in order to keep Chinese vessels competitive internationally.[32] This means the industry as a whole can no longer afford to expand in physical size, but rather must engage in a period of reorganization or recombination, focusing on cooperative use of existing facilities to expand individual enterprises' business.[33] Accordingly, the 2013 Implementation Plan directs the state to assist "qualified enterprises" in achieving this sort of restructuring by multiple means, including mergers, joint ventures, and simple cooperation between enterprises. The point of this cooperation is to enable enterprises to better pool their research, development, and production resources, as well as their overseas relationships and marketing networks, all toward the larger goal of producing more technologically advanced ships able to compete in the global marketplace.[34]

Thus, curbing overexpansion and reducing excess capacity (especially backward and outdated production capacity) are critical to the industry's future, but so too are steady progress in corporate mergers and acquisitions, increasing industrial concentration, the integration of shipbuilding infrastructure, and the development of a more reasonable industrial layout.[35] Unsurprisingly, state planning documents include provisions directly tackling the problem. The State Council's 2009 plan included draconian limits on infrastructure investment, specifically limiting the ability of maritime, environmental, financial, and other state planning agencies at all levels of government to independently approve the expansion of production facilities at existing shipyards during 2009–11.[36] The limited effectiveness of this prohibition is likely indicated by the fact that the State Council's 2013 Implementation Plan likewise imposed restrictions on infrastructure expansion. In particular, the plan emphasized continuing problems with local actors approving projects in contravention of plans and reinforced the restrictions on local approval by creating financial controls to prohibit institutions such as banks and investment firms from funding shipbuilding infrastructure projects that had not received central approval.[37] Such approval, in turn, is conditioned upon an enterprise (and its associated project) meeting a set of more than two dozen strict criteria developed by the Ministry of Industry and Information Technology and issued as the 2013 Shipbuilding Industry Specification Requirements.

These criteria cover manifold issue areas, including production facilities, equipment, test and measurement facilities, construction technology, technological innovation, quality assurance, and environmental protection. Indeed, they reach a considerable degree of specificity, mandating, for instance, that digital design tools be used for no less than 85 percent of design work, that up to 65 percent of welding be (semi-)automated, and that yards be able to achieve at least 80 percent completion of a vessel's pre-launch construction and outfitting (implying that considerable outfitting and systems integration work should occur beforehand).[38] The overall objective is to ensure that investment funding is being directed toward facilities that use modern equipment and processes and that possess sufficient physical facilities (buildings, utilities, docks, testing equipment, laboratory/research facilities, etc.) to sustain themselves in the long run. The 2013 requirements are, in turn, operationalized in the form of a "white list" controlled by the Ministry of Industry and Information Technology and comprising those enterprises successfully meeting the requirements. This list did not, apparently, become operational until fall 2014; companies were given more than a year to implement internal reforms.[39] The initial list included sixty enterprises, nearly half concentrated in Jiangsu, Zhejiang, and Shandong provinces.[40] Such a number, when compared to China's several hundred existing shipbuilding enterprises, augurs the prospect of vast swathes of the industry being denied financing for expansion, and thereby faced with financial strangulation; but then this is perhaps not far from the express intention of the white list, which is described as a discriminatory tool intended to keep inadequate firms/enterprises out of the shipbuilding industry.[41]

As noted earlier, a key element of the industry's transformation and reorganization is achieving a higher degree of industrial concentration; thus, while infrastructure investment intended simply to expand capacity is discouraged, that seeking to recombine and concentrate enterprises' facilities and production capacity is welcomed. In Beijing's view, it is essential that research, design, and production facilities be more tightly integrated and located as closely as possible.[42] This is important in terms of increasing not only ships' technical sophistication and expanding the industry's sphere of business, but also efficiency. As Chinese analysts note, modern destroyers contain 600,000–700,000 components and require multifarious welding and systems integration. The simultaneous execution of such complex, interlocking activities on anything like an affordable and sustainable basis thereby necessitates wholesale digitization, logistics management, and information technology upgrades within individual yards.[43] Such upgrades enable the use of a lean (just-in-time) production model, which are most cost-effective when as many moving parts as possible are concentrated in close proximity.[44] Similar advantages pertain to almost any complex product, from a missile destroyer to a radar or communications system.

It is thus unsurprising to read of plans on the part of CSSC's Jiujiang subsidiary to implement a "1236 strategy" wherein the company will be based on one center and two industrial zones while focusing on three service segments and six industrial foci. The company is concentrating its technical resources at a research and development center to develop more advanced products to be produced at two industrial zones, one each for general maritime and defense electronic equipment.[45] Seemingly exemplifying intended reforms, this reorganization was undertaken in direct response to the need for regional concentration and specialization. Likewise, CSSC as a whole is currently engaged in similar concentration, consolidating central research and development platforms for each of its five main business sectors. These platforms are apparently being collocated with production facilities, with the electromechanical platform intended for Nanjing's Luzhou Yard.[46]

This concentration's further stated purpose is to raise the technological levels of industry products, particularly those of shipboard systems, which historically underperform foreign models and therefore are less utilized, even on Chinese vessels. Thus, the maritime equipment market represents a major growth opportunity for the industry, which can afford new income streams vital to the industry's long-term sustainability, provided that its products can compete.[47] In addition to relatively simple ships, the industry must increasingly produce sophisticated, first-class marine equipment. From this imperative proceeds the drive to "localize production," especially of power and propulsion systems and communications and navigation equipment.[48] According to CANSI head Guo Dacheng, the best means of achieving this lie in promoting greater vertical integration, especially by promoting deeper cooperation between the research institutes and the enterprises that would produce their designs, thereby fostering greater research-production integration, to improve quality and achieve faster technological breakthroughs.[49]

In CSSC chairman and party secretary Hu Wenming's view, the primary categories of equipment on which the industry should focus are maritime security, research, transportation, and exploration equipment. Maritime security encompasses sensors, weapons systems, and any other equipment needed specifically by maritime security forces, and a blue-water navy. Maritime research comprises equipment needed for activities such as environmental monitoring and polar expeditions. Maritime transport includes a wide range of equipment, from fuel-efficient, environmentally friendly power and propulsion systems to advanced dry/liquid cargo handling systems. Maritime exploration encompasses all manner of equipment needed for identifying and exploiting marine resources, including oil, gas, minerals, and fish.[50] According to Hu, it is ultimately imperative that industry more clearly and actively diversify beyond mere hulls to advanced systems and their integration.

This diversification, in turn, is directly embodied within the effort to increase demand and expand export orders. According to both the 2009 and 2013 plans, the key to growth (and stability) in orders is to produce ships and equipment meeting ever-increasing global industry standards. This is especially true of next-generation shipbuilding technology: focused energy conservation, low-carbon "green" shipbuilding, information technology–based communications and navigation systems, and more intelligent, user-friendly designs.[51] Though the aforementioned are not necessarily military technologies per se, it is clear that Chinese analysts consider them as such, emphasizing the fact that increased technology export can draw navies together and improve political and military relationships (viewing it essentially as a form of soft power).[52]

In the end, however, the ultimate objective is developing an SBI capable of producing "high value added" vessels. Of course, designing and producing such complex, high-quality ships and equipment at a competitive cost necessitates "intelligent manufacturing," requiring lean production and resource concentration.[53] Conversely, stricter adherence to increasingly stringent international technical, environmental, and other standards also pays dividends in the domestic market, in that they are useful means of compelling operators to retire and replace otherwise serviceable vessels (or other equipment) presently in service. Indeed, the State Council's 2013 plan specifically advocates using stricter international standards concerning ship safety, environmental protection, and energy efficiency to encourage early replacement or modification of everything from coastal fishing vessels to oil tankers.[54] Accordingly, the state can stimulate demand for both new ships and new equipment from China's merchant marine and fishing fleets.

Beyond these major concerns of technological innovation, organizational restructuring, and fostering demand, there are less obvious, but nonetheless profound, issues with which the industry must contend. Among them is the perennial issue of civil-military integration, the advancement of which is the sixth principal task promulgated in the State Council's 2013 plan. The objective is to more tightly integrate military and civilian systems and equipment research, development, and production, so that each sector can more readily and effectively benefit from developments and achievements made in the other. Such fusion will ideally afford the civilian sector cutting-edge technology developed in support of the military, while civilian work can occupy excess research and production capacity as military demand varies with policy decisions.[55] Additionally, Chinese analysts emphasize the SBI's struggles to form a stable and fully proficient workforce.[56] Strengthening the industry's workforce is also identified as an important element of the seventh principal task in the State Council's 2013 plan, namely "strengthening enterprise management and industrial service." That plan contends that establishing stricter personnel training, selection, appraisal, and retirement mechanisms is critical to improving workforce quality, which is essential to sustaining industry development.[57] Chinese analysts emphasize several key problems with the shipbuilding personnel base. Chief among these is that most shipbuilding employees have only a middle/high school education, severely limiting their utility in an industry increasingly responsible for design, production, installation, and maintenance of high-technology equipment and systems. It is no longer sufficient for the industry to bring in relatively unskilled, uneducated workers and slowly impart skills over a long career. Rather, new employees must possess higher educational levels and more advanced skills upon employment.[58] Furthermore, many enterprises lack formalized personnel evaluation systems, making it hard to evaluate skills and tie compensation to performance and certifications.[59]

Among these deficiencies' many serious consequences are enormous workloads for the better educated managers and designers. For instance, a recent profile of the deputy head of Jiangnan Shipyard's military design work heavily emphasizes the degree to which he is compelled to personally address even relatively minor details during the construction process, with the unspoken subtext that he must do so because he lacks enough workers and subordinates sufficiently qualified to enable him to delegate such responsibilities. In his particular case, the result has been regular sixteen-hour days and enormous physical and psychological strain.[60] Obviously, having a senior designer supervising comparatively minor details of the construction process constitutes suboptimal personnel utilization. Solutions suggested include closer, more formal partnerships between the shipbuilding enterprises and the vocational schools that are training many prospective employees. Closer cooperation would provide vocational schools with better access to resources and equipment for training, education, and hands-on experience while allowing shipbuilding enterprises to effectively utilize them as a personnel feeder system.[61] The development of such mechanisms would enable the industry to better identify, promote, reward, and retain its most capable personnel—all critical to its future international competitiveness.

Case Study: Amphibious Shipbuilding

In an effort to highlight in more concrete terms the pertinence of the various issue areas outlined above, the present section examines China's amphibious shipbuilding efforts, in terms of both the military requirements driving them and the various factors affecting industry efforts to meet those requirements. Though the PLA's amphibious contingencies have expanded outward in recent years, its amphibious requirements continue to be focused on a potential Taiwan invasion. However, as was the case in the 1950s, Chinese campaign planners see the PLA's lack of adequate sealift capacity as dramatically reducing their odds of success. According to recent PLA assessments, a massive fleet of specialized military transport aircraft and amphibious ships would be needed for projecting an invasion force of overwhelming size across the Taiwan Strait. Such an armada does not yet exist in China. Nonetheless, Chinese analysts note that they have growing amphibious power projection capabilities. While inadequate, these could theoretically be bolstered by dual-use civilian ships and aircraft.

Amphibious plans regarding Taiwan appear to call for supplementing China's relatively modest military transportation fleet with enormous numbers of civilian vessels.[62] The PLAN would use container ships, merchant oilers, ferries, cargo boats, fishing trawlers, maritime rescue ships, and even motorized lifeboats for the mission.[63] The problem for the PLAN is that dual-use civilian vessels are not optimized for amphibious invasion operations. They would be difficult to load and unload and extremely difficult to coordinate.[64] Moreover, PLA writers do not think it probable that China could produce enough landing craft or convert enough civilian ships in time for the mission. Nonetheless, they state that emergency production and refitting work could be attempted to prepare as many vessels as possible.[65] Recently published Taiwanese military assessments agree that the PLA's amphibious lift capacity is currently insufficient to credibly threaten Taiwan with a full-scale amphibious invasion.[66] Yet Chinese military officers soberly note that the threat has grown at a remarkable pace over the past decade and could accelerate in the future. According to authoritative Taiwanese assessments, the PLA has set a goal for itself of being able to invade Taiwan by 2020.[67] To achieve this goal, the PLA is expanding the quality and size of its amphibious units and transport ships.

At present, the PLAN boasts Asia's largest amphibious ship force (fifty-seven medium and large vessels).[68] The PLAN has thirty-two landing ship tanks capable of transporting either five tanks or an infantry company equipped with three amphibious fighting vehicles.[69] The PLAN also has at least twenty-one medium landing ships capable of landing an infantry company and three medium tanks.[70] Demonstrably reliable open sources suggest that China has no more than twenty operational hovercraft total of all types, and perhaps even fewer than fifteen.[71]

The most capable amphibious ships currently in the PLAN inventory are its four *Yuzhao*-class (Type 071). *Yuzhao*s have an estimated displacement of 18,500 tons, making them larger than the U.S. *Harpers Ferry*–class (LSD-49) amphibious ships, the latter displacing 16,700 tons.[72] These ships are thought to be capable of carrying four helicopters and a naval infantry battalion with twenty armored fighting vehicles. This would typically total five hundred to eight hundred assault troops per ship.[73]

Indeed, *Yuzhao*s may best serve as a concrete illustration in that they are intended for use in multiple missions beyond amphibious assault, including military visits, disaster relief, and escort missions. As a result, the ship is very large (about 25,000 tons with a full load) and complex, with a full command and control system, extensive medical facilities, docking and aviation facilities, and a water distillation plant. In addition, the ships' size and structure optimized for amphibious operations impose an especially heavy and complex welding burden on workers. Thus, when it fell to selecting a yard for building these advanced vessels, CSSC's Hudong Shipyard was able to exploit its widespread reputation within the industry for reliable welding to obtain the orders for all six hulls planned in the class.[74] In this instance, Hudong was actually proactive in tackling the diverse technical challenges involved in building amphibious ships. Prior to selection, the yard sought to demonstrate its proficiency in such tasks as installing special propulsion shafts and tail fin end supports by undertaking internal projects to develop the necessary technologies and processes to do the job.[75] In this, one can likely see the fruits of the emphasis on specialization and reputation building, as well as actively seeking to increase and demonstrate yards' technical capabilities. Nevertheless, the complexity of the *Yuzhao*-class can perhaps be seen straining Hudong's capacities as well. In particular, the complexity of *Yuzhao* construction is such that the engineers and General Armament Department representatives in the yard were constantly scrambling to coordinate and revise work schedules and plans at a much higher tempo than normal, often on a daily or even hourly basis, likely indicating continued problems with instituting a true lean production model. Moreover, specialists were brought in to advise on and assist in the installation of much equipment, perhaps due to problems with the yard's personnel quality.[76] Nonetheless, Hudong is also known as the "cradle of missile frigates and amphibious craft" and is actively seeking to exploit this reputation in an effort to export its naval ships and equipment to foreign countries such as Algeria, Thailand, and Pakistan, consistent with the wider directive to further expand exports.[77] Thus, in many ways, the *Yuzhao* typifies many Chinese SBI strengths, struggles, and weaknesses as it seeks to strengthen and reconstitute itself in the wake of the global financial crisis to fulfill the broader strategic role decreed by the party-state.

Going Forward

The industry's path forward is fraught and complex. On the one hand, it has received, and will likely continue to receive, significant state financial support and state guidance that may underwrite technological development and long-term stability. On the other hand, the challenges confronting the industry are complex. While the changes and policies necessary to overcome them may benefit the industry as a whole, they will also lead to the closure of many individual yards and other enterprises, creating not only uncertainty but also local economic dislocation (possibly leading to local disaffection, with attendant political consequences). Indeed, Chinese leaders cannot be clearer about the fact that they expect current policies to result in massive consolidation and downsizing within the industry, with one expert estimating that there may only be thirty shipbuilding enterprises operating in China by 2018.[78] Nonetheless, the struggle for organizational reform and transformation is far from over, with former CANSI president Zhang Guangqin predicting that the problem of overcapacity will not be solved until nearly the end of the decade.[79] Moreover, as the financial crisis has already shown, shipbuilding is highly susceptible to external factors beyond party-state control. The recent decline in energy prices, for instance, may impede (though by no means thwart) the demand for both more fuel-efficient ships as well as maritime energy-exploitation equipment, both intended to be important growth areas for the Chinese SBI.

How policy toward the industry will change in the coming years remains unclear. Even now, initial preparations are under way at all levels for the upcoming thirteenth Five-Year Plan, which will certainly devote considerable attention to the industry. Yet seeing as how firmly the state has advocated the current policy course, and the lengthy period that such a policy requires to achieve its aims, it is unlikely that the new Five-Year Plan will offer substantial changes. Ultimately, the Communist Party has charged the industry with the dual role of contributing directly to China's economic development and equipping the PLAN to execute its own strategic tasks in support of China's continued rise. As we have argued, if the industry is to perform this dual role successfully and sustainably over the long term, it must undergo a series of profound (even wrenching) internal changes. The political will to effect these changes certainly exists; the question remaining is whether the industry can achieve them in a timely and organized manner that does not excessively tax the state's fiscal resources or retard the industry's ability to equip the Navy effectively and affordably.

Notes

1. "张广钦：明确航向 建设造船强国" ["Zhang Guangqin: A Clear Course—Building a Shipbuilding Power"], 中国船舶报 [*China Shipping News*], August 11, 2014, http://www.cssc.net.cn/component_news/news_detail.php?id=17661.

2. Unless otherwise noted, information in this section is derived from Gabriel Collins and Michael C. Grubb, *A Comprehensive Survey of China's Dynamic Shipbuilding Industry* (Newport, RI: China Maritime Studies Institute, 2008).

3. Asian Technology Information Program (ATIP), *China's Shipbuilding Strategy* (Beijing: ATIP, 2008), Report No. 08.004.

4. Nonetheless, a considerable proportion of the industry is located inland, especially along the Yangzi River, which is navigable for ocean-going vessels up to one thousand miles inland.

5. There are two conglomerates each for China's ordnance, nuclear, and aerospace industries, and one each for aviation and electronics.

6. The balance of output was largely accounted for by the China Shipping Group and the China Ocean Shipping Company, China's two largest cargo carriers. Each operates several yards, allowing them to build their own fleets.

7. "Zhang Guangqin."

8. 王敏 [Wang Min], "加快结构调整促进转型升级实施方案公布" ["Announcement of the Implementation Plan for Accelerating Structural Reorganization and Promoting Transformation"], 解放军报 [*PLA Daily*], August 5, 2013, http://navy.81.cn/content/2013-08/05/content_5429792.htm.

9. 蒋乾麟 [Jiang Qianlin], "加快推进国防和军队现代化的科学指南－深入学习习近平关于国防和军队建设重要论述" ["A Scientific Guidance for Accelerating Modernization of National Defense and the Armed Forces—Thoroughly Studying Xi Jinping's Important Expositions on Building National Defense and Armed Forces"], 中国军事科学 [*China Military Science*] 1 (2014): 12.

10. 周新胜 [Zhou Xinsheng], ed., 军种战略教程 [*Service Strategy Course Material*] (Beijing: Academy of Military Science Press, December 2013), 175.

11. 任海泉 [Ren Haiquan], "加强新时期新阶段国防和军队建设" ["Strengthening National Defense and the Armed Forces Building at the New Stage in the New Period"], 中国军事科学 [*China Military Science*] 3 (2013): 9–10.

12. 邓红洲 [Deng Hongzhou], "强军要运用底线思维运筹未来军事斗争" ["A Strong Army Necessitates the Use of Bottom Line Thinking in the Course of Future Military Struggles"], 学习时报 [*Study Times*], October 21, 2013, http://news.ifeng.com/shendu/xxsb/detail_2013_10/21/30505518_0.shtml.

13. Zhou, ed., *Service Strategy Course Material*, 176–78.

14. Ibid., 183.

15. "Zhang Guangqin."

16. Zhou, ed., *Service Strategy Course Material*, 183.

17. 王智辉 [Wang Zhihui], "全面深化改革 让转型之路越走越宽" ["Comprehensively Deepening Reform—Step-by-Step Down the Road of Transformation"], *China Ship News*, March 11, 2015, http://chinashipnews.com.cn/show.php?contentid=8679.

18. Ibid.

19. "Zhang Guangqin."

20. The article in question plainly anticipates a painful degree of consolidation and downsizing within the shipbuilding industry. SASTIND's attitude is perhaps best summarized by a harsh encapsulation: "survival of the fittest is most cruel" (优胜劣汰很残酷). SASTIND, "造船业面临史上最大规模结构调整" ["The Shipbuilding Industry

Is Facing the Largest-Scale Structural Changes in Its History"], October 25, 2013, http://cheos.org.cn/n137/n248/c67146/content.html.

21. Ibid. SASTIND also notes the critical role the South Korean government played in helping to arrange and bring about such relationships.

22. State Council, "船舶工业调整和振兴规划" ["Shipbuilding Industry Restructuring and Revitalization Plan"], 2009, http://www.miit.gov.cn/n11293472/n11293832/n11294 072/n11302450/12402840.html.

23. Ibid.

24. Ibid.

25. Ibid.

26. State Council, "船舶工业加快结构调整促进转型升级实施方案" ["Implementation Plan for Accelerating Structural Adjustment and Advancing Transformation in the Ship Building Industry"], 2013, http://www.gov.cn/zwgk/2013-08/04/content_2460962.htm.

27. 何育静 [He Yujing] and 刘树青 [Liu Shuqing], "我国造船企业竞争力研究" ["Research on Competitiveness of China's Shipbuilding Enterprises"], 船舶工程 [Ship Engineering] 37.1 (2015): 103–4.

28. Wang Zhihui, "Comprehensively Deepening Reform."

29. The figure of eight hundred can be compared to the less than seven hundred shipyards and maritime equipment factories existing in the 1980s, according to http://fas .org/nuke/guide/china/contractor/cssc.htm. The exact number of shipyards and other shipbuilding enterprises in China varies widely by source, depending on how physically separate but jointly owned facilities are counted. For instance, one newspaper stated that in 2014 there were some 1,600 shipyards in China, down from more than 3,000 in 2012. Jing Yang, "China's Shipbuilding Industry Faces Further Consolidation, Says Yangzijiang Chairman," South China Morning Post, February 27, 2015, http:// www.scmp.com/business/china-business/article/1725245/chinas-shipbuilding-indus try-faces-further-consolidation.

30. "产能过剩800家船企面临行业洗牌 中小企业或遭淘汰" ["Excess Capacity: 800 Shipbuilding Enterprises Face Industrial Reshuffling—Small-and-Medium-Sized Enterprises May Suffer Elimination"], 证券日报 [Securities Daily], November 23, 2013, http://finance.cnr.cn/gundong/201311/t20131123_514215210.shtml.

31. "Zhang Guangqin." Local and provincial governments that own or manage shipyards would have especial motivation for engaging in such behavior. They face intense pressure from above to foster local employment and economic growth while at the same time being less constrained by financial pressures (since they would be using tax money).

32. State Council, "Implementation Plan."

33. "Zhang Guangqin."

34. State Council, "Implementation Plan."

35. "Excess Capacity."

36. State Council, "Shipbuilding Industry Restructuring Plan."

37. State Council, "Implementation Plan."

38. Ministry of Industry and Information Technology, "船舶行业规范条件" ["Shipbuilding Industry Specification Requirements"], 2013, http://www.gov.cn/zwgk/2013–11/13/content_2526496.htm.

39. "金融支持船舶工业意见将出台" ["Suggestions for the Financial Support of the Shipbuilding Industry Will Be Publicized"], 中国证券报 [*China Securities*], January 28, 2015, http://stock.jrj.com.cn/hotstock/2015/01/28062518777588.shtml.

40. "造船业陷噩梦: 船东弃船　造船大省密集救市" ["The Shipbuilding Industry's Nightmare Trap: Owners Abandoning Ship"], 华夏时报 [*Huaxia Times*], April 13, 2015, http://www.cnss.com.cn/html/2015/currentevents_0413/173445.html.

41. "Excess Capacity."

42. "郭大成: 服务国家大战略　打造增长双引擎" ["Guo Dacheng: In Service of the National Grand Strategy—Building and Growing Two Engines"], 中国船舶报 [*China Ship News*], March 16, 2015, http://chinashipnews.com.cn/show.php?contentid=8755.

43. "数字化应用成就现代船厂与优异装备" ["Digital Applications Yield Outstanding Modern Shipyard Equipment"], Jiangnan Shipbuilding Corp., April 7, 2015, http://jnshipyard.cssc.net.cn/compay_mod_file/news_detail.php?cart=3&id=401. The article notes that under the previous dispersed shipbuilding model, which did not use lean production methods, workers typically spent 30–40 percent of an eight-hour shift simply locating tools, parts, and other supplies, thereby greatly lengthening construction times and increasing construction costs.

44. Ibid.

45. "中船九江海洋装备配套产品产业区开工奠基" ["Breaking Ground at the CSSC Jiujiang Maritime Equipment Products Industrial Zone"], Eworldship, January 22, 2015, http://www.eworldship.com/html/2015/Manufacturer_0122/97839.html.

46. "胡问鸣调研海洋机电装备产业园项目" ["Hu Wenming Investigates the Marine Power Machinery Industrial Park Project"], Nanjing Luzhou Machinery Co. Ltd., March 1, 2015, http://luzhou.cssc.net.cn/compay_mod_file/news_detail.php?cart=3&id=493.

47. "Excess Capacity."

48. *Guochanhua lü* (国产化率), literally "the rate [of] increasing [products] produced at home."

49. "Guo Dacheng."

50. "胡问鸣: 当好海洋装备领域的排头兵" ["Hu Wenming: Suitable Frontline Troops in the Field of Marine Equipment"], Ministry of Industry and Information Technology Department of Civil-Military Integration Promotion, March 18, 2014, http://jmjhs.miit.gov.cn/n11293472/n11295193/n13667576/15930273.html.

51. Wang Min, "Announcement of Implementation Plan."

52. Kong Defeng, "国际舰船市场需求及营销策略分析" ["The International Naval Ship Demand and Marketing Strategies"], 價格月刊 [*Pricing Monthly*] 1 (2014): 79–81. Of course, such relationships could very well be made into two-way streets, with much to offer technologically to China itself.

53. "Guo Dacheng."

54. State Council, "Implementation Plan."

55. Ibid.

56. "Zhang Guangqin."

57. State Council, "Implementation Plan."

58. 严慧 [Yan Hui], "船舶制造业技能人才供需问题及对策研究" ["Skilled Shipbuilding Personnel Supply-Demand Problems and Policy Solutions"], 江苏船舶 [*Jiangsu Ship*] 31.2 (April 2014): 30–32.

59. Ibid.

60. "激情铸舰 为舰船国产化添砖加瓦" ["Passionately Building Warships—Doing One's Part to Localize Warship Production"], 中国船舶报 [*China Ship News*], March 2, 2015, http://www.cssc.net.cn/component_news/news_detail.php?id=19000.

61. Yan Hui, "Skilled Shipbuilding Personnel Supply-Demand Problems and Policy Solutions."

62. Cao Zhengrong et al., eds., *Informatized Army Operations* [信息化陆军作战] (Beijing: National Defense University Press, 2014), 123–24. This is a military publication produced by the Nanjing Army Command Academy that describes a joint landing campaign against Taiwan.

63. Ibid., 124.

64. Ibid., 131.

65. Ibid.

66. [Yang You-hung], Lieutenant Colonel, ROC Army, Commander of the Taoyuan County Reserve Command Post, "共軍聯合島嶼進攻戰役能力研究" ["Research into Communist Military's Joint Island Landing Offensive Campaign Capabilities"], 後備半年刊 [*Reserve Force Journal*] 88 (October 2013): 109.

67. [Tsai Ho-Hsun], Lieutenant Colonel, National Defense University Army Command Academy Intelligence Cell, "共軍師登陸作戰之研究" ["Research on the Communist Military's Division Landing Operations"], 陸軍學術雙月刊 [*Army Studies Bimonthly*] 50.537 (October 2014): 61.

68. Ronald O'Rourke, *China Naval Modernization: Implications for U.S. Navy Capabilities—Background and Issues for Congress* (Washington, DC: Congressional Research Service, June 17, 2016), RL33153, 54, http://www.fas.org/sgp/crs/row/RL33153.pdf.

69. This includes seven *Yukan*s, ten *Yuting-I*s, and fifteen *Yuting-II*s, with six new ones as of last year. ONI, "China People's Liberation Army Navy (PLA[N]) and Maritime Law Enforcement (MLE) 2015 Recognition and Identification Guide," April 2015, http://www.oni.navy.mil/Portals/12/Intel%20agencies/China_Media/PLA_Navy_Identification_Guide.pdf?ver=2015-12-10-103823-167.

70. This includes ten Type 073A *Yunshu*s, one Type 073-II *Yudeng*, and ten to twelve Type 074 *Yuhai*s. Ibid.; Yang You-hung, "Research into Communist Military's Joint Island Landing Offensive Campaign Capabilities," 103.

71. This includes two *Pomornik*s ("Zubr"), roughly five Type 726 *Yuyi*s, and roughly ten Type 724 *Payi*s.

72. Ronald O'Rourke, *China Naval Modernization*, 38.

73. Yang You-hung, "Research into Communist Military's Joint Island Landing Offensive Campaign Capabilities," 103.

74. "沪东中华: 为中国海军打造'靓丽名片'" ["Hudong Zhonghua: Forging Beautiful 'Calling Cards' for the Chinese Navy"], 中国船舶报 [*China Ship News*], August 28, 2014, http://www.cssc.net.cn/component_news/news_detail.php?id=17797.

75. Ibid.

76. Ibid.

77. 严风华 [Yan Fenghua], "中船集团所属沪东中华建造的新型护卫舰吉安舰入列" ["The New Corvette *Ji'an*, Built by CSSC's Hudong-Zhonghua, Enters Service"], Shanghai Jiaotong University, January 16, 2014, http://www.cssc.net.cn/component_news/news_detail.php?id=16365.

78. Kyunghee Park, "China Shipbuilding Sector Set to Contract, Yangzijiang Says," *Bloomberg Business*, April 30, 2015, http://www.bloomberg.com/news/articles/2015-04-30/china-shipbuilding-industry-is-set-to-contract-yangzijiang-says.

79. "Chinese Shipbuilding Industry Rides Wave of Restructuring," *Xinhua*, January 19, 2014. At that time, Zhang specifically estimated five years.

Gabe Collins and Eric Anderson

Resources for China's State Shipbuilders
Now Including Global Capital Markets

CHINA SHIPBUILDING INDUSTRY CORPORATION (CSIC) and its state-owned enterprise (SOE) sister, China State Shipbuilding Corporation (CSSC), are now the world's most prolific builders of large surface combatants and submarines. This chapter examines the sources and magnitude of financial resources available to China's state shipbuilders. It focuses in particular on the capital market activities of CSIC and CSSC's listed arms, which allow investors to buy stock in the companies. CSSC and CSIC were a single company until the government split them in 1999 during the wave of pre–World Trade Organization reforms.

The shipbuilders are leading a push to access local and global capital markets that other Chinese defense enterprises will likely emulate. Capital market access is a strategy increasingly driven by necessity, since China's civilian shipyards face years of doldrums due to severe overcapacity and anemic global demand for the commodity vessel classes in which they are most competitive. CSIC and CSSC are both beginning to market military assets to private investors who universally recognize that China's naval budget is likely to continue growing strongly for some years.

Potential investors are also increasingly aware that the military yards get the most skilled staff and have a virtual monopoly on supplying warships,

62

submarines, and parts to the world's next aspiring naval superpower. Beijing's clumsy response to the July 2015 stock market crash will deter some foreign investors. Yet markets generally forgive relatively quickly, especially when the companies in question offer exposure to something as politically supported as the world's largest ongoing comprehensive naval buildup.

The efforts of CSSC and CSIC to access the domestic and global capital markets could significantly boost the quantity of financial resources available for modernizing and expanding China's navy. Every dollar or renminbi (RMB) that CSSC and CSIC can raise on the market and plough into upgraded yard infrastructure, staff, and warship equipment frees up state-granted military budget funds for other uses. To put the dollar figures in perspective, each Type 054A frigate delivered to the People's Liberation Army Navy (PLAN) likely costs approximately US$350 million–$375 million.[1] Each billion dollars raised on the market thus effectively funds activity equivalent to the delivered cost of nearly three Type 054As—a substantial impact.

This analysis consists of three major sections. Section one illustrates the scale of China's naval shipbuilding program and its structure in shipyard and geographical terms. Section two offers a detailed analysis of the debt and equity sales conducted by CSIC Limited and CSSC Holdings over the past decade, including their volume, issue terms, and timing. Section two also examines the origins and magnitude of financial resource flows into CSSC and CSIC and the evolving trend of asset injections and increasing securitization in the Chinese naval shipbuilding sector. Section three concludes the chapter by examining the strategic implications of CSSC and CSIC's turn to the domestic and global capital markets.

China's Rapid Naval Buildup

Available data clearly demonstrate that China is engaged in a substantial naval buildup. Between 2005 and the first three months of 2015, Chinese yards launched sixty-seven large surface combatants (not counting the Type 022 *Houbei*-class), sixteen submarines, and five merchant vessels. Today Type 052D destroyers, Type 056 corvettes, China Coast Guard (CCG), and maritime militia craft are all under construction in significant numbers. In addition, the PLAN is building a second aircraft carrier, along with additional, more modern nuclear attack submarines. Projected to 2020, it would not be unreasonable to add another 12 to 18 large surface combatants, 2 to 3 nuclear submarines, and 2 to 3 replenishment vessels, for a total of 104 to 112 naval vessels built since 2005—a staggering number.

Seven shipyards—four controlled by CSIC and three by CSSC—produce the armada of modern vessels entering PLAN service. Among these seven, as of early 2015, four specific yards—Hudong Zhonghua, Jiangnan Changxing, Huangpu, and Wuchang—accounted for 89 percent of the surface combatants and for all conventional submarines launched since 2005.

CSSC and CSIC have four primary financial sources that are accessible to their domestically oriented military ship construction operations: state defense budget funds, capital markets (debt and equity sales), military ship exports, and bank loans. Given the lack of defense budget transparency, this analysis focuses primarily on capital market transactions, with a secondary analysis of how military ship exports and CCG vessel construction factor into the companies' overall financial pictures. The bottom line is that China is now attempting to use securitization to enhance defense enterprises' operational performance (a goal that preferential state loans do not facilitate), reduce enterprises' relative reliance on the state budget, and foster deeper civil-military industrial integration.

Financial Resources Available to China's Military Shipbuilders

The official defense budget is most likely the largest single source of usable funds for CSSC and CSIC's military shipbuilding operations. It is also the PLAN's least transparent financial resource stream. Bernard Cole estimates that the PLAN receives more than one-third of China's officially stated defense budget, a figure we consider a reasonable approximation.[2] Conservatively estimating that the PLAN receives 30 percent of the defense budget would suggest that, based on the 2015 announced defense budget of 886.9 billion RMB (US$141.5 billion), the PLAN's share is approximately US$45 billion.[3] The navy must devote a substantial portion of its funds to personnel and routine operational expenses, and our estimate assumes that 35–40 percent of the PLAN budget is actually available for hardware purchases.

Entry of Defense Shipbuilding SOEs into Capital Markets

For this analysis, we compiled a unique proprietary data set showing CSSC and CSIC's post-2004 number, type, and volume of capital markets transactions. These include both debt sales and equity issuances and typically involve the companies' respective listed arms: CSSC Holdings, Ltd. (trading symbol SHA:600150) and CSIC Limited (SHA:601989).

Between January 2004 and January 2015, the authors count thirty-one transactions by the companies, for a combined total capital raised of US$22.26 billion. Twelve transactions were by CSIC Limited, nineteen by CSSC

Holdings. Despite the public listings of CSSC in 2007 and CSIC in 2009, over-all the companies have thus far issued far more debt than equity. As of January 2015, CSSC Holdings had raised a total of US$8.63 billion from the debt mar-kets and US$3.02 billion from equity sales, while CSIC Limited had raised US$7.04 billion from debt issuances and US$3.57 billion from equity sales.

These strides into the capital market come in part as a result of a series of policy guidelines implemented over the past several years to encourage pri-vate capital to enter China's defense enterprises. In 2003, the China Securities Regulatory Commission began tightly restricting related party transactions (including prohibiting various fund transfers) between listed subsidiaries and unlisted state-owned parent companies.[4] While official sources do not con-firm the new regulations' intent, the authors suspect a primary reason was to increase investors' confidence that they were buying more of a real asset and less of a shell company, which in turn would help boost securitized assets' mar-ket value.

Then in 2007 five guidelines promulgated by the Commission for Science, Technology, and Industry for National Defense (now the State Administration for Science, Technology, and Industry for National Defense) enabled defense industries to begin taking steps toward securitizing defense assets. This marked a push to make the state-owned defense industry more efficient in funds allocation and to allow nonstate firms to begin to invest in and com-pete with monopolized state-owned firms in particular areas, thereby sup-plementing central allocations to the defense industry. Soon after the release of these guidelines, both shipbuilding SOEs issued their initial public offer-ings, followed by CSIC and CSSC issuing their first bonds in 2008 and 2009, respectively. From 2008 to 2011, CSSC issued US$1.39 billion in bonds, CSIC US$2.93 billion.

Bond issuances spiked in 2012, when CSIC issued US$3 billion in bonds and CSSC US$2.63 billion. This substantial increase from previous years indi-cates an additional significant change in the shipbuilding companies' atti-tude toward the capital markets. Two transactions highlight this new attitude. First, CSIC Limited raised 8 billion RMB (US$1.26 billion) in June 2012 from a convertible bond issue to buy Wuchang Shipbuilding and five other CSIC-controlled companies from its parent. Second, and particularly noteworthy, is CSIC's September 2013 8.48 billion RMB (US$1.4 billion) private share sale. This marked the first time that China's defense industry explicitly advertised military modernization as the purpose for raising the funds, and it is illustra-tive of the process by which a Chinese defense enterprise asset injection works in actual practice. Out of the total amount raised, over one-third (3.275 billion

RMB, US$540.7 million) was earmarked for the acquisition of medium and large surface ships, conventional submarines, and large landing ships; 2.66 billion RMB (US$439.2 million) for military equipment arms trade and civil-military industrialization projects; and the remaining 2.54 billion RMB (US$419.3 million) to supplement working capital.[5]

The asset injection brought two of CSIC's three primary military ship construction assets—Wuchang Shipbuilding and Dalian Shipbuilding—into its listed arm (along with eight other assets). This confers more direct access to investors, especially those outside China. The injection also had a very positive effect on CSIC Limited's rapidly depleting ship orderbook. China Securities Net reports that at the end of June 2014, CSIC Limited derived nearly 19 percent of its revenue from military goods (up from roughly 8 percent a year prior) and that the listed company's military and marine engineering orderbook was 68 percent larger than a year prior.[6] Upon announcing the bond issue, CSIC stated on the Shanghai Stock Exchange website, "The deal will expand the financing channels for China's military defense. It would also herald an overall securitization of China's military assets."[7]

In November 2014, Guangzhou Shipyard International (GSI) purchased Huangpu Wenchong Shipbuilding from the CSSC parent company for 4.35 billion RMB (US$718.2 million), paying for the purchase by issuing 271.6 million shares of stock to the parent and the balance in cash.[8] Since May 11, 2015, GSI has been known as CSSC Offshore and Marine Engineering (Group) Company Limited (COMEC), following a decision three days prior by shareholders to rename the enterprise.[9] The renaming does not appear to have fundamentally altered the corporate structure or its mission in any material way and the company's shares continue to trade on the Hong Kong Exchange (ticker HKG:0317). Following its announcement of the Huangpu Wenchong purchase in late 2014, GSI/COMEC issued a public statement emphasizing that securitization will help it "carry out asset securitization for relevant military assets, [and] enhance protection for military construction assignments through means such as financing from the listing platform, so as to exert the supporting function of the capital markets towards the development and growth of military enterprises."[10] The companies consummated the transaction on March 9, 2015.[11]

COMEC's acquisition of the CSSC Huangpu Wenchong assets, among other new subsidiaries, reflected a shift aimed at diversifying the capital streams that China's defense-industrial enterprises can access. While the bulk of debt and equity investment in China's military shipbuilders to date likely came from domestic "strategic parties," such as state banks and insurance companies, injecting assets into a vehicle traded in Hong Kong strongly suggests that Beijing wants to make its military-industrial complex more accessible to potential investors from around the globe. If potential upside from military ship and equipment purchases motivate non–People's Republic of China investors to meaningfully buy into COMEC, we would expect additional injection deals that foreign investors can gain exposure to via Hong Kong traded shares.

Further securitization will likely boost the volumes of capital CSIC and CSSC can raise. The companies' listed arms have already proven to be a formidable fundraising force. Allowing investors to gain exposure to more of the companies' prime assets will likely enhance domestic and foreign investors' appetite for debt and equity issuances. A key question here is, "What assets might be injected into listed companies next?" Based on a CITIC Securities analysis, research institutes within CSIC and CSSC are viewed as a next likely target. Steps have already been made to move these assets to the capital market, such as CSIC's October 2014 announcement that it would restructure sixteen of its subsidiary science and technology industry companies—all positioned within four of its twenty-eight research institutes—into four holding companies that would later become listed companies.[12] CITIC Securities also predicts that CSSC will inject Hudong Zhonghua and Jiangnan Shipbuilding into publicly traded entities.[13] Continued obstacles and embedded interests from within research institutes, however, will likely hinder attempts to securitize all of them.[14] Furthermore, the government's priorities and those of investors diverge somewhat on the research institute question. The government wants to get these institutes off the official balance sheet, while investors seek the assets they see as being most likely to yield real economic returns. Preliminary evidence suggests that the military asset injection may have helped boost revenue at CSIC. Even as most segments of the global commercial ship market remain badly depressed, the company reported a 12 percent increase in revenues for 2015.[15] COMEC itself enjoyed a 21.25 percent increase in operating income, "mainly due to the injection of high-quality core military assets of Huangpu Wenchong and enhanced production efficiency."[16]

Military Ship Exports

China uses military ship exports as a source of revenue and also to maintain shipyard activity during times of low ship orders. Between January 2005 and January 2015 there were twenty-three separate orders for naval ship exports from China totaling fifty-four different vessels.[17] Approximately one-third of China's military ship exports since 2005 are frigates, and a slightly larger percentage are small patrol craft. However, a large number of the frigates have been second-hand retired PLAN vessels. Hudong-Zhonghua Shipyard and Wuchang Shipyard are the major build sites for exported military ships.

Unlike civilian exports, military ship exports likely carry high purchasing prices with large profit margins for the seller.[18] These may not be as large for China, however, with its typical export of small, low-tech ships to developing nations who are primarily concerned with coastal or regional defense, not blue-water capabilities.[19]

China Coast Guard Ships

CCG orders offer important revenue for Chinese shipyards. For this analysis, data gathered includes all CCG vessels three thousand tons and larger that were launched since 2005 (including newly launched vessels but excluding CCG refitted from retired PLAN vessels). Dozens of smaller CCG vessels (one thousand tons and smaller) were also launched in this time period, but individual ship data for these classes remain sparse. Since 2005 there have been thirty-eight coast guard cutters in this classification launched or currently under construction. Twenty-five are 3,000-ton class cutters, four are 4,000-ton, seven are 5,000-ton, and two are 10,000-ton class cutters.

In late 2013/early 2014, Chinese yards—primarily Wuchang and Huangpu—begin launching a massive wave of new cutters and increasingly focused on building larger vessels. The Chinese military and paramilitary ship construction lines overall launched more cutters and large patrol vessels in 2014 than they did naval surface ships and submarines. This large CCG ship volume plays a strong role in keeping shipyards active while infusing much-needed revenue to help compensate for a slowdown in commercial shipbuilding. For example, nine relatively small CCG vessels will help the yard generate at least as much economic activity as a million-deadweight-tonnage worth of crude oil tankers. While CCGs are not as expensive and complex as warships, they help core CSSC and CSIC yards weather a prolonged commercial ship order slowdown while also boosting China's paramilitary maritime capabilities.

Strategic Outlook and Implications

The COMEC-Huangpu Wenchong transaction in November 2014 marked a turning point in the relationship between China's state shipbuilders and the ability to raise money through capital markets specifically for military modernization. Former CSSC chairman Hu Wenming noted that this deal "broke through regulatory restrictions and opened the pathway to securitization for the military product and general assembly industry or rather for security assets." He expects that many more military industrial assets will be securitized to secure good returns.[20]

China's military shipbuilding SOEs have historically relied heavily on state allocations from the People's Liberation Army (PLA) budget to fund shipbuilding activity. This continues to the present, with China's defense industries riding the wave created by double-digit year-on-year growth in PLA budgets. Greater access to the domestic and global capital markets will not replace defense budget funding but does hold the potential to augment it to a degree that will facilitate significant additional naval modernization activity without a commensurate burden on the national balance sheet.

The issues analyzed here therefore have important political and national security implications extending beyond the shipbuilding sector. Consider some plausible scenarios that could arise as China's shipbuilders and other defense enterprises seek more market-based sources of funding, including foreign investors:

- How would policymakers react if U.S.-domiciled investors purchased a major debt issue by CSSC Holdings or CSIC Limited that was in part earmarked to upgrade military ship production capabilities?

- What if a European or Canadian pension fund participated in such a transaction?

- What if investment banks with major U.S. ties helped CSSC or CSIC raise funds that, due to the fungibility of money, effectively helped underwrite part of China's naval buildup?

These questions merit discussion: in today's interconnected financial world, transactions that pass formal legal muster may in fact still engender substantial diplomatic and security consequences. Indeed, Barclays, Société Générale, and ANZ have already facilitated a €500 million bond sale by CSSC Holdings in February 2015.[21] As China's defense enterprises pursue additional resources from the capital markets, international investors will also likely seek to buy into deals, as opposed to simply brokering them.

Notes

1. Gabe Collins, "How Much Do China's Warships Actually Cost?" *The Diplomat*, June 18, 2015, http://thediplomat.com/2015/06/how-much-do-chinas-warships-actually-cost/.

2. Edward Wong, "Chinese Military Seeks to Extend Its Naval Power," *New York Times*, April 23, 2010, http://www.nytimes.com/2010/04/24/world/asia/24navy.html?_r=0.

3. Budget data from Andrew S. Erickson and Adam P. Liff, "China's Military Spending Swells Again Despite Domestic Headwinds," China Real Time Report, *Wall Street Journal*, March 5, 2015, http://blogs.wsj.com/chinarealtime/2015/03/05/chinas-mili tary-spending-swells-again-despite-domestic-headwinds/.

4. 中国证监会 [China Securities Regulatory Commission], "关于规范上市公司与关联方资金往来及上市公司对外担保若干问题的通知" ["Notice Regarding Several Issues Relating to the Standardization of Listed Company-Related Party Funds Flows and Listed Company External Guarantees"], August 28, 2003, 56, http://www.csrc.gov .cn/pub/newsite/flb/flfg/bmgf/ssgs/gljy/201012/t20101231_189866.html.

5. "中国重工84.8亿定增预案出炉 开创重大军工资产注入先河" ["CSIC Releases Plan for 8.48 Billion Set, Creates Precedent for Defense Asset Injection"], 上海证券报 [*Shanghai Securities Report*], September 11, 2013, http://finance.sina.com.cn/stock/s/20130911/023716724295.shtml.

6. Chen Jing, "中国重工: 军工资产注入成效初显" ["CSIC: Results Clear from Military Industrial Asset Injection"], 中国证券报 [*China Securities Journal*], August 27, 2014, http://www.cs.com.cn/ssgs/gsxw/201408/t20140827_4495207.html.

7. Yimou Lee and Michael Martina, "State-backed China Shipbuilding to Raise $1.4 Billion for Naval Buildup," *Reuters*, September 11, 2013, http://www.reuters.com/arti cle/2013/09/11/us-china-shipbuilding-idUSBRE98A02L20130911.

8. Guangzhou Shipyard International Company Limited, "Announcement," October 31, 2014, http://www.hkexnews.hk/listedco/listconews/SEHK/2014/1031/LTN20141031 915.pdf.

9. CSSC Offshore and Marine Engineering (Group) Company Limited, "Change of Company Name, Logo, Stock Short Name and Company Website," www.hkexnews .hk/listedco/listconews/sehk/2015/0603/LTN20150603649.doc.

10. Guangzhou Shipyard International Company Limited, "Announcement."

11. COMEC, "Company Profile," http://comec.cssc.net.cn/en/component_general_situa tion/index.php?typeid=1.

12. Li Jiexue, "中国重工: 民船回升军船爆发, 优质资产注入预期强烈" ["CSIC: Civilian Ships Rebound, Military Ships Breakout; Strong Expectations of High Quality Asset Injection"], 理财周报 [*Moneyweek*], February 14, 2015, http://www.lczb.net/channel/view/id/21146/index.html.

13. Gao Song, "中信军工 – 军临天下- 改革专题: 多管齐下 估值提升" ["CITIC Defense—Reform Topic: A Multi-Pronged Valuation Increase"], 中信证券 [CITIC Securities], February 24, 2014, 27, http://pro790512df.pic10.websiteonline.cn/upload/rQUX.pdf.

14. Ibid.

15. Jon Grevatt, "China Shipbuilding Industry Merges Key Subsidiaries," *Jane's Defence Weekly*, May 25, 2016; "XSHG:601989 China Shipbuilding Industry Corp Annual Report," December 31, 2015, http://quote.morningstar.com/stock-filing/Annual-Report/2015/12/31/t.aspx?t=XSHG:601989&ft=&d=79f038fa4ad69e48ce06fa9f1e6

bo30c. For related CSIC reports, see http://quicktake.morningstar.com/stocknet/secdocuments.aspx?symbol=601989&country=chn. For related CSSC reports, see http://quicktake.morningstar.com/stocknet/secdocuments.aspx?symbol=600150&country=chn.

16. CSSC Offshore and Marine Engineering (Group) Company Limited, *Annual Report 2015*, 9, http://comec.cssc.net.cn/en/upload_img/E0031720160422.pdf.

17. Military ship export data from SIPRI. See *SIPRI Arms Transfer Database*, http://www.sipri.org/databases/armstransfers.

18. Li Chao, "基于市场机构理论的军船国际贸易研究" ["Research on the International Trade of Warships Based on Market Structure Theory"], master's thesis, Jiangsu University of Science and Technology, 2011.

19. John Birkler et al., *Differences between Military and Commercial Shipbuilding: Implications for the United Kingdom and Ministry of Defence* (Santa Monica, CA: RAND, 2005), http://www.rand.org/content/dam/rand/pubs/monographs/2005/RAND_MG236.pdf.

20. "胡问鸣: 跨国企业集团单一经营是个错误" ["Hu Wenming: Multinational Companies Running a Single Business is a Mistake"], 英才 [*Talent Magazine*] (September 2014): 32–35.

21. Moody's Investors Service, "Rating Action: Moody's Assigns A1 to BOC Supported Bonds of China State Shipbuilding Corporation," February 17, 2015, https://www.moodys.com/research/Moodys-assigns-A1-to-BOC-supported-bonds-of-China-State-PR_318535.

Shipyard Infrastructure

Sue Hall and Audrye Wong

Key Factors in Chinese Shipyards' Development and Performance

Commercial-Military Synergy and Divergence

SHIPBUILDING IN CHINA has for some time been a focus of international interest, and—in some instances—concern. In 2002, following then-premier Zhu Rongji's challenge to Chinese shipbuilders to achieve preeminent status, the State Commission of Science, Technology, and Industry for National Defense set a target of 2015 for China to become the world's leading shipbuilder. In fact, this turned out to be a conservative target, as China achieved first place in merchant shipbuilding production in 2010, when it delivered 18.8 million compensated gross tons (CGT), ahead of South Korea's 15.6 million CGT.[1] With world output (for vessels over 500 gross tons) at 52.5 million CGT, this meant that China accounted for over 35 percent of world production. China has retained this leadership position in subsequent years. Statistics for 2014 show that China again maintained a narrow lead in production, with a 32.7 percent share of world completions by CGT against South Korea's 31.8 percent.[2]

Recent Merchant Shipbuilding Trends

To understand the context within which China has achieved this position, it is important to examine long-term global shipbuilding production trends.

Exhibit 4-1. Shipbuilding Production Trends since 1990
(in millions of compensated gross tons)

Year	Europe	China	Japan	Korea	Others	World
1990	4.2	0.3	4.2	1.6	1.0	11.4
1991	4.2	0.4	4.0	1.7	0.9	11.3
1992	4.5	0.4	4.2	1.9	1.1	12.1
1993	4.3	0.5	4.7	1.9	1.0	12.5
1994	4.0	0.7	5.0	2.2	1.0	12.8
1995	4.2	0.6	5.3	2.9	1.0	14.0
1996	5.5	0.7	5.5	3.5	1.0	16.2
1997	4.3	1.0	6.1	4.0	1.3	16.6
1998	5.1	1.2	6.5	3.4	1.4	17.7
1999	4.7	1.1	6.0	4.4	1.5	17.6
2000	4.3	1.2	5.9	5.5	1.2	18.1
2001	5.0	1.4	6.4	5.7	1.2	19.6
2002	5.0	1.5	6.3	6.3	1.4	20.5
2003	4.7	2.6	6.7	6.7	1.5	22.3
2004	4.6	3.0	7.8	7.7	1.6	24.7
2005	4.1	4.4	8.3	9.3	2.3	28.5
2006	4.8	5.0	9.3	10.7	2.3	32.1
2007	5.6	6.8	9.1	12.0	2.7	36.2
2008	5.7	9.1	9.9	15.3	3.1	43.0
2009	4.7	12.4	9.7	15.4	3.3	45.4
2010	4.7	18.8	9.9	15.6	3.5	52.4
2011	3.0	19.7	9.2	16.2	3.3	51.4
2012	3.0	19.7	8.4	13.7	4.5	49.3
2013	2.5	13.2	7.0	12.4	2.9	37.9
2014	2.1	11.0	6.4	11.0	3.1	33.6

Source: SHE Database

Exhibit 4-1 documents China's rise to prominence, which coincided with an explosion of shipbuilding worldwide.[3] Not evident from this table is the fact that this is part of the industry's cyclical nature; to see this we need to look further back. As the present system of CGT, the favored measure of ship-building activity, was not adopted until 1984, exhibit 4-2 shows the longer-term perspective from the mid-1950s, measured in gross tons (which reflects ships' physical volume, ignoring complexity). Japan's emergence in the 1970s also occurred during an explosion of shipbuilding demand—leading to Japan's establishment as the leading shipbuilding nation. So in hindsight, it may now be evident that there was little coincidence about the context of China's rise to shipbuilding prominence.

Although shipbuilding's cyclical nature has been evident since those production peaks were reached in the mid-1970s, the recent production peak in 2010 was approximately 2.5 times the previous apogee. In fact, the individual production of both South Korea and China in 2010 was roughly equivalent to total world production in 1975.

This recent production peak, occurring some two to three years after the global financial crisis in late 2007, reflects an important phenomenon—the lag between vessel ordering and delivery. This lag is *not* the result of the production timescale for building individual ships, but rather the size of the forward orderbook of shipbuilding orders, which itself can vary significantly.

At the peak of the recent ship-ordering boom, leading yards' forward workloads typically represented three to five years of production at then-current output levels. In fact, some leading shipbuilders had closed their orderbooks because of the inherent risks associated with contracting production for so far ahead. It is hence easier to understand how peak production lagged world economic trends. Although a substantial orderbook existed at the outset of the financial crisis, this suffered some problems, and many orders were either canceled or frustrated (generally due to failure of buyer, builder, or finance). Nevertheless, this still left a significant accumulated orderbook, which bolstered subsequent years' output.

Counterintuitively, ship orders continued throughout 2008, albeit at lower levels than the previous year. Not until 2009 did the shipping community show any real recognition of the worldwide economic downturn. For one year, new ship orders plummeted to very low levels, indicating to many that orders would imminently evaporate completely while the markets and fleets adjusted. But 2010 saw a return to placing orders at a significant level—evidence of the shipbuilding industry's tendency to react illogically or irrationally to the external factors that regulate most other economic activity. Exhibit 4-3 gives a clearer view of delivery and ordering activity and its impact on the accumulated forward workload orderbook.

Exhibit 4-2. Historical Shipbuilding Production (in millions of gross tons)

Year	Europe	Japan	Korea	China	Other	World
1954	4.3	0.4			0.7	5.5
1955	4.2	0.6			0.2	5.0
1956	4.6	1.5			0.2	6.3
1957	5.4	2.3			0.4	8.1
1958	6.1	2.2			0.7	9.1
1959	6.0	1.7			1.0	8.7
1960	6.0	1.8			0.6	8.4
1961	5.8	1.7			0.6	8.1
1962	5.5	2.1			0.6	8.2
1963	6.0	2.3			0.8	9.0
1964	5.4	3.8			0.5	9.7
1965	6.3	4.9			0.5	11.8
1966	7.1	6.5			0.5	14.1
1967	7.3	7.2			0.6	15.2
1968	7.7	8.4			0.9	16.9
1969	8.6	9.2			1.0	18.7
1970	9.6	10.1			1.3	21.0
1971	10.4	11.1			2.9	24.4
1972	10.6	12.9			3.3	26.8
1973	11.9	14.8			3.8	30.4
1974	12.5	16.9	0.3		3.8	33.5
1975	13.1	17.0	0.4		3.7	34.2
1976	12.7	15.9	0.8		4.5	33.9
1977	11.7	13.8	0.7		4.5	30.7
1978	10.7	11.7	0.6		4.5	27.6
1979	6.6	6.3	0.6		1.7	15.2
1980	4.7	4.7	0.5		4.4	14.3
1981	4.1	8.4	0.9		3.5	16.9
1982	3.9	8.2	1.4		3.4	16.8
1983	4.2	6.7	1.5		3.5	15.9
1984	3.5	9.7	1.5		3.7	18.3

Exhibit 4-2. Historical Shipbuilding Production *cont.*

Year	Europe	Japan	Korea	China	Other	World
1985	3.0	9.5	2.6		3.1	18.2
1986	2.1	8.2	3.6		3.0	16.9
1987	2.0	5.7	2.1		2.5	12.3
1988	1.7	4.0	3.2		2.0	10.9
1989	2.0	5.4	3.1		2.8	13.2
1990	4.2	6.6	3.6	0.4	1.4	16.1
1991	4.2	7.0	3.5	0.5	1.1	16.3
1992	4.7	7.4	4.5	0.5	1.3	18.6
1993	4.9	9.1	4.5	0.8	1.3	20.6
1994	4.4	8.7	4.3	1.0	1.3	19.7
1995	5.0	9.3	6.3	1.0	1.1	22.6
1996	6.2	9.8	7.3	1.0	1.2	25.5
1997	4.3	10.0	8.1	1.5	1.3	25.1
1998	5.3	10.2	7.1	1.7	1.5	25.8
1999	4.6	11.1	9.3	1.4	1.4	27.7
2000	4.4	11.5	11.6	1.6	1.3	30.4
2001	4.8	12.5	11.7	2.0	1.4	32.4
2002	5.0	12.1	13.1	2.0	1.6	33.7
2003	4.6	12.7	13.7	3.9	1.7	36.7
2004	4.8	14.5	14.7	4.8	1.7	40.5
2005	4.5	16.4	17.5	6.8	2.2	47.4
2006	5.3	18.1	18.6	7.7	2.3	51.9
2007	6.2	17.5	20.6	10.4	2.6	57.3
2008	6.0	18.7	26.2	13.9	2.8	67.6
2009	4.6	19.0	29.1	21.7	2.9	77.3
2010	4.7	20.2	31.7	36.2	3.6	96.5
2011	2.8	19.3	35.8	39.2	4.3	101.5
2012	2.4	17.4	31.6	38.8	5.6	95.8
2013	2.1	14.5	24.5	25.8	3.5	70.4
2014	1.8	13.0	20.1	21.3	3.8	60.0

Source: SHE Database

Exhibit 4-3. Trends in Production, Ordering, and Forward Orderbook for World Shipbuilding (in millions of compensated gross tons)

Year	New Orders	Orderbook	Deliveries	Orderbook/ Delivery Ratio
1990	14.0	27.9	11.4	2.4
1991	11.8	28.4	11.3	2.5
1992	8.7	25.0	12.1	2.1
1993	14.9	27.4	12.5	2.2
1994	16.4	31.0	12.8	2.4
1995	17.7	34.7	14.0	2.5
1996	17.4	35.9	16.2	2.2
1997	20.6	39.9	16.6	2.4
1998	17.0	39.2	17.7	2.2
1999	18.6	40.2	17.6	2.3
2000	23.5	45.6	18.1	2.5
2001	21.9	47.9	19.6	2.4
2002	19.4	46.8	20.5	2.3
2003	43.1	67.6	22.3	3.0
2004	50.6	93.5	24.7	3.8
2005	41.3	106.3	28.5	3.7
2006	61.3	135.5	32.1	4.2
2007	91.2	190.5	36.2	5.3
2008	49.6	197.1	43.0	4.6
2009	6.4	158.1	45.4	3.5
2010	30.8	136.5	52.4	2.6
2011	24.9	110.0	51.4	2.1
2012	27.3	88.0	49.3	1.8
2013	42.9	96.0	37.9	2.5
2014	40.1	109.1	33.6	3.2

Source: SHE Database

This more comprehensive view of shipbuilding trends demonstrates that continued ordering since 2010, while volatile, has been sufficient for the forward workload of accumulated shipbuilding orders to resume growth in 2013. In brief, volumes of new orders placed exceeded volume of ships delivered in both 2013 and 2014. Orderbooks at the end of 2014 represented three years' forward production at 2014 output levels.

In reality, however, this orderbook is phased across a longer period—seven years—with the latest delivery for 2021.[4] Exhibit 4-4 shows this forward order-book together with historical deliveries. This reflects only a point in time: moving forward, completion of ships on order will deplete the orderbook, and further orders will supplement it. The orderbook for 2014 reflects the poten-tial for late reporting to increase the final total production for 2014, although in practice a proportion of this is likely to be slippage, comprising vessels origi-nally scheduled for delivery in 2014 that are actually delivered in 2015, as well as cancellations (vessels currently in the orderbook that for some reason are never ultimately constructed).

On this basis, exhibit 4-5 makes it easy to compare the situation in China with that worldwide—most notably, the much faster rate of increase from 2002 onward. This is unlikely to all have resulted from Premier Zhu Rongji's chal-lenge to the industry in 2002, because most deliveries scheduled for 2003–5 would already have been on order at the time of the announcement.

In China, production peak occurred in 2011–12, versus 2010 in world terms, with production levels in both years reaching 19.7 million CGT. This time lag at least partially reflects the historical problem of orderbook slippage evident in Chinese production. Although slippage has been a factor for many countries in recent years, Chinese orders seem to have been disproportionately susceptible. Production decline, arriving 2013, exceeded global trends.

Perhaps the clearest indicators of the explosion in Chinese shipbuilding activity are the over 13-fold increase in production from 2002 to 2012—over 5 times the 2.4-fold increase in global output over the same period—and the fact that China's 2012 production roughly equaled world production for 2002.

Chinese Shipbuilding Industry Development

To understand the challenges and issues currently facing Chinese shipbuild-ers, one must understand the structure of the industry sector that developed so rapidly between 2002 and 2012. Unlike South Korea, the previous shipbuilding leader, China's capacity comprised numerous individual yards—at one point reportedly exceeding one thousand, per government statistics—of hugely varying production volumes and capabilities. South Korean capacity was built predominantly upon the "big five" conglomerates (Daewoo, Samsung, Hyundai, Hanjin, and STX), accounting for over 80 percent of South Korean production. Each comprised one or two individual yards with enormous

Exhibit 4-4. World Historical Production and Orderbook Phasing
(in millions of compensated gross tons)

Year	Deliveries	Orderbook	Total
1990	11.4		11.4
1991	11.3		11.3
1992	12.1		12.1
1993	12.5		12.5
1994	12.8		12.8
1995	14.0		14.0
1996	16.2		16.2
1997	16.6		16.6
1998	17.7		17.7
1999	17.6		17.6
2000	18.1		18.1
2001	19.6		19.6
2002	20.5		20.5
2003	22.3		22.3
2004	24.7		24.7
2005	28.5		28.5
2006	32.1		32.1
2007	36.2		36.2
2008	43.4		43.4
2009	45.7		45.7
2010	52.5		52.5
2011	51.4		51.4
2012	49.3		49.3
2013	37.9		37.9
2014	33.6	8.2	41.8
2015		49.2	49.2
2016		35.8	35.8
2017+		15.8	15.8

Source: SHE Database

Exhibit 4-5. China's Historical Production and Orderbook Phasing

Year	Deliveries	Orderbook
1990	0.3	
1991	0.4	
1992	0.4	
1993	0.5	
1994	0.7	
1995	0.6	
1996	0.7	
1997	1.0	
1998	1.2	
1999	1.1	
2000	1.2	
2001	1.4	
2002	1.5	
2003	2.6	
2004	3.0	
2005	4.4	
2006	5.0	
2007	6.8	
2008	9.2	
2009	12.5	
2010	18.8	
2011	19.7	
2012	19.7	
2013	13.2	
2014	11.0	3.7
2015		19.6
2016		14.6
2017+		4.4

Source: SHE Database

production scale. In contrast, in China the industry was heavily diversified. Even the state-owned "majors," China State Shipbuilding Corporation (CSSC) and China Shipbuilding Industry Corporation (CSIC), themselves comprised numerous different shipyards, thereby diluting the actual production volumes of even their largest constituent shipyards.

In 2012, China's largest yards were Jiangnan Changxing Shipyard (a member of CSSC) and Dalian Shipbuilding (a member of CSIC), both recording output of just over one million CGT. Although Dalian theoretically comprises two shipyards (Dalian and New Dalian), they are collocated and seem to have been operating as a single entity for many years. After this came STX Dalian and Waigaoqiao Shipyard in Shanghai (a CSSC member), each with approximately 0.7 million CGT of production. These top four producers produced 18 percent of China's output. The remaining 16.2 million CGT was delivered from over 250 shipyards, the smallest of which produced just 1,500 CGT. Indeed, there were nearly eighty shipyards with reported output of under ten thousand CGT.

That year, South Korea's largest shipbuilder was Hyundai Heavy Industry (HI), which delivered 2.87 million CGT, followed closely by Daewoo Shipbuilding and Samsung HI with just under 2.5 million CGT each. These three shipbuilders combined accounted for 57 percent of China's total shipbuilding production, with nineteen other shipbuilding enterprises producing the remainder (seven of which produced under ten thousand CGT).

Shipbuilding industry analysts have struggled to keep track of Chinese shipyards, many of which seem to have appeared and disappeared without foreign notice. While some oversights may have stemmed from name changes, translation issues, and how shipyard names were reported, there is no doubt that some were beach yards with primitive vessel-launch methods and little or no major shipbuilding facilities. It became unremarkable for individual yards to appear on the list of builders one year only to disappear a few years later. The sheer volume of separate reported operations made it almost impossible to follow industry development from outside China, and identifying the location of a new shipyard became increasingly difficult. In every prime shipbuilding location, new shipyards lined major rivers and coastlines.

Despite such difficulties in tracking the industry, there has unquestionably been massive facilities investment in almost every conceivable Chinese shipbuilding location. New shipyards and additional shipbuilding docks/berths have emerged in both the state-owned groups and the private sector, with quasi-state groups (such as national shipping companies) and the municipal or provincial government developments sitting somewhere in between.

There is no easy way to summarize this capacity development, but the first author of the present chapter was the prime author of one of the first seminal reports on Chinese shipbuilding: Drewry Shipping Consultants' *China's Shipyards: Capacity, Competition, and Challenges* (2003). This report is employed here as a baseline against which Chinese shipbuilding development can be viewed.[5]

At the time of the report's analysis, the top twenty list of Chinese shipbuilders was as shown in exhibit 4-6. Most of the shipyards were from the two large state-owned shipbuilding groups, CSSC and CSIC. Apart from one shipyard, the others were owned by national shipping companies or municipal/provincial governments. The sole exception was Yangzijiang Shipyard, then the only significant privately owned yard.

In contrast, exhibit 4-7 shows the top twenty Chinese shipbuilders in 2012, at production's peak. While some names still feature, there are many new ones and a much greater mix of private and state or quasi-state owned facilities.

Analysis of all the development trends and issues for the diversity of enterprises that have contributed to China's explosion of shipbuilding capacity is impracticable, as is accounting for all the yards that have emerged, developed, disappeared, or flourished. However, comparing the top twenty shipbuilders by output from 2000 and 2012 highlights most of the broader trends that have occurred, and in many cases repeated themselves.[6] Following are the 2012 rankings:

- Jiangnan Changxing Island Shipyard, a megayard development for CSSC, was developed under the patronage of the long-established Jiangnan Shipyard to provide a facility for its relocation in 2008 to clear the site for the Shanghai Expo in 2010. Changxing Island has four docks, three for ultra large crude carriers (ULCCs) and one for very large crude carriers (VLCCs).

- Dalian Shipbuilding, CSIC's flagship yard, is the integration of Dalian Shipyard and Dalian New Shipyard (listed separately in 2000).

- STX Dalian China Shipbuilding, an inward investment development by South Korea's STX Group, delivered its first ship in 2009. In 2013, STX withdrew due to STX Group financial problems, leaving the shipyard to Chinese authorities. Among many other ideas, it has been cited as a possible location to bring Dalian Shipbuilding from downtown Dalian.

- Shanghai Waigaoqiao Shipyard, nearing completion for CSSC at the time of the 2003 report, delivered its first ship in June 2003. One of the first megayard projects, with two VLCC/ULCC-sized docks, it is now one of CSSC's flagship yards.

Exhibit 4-6. Top 20 Chinese Shipbuilders from *China's Shipyards Report 2003*

Yard	Group	Output 000 CGT	% Util'n	Capacity 000 CGT	Max Ship Size (dwt)	No of Berths	Province
Dalian New	CSIC	120	69	214	"300,000"	2	Liaoning
Hudong	CSSC	174	102	410	"300,000"	3	Shanghai
Jiangnan	CSSC	163	65	216	"80,000"	4	Shanghai
Dalian	CSIC	111	62	180	"60,000"	3	Liaoning
Guangzhou Int'l	CSSC	108	66	163	"60,000"	3	Guangdong
Zhonghua	CSSC	64	77	83	"28,000"	2	Shanghai
Shanghai	CSSC	62	60	103	"70,000"	2	Shanghai
Jinling	CNSC	33	34	97	"30,000"	10	Jiangsu
Liaoning Bohai	CSIC	43	46	93	"150,000"	5	Liaoning
NACKS	COSCO/KHI	42	44	93	"300,000"	1	Jiangsu
New Century	(Municipality)	39	31	127	"300,000"	2/3	Jiangsu
Wuhu	CSSC	32	105	31	"28,000"	2	Anhui
Wenchong	CSSC	30	43	69	"25,000"	2	Guangdong
Jiangyang	Jiangyang SG	27	52	52	"50,000"	4	Jiangsu
Xingang	CSIC	22	40	78	"35,000"	3	Tianjin
Qiuxin	CSSC	22	28	78	"15,000"	4	Shanghai
Yangzijiang	(non-state owned)	20	24	140	"50,000"	4	Jiangsu
Qinshan	CSNC	18	14	124	"20,000"	10	Hubei
Shanghai Edward	CSSC	17	52	32	"20,000"	1	Shanghai
Mawei	Fujian SIGC	12	38	31	"35,000"	3	Fujian
Total		1,159	55	2,412			

CGT: compensated gross tons
dwt: deadweight tonnes
CSIC: China Shipbuilding Industry Corp.
CSSC: China State Shipbuilding Corp.
CNSC: China National Service Corp.
NACKS: Nantong COSCO/KHI Ship Engineering
COSCO: China Ocean Shipping Co.
SG: Shipping Group
SIGC: Shanxi Investment Group Co.

Source: Drewry Shipping Consultants, *China's Shipyards: Capacity, Competition, and Challenges* (London: Drewry, July 2003)

- Nantong Rongsheng Shipbuilding has been one of the more successful of the new privately owned megayards, with four ULCC-sized docks. It delivered its first ship in 2008 and grew rapidly. It aspired to purchase Qanchai Engine Works in 2012 but subsequently withdrew, just prior to an announcement of financial difficulties and possible bankruptcy in September 2012.

- Jinhai HI, formerly Zhoushan Jinhaiwan Shipyard, another private yard, delivered its first vessel in 2009 and had built exclusively bulk carriers up to 2012. It has four docks: one each for ULCC, VLCC, 150,000 deadweight tonnes (dwt), and 70,700 dwt. Jinhai too seems to have had financial problems, with no deliveries reported in 2013 but with deliveries recommencing in 2014 at reduced levels.

- New Yangzijiang Shipbuilding is the Yangzijiang Group's second yard. The group also includes Yangzijiang Shipbuilding—the only top-twenty private yard from the 2003 report. New Yangzijiang was originally built to replace the existing yard, but when it delivered its first ship in 2009, it provided a second stream of production that eventually exceeded the original shipyard. New Yangzijiang has two docks: one ULCC-sized, one 200,000 dwt.

- NACKS (Nantong COSCO/KHI Shipbuilding), a longstanding Sino-Japanese joint venture between COSCO Shipping and Kawasaki HI of Japan, delivered its first vessel in 1999 and enjoys continued success. Subsequent improvements include a second dock (ULCC-sized) opened in 2007 and the construction of a third dock approved in 2011.

- Hudong-Zhonghua Shipbuilding, part of CSSC, is an amalgamation of the Hudong and Zhonghua shipyards on opposite river banks. These were ranked second and sixth, respectively, in 2000. They formerly also included Shanghai Edward Shipyard (the first-ever Sino-foreign shipyard joint venture, with the German Hansa Group), no longer operational.

- Bohai Shipbuilding Industry, part of CSIC, is synonymous with the Liaoning Bohai yard ranked ninth in 2000. Output increased tenfold by 2012.

- Yangfan Group, a privately owned conglomerate, comprises several yards. Best known is Zhoushan Shipyard, which delivered its first vessel in 2001. Shipyard relocations and new developments have progressively increased the group's capacity.

- New Times Shipbuilding is the second yard of the privately owned New Century group, which has overtaken the parent New Century

Exhibit 4-7. Top 20 Chinese Shipbuilders, 2012

Shipyard	Ownership	Output CGT (in hundred thousands)
Shanghai Jiangnan Changxing Heavy Industry	China State Shipbuilding Corporation (CSSC)	1,094
Dalian Shipbuilding Industry	China Shipbuilding Industry Corporation (CSIC)	1,010
STX Dalian Shipbuilding Co Ltd	STX Group of South Korea	704
Shanghai Waigaoqiao Shipbuilding	CSSC	698
Nantong Rongsheng Shipbuiding	Private	616
Jinhai Heavy Industry Co Ltd	Private	555
New Yangzijiang Shipbuilding	Yangzijiang Group	546
Nantong China Ocean Shipping Company (COSCO) KHI Ship Eng	COSCO/KHI joint venture	452
Hudong-Zhonghua Shipbuilding	CSSC	424
Bohai Shipbuilding Heavy Industry	CSIC	416
Yangfan Group Co Ltd	Private	413
New Times Shipbuilding Co Ltd	New Century Group	405
Guangzhou Shipyard Intl Co Ltd	CSSC	389
Tsuneishi Zhoushan Shipbuilding	Tsuneishi Heavy Industry of Japan	378
Hantong Ship Heavy Industry	Joint venture with South Korea	365
Jinling Shipyard	Sinotrans-CSC	344
Yangzhou Dayang Shipbuilding	Sinopacific Group	323
Huanghai Shipbuilding Co Ltd	Private	295
Shanghai Shipyard Co Ltd	CSSC	289
Guangzhou Longxue Shipbuilding	CSSC	288

Shipbuilding (formerly Jingjiang Shipyard) in output. In 2003, New Century (ranked eleventh in 2000) was owned by the municipality, but it was privatized in 2004. The New Times yard has a single ULCC-sized dock; New Century yard has two operational large docks, for ULCCs and VLCCs respectively. New Century Group likewise appears to have experienced difficulties, with output stalling for a period in 2014.

- Guangzhou Shipyard International (GSI), one of CSSC's flagship yards, was long its leading yard in the southern Pearl River cluster. It was best known as the first Chinese shipyard to be listed on a stock exchange (Hong Kong and Shanghai) back in 1993. It was ranked fifth in 2000, but—despite increasing output nearly fourfold—only thirteenth in 2012. Subsequently, as detailed by Gabe Collins and Eric Anderson in their chapter in this volume, it has grown through acquisition and been renamed CSSC Offshore and Marine Engineering (Group) Company Ltd. (COMEC).

- Tsuneishi Zhoushan Shipbuilding, one of the few foreign-owned shipbuilding ventures, opened in 2003 originally as a hull-building operation for Japanese parent Tsuneishi HI. Since delivering its first complete vessel in 2007, while concentrating only on building bulk carriers, it has thrived with twenty deliveries recorded in 2012.

- Hantong Ship HI, a joint venture with South Korean investors, was one of the earlier overseas involvements. Founded in 2005, it delivered its first ship in 2008. The yard undertakes floating production storage and offloading work as well as shipbuilding and is equipped with a dock (max length 260 meters) and two building berths (both max length 220 meters). Its shipbuilding production has almost exclusively comprised 30,000–55,000 dwt bulk carriers.

- Jinling Shipyard, Changjiang National Shipping Corporation's largest shipyard, was ranked eighth in 2000 but only sixteenth in 2012 despite tenfold output growth. The group was renamed Sinotrans-CSC when the parent company merged with Sinotrans.

- Yangzhou Dayang Shipbuilding is part of Sinopacific's yard group. Sinopacific acquired two established shipyards in 2003: Zhejiang and the former Binjiang yard. To upgrade capacity, it undertook extensive development of these and new sites. The group's output is a mixed stream of large bulk carriers from this yard with smaller offshore support and anchor handling vessels predominantly from the Zhejiang facility.

- Huanghai Shipbuilding, a long-established shipbuilder previously owned by the municipality, built a second new yard under private ownership to expand capacity. This opened in 2009. Now both yards contribute to production.

- Shanghai Shipyard, a long-established CSSC yard, originally comprised two yards on opposite river banks—one for shipbuilding, the other for ship repair. Pudong Shipyard was closed in 2004 and shipbuilding relocated to a new Chongming Island facility, one of the new megayards. The group also includes Chengxi Shipyard, which ceased reporting its production separately for a period. The new Chongming facility opened in 2002 with one VLCC building berth. A drydock for shipbuilding opened around 2009–10.

- Guangzhou Longxue facility is another of the megayard developments of the CSSC group, originally intended mainly for ship repair (with two docks) and limited shipbuilding (one dock). Largely utilized entirely for shipbuilding during its early days, Longxue now has a mix of building, repair, and—more recently—offshore engineering. Through acquisitions made by GSI (now a subsidiary of COMEC) effective June 16, 2014,[7] the site seems to have been reunited for multipurpose use. This may involve future relocation of former GSI shipbuilding activity from its original site.

In summary, Chinese shipbuilding development has stemmed from a combination of mergers and integrations, relocations, new developments, privatization, inward investment, and evolution of existing yards.

In the state-owned sector, both CSSC and CSIC have merged and integrated some of their older shipyards, such as Hudong-Zhonghua and Shanghai Edward, Dalian SY and Dalian New Yard, Jiangnan and Qiuxin, and Shanghai Shipyard and Chengxi Shipyard. CSSC has built four new megayards—Waigaoqiao, Chongming, and Changxing island sites in Shanghai and Longxue in Guangzhou—whereas CSIC constructed a new facility at Haixiwan near Qingdao. Three of these new developments have enabled the relocation of existing shipbuilding facilities—Jiangnan (to Changxing Island), Shanghai Shipbuilding (to Chongming Island), and Qingdao (to Haixiwan)—with increased capabilities.

The domestic private sector has seen sweeping new developments, such as the emergence of Nantong Rongsheng and Jinhai HI, as well as new shipyards for existing shipbuilders, such as the New Yangzijiang yard for the Yangzijiang group and the New Times yard for the New Century Group. Other established shipbuilders, such as Sinopacific, have expanded their capabilities through a combination of acquisition, expansion, and new developments.

In the municipal sector, groups such as Fujian SIGC have expanded and flourished. Privatization has contributed to the domestic sector's growth—for example, Huanghai Shipbuilding has subsequently expanded under private ownership. Inward investment by both Japanese and South Korean shipbuild- ers, initially in hull and block-building, has triggered new facilities such as Tsuneishi's Zhoushan and DSME's Weihai, which have subsequently converted to shipbuilding. Further inward investment from South Korea resulted in new facilities by STX at Dalian and Hantong Ship HI in Jiangsu. These factors are in addition to the innumerable individual shipyard startups, some of which have lasted, while others have not.

Shipyard Performance

Contrary to sector outsiders' expectations, shipyard performance is a complex, multifaceted issue. There are many different parameters by which it can be measured and different aspects that influence it. The most common parameters regarded as important include technology, productivity, labor cost, profitability, and technical complexity. The reality is more complicated, however. The most high-technology shipyard or the shipyard with the highest productivity or lowest labor cost may not be the best overall performer. It is helpful to go back to basics to probe what actually most influences shipyard performance. The key measures of efficiency are cost, timescale, and quality. Most fundamentally, a shipyard needs to be able to deliver ships on time and to specification, at the lowest cost possible. Shipyards have little control over the sales price of ships and so must concentrate on these measures to maximize performance. But to perform well in the future, a shipyard must remain in operation. Even profitability, which is simply an accounting concept, is not a guarantee of this. In a project-based industry, profitability can vary hugely from year to year. Many shipyards experience protracted losses.

Shipbuilding is unusual in that it is both labor- and capital-intensive. It is more common for businesses to be one or the other rather than both. Accordingly, effective operations need to manage the benefits and disadvantages of both.

Perhaps the greatest misconception is that technology, productivity, and labor cost are intrinsically linked to profitability such that high productivity or low labor cost ensures improved profitability. In reality, shipbuilding can be equally cost competitive under different economic conditions. Thus, a high-labor-cost/high-productivity producer and a low-labor-cost/low-productivity producer *may* be equally cost-efficient, although not necessarily so.

Less well understood is the cost effect of technology and capital investment on shipyard performance. Technological investment needs to be *appropriate* to the productivity and labor cost context of a particular shipbuilder; otherwise it will harm performance.

If a shipbuilder invests in a particular technology, the productivity improvement required to make it cost-effective needs to be far higher for a low-labor-cost yard than for a high-labor-cost yard. In essence, the saving (and hence payback) is man-hours saved times the unit cost of man-hours. In many instances the man-hours saved may be the same, but the labor cost may vary significantly. So investing in, for example, plasma or laser-cutting machines to improve cut accuracy and reduce heat distortion may be cost-effective for one shipbuilder but not another.

At a higher level, the capital investment of constructing or upgrading a shipyard has considerable effect on its cost performance potential. Reasons include:

- inappropriate technology that is too "high" for the "labor cost" to recover the investment
- significant overhead burden (amortization or use of asset charges) that must be recovered from project contribution levels
- high financing costs.

Economies of scale are a key component of shipyard performance. While capacity or throughput capability of a shipyard is notoriously difficult to define, a high-throughput facility has an inherent competitive advantage.

Construction timescales, in particular the time the vessels spend under construction in the dock or on the building berth, are a key element in maximizing the capacity of these key assets and hence a shipyard. Hence, dock cycle times are a key measure of a shipyard's performance. The capacity of lifts at the build location is important, dictating the maximum size of lift for the blocks from which the ship is constructed on the berth/dock. This is a principal determinant of overall dock cycle times. It is much faster to construct a given vessel out of one-thousand-ton blocks than it is out of two-hundred-ton blocks. However, this necessitates an adequate supply of steelwork capability to assemble these blocks and areas for them to be painted, pre-outfitted, and so forth. All of these facilities generally involve expensive investment in capital facilities.

Exhibit 4-8. Shipbuilding Throughput Comparison of Major Shipbuilders

South Korea		China		Japan		Southeast Asia	
Shipbuilder	CGT (m)	Shipbuilder	CGT (m)	Shipbuilder	CGT (m)	Shipbuilder	CGT (m)
Hyundai Heavy Industry	2.355	Dalian Shipyard	0.705	Universal Shipbuilding	0.945	Tsuneishi Philippines	0.292
Samsung Heavy Industry	2.320	Waigaoqiao Shipyard	0.653	Imabari Shipbuilding	0.934	CSBC	0.255
Daewoo Shipbuilding and Marine Engineering	2.009	New Yangzijiang	0.580	Oshima Shipbuilding	0.625	Hanjin Heavy Industry and Construction Philippines	0.241

Fixed or semi-variable costs form a significant part of the overall cost of shipbuilding, particularly for a newly constructed shipyard with great capital investment costs that need to be both financed and then recovered through project contributions. The most widely used measure of capacity in shipbuilding is CGT (which reflects the added value element of ship construction), and the following examples show the huge variations in scale that can exist, even among some of the largest shipbuilders in the world's leading shipbuilding regions (see exhibit 4-8).

Based on these figures, it is perhaps easier to understand how the large South Korean shipbuilders have a built-in performance advantage over even the largest of the Chinese shipbuilders, whose throughputs (in 2013) were less than one-third those of their South Korean counterparts. Certainly, the state-owned Chinese shipyards that are part of CSSC and CSIC (which have larger total throughputs) may gain some economies of scale. But much of the overhead function, and hence cost, of the operation is generated by the shipyard itself; therefore, groups of yards are generally not as cost-efficient as a single yard of the same capacity. Additionally, of course, both Waigaoqiao and New Yangzijiang are new shipyards that likely bear a high depreciation cost. In Korean shipyards, by contrast, at least part of the main facilities will be fully depreciated.

In addition to the overhead and fixed cost element of shipbuilding, economies of scale can also generate significant purchasing economies or efficiencies for high-volume shipyards and individual yard members of large shipbuilding groups.

The volatility of shipbuilding workload can result in significant throughput variations within a given shipyard over time; this alone may significantly affect the profitability of a particular shipyard at a given time. Exhibit 4-9 shows how the throughput volumes of China's top twenty shipyards from 2012 (the peak output year) had changed by 2013. In most cases the throughputs had dropped to between 50 and 75 percent of the previous year, which will have contributed to reduced profitability potential. Only three shipyards from this list showed any increase in throughput. In two of those, it was only slight; three other yards experienced less significant reductions.

Preliminary figures for 2014 show that many Chinese shipyards saw a further fall in merchant shipbuilding throughput. These changes are largely due to fluctuations in demand. The supply capacity of these shipyards is extremely unlikely to have reduced, but as overall demand for shipbuilding has dropped, these facilities' throughput, and hence utilization, has dropped.

Exhibit 4-9. Shipbuilding Throughput Changes for Chinese Shipbuilders

Shipyard	Ownership	Output CGT (in hundred thousands)		
		2012	2013	%2012
Shanghai Jiangnan Changxing Heavy Industry	China State Shipbuilding Corporation (CSSC)	1,094	677	61.9
Dalian Shipbuilding Industry	China Shipbuilding Industry Corporation (CSIC)	1,010	705	69.8
STX Dalian Shipbuilding Co Ltd	STX Group of S Korea	704	469	66.6
Shanghai Waigaoqiao Shipbuilding	CSSC	698	653	93.6
Nantong Rongsheng Shipbuiding	Private	616	345	56.0
Jinhai Heavy Industry Co Ltd	Private	555		0.0
New Yangzijiang Shipbuilding	Yangzijiang Group	546	580	106.2
Nantong COSCO KHI Ship Engineering	COSCO/KHI joint venture	452	388	85.8
Hudong-Zhonghua Shipbuilding	CSSC	424	337	79.5
Bohai Shipbuilding Heavy Industry	CSIC	416	238	57.2
Yangfan Group Co Ltd	Private	413	219	53.0
New Times Shipbuilding Co Ltd	New Century Group	405	243	60.0
Guangzhou Shipyard Intl Co Ltd	CSSC	389	163	41.9
Tsuneishi Zhoushan Shipbuilding	Tsuneishi Heavy Industry of Japan	378	325	86.0
Hantong Ship Heavy Industry	Joint venture with South Korea	365	186	51.0
Jinling Shipyard	Sinotrans-CSC	344	141	41.0
Yangzhou Dayang Shipbuilding	Sinopacific Group	323	374	115.8
Huanghai Shipbuilding Co Ltd	Private	295	223	75.6
Shanghai Shipyard Co Ltd	CSSC	289	302	104.5
Guangzhou Longxue Shipbuilding	CSSC	288	127	44.1

Exhibit 4-10. New Ship Price Volatility

Ship Type	Size	Year Average Price (US$ million)								
		2000	2002	2004	2006	2008	2010	2012	2014
Bulk carrier	30k deadweight tonnes (dwt)	16.6	14.3	19.3	22.3	37.0	24.8	19.6	21.7
	170k dwt	36.8	35.1	54.8	62.1	93.6	57.9	46.0	50.7
Oil tanker	75k dwt	33.2	31.1	38.9	48.0	62.9	44.7	42.5	45.4
	160k dwt	46.0	44.8	60.1	75.5	95.4	65.8	58.5	64.8
	300k dwt	72.3	67.5	90.5	124.9	155.7	102.7	94.3	98.5
Chemical tanker	37k dwt	67.6	50.0	55.0	64.0	64.0	64.0	54.0	65.9
Container ship	3,500 twenty-foot equivalent units (teu)	39.0	33.8	50.3	54.5	63.5	38.6	43.1	40.8
	6,500 teu	67.1	63.5	86.0	95.1	109.5	74.8	63.1	60.3
	10,000 teu				134.2	151.5	100.0	93.8	93.8
Liquefied natural gas carrier	125k–155k cubic meters (cbm)	150.0	160.0	173.0					
	160k cbm				222.0	249.0	207.8	201.1	205.3
Liquefied petroleum gas carrier	78k cbm	61.4	57.5	71.0	92.6	93.5	72.3	75.4	78.3

Source: Drewry Shipping Consultants

Demand-side variations in the shipbuilding market are beyond shipbuilders' control, but they greatly affect shipyards' profitability. Demand is volatile; so are shipbuilding prices. Exhibit 4-10 shows the changes in prices of particular ship types during recent years.

Prices for new ships are heavily market-driven; in reality the cost of construction is irrelevant. Factor costs of production, however, are generally influenced by entirely different factors, such as locality for wages, general economic conditions for many commodities, and other market trends for others. Generally, only steel and marine engines are likely to vary with any element of congruence with shipbuilding prices. Exchange rate fluctuations between the U.S. dollar (the currency in which ship prices are still mainly denominated) and the currencies in which a shipbuilder incurs costs also affect the shipbuilder's real income. Therefore, the income that the shipbuilder receives to recover direct and overhead costs of production is both outside the control of the shipbuilder and highly volatile.

In terms of overall profitability, therefore, perhaps the key criterion that influences shipyard performance is a shipbuilder's ability to weather the volatility of shipbuilding over the long timescales inherent in such a capital-intensive industry. Additionally, having built a shipyard, there are significant barriers to easy exit and limited opportunities to access other industry markets; it is survival in the long term that is key. Traditionally, shipbuilders look to make money in the boom years in order to survive inevitable market downturns. It is therefore not abnormal to find that shipbuilders can be loss-making for extended periods of time during market slumps.

Experience has shown that the following characteristics positively influence shipbuilding success (i.e., continued survival):

- technical competence (essential)
- product mix diversity to deal with differing cycles of the mainstream ship types
- cost-effective capital investment
- ability to maximize output of key assets
- economies of scale and throughput flexibility to respond to demand variations
- ability to evolve up the ship complexity scale to gain greater added-value potential, especially as labor and capital investment costs increase
- diversification or cross-subsidy within the ownership group to withstand market downturns

- vertical integration between shipowners and shipbuilding
- government subsidies
- shipyard owners' finances
- captive home markets, such as military shipbuilding, to provide support during market downturns—particularly important for Chinese shipbuilders today.

Challenges Facing Chinese Merchant Shipbuilders

The rapid development of Chinese merchant shipbuilding capability during the early twenty-first century occurred during an almost unprecedented shipbuilding boom period, wherein both prices and demand skyrocketed against historical conditions. Even the previous 1970s boom was on a much smaller, slower scale in almost every respect. Perhaps the only similarity is that they both birthed a new emergent shipbuilding nation.

The rapid explosion of shipbuilding output yielded an enormous number of new shipyards, so many that most shipbuilding analysts found it difficult to keep track. Key growth components included expansion of the existing state-owned sector, in the form of CSSC and CSIC, including the construction of new mega-shipyards; development of a quasi-state-owned sector in the form of shipyard groups developed from national shipping operations such as COSCO, China Shipping, and Changjiang; inward investment by foreign shipbuilders, mostly from Japan and South Korea; emergence of a private sector of domestically owned shipyards and joint ventures with overseas investment; and evolution of existing provincial shipyards, with some greatly expanded and others privatized.

Much of this growth has involved significant investment in facilities, with the possible exception of the low-tech beach yards that burgeoned haphazardly. The enormous increase in world shipbuilding capacity has meant that with the significant decline in demand, the shipyards will have lower utilizations. Prices have also dropped significantly; on almost all significant fronts, financial levers have retrogressed.

Many Chinese shipyards are now experiencing severe financial pressures through high capital costs, reduced ship prices (and hence contribution), and reduced throughputs. Credit is also dear, particularly for the yards that do not have state or group owners with significant financial strength. There have already been bankruptcies and closures among private shipyards, and many others appear to have simply vanished as quietly as they came. Additionally,

China's ship-building industry faces government-driven restructuring, in particular the "white list" phenomenon; protecting prioritized operations makes it difficult for those not meeting criteria to survive.

It is almost inevitable that the Chinese government would not let its own state-owned yards "go to the wall." Instead, intensive consolidation in both CSSC and CSIC appears to be under way, alongside relocation of longer-established yards to modern, larger-capacity, newly developed shipyards. The absence of detailed financial information obscures the true economics of these operations, but they certainly enjoy moneyed owners. Importantly, it appears that China's government may be underpinning its flagship yards with military workloads.

Consolidation also seems slated with the quasi-state sector in the form of the major shipping lines' shipyard groups. The only true market test is likely to be the privately owned shipbuilding enterprises, already suffering bankruptcies and other financial problems. The orderbook lead times mean that there can be a time delay in financial outcomes: not only have throughput volumes started to decline, but also the effects of the lower margins stemming from lower prices for vessels contracted two or three years ago keep emerging.

Evolution of Technical Complexity and Size within Chinese Merchant Shipbuilding

Traditionally, when the world shipbuilding industry faces financial difficulties, one response has been for yards to try to move up the ship complexity scale. In relative terms, the added-value contribution level there can be higher and the competition reduced.

Probably the simplest way to determine complexity is through the compensation factor that forms part of the industry's CGT measure of workload. Certain ship types are inherently more complex (and work-intensive) than others; however, size also affects complexity, with smaller vessels requiring more work per gross ton (volume measure) of ship constructed.

Exhibit 4-11 shows a simplified ranking of vessel complexity using the average "compensation factor" from world production over the last three years for each ship type. Ship types have been grouped into three size categories—large, medium, and small—because to benefit, a high throughput producer needs to capture both volume and complexity.

Exhibit 4-12 shows the percentage of Chinese shipbuilding output that each ship type accounted for during 2012 to 2014. China's production remains

Exhibit 4-11. Complexity Ranking of Ships According to Average Compensated Gross Ton (CGT) Coefficient

Large Ships (>20k Gross Tons [GT])

Ship Type	Average Ship GT	Average CGT Coefficient	% World CGT
Liquefied natural gas carrier	98,499	0.799	3.6
Car carrier	56,684	0.557	2.0
Container	71,556	0.498	18.4
Bulk carrier	43,662	0.429	39.2
Oil Tanker	40,097	0.389	10.0

Medium Ships (7–20k GT)

Ship Type	Average Ship GT	Average CGT Coefficient	% World CGT
Special tanker	7,404	1.436	0.4
Passenger	15,819	1.307	2.4
Ferry	7,127	1.294	0.7
Liquefied petroleum gas carrier	13,708	0.961	1.6
Chemical tanker	16,724	0.953	5.7
General cargo	8,453	0.935	3.8
Roll-on/roll-off	9,425	0.835	1.1
Special cargo	14,122	0.788	0.4

Small Ships (<7k GT)

Ship Type	Average Ship GT	Average CGT Coefficient	% World CGT
M-hull/ fast passenger	1,581	3.845	0.1
Tug	920	3.602	0.7
Fishing vessel	1,503	2.859	0.6
Service vessel	2,244	2.189	0.8
Reefer	3,004	2.033	0.1
Dredger	5,363	1.669	0.4
Offshore vessel	5,860	1.407	7.5

Note: Based on world production of ships > 500 GT between 2012 and 2014.

skewed toward simpler types, particularly in the large ship category, in which production is still dominated by bulk carriers and oil tankers. To achieve higher complexity and potentially higher added-value at the production levels that China has reached, it needs to penetrate the liquefied natural gas ship sector. Although it builds a significant volume of container ships, the average size of its production in this sector is less than 60 percent of the world average for this type of vessels, so it would also need to build more of the very large container ships.

In the medium ship category, it is notable that China is not yet active in significant passenger vessel construction. In addition, the average size of its chemical tanker output is only about 70 percent of the average size of these ships worldwide.

Interaction between Merchant and Naval Shipbuilding—Facts and Fallacies

From the perspective of merchant shipbuilding, naval and merchant shipbuilding are not a good mix operationally. The exceptions are the provision of a "captive" client and the opportunity for "state support" through naval contracts during downturns in the merchant shipbuilding market. To be specific:

- client: there is little synergy between the requirements of the national government/military (even overseas naval customers) and commercial shipowners.

- culture: because of the client and product differences, the culture in military shipyards is not commercially honed and often depresses productivity and efficiency in merchant shipbuilding activities.

- timescales: military shipbuilding design and production timescales are far longer than those in merchant shipbuilding.

- engineering: is generally more complex in military shipbuilding and both design and production competence in weapons systems is required.

- ship design: criteria for military ships differ significantly from those of mainstream merchant ships.

- propulsion systems: those for military vessels are more complex, sometimes technologically sensitive nuclear reactors, gas turbines, and diesel/gas combinations rather than the slow- and medium-speed diesels common to most merchant ships.

Exhibit 4-12. Composition of Chinese Shipbuilding Production by Size and Complexity

Ship Type	Average Compensated Gross Tons Coefficient World	Size Category	Average Gross Tons China	Percent China Compensated Gross Tons		
				2012	2013	2014
Liquefied natural gas carrier	0.799	Large	43,145	0.4	0.1	0.0
Car carrier	0.557	Large	15,352	1.5	0.0	0.0
Container	0.498	Large	41,372	7.1	14.8	23.6
Bulk carrier	0.429	Large	43,145	62.0	56.6	48.9
Oil tanker	0.389	Large	35,528	8.2	9.5	8.2
Special tanker	1.436	Medium	3,161	0.3	0.0	0.2
Passenger	1.307	Medium	71	0.0	0.0	0.0
Ferry	1.294	Medium	11,804	0.6	0.1	0.5
LPG carrier	0.961	Medium	7,638	0.7	1.2	1.0
Chemical tanker	0.953	Medium	11,449	4.6	2.7	2.2
General cargo	0.935	Medium	10,640	6.0	5.1	3.2
Roll-on/roll-off	0.835	Medium	5,596	0.5	0.9	0.4
Special cargo	0.788	Medium	16,537	2.4	1.2	1.0
M-hull and fast passenger	3.845	Small	329	0.0	0.0	0.0
Tug	3.602	Small	1,011	0.6	0.1	0.3
Fishing vessel	2.859	Small	1,046	0.3	0.4	0.7
Service vessel	2.189	Small	3,797	0.2	0.3	0.2
Reefer	2.033	Small	1,782	0.0	0.0	0.1
Dredger	1.669	Small	6,078	0.6	0.1	0.3
Offshore vessel	1.407	Small	3,443	3.6	6.4	8.9

- hull construction: military ships traditionally involve much thinner plate thicknesses than merchant vessels and may involve a greater variety of alternative hull materials. This necessitates more sophisticated production equipment and assembly skills.

- technical standards: military specifications frequently require different technical standards from ship classification societies or merchant ship specifications.

- security: restrictions required for military shipbuilding complicate access for owners, suppliers, technical advisers, and so forth that merchant shipbuilding might require.

In many respects, military shipbuilding will tend to increase overhead costs of a shipyard's operation and depress productivity and efficiency. This can manifest itself in many areas, including more extensive design capability, specialized production workshops, different procurement policies and practices (driven by public spending requirements), specialized supplier base for certain materials and equipment, and more intensive project management requirements.

Given the differences between military and merchant shipbuilding, in many instances the only way to successfully operate in both sectors is to run both as entirely separated operations—often with physical separation of facilities—even if these are located adjacent to each other on a single site.

The potential of cross-subsidy between military and merchant shipbuilding has had a significant impact on shipbuilding within the European Union (EU). Cross-subsidy, like almost all forms of subsidy, causes a conflict with the European Commission's Competition Policy. Because of the difficulties experienced over two decades by EU shipbuilders as a result of the drive to eliminate subsidy and support from shipbuilding, this has attracted considerable controversy. Cross-subsidy has been identified and remedies and/or penalties have been imposed on several occasions. Some have radically altered the structure of Europe's shipbuilding sector, particularly for those countries that retained nationalized shipbuilding capacity, such as Spain and Greece. Many analysts are "watching this space" as far as Spain's state-owned Navantia group is concerned, which could be next in line for an EU investigation. As a result, shipyards that regularly undertake both military and merchant shipbuilding within the EU are now more of the exception than the rule and are subject to a high level of scrutiny from the European Commission's authorities and other member states.

Many naval shipbuilders in Europe, therefore, seem to have concentrated on building military vessels for foreign navies, in addition to their own, rather than integrating merchant and military shipbuilding activities. While China may not have such concerns, the operational conflicts between naval and merchant shipbuilders are likely to be detrimental to both activities.

In contrast, however, both in Europe and some other regions of the world, there has been an increase in the use of merchant shipbuilding standards within naval shipbuilding—perhaps the most obvious of which is the use of merchant hulls as the platforms for logistics vessels, and the application of merchant shipbuilding standards to elements of warship construction.

Interaction between Naval and Merchant Shipbuilding in China

Despite the lack of natural synergy between naval and merchant shipbuilding activities, in China there may be an increasing level of integration between the two. Whether this is because of the support that military work can provide to merchant shipbuilding during market hard times remains unclear. What is apparent is that not only is there consolidation happening in the state-owned sector, resulting in the emergence of a group of state-owned megayards, but also that these are in many instances incorporating both merchant and military capabilities.

Dalian Shipyard, traditionally the largest Chinese shipbuilder, has a long-term record of military shipbuilding in a collocated site in downtown Dalian. Following its refit of China's first aircraft carrier (an unfinished hull purchased from Ukraine), it appears to be the shipyard building the first of the Chinese-designed and -constructed aircraft carriers. With further aircraft carriers possibly following, this would afford Dalian a significant military shipbuilding program. Expansion of Dalian's facilities has been a continuous theme since the construction of Dalian New Shipyard, which opened in the early 1990s. Although expansion away from the core site has occurred with the construction of a separate offshore construction facility, there seems to be a desire to move Dalian away from of its current downtown site. Relocation to the company's associated ship repair site on Changxing Island was rumored several years ago, and recently there was speculation that the business might take over the former STX Dalian Shipbuilding site. Much remains unclear.

Jiangnan Shipyard is China's largest joint merchant yard since relocating in 2008 to its new Changxing Island site, greatly increasing capacity. In addition to its merchant shipbuilding production, it appears to be busy constructing several destroyers. It has built a series of six Type 052C destroyers, with the last entering service in 2015. Three Type 052D destroyers entered service by the end of 2015, with a total of ten to twelve anticipated.[8] In addition, Jiangnan has built two twelve-thousand-ton cutters, both in service in the China Coast Guard.

Hudong Zhonghua, although no longer one of China's largest merchant shipbuilders, remains an established player. In addition to its merchant ship-building production, it appears to be busy with frigate production, including three for Algeria's navy.

COMEC, traditionally much more of a merchant shipbuilder than a military one while known as GSI pre-May 2015, recently achieved a "double play." The former GSI's acquisition, as subsidiaries, of the Guangzhou Longxue facility in June 2014 and Wenchong Huangpu in March 2015 expanded its capacity. The latter brought both military shipbuilding expertise and a significant stream of military work through its incorporation of Huangpu Shipyard (one of China's long-established military shipbuilders). Huangpu Shipyard's frigate building experience supplemented the former GSI's more limited military experience, which has been with smaller vessels such as minesweepers and landing craft. Huangpu has built several Type 056 corvettes and Type 054A frigates, and is also heavily involved in the production of cutters for the coast guard and maritime law enforcement agencies. In contrast, shortly before its renaming, GSI had built five supply ships and a fifteen-thousand-ton logistics ship rather than front line warships. On its website, COMEC states, "Our position as the largest manufacturer of . . . military auxiliary ships has been further enhanced."[9] Its 2015 annual report elaborates extensively on the benefits of its successful incorporation of "the core military assets of Huangpu Wenchong": "ability to build military ships . . . has been further improved, achieving overall optimization and comprehensive development in military ships"[10] "as well as the strong growth of its military business."[11]

Conclusion

While the major players in the private sector of Chinese shipbuilding face financial problems and some collapses, consolidation in the state-owned sector seems to be the order of the day, together with an increase and broadening of military shipbuilding activity. Several new megayards are emerging as a result of recent relocations, and these may form a secure core of state-owned shipbuilding capacity. It may well be that this will provide for that most essential but often elusive shipbuilding attribute—survivability. Operationally, however, the intermingling of merchant and naval construction is more likely to be detrimental to both, as a result of the conflicts and complexities it brings to shipyard management.

Notes

1. Compensated gross tons is the preferred measure of work content within merchant shipbuilding, which takes into account the relative complexity of different ship types; it reflects work content more accurately than deadweight or gross tons.

2. SEA Europe Market Monitoring Report no. 38, April 2015.

3. Exhibits are based on the preliminary figures for 2014. Specific entries in the text have been updated for final year figures.

4. The time distribution has a "feathered edge," with the vast majority of vessels currently on order being scheduled for delivery during 2015–18.

5. Drewry Shipping Consultants, *China's Shipyards: Capacity, Competition, and Challenges* (London: Drewry, July 2003).

6. The listing in the 2003 report was based on average output of 1999–2001.

7. "Company Overview of CSSC Guangzhou Longxue Shipbuilding Co., Ltd.," *Bloomberg*, July 26, 2016, http://www.bloomberg.com/research/stocks/private/snap shot.asp?privcapId=38682164.

8. Ronald O'Rourke, *China Naval Modernization: Implications for U.S. Navy Capabilities—Background and Issues for Congress* (Washington, DC: Congressional Research Service, June 17, 2016), RL33153, 30-31, http://www.fas.org/sgp/crs/row/RL33153.pdf.

9. COMEC, "Company Profile," http://comec.cssc.net.cn/en/component_general_situation/.

10. CSSC Offshore and Marine Engineering (Group) Company Limited, *Annual Report 2015*, 9, http://comec.cssc.net.cn/en/upload_img/E0031720160422.pdf.

11. Ibid., 11.

Alex Pape and Tate Nurkin

China's Naval Strength
Current and Future

THE PEOPLE'S LIBERATION ARMY NAVY (PLAN) has undergone a dramatic revitalization that began in the mid-2000s but has accelerated since 2010. IHS *Jane's Defence and Security Forecast* estimates that the PLAN will have committed approximately US$65.7 billion to $84.8 billion on new naval construction projects over the fifteen-year period from 2010 to 2024. Recent spending peaked at around US$5.2 billion in 2012, mainly due to the large number of destroyers, frigates, and corvettes under construction at the time, but is now projected to regularly exceed this level, with annual spending in excess of US$5 billion from 2015 to 2024.

In examining the various fleet segments, the submarine force emerges as a key recipient of funding, with more than US$27 billion projected to be allocated toward nuclear-powered ballistic missile submarine (SSBN), nuclear-powered attack submarine (SSN), and conventionally powered attack submarine (SSK) procurement—the last category including boats with air-independent power (AIP), designated as SSPs. The surface combatant fleet is also receiving substantial investment, with more than US$19.2 billion on the destroyer fleet, US$12.1 billion on frigates, and around US$4 billion on corvettes in this fifteen-year timeframe. By contrast, the level of spending on carriers and amphibious warfare ships appears modest, at around US$5.5 billion and US$4 billion respectively. Exhibit 5-1 summarizes these projections, which are of course subject to change.[1]

Exhibit 5-1. Estimated Chinese Investment in Naval Ship Construction by Type, 2010–24

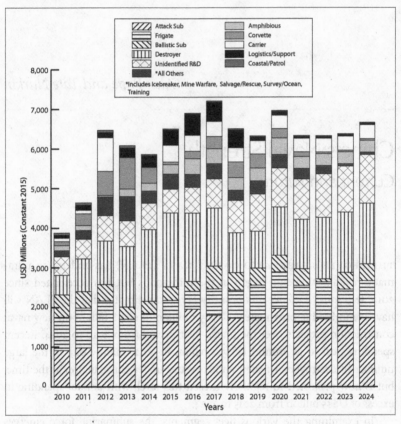

Submarine Programs

Type 094 SSBN (*Jin*)

Four Type 094 SSBNS have been completed at Bohai Shipyard in Huludao and been deployed, with one more expected to enter service in 2017.[2] The Type 094's design heritage is concurrent with the Type 093 SSN. And while the hulls are different, both submarines likely share similar propulsion, auxiliary, and sensor systems. Interestingly, the Type 094 *Jin*-class has what resembles a Russian-designed towed array deployment tube on the upper rudder, suggesting increased interest in the *Jin*'s ability to detect and avoid adversary submarines. The Type 094 carries twelve JL-2 submarine-launched ballistic missiles (SLBMs) with a range of 7,200 kilometers.[3] This would allow it to strike the U.S. mainland from the Yellow Sea and Bohai Sea bastion.

The first-of-class had begun sea trials by early 2006 and was ready for deployment as of early 2007. The boat is based at Yalong Bay with the South Sea Fleet. Full operational capability was probably delayed until the JL-2 missile completed its test firings in 2008–12; however, another test firing was conducted on January 23, 2015.[4] There has been no public evidence to indicate that a Type 094 *Jin*-class submarine has conducted a strategic deterrent patrol; the Pentagon projects this to occur later in 2016.[5]

The second boat was launched around 2006, conducted trials in 2008, and entered service with the North Sea Fleet around 2010. The third boat was launched in late 2009 and entered service around 2012. The fourth was launched around 2011, commenced trials in 2013, and entered service in 2015.

Reports of a pause in construction ensued, with a new Type 093 SSN reported at Huludao in the interim. A fifth and final Type 094 boat is now thought to have been started around 2008. It should be launched in 2016 and enter service in 2017. Construction may then switch to a new SSBN, currently dubbed Type 096.[6]

Type 096 SSBN

This SSBN, of a class yet to be determined, is expected to follow on from the Type 094s, likely using a modified design. Changes are expected to include an increased missile load (potentially sixteen to twenty-four JL-2s). Construction is projected to commence at Huludao Shipyard around 2017–18, with entry into service of the first hull around 2024.

Type 093 SSN (*Shang*)

Two type 093 SSNs were launched from Huludao in 2002 and 2003 and were commissioned in 2006 and 2007 after lengthy trials.[7] Construction of an improved 093A variant with a hydrodynamic rounded sail and a fillet between the sail's base and the hull to reduce drag and wake-related noise sources (particularly at higher speeds) commenced around 2009, with the first boat reportedly launched in 2012 and entering service in 2015.[8] A second was launched in 2013 and entered service in 2016. Initial photographs suggest changes to the sail along with a possible fillet at the sail's base. The boats are rumored to have been fitted with a vertical launching system (VLS),[9] capable of accommodating the YJ-18 antiship cruise missile (ASCM).

Two additional improved Type 093As are estimated by around 2020, for an eventual total of six *Shangs*.[10] By the early 2020s, DoD expects China to produce a substantially new design in the form of a guided-missile attack submarine (SSGN). DoD designates this SSGN the Type 095 (without VLS tubes it would be an SSN) and states that it "not only would improve the PLAN's anti-surface warfare capability but might also provide it with a more clandestine land-attack option."[11] Additionally, the potential exists to increase the SSBN fleet to seven or eight, and SSN fleet to more than ten by 2030, as well as to engage in other nuclear-powered vessel work.

Type 039A/B SSP (*Yuan*)

The launch of a new class of conventional submarine in May 2004 came as a surprise to many. The first boat likely entered service around 2006. The second boat, delayed somewhat, was eventually launched in August 2007. The third is thought to have been launched in November 2007 and the fourth in April 2008. Six additional units were launched at Wuhan between October 2010 and August 2011 and entered service in 2011–12. A second production line at Jiangnan was also noted in 2011, with two boats launched there in 2011 and completed in 2012, for a total of twelve boats by 2013. Two additional boats with a more hydrodynamic sail to reduce drag, incorporating a fillet at the base and a rounded top, were launched in 2014 at Wuhan, and accepted into service in 2015—for a total of fourteen hulls operational by 2015. Six additional boats are expected (for a total of twenty). The Type 039A/B is fitted with a Stirling engine–type AIP system developed by the No. 711 Research Institute.[12]

At an average rate of two boats per year delivered from 2016 to 2030 and the retirement of existing boats, the potential exists to increase the conventional submarine fleet by eight boats to around sixty-one or to maintain the fleet at around fifty boats at a lower production rate or procurement in batches with time allowed for testing, trials, and modifications.

The PLAN conventional submarine force hovers at around fifty-five boats at present, a decline from around 2006 when more than sixty were thought to be in service. However, the obsolete Type 033 *Romeo*-class boats have now been retired and are being followed by the Type 035 *Ming*-class, of which around sixteen remained as of 2015 and are estimated to be retired by 2025 at the latest. The older Project 877/636 *Kilo*-class boats are projected to reach the end of their service lives in the late 2020s, as will the initial Type 039G *Song*-class boats.

Amur 1650 SSK (*Lada* Project 677E)

The Amur 1650, the export variant of the Russian Project 677 *Lada*, has long been rumored as a possible acquisition by China. After problems reported with the AIP performance and other technical challenges on the first-of-class boat, *Sankt Peterburg*, the design has been subject to engineering and design improvements. While Russian construction has resumed on the second and third hulls, it is becoming increasingly unlikely that the submarines will be fitted with an AIP system, and the class is reportedly to be halted after three units.[13] The first boat arrived at the Russian Northern Fleet in October 2013; the second unit, *Kronstadt*, is scheduled for delivery to the Russian fleet in 2019.[14]

Reports in late 2012 suggest two boats may ultimately be built for China in Russia, with transfer of technology for subsequent construction of two additional boats in China. It remains to be seen if Russian fourth-generation submarine technology finds its way into future classes of indigenously designed submarines. "Rosoboronexport signed a framework contract with the Chinese side to jointly design and construction [*sic*] for China's four Project 677E non-nuclear submarines," reported Russia's *Kommersant* in December 2012. "The signing of the firm contract is not expected before 2015."[15] To date, however, no other Russian news media, including TASS and Lenta.ru, have addressed this subject, and there has been no confirmation that a final contract *has* been signed. As this volume went to press, it appeared that China and Russia were still pursuing a deal, with a formal sales agreement not yet signed. But with the cancellation of Russia's Project 677, it is rather unlikely that China would conclude such a purchase.[16]

Type 032 Auxiliary Submarine (*Qing*)

After four Type 039A/B *Yuan*-class submarines were launched at Wuhan, a new submarine of an unknown type was noted to have been launched in September 2010 and commissioned in 2012. Based on imagery to date, the new boat combines features from Russia's *Kilo*-class and Chinese designs.

Length is estimated to be around 92 meters (m), with a beam of around 10m. Dived displacement exceeds 4,000 tons. Images show a large sail (approximately 22m long) with hydrodynamic fairings, new rudder, bow planes rather than sail planes, as well as what may be an intercept array on the bow. It remains uncertain whether AIP is fitted.

A model subsequently displayed indicates the submarine's role as a comprehensive weapons test platform, replacing the aging Type 031 *Golf*-class conventionally powered ballistic missile submarine. This offers a test platform for future SLBM systems, subsurface-launched cruise missiles, and torpedoes, as well as research into other warfare areas. No additional units have been noted.

Aircraft Carriers

China reportedly has investigated the possibility of buying a light aircraft carrier from a European shipbuilder, but it is highly unlikely to be able to secure such a deal. Subsequent reports suggest China has opted to build aircraft carriers indigenously. Reactivation of former Russian Project 1143 (*Kuznetsov*) carrier *Varyag* (which China purchased from the Soviet navy in 1998 and completed as *Liaoning* by 2012) at Dalian Shipyard provides a training platform, enabling the PLAN and its naval aviation wing to gain experience in carrier-borne fixed wing aircraft operations while local design and construction capabilities are refined.

The eventual outcome of a local venture is expected to be based to a certain extent on Russian designs and know-how; however, it may ultimately be replaced by indigenous capabilities or materials acquired from other sources.

Unconfirmed reports suggest existing plans are designated Type 085 and Type 089, with the latter reportedly to be powered by a nuclear propulsion system. It is as yet uncertain whether a new system would be developed for this purpose; or whether existing pressure water reactors as used in the submarine fleet can be adapted for operations on board a surface vessel—a suboptimal approach given the lower power available.

Construction of China's first indigenous aircraft carrier began at the Dalian Shipyard in early 2015. The carrier is being built in the same graving dock that *Liaoning* used. This ship likely will be delivered around 2020–21, with entry into service after extensive trials and work-up. A second indigenous carrier is estimated for around 2030, but it remains unknown whether this carrier would be the same class as the one possibly under construction, or if the PLAN would pursue a larger, nuclear-powered carrier with an electromagnetic launch system.

China will move slowly into the aircraft carrier construction business. Even the conventionally powered variant currently under construction is larger and more complex than anything it has built to date. Proceeding to an even larger, nuclear-powered design could further slow the pace.

Cruisers

Aside from the United States, China is the only country currently building cruiser-sized warships—vessels with great firepower and range. In early 2015, China began construction of a Type 055D multi-role guided-missile cruiser (CG). The 11,000- to 12,000-ton behemoth may have as many as 128 VLS launchers. The Pentagon expects the first hull to be commissioned in 2017–18.[17]

Destroyers

A spate of different classes (six new ones since the early 1990s, including three variants of one class) containing a few hulls each until recently reflected persistent attempts at incremental improvement amid stopgap foreign purchases. Two Type 052A *Luhus* were modernized in 2010–12. Beginning in 2013, a single Type 051B Luhai underwent extensive modernization. Hand-held photos from September 2015 showed that a new main mast structure had been installed. Meanwhile, three of the four Project 956 *Sovremenny* guided-missile destroyers (DDGs) acquired from Russia in the 1990s were noted in refit as of June 2015. This mid-life overhaul appears designed to address normal wear and tear on the chronically problematic steam plants and to upgrade air defense systems and sensors. By this time, however, Jiangnan had given birth to a more advanced DDG worthy of serial production, the Type 052C (*Luyang II*). In 2005 it delivered two ships, then four additional ones in 2012–15.

After introducing four Type 051C and Type 052C anti-air warfare (AAW) DDGs between 2004 and 2007, China had developed a fleet air defense capability; however, it still faced a significant shortfall in the PLAN order of battle, particularly given its plans for aircraft carriers and large-deck amphibious assault ships. After a brief interlude in 2007–8, production resumed and a second batch of four Type 052C destroyers emerged from Jiangnan's new Changxing Island shipyard.

Launched in November 2010, the first vessel (150) completed initial trials in late October 2011 and entered service in January 2013. The second vessel (151), launched in the second half of 2011, was commissioned in December 2013. The third vessel (152), launched in late 2011, was reportedly commissioned in December 2014. The fourth vessel was commissioned in February 2015, completing the class at six ships.

Type 052D DDG (*Luyang III*)

A new Type 052 *Luyang*-class destroyer, considered a modified design, was noted at Changxing by early 2012 and confirmed by the time of launch in August 2012. The first ship, *Kunming* (172), was commissioned in March 2014. The second, *Changsha* (173), followed in July 2015. The third, *Hefei* (174), was commissioned in December 2015; the fourth, *Yinchuan* (175), in July 2016. At least six more are now under construction, including four at Jiangnan and two at Dalian. As this volume went to press, four hulls had been commissioned in total. Eight more are expected, for a projected total of twelve.[18]

Design changes for the modified type include new active phased array radar on the superstructure and changes to the aft superstructure and missile launchers now comprising two thirty-two-cell VLSs (totaling sixty-four cells) of a new design that could support hot- and cold-launched missiles, including the YJ-18 ASCM and possibly a land-attack cruise missile—the latter a first for the PLAN.[19] The ship is also fitted with a twenty-four-cell HHQ-10 surface-to-air missile, an H/PJ-11 close-in weapon system forward, and a new PJ-38 130 millimeter (mm) gun.

Future DDG

To further expand its surface combatant fleet and AAW capabilities, China is expected to build additional batches of destroyers following the six Type 052C and twelve Type 052D anticipated before 2020. The current fleet comprises indigenously built Type 051 and Type 052 variant destroyers as well as four Project 956E/956EM destroyers, which will be approaching the end of their service lives by around 2030.

These new ships would be aimed at developing greater blue-water and escort capabilities rather than replacing aging Type 051 *Luda*-class destroyers. A requirement of around eighteen AAW vessels to support aircraft carrier and amphibious groups is estimated by 2030 as this element of the fleet grows.

The Type 052D evolved design displaces over seven thousand tons. There were reports in October 2009 that a larger design of over ten thousand tons was under consideration. The Type 055D fits this description, but it is unclear whether this should strictly be considered a new larger destroyer or can be considered a cruiser (a full-fledged long-range combatant). The bottom line is that based on current production alone, China will operate around twenty new ships with area air defense by 2020 and possibly around thirty-six by 2030. This will bolster its anti-access/area denial and power projection capabilities significantly.

Frigates

Type 054A FFG (*Jiangkai II*)

Since the early 1990s, China has commissioned four new classes of indigenous frigates. Now, in succession similar to the aforementioned destroyer improvement, *Jiangkai II* guided missile frigates are expected to replace the *Jianghu* class. Two Type 054 vessels, with point-defense AAW capability only, have been in service since September 2005. Construction subsequently switched to a series of modified vessels known as Type 054A at Huangpu and Hudong Shipyards. These versatile workhorses have performed reliably throughout China's eight-plus-year antipiracy operations in the Gulf of Aden.

The first vessel was launched in September 2006 and entered service in January 2008. A total of twenty vessels was completed as of mid-2015. The shipyard allocation for subsequent ships may have been changed following disruption at Hudong involving a 2008 crane collapse.

Huangpu launched its fifth vessel in August 2010. The ship commenced trials by late 2010 and entered service in 2011. Confirmed in late 2010, the sixth vessel under construction at Huangpu was delivered in 2012. Work on the seventh ship was also well advanced as of mid-2011, with commissioning in December 2012. The eighth vessel was launched in May 2012 and delivered in 2013. The ninth was launched in September 2013 and entered service in January 2015. The tenth was launched in July 2014 and was commissioned in July 2015. This tenth ship is noted to feature some modifications, including an active towed array sonar system at the stern that is being retrofitted on other units of the class. An eleventh vessel at Huangpu was delivered in 2016, and a twelfth is expected in 2017.

Launched in 2011, the sixth vessel at Hudong was delivered in late 2012. A seventh vessel, launched at Hudong in July 2012, was delivered in mid-2013. The eighth vessel, launched in November 2012, was commissioned in December 2013. The ninth was launched in September 2013 and commissioned in mid-2015. The tenth was launched in January 2015 and entered service in 2016. The eleventh and twelfth at Hudong have likewise been completed.

All told, as this volume went to press, twenty-five *Jiangkai II*s had been launched—likely the total for the class—with twenty-two already operational.[20]

Possible Future Type 054B (*Jiangkai III*)

Unconfirmed reports and numerous computer graphic images show a new frigate with a new radar and VLS. After an initial pair of Type 054 *Jiangkai I*-class frigates in 2005, a large number of the improved Type 054A *Jiangkai II*-class followed at a rate of up to four vessels per year.

Replacement of the legacy fleet with modern frigates (and corvettes) is likely to continue into the 2020s. Additional 054As may be built, but improvements and design modifications or a more substantially new design are likely. Construction of new vessels is estimated to start around 2016–17, and they should be ready to enter service from approximately 2019, with around two vessels per year through 2029.

Based on replacement of the legacy fleet of *Jianghu I* through *V* and Jiangwei frigates, and assuming not all *Jianghu* are due to be replaced by Type 056 corvettes, some twenty units could be required. This would require the production rate to continue at up to four ships per year, split between Hudong and Huangpu yards, if this is to be achieved by the mid-2020s versus 2030.

Corvettes

Type 056/056A (*Jiangdao*)

The PLA Navy has acquired several dozen corvette-type light surface combatants, in part to begin replacement of its aging large patrol craft and Type 053 *Jianghu*-class light frigates. The resulting fast, highly networked, and lightly armed Type 056 guided missile corvette is fast becoming China's leading patrol vessel and first responder for the near seas.

In late 2010 images surfaced of the Type 056. Estimated to displace around 1,800 tons, it is armed with a PJ-26 76mm gun, four YJ-83 antiship missiles, and the short-range air defense HHQ-10 missile system (eight cells). A flight deck to allow operation of light to medium helicopters such as the Z-9 is featured, although the aircraft cannot be permanently embarked given the lack of a hangar.

In November 2013 a modified variant expected to provide enhanced antisubmarine warfare (ASW) capability was noted. The ASW variant features a hatch at the stern for an active towed array system that uses a separate towed body (transmitter) and a towed array (receiver). Around seven of the ASW variant had been noted as of early 2015.

Fast Attack Craft

Type 022 PTG (*Houbei*)

Construction of these forty-two-meter catamarans, each carrying eight C-802 ASCMs, ended abruptly around 2009. Sixty have been completed at multiple yards and are based at the North, East, and South Sea fleets.

Amphibious Warfare Ships

Type 071 Landing Platform/Dock (*Yuzhao*)

To develop force projection capabilities, China is undertaking multiple amphibious warship programs. In 2005 there were reports that construction of a large unit was under way at Shanghai's Hudong Shipyard. The first 18,500-ton Type 071 landing platform/dock (LPD) was launched on December 21, 2006, and entered service in late 2007 after extensive trials. The Type 071 features a large flight deck aft and hangar space for around four medium helicopters and a well deck for landing craft and air cushion vehicles.

Testing of the first ship is thought to have informed planning for additional units. Launched in November 2010, the second Type 071 entered service in October 2011. The third, launched in September 2011, entered service in September 2012. A fourth unit has been built. Launch occurred in early 2015, trials from September 2015, and commissioning in February 2016. Construction of a fifth ship is reportedly in progress, with delivery estimated for 2017. A sixth is currently forecast to follow in 2018.

Landing Helicopter Dock

Designs have been reported over the years, but no new landing helicopter dock (LHD) has been confirmed, although the Pentagon states that "construction is expected in the near-term" and anticipates "a full flight deck for helicopters."[21] There are reportedly plans to acquire three to six larger amphibious assault ships like an LHD-type vessel with a through-deck flight deck. A new design, dubbed Type 081 and displacing around 22,000 tons, is mooted.

Taiwan's *Defense Technology Monthly* supplied images of the construction model and declared that the proposed LHD should have a length of 211 meters and maximum speed of 23 knots. It may embark eight helicopters, with hangar space for four. Endurance would be twenty-five to thirty days at sea, with accommodation provided for more than one thousand embarked marines. The first vessel is estimated from around 2020, although the lack of firm evidence of construction makes this projection tentative. Additional units could be accepted from around 2025 after operational evaluation of the lead hull.

Project 1232.2 (*Pomornik*-class "Zubr") Landing Craft Air Cushion

These craft have "a range of 300 nautical miles, a maximum speed of 63 knots, and a payload capacity of 150 tons."[22] Two hulls delivered from Ukraine in 2012 and 2014 are in service. In July 2015, the PLAN employed one in a South Sea Fleet amphibious assault drill.[23] China is completing construction of two indigenously produced units.[24]

Mine Countermeasures

Type 081/081A (*Wochi*)

New mine countermeasure vessels (MCMVs) are under construction to replace the aging Type 6610/T43 class units and other aging assets. Four Type 081 *Wochi*-class MCMVs were delivered between 2005–8 from Jiangnan Qiuxin. Additional units had been expected, but construction switched to a modified design.

The first vessel of this version (*Xiaoyi* 841) was launched at Jiangnan in November 2010 and entered service in 2012. Three further vessels were launched in 2011–12. The fourth (*Heshan* 844) entered service in October 2013. The fifth (*Qingzhou* 845) was completed at Wuhan by October 2013 and commissioned in January 2014. The sixth (*Yucheng* 846) was commissioned at Dalian in October 2014. As of February 2015, more than nine hulls were in service.[25]

Type 082B (*Wozang*)

New MCMVs are under construction to replace the aging Type 6610/T43 minesweeping ships. The lead unit (*Houqiu* 804) underwent sea trials in 2005. This class, Type 082B, may be the first fiberglass-reinforced plastic hulled MCMV unit built in China. Subsequently, there was a gap of several years, and construction focused on another new MCMV, the Type 081A *Wochi* class.

In 2011, however, there were indications that construction of the *Wozang* class had resumed at Jiangnan, with a second hull nearing launch in October 2011 and eventually commissioned as *Kunshan* 818. Trials, evaluation, and work to mature the glass-reinforced plastic technology may have been behind the gap in production. Additional units are expected, and unconfirmed reports suggest two may be in production. All units serve as motherships for the six remote-controllable *Wonang*-class inshore minesweepers in the PLAN inventory as of February 2015 that supplement an older fleet of Type 312 *Troika*-type remote sweeps. A requirement to continue replacement of the remaining (fewer than five) T-43/Type 6610 and ten Type 082 (*Wosao*) units is expected.[26]

Auxiliaries

Type 903/903A (*Fuchi*) Auxiliary Oiler and Replenishment

Fuchi-class auxiliary oiler and replenishment (AOR) tankers of over 23,400 tons were built from 2002 at Hudong and Guangzhou, entering service in 2004–5. The type is similar to the Type R22T AOR Similan built in the mid-1990s for Thailand. Additional fleet replenishment ships were projected to be procured to replace aging 1970s-vintage vessels and to enhance the reach of the PLAN on more frequent overseas deployments.

Construction of the Type 903A started around 2011 at both Hudong and Guangzhou, with the first two launched between March and May 2012. In June 2013 *Taihu* (889) became the first new unit commissioned. The second, *Chao Hu* (890), followed in September 2013. A third Type 903A tanker was noted under construction in October 2013 and was commissioned in 2016. A fourth unit, launched in September 2014, appears to feature some design changes. A fifth unit was reported under construction at Guangzhou in November 2014, launched in December 2014, and entered service in 2016.

A total of eight *Fuchi*-class AORs are in service today,[27] with perhaps ten in service by 2020. Moreover, to support its emerging carrier fleet, China is now constructing the Type 901 *Fuyu*-class integrated supply ship, which at 45,000–50,000 tonnes is twice as large as the *Fuchi*-class and similar in all major parameters save munitions transfer rate to the U.S. *Supply*-class. The first hull was launched in December 2015.[28]

Type 904 (*Danyao I/II*) Combat Stores Ship

This comprehensive resupply vessel was built at Guangzhou Shipyard in 2006 and entered service around late 2007. Based in the South Sea Fleet, it carries troops, ammunition, water, fuel, and other supplies to support outposts and basic ship replenishment vis-à-vis the Spratly and Paracel Islands in the South China Sea. Equipped with aviation facilities to operate a helicopter, it is fitted with four davits for small landing craft. An enlarged variant, the *Danyao*-II, can carry additional cargo and troops. The first underwent outfitting at Guangzhou Shipyard International in late 2014 and was commissioned in July 2015. A third was launched in March 2015. Additional ships may follow, with three more anticipated by 2020.

Type 909 (*Dahua*) Auxiliary General Experimental

At least two hulls of this experimental trials support vessel have been constructed at Hudong, and are currently in service.

Type 815/815A (*Dongdiao*) Auxiliary General Intelligence

These space event/intelligence collecting ships are built by Hudong Zhonghua. The first unit entered service in 2000. In 2010, the second unit—the first in the enhanced 815A series—was commissioned. Three more followed in 2015, for a total of five in service at present.[29] Internet photos show a sixth hull being launched at Hudong Zhonghua in early 2016.

Kanhai Auxiliary General

China's new catamaran survey vessel has a swath hull but otherwise differs significantly from the U.S. Navy's much larger towed array sensor system ocean surveillance (T-AGOS) vessels. The first was launched in 2011, followed by two more in 2012 and 2013. A total of five are now in service, with one more likely to join them soon.[30]

Type 926 (*Dalao*) Submarine Rescue

Three hulls employing the LR-7 submersible, launched in 2008–12, are currently in service. It is unknown whether more submarine rescue capability is required.

Type 272 (*Yanrao*) Icebreaker

The icebreaker *Haibing* 722 was commissioned in 2015. It replaces its eponymous predecessor *Haibing* 722, as well as two decommissioned Type 071 *Yanha*-class light icebreakers.[31]

China's Current and Future Naval Vessel Requirements

In its latest unclassified report, the U.S. Office of Naval Intelligence offered the following summation:

> In contrast to its narrow focus just a decade ago, the PLA(N) is evolving to meet a wide range of missions including conflict with Taiwan, enforcement of maritime claims, protection of economic interests, as well as counterpiracy and humanitarian missions. The PLA(N) will also soon assume a central role in China's nuclear deterrent with the first ballistic missile submarine patrols with an intercontinental-range missile. In the next decade, China will complete its transition from a coastal navy to a navy capable of multiple missions around the world. China's leaders see the evolution of naval strategy as necessary to preserve China's interests and commensurate with its role as an emerging major power.[32]

There are signs that all elements outlined by the assessment are being addressed. For instance, the sea-based strategic deterrent now has four SSBNs at its disposal and is expected to grow further. The SSN fleet has to date not grown substantially and is likely to enjoy prioritization in the next decade to provide a capability to disrupt potential opponent's sea lanes. The conventional submarine force has seen rapid modernization, and replacement of the remaining twenty-five to thirty older boats (still comprising 50 percent of the fleet) in the next fifteen years will further enhance its capability to deny near seas waters (including those around Taiwan) to opponents.

Meanwhile, the large fleet of legacy frigates and destroyers with limited utility beyond coastal waters and based on obsolete Soviet designs or concepts is well on its way to being replaced with a new fleet of larger ships with better endurance, sensors, and armaments. The new fleet is capable of deploying farther afield, both in region and on extended international missions, including a sustained engagement off the Horn of Africa to deter piracy, and several humanitarian missions and civilian evacuations.

With the surface combatant force thus engaged, a new fleet of corvettes and support assets has been commissioned to provide enhanced presence in the near seas. Since 2014 a number of surface ships have been noted to be equipped with advanced active towed array sonar systems, thereby starting to address a shortfall in capability in antisubmarine warfare. If the new Chinese system performs as well as its European cousins, the PLAN will have an improved submarine detection capability in both deep and shallow water. As noted, Chinese capabilities on a regional level are being enhanced with the introduction of the corvettes, new submarines, and support assets. This also includes the large-scale construction of coast guard–type ships.

Requirement for support capability grows with the PLAN's increasing long-distance operations. Construction of Type 903/903A AORs provides at-sea replenishment capability, but the current total of eight ships may prove insufficient as additional carriers and amphibious units are added to the fleet in coming years. Meanwhile, the far larger and more specialized Type 901 is emerging to provide the required levels of support for a carrier group.

There are multiple areas where replacements had been estimated; however, they have not yet happened, or are not direct replacements. The question is whether any capability gaps emerge as a result. For example, the PLAN currently has roughly one hundred older coastal patrol and fast missile vessels, comprising fewer than thirty Type 037 (*Hainan*) patrol craft (PC), six 037-I (*Haiqing*) PC, roughly twenty Type 037-1G (*Houxin*) patrol/missile craft (PGG), six Type 037-II (*Houjian*) PGG, and approximately forty Type 062-I (*Shanghai II/III*) PC.[33] All Type 021 (*Huangfeng/Osa*) missile craft have been decommissioned. Replacement is understood to have commenced with the introduction of around sixty Type 022 missile boats and perhaps soon a similar contingent of Type 056 corvettes, which provide a high-endurance, better-armed near seas platform. But will this be enough to cover all aspects of the coastal patrol mission? Is there overlap with China's huge coast guard construction program and a shift in responsibilities, or can we expect a new program for fast missile boats and coastal patrol boats in due course?

In the amphibious arena, similarly, numerous older landing ships built in the 1980s and 1990s may soon be due for replacement. This includes seven Type 072/-IIG (*Yukan*) landing ship/tank (LST) and ten Type 072 II (*Yuting*) LST. Already, all Type 079 (*Yuliang*) LSM vessels have been decommissioned. Beginning in 2002–2005, a program rapidly began to acquire thirty new landing ships in three classes—including ten of the Type 073A (*Yunshu*) LSM, three of the Type 074A (*Yubei*) landing craft utility, and eleven of the Type 072A (*Yuting II*) LST. We do not expect any significant construction programs for new LSM or LST. Perhaps a few classes will be built in small numbers. LPD/Landing Helicopter Assault (LHA) acquisition appears to be the wave of the future.

Evolution of the PLAN over Time

Over the last decade, a number of centers of excellence have emerged for various sectors, some solidifying their position as key suppliers, and some also adding capabilities.

For the submarine fleet, nuclear-powered boats continue to be built at Huludao (see exhibit 5-2). During 2010–20, the yard is projected to deliver about four SSBNs and up to four SSNs. While this means the strategic deterrent has been developed to a meaningful capability potentially providing continuous at-sea deterrence, the SSN fleet is projected to remain static until then and will only grow in the 2020–30 timeframe, with a doubling in size from five to around ten boats estimated (unless there are competing requirements like the need to establish a production line for a nuclear-powered aircraft carrier).

Based on existing production rates, it may still be possible to expand both SSN and SSBN fleets and build a first nuclear-powered aircraft carrier by 2030. The shipyard would likely require modifications to accommodate a carrier-sized vessel for extended construction and outfitting without disrupting submarine work. Inter-yard collaboration—not yet observed in Chinese shipbuilding—would alleviate this pressure, with, for instance, the hull and nuclear machinery built at Huludao and completed at Dalian (although a return to Huludao for setting-to work may be required). This option could be less costly than establishing a second nuclear-capable shipyard, but unless a long-term planning approach is taken for the nuclear fleet, it would offer less redundancy and risk occasional bottlenecks.

Exhibit 5-2. Bohai (Huludao) Shipyard Military Output, 2006–30

Year	Number Delivered	Vessel Class	Vessel Type	Class Inventory
2006	1	Type 093	Nuclear-powered attack submarine (SSN)	4
2007	1	Type 093	SSN	4
	1	Type 094	Nuclear-powered ballistic missile submarine (SSBN)	2
2008				
2009				
2010	1	Type 094	SSBN	3
2011				
2012	1	Type 094	SSBN	4
2013				
2014				
2015	1	Type 094	SSBN	4
2016	1	Type 093A	SSN	4
2017	1	Type 093A	SSN	5
2018	1	Type 094	SSBN	5
2019	1	Type 093A	SSN	6
2020				
2021	1	Type 095?	SSN	7
2022	1	Type 095?	SSN	8
2023				
2024	1	Type 096	SSBN	6
2025	1	Type 095?	SSN	9
2026				
2027	1	Type 096	SSBN	7
2028				
2029	1	Type 095?	SSN	10
2030	1	Type 095?	SSN	11

Exhibit 5-3. Wuchang (Wuhan) Shipyard Military Output, 2006–30

Year	Number Delivered	Vessel Class	Vessel Type	Class Inventory
2006	1	Type 039A/B	Conventionally powered attack submarine (SSK)	1
	1	Type 039	Cruise missile submarine (SSG)	13
2007				
2008				
2009	2	Type 039A/B	SSK	3
2010	1	Type 039A/B	SSK	4
2011	3	Type 039A/B	SSK	7
2012	3	Type 039A/B	SSK	12
	1	Type 032	Cargo submarine (SSA)	1
2013	1	Type 056	Guided missile corvette (FSG)	8
	1	Type 081A	Mine countermeasure vessel (MCMV)	5
2014	2	Type 056	FSG	18
	1	Type 081A	MCMV	6
2015	2	Type 039A/B	SSK	14
	2	Type 056	FSG	28
	1	Type 07 III	Landing ship/tank (LST)	1
	1		MCMV	?
2016	2		SSK	16
	1	Type 056	FSG	32
2017	2		SSK	18
	1	Type 056	FSG	36
2018	2		SSK	20
	1	Type 056	FSG	40
2019	2		SSK	2
2020	2		SSK	4
2021	2		SSK	6
2022	2		SSK	8
2023	2		SSK	10
2024	2		SSK	12

Exhibit 5-3. Wuchang (Wuhan) Shipyard Military Output, 2006–30 *cont.*

Year	Number Delivered	Vessel Class	Vessel Type	Class Inventory
2025	2		SSK	14
2026	2		SSK	16
2027	2		SSK	18
2028	2		SSK	20
2029	2		SSK	22
2030	2		SSK	24+

Surface combatant construction is split between destroyers at Jiangnan (see exhibit 5-4) and Dalian and frigates and corvettes primarily at Hudong and Huangpu, with some assistance by Wuhan (see exhibit 5-3) and Liaonan. Particularly since the move to a new facility at Shanghai's Changxing Island, no bottlenecks have been evident for Jiangnan, which has surprised observers with the rate at which major Type 052C/D destroyers have been launched, all while other naval and paramilitary projects progress without apparent delays.

No frigates or corvettes have been noted at Jiangnan; their production continues to be firmly centered at Hudong (see exhibit 5-5) and Huangpu (see exhibit 5-6). Simultaneous construction of corvettes in large numbers at these two yards and at Wuhan and Liaonan came as a surprise, seeming to go against the previously observed model of building a few ships, testing, modifying the design if required, and building more. This suggests a high degree of confidence in the maturity and suitability of the design (adapted from ships exported to Thailand previously but also perhaps subject to extensive simulation). In parallel, Huangpu is building multiple classes of less complex paramilitary ships, with Wuhan in turn finishing up export orders for offshore patrol vessels (OPVs) and corvettes. Hudong, meanwhile, is building the Type 071 LPDs, auxiliaries, and corvettes for export to Algeria (prepared for a Western combat system). The yard may become the primary supplier of modern amphibious warfare ships with floodable well decks if it is selected to build the LHDs as well. It remains to be seen if the new model of building larger batches of a design (like Type 056 and 052D) model will be sustained, or whether the more cautious approach may again be adopted for future projects, such as the projected LHDs. Last but not least, having refitted *Liaoning*, Dalian has commenced work on a batch of Type 052D destroyers, as well as China's first indigenous carrier.

Exhibit 5-4. Jiangnan (Shanghai) Shipyard Military Output, 2006–30

Year	Number Delivered	Vessel Class	Vessel Type	Class Inventory
2006	1	Type 039	Cruise missile submarine (SSG)	13
	1	Type 081	Mine countermeasure vessel (MCMV)	2
2007	1	Type 081	MCMV	3
2008	1	Type 081	MCMV	4
2009				
2010				
2011	1	Type 081A	MCMV	1
2012	2	Type 039A/B	Conventionally powered attack submarine (SSK)	12
	1	Type 081A	MCMV	2
	1	Type 082B	MCMV	2
2013	2	Type 052C	Guided missile destroyer (DDG)	4
	2	Type 081A	MCMV	4
2014	1	Type 052C	DDG	5
	1	Type 052D	DDG	1
	1	Type 081A	MCMV	6
2015	1	Type 052C	DDG	6
	2	Type 052D	DDG	3
	1		MCMV	?
2016	2	Type 052D	DDG	5
2017	3	Type 052D	DDG	10
2018	2	Type 052D	DDG	12
2019	2		DDG	2
2020	2		DDG	4
2021	2		DDG	6
2022	2		DDG	8
2023	2		DDG	10
2024	2		DDG	12
2025	2		DDG	14
2026	2		DDG	16

Exhibit 5-4. Jiangnan (Shanghai) Shipyard Military Output, 2006–30 *cont.*

Year	Number Delivered	Vessel Class	Vessel Type	Class Inventory
2027	2		DDG	18
2028	2		DDG	20
2029	2		DDG	22
2030	2		DDG	24+

Most projections in the preceding sections estimate future production capacity conservatively, below the peak rates seen only a few years ago, but rather with a steady average that appears well within capability. The resulting production estimate suggests China's navy will be able to complete a whole-sale renewal and modernization, replacing obsolete designs with more modern submarines, surface combatants, and other warships on a near one-to-one basis. Changes are noticeable for the patrol and light surface combatant fleet, where fewer, larger units are being procured, although a direct replacement with vast numbers of simple patrol boats are certainly within the shipyards' capability. The existing landing ships may be retained, although the fleet somewhat shrunk, but are supplemented by an entirely new force of LPDs and LHDs, primarily built at Hudong. To date, this appears to have had little to no impact on the production rates of other ships out of this yard. With Huangpu, Wuhan, and now Liaonan also engaged in the light surface combatant sector, there appears to be flexibility in the system should a future LHD program entail construction of several units in parallel.

In terms of quality of contemporary naval ship construction, we see no reliable reports. Anecdotal reports from previous export ships to Thailand noted problems that had to be corrected post-delivery, and exports remained few and far between. Over the last five years, this has seen a major change with exports of both simple ships such as patrol boats (to Nigeria, Ghana, Bangladesh, and Pakistan) and more complex units such as OPVs, corvettes, and frigates (to Nigeria, Bangladesh, Pakistan, and Algeria) now nearing completion and with further orders rumored, not least of which are submarines for Pakistan. While pricing is reported to be a key differentiator, likely facilitated by financing on favorable terms, other yards (South Korean or Dutch, for instance) can offer affordable ships due to economies of scale. Political factors, helped by Chinese engagement in local economies in areas such as resource extraction and building of infrastructure, may have a role to play as well. While the new export

Exhibit 5-5. Hudong (Shanghai) Shipyard Military Output, 2006–30

Year	Number Delivered	Vessel Class	Vessel Type	Class Inventory
2006	1	Type 909	Auxiliary general (AG)	2
2007	1	Type 071	Landing platform dock (LPD)	1
2008	2	Type 054A	Guided missile frigate (FFG)	4
2009				
2010	1	Type 054A	FFG	7
2011	1	Type 054A	FFG	9
	1	Type 071	LPD	2
2012	2	Type 054A	FFG	13
	1	Type 071	LPD	3
	1	Type 909	AG	3
2013	2	Type 054A	FFG	16
	2	Type 056	Guided missile corvette (FSG)	8
	1	Type 903A	Auxiliary Oiler and Replenishment (AOR)	4
2014	3	Type 056	FSG	18
	1	Type 909	AG	4
2015	2	Type 054A	FFG	20
	2	Type 056	FSG	28
	1	Type 071	LPD	4
	1	Type 903A	AOR	6
2016	1	Type 054A	FFG	22
	1	Type 056	FSG	32
	1	Type 903A	AOR	8
2017	1	Type 054A	FFG	24
	1	Type 056	FSG	36
	1	Type 071	LPD	5
2018	1	Type 056	FSG	40
	1	Type 071	LPD	6
2019	2		FFG/FSG	4

Exhibit 5-5. Hudong (Shanghai) Shipyard Military Output, 2006–30 *cont.*

Year	Number Delivered	Vessel Class	Vessel Type	Class Inventory
2020	2		FFG/FSG	8
	1		Landing helicopter dock (LHD)	1
2021	2		FFG/FSG	12
2022	2		FFG/FSG	16
2023	2		FFG/FSG	20
2024	2		FFG/FSG	24
	1		LHD	2
2025	2		FFG/FSG	28
	1		LHD	3
2026	2		FFG/FSG	32
2027	2		FFG/FSG	36
2028	2		FFG/FSG	40
2029	2		FFG/FSG	44
2030	2		FFG/FSG	48

orders hint at improved quality, repeat orders are a better indicator, as seen in Thailand and Pakistan.

China's shipbuilding industry, low prices or not, lacks immunity to the trend of countries requesting transfer of technology and local construction. The most complex program to date is the Pakistani F-22P frigate program, followed by fast attack craft, and possibly submarines soon. Another change that has been noted is the transfer of PLAN ships that are being decommissioned. This has seen Type 053H1/2 (*Jianghu II/III*) frigates going to Myanmar and Bangladesh over the last few years, with the temporary increase in fleet numbers possibly offsetting any quality issues that linger on these older ships. Nevertheless, China is unlikely to export its best naval ships in any form.

Even a snapshot of technical publications from the last three years indicates research in multiple areas. For example, *Ship Research Journal* has covered themes on aircraft carrier operations such as sortie generation models, launch and recovery workflows, principles, technologies, and analysis of U.S. carrier operations. Work on combat systems included cloud-based computing combat system architecture and combat system mission profile optimization.

Technical studies also cover assorted materials (composites, steel sandwich), damage (analysis of impact, material and structural strength, and damage control technology and methods), platform systems, computational fluid dynamics, shock effects and mitigation, and stealth (water mist, acoustic).

Unmanned systems technology has also made inroads in Chinese publications, covering similar topics as in Western conferences, such as unmanned underwater vehicle launch/recovery challenges, control systems, and ocean gliders. On the sensor side, performance modeling of existing and new sensors is being examined further, as are countermeasures, and guided or smart munitions where targeting and fusing challenges appear to remain. We noted propulsion-related studies, the subject of the chapter by Erickson, Ray, and Forte in this volume. Looking forward, it will be interesting to see if electric propulsion and topics such as directed energy weapons feature prominently.

Key Knowledge Gaps

Much of our research and analysis is reactive in nature, based on new imagery and reports emerging from China when a new ship has already been launched, for instance, and then deducing the role in the fleet, trends, and projections.

Accordingly, perhaps the biggest question is: What is the underlying plan? Is there a long-term fleet development plan that balances capabilities and investment in the sea-based deterrent, carriers and amphibious groups, escorts, conventional submarines, patrol assets?

Many related questions remain. Does this plan account for production capacities at the various government-owned yards and adjust accordingly, or do the yards respond to the plan and try to meet volume and time targets? How responsive are the yards expected to be to accommodate alternating production of various types of updated designs? And where does planning for the paramilitary patrol fleet come in? Is this coordinated at all with the PLAN's plan in general or based on capacity at the individual yards over a limited timeframe?

How far from capacity are the yards operating and what limits are there to further expansion or increases in efficiency? Have any bottlenecks that we wonder about already been addressed by internal planning and resolved? How much resilience and redundancy is there in the system in case of problems (e.g., damage from natural disasters, major industrial accidents, or labor disputes)?

There are some uncertainties regarding the planning stage. For instance, what are lead times from requirement to design to build? Has this increased to incorporate more studies and modeling and simulation before the decision to

Exhibit 5-6. Huangpu (Guangzhou) Shipyard Military Output, 2006–30

Year	Number Delivered	Vessel Class	Vessel Type	Class Inventory
2006				
2007				
2008	2	Type 054A	Guided missile frigate (FFG)	4
2009				
2010	2	Type 054A	FFG	7
2011	1	Type 054A	FFG	9
2012	2	Type 054A	FFG	13
2013	2	Type 054A	FFG	16
2013	2	Type 056	Guided missile corvette (FSG)	8
2014	3	Type 056	FSG	10
2015	2	Type 054A	FFG	20
2015	2	Type 056	FSG	28
2016	1	Type 054A	FFG	22
2016	1	Type 056	FSG	32
2017	1	Type 054A	FFG	24
2017	1	Type 056	FSG	36
2018	1	Type 056	FSG	40
2019	2		FFG/FSG	4
2020	2		FFG/FSG	8
2021	2		FFG/FSG	12
2022	2		FFG/FSG	16
2023	2		FFG/FSG	20
2024	2		FFG/FSG	24
2025	2		FFG/FSG	28
2026	2		FFG/FSG	32
2027	2		FFG/FSG	36
2028	2		FFG/FSG	40
2029	2		FFG/FSG	44
2030	2		FFG/FSG	48

build is taken? Does the production model of "build a few, test, improve, and build more" still exist? If so, where would it be applied in the future?

Notes

Unless otherwise specified, all data are derived from IHS Jane's Defence Procurement, IHS Jane's DS Forecast databases, *IHS Jane's Fighting Ships 2016–17*, and Commodore Stephen Saunders, *IHS Jane's 2017*.

1. This is particularly true for the *extremely tentative* projections for 2025–30 supplied in exhibits 5-2 through 5-6 at the end of the chapter.
2. Ronald O'Rourke, *China Naval Modernization: Implications for U.S. Navy Capabilities—Background and Issues for Congress* (Washington, DC: Congressional Research Service, June 17, 2016), RL33153, 17, http://www.fas.org/sgp/crs/row/RL33153.pdf.
3. Department of Defense, *Annual Report to Congress: Military and Security Developments Involving the People's Republic of China, 2016* (Washington, DC: Department of Defense, 2016), 26 (hereafter, DoD [2016]).
4. Bill Gertz, "China Conducts JL-2 Sub Missile Test," *Washington Times*, February 18, 2015, http://www.washingtontimes.com/news/2015/feb/18/inside-the-ring-china-tests-nuclear-missile-for-su/?page=all.
5. DoD (2016), 26.
6. O'Rourke, *China Naval Modernization*, 17.
7. Ibid., 17.
8. Initial reports anticipated a new batch stretched by less than 10m, but Google Earth measurements of the three Type 093 mod submarines at Huludao shows they are the same length as the initial two.
9. Andrew Tate, "PLAN Launches New Type 052D, Multirole Destroyer Numbers Grow," Jane's Navy International, December 17, 2015.
10. DoD (2016), 26.
11. Ibid.
12. Office of Naval Intelligence (ONI), *The PLA Navy: New Capabilities and Missions for the 21st Century* (Suitland, MD: ONI, April 9, 2015), 16, http://www.oni.navy.mil/Intelligence_Community/china_media/2015_PLA_NAVY_PUB_Interactive.pdf.
13. Nikolai Novichkov, "Russia's Lada-class Submarine Project Suffers Further Delays," *Jane's Defence Weekly*, January 20, 2016.
14. "Diesel Submarine *Saint Petersburg* Has Arrived in the Northern Fleet," *Ria Novostoi*, October 17, 2013; "Russia's Newest Diesel Sub to Continue Barents Sea Trials," *Sputnik News*, October 17, 2013, http://sputniknews.com/military/20131017/184203871/Russias-Newest-Diesel-Sub-to-Continue-Barents-Sea-Trials-.html.
15. "На китайских берегах 'Амуры': Россия прорвалась на рынок крупнейшего импортера вооружений из-под воды" ["On the Chinese Banks of the 'Amur':

Russia Breaks into a Large Import Market for Undersea Weapons"], Коммерсантъ [*Kommersant*], December 20, 2012, http://www.kommersant.ru/doc/2094362.

16. "Russia Scraps Plans of Additional Project 677 Submarines Construction," *Sputnik International*, January 19, 2016, http://sputniknews.com/russia/20160119/1033354924/russia-plans-additional-submarines-construction.html.

17. DoD (2016), 69.

18. O'Rourke, *China Naval Modernization*, 30.

19. DoD (2016), 27.

20. Ibid., 26; O'Rourke, *China Naval Modernization*, 31.

21. DoD (2016), 27.

22. O'Rourke, *China Naval Modernization*, 41.

23. DoD (2016), 92.

24. Ibid.

25. ONI, "China People's Liberation Army Navy (PLA[N]) and Maritime Law Enforcement (MLE) 2015 Recognition and Identification Guide," April 2015, http://www.oni.navy.mil/Portals/12/Intel%20agencies/China_Media/PLA_Navy_Identification_Guide.pdf?ver=2015-12-10-103823-167.

26. Ibid.

27. "China's 7th and 8th Type 903A Fleet Replenishment Oilers Commissioned into PLAN South Sea Fleet," *Navy Recognition*, July 16, 2016, http://www.navyrecognition.com/index.php?option=com_content&task=view&id=4206.

28. Andrew S. Erickson and Capt. Christopher P. Carlson, USNR (Ret.), "Sustained Support: the PLAN Evolves Its Expeditionary Logistics Strategy," *Jane's Navy International*, March 9, 2016.

29. ONI, "PLAN Recognition Guide."

30. Ibid.; ONI, *The PLA Navy*, 15.

31. "New Icebreaker Joins PLA Navy in Liaoning," *China Military Online*, January 5, 2016, http://english.chinamil.com.cn/news-channels/2016-01/05/content_6844781.htm.

32. ONI, *The PLA Navy*, 9.

33. ONI, "PLAN Recognition Guide."

Sean O'Connor and Jordan Wilson

Monitoring Chinese Shipbuilding Facilities with Satellite Imagery

AS FEATURE AND MARITIME claims disputes in the East and South China seas make China's navy an increasingly important geopolitical force, thorough analysis of China's ability to produce modern warships is critical to understanding its future. Given Beijing's opacity, commercially available satellite imagery represents a useful component of any analysis of China's naval power.

Open Source Imagery Intelligence Procedures and Issues

Commercial satellite imagery is a revealing analytical tool, especially when monitoring fixed-site locations such as shipyards or military installations. Particularly useful for gaining insight into the use, layout, and occupants of closed or secure facilities, imagery offers the ability to accurately gauge facility makeup, type, and the presence and categorization of military components.

Proper imagery exploitation, however, results in the image itself representing a secondary facet of the overall analysis, akin to any other reference source consulted in making an assessment. Imagery does not provide a completely accurate indicator of intent, capability, or activity level. Additional information is typically required to assess these areas effectively. Often, spatial or contextual analysis is combined with imagery data to present a more complete assessment, demonstrating that a competent interpreter must also be a credible researcher.

Imagery analysis has certain inherent limitations. The most obvious relate to the general characteristics of satellite imagery. Commercial imaging satellites are largely bound to predetermined orbits, which can result in a lack of imagery availability due to a satellite's ground track not bringing it within range of a target of interest within a given period. With an increasing number of satellites and their associated imagery providers for the analyst to consider, however, this concern relates mostly to acquiring archived imagery from previous passes; the wealth of current options results in far fewer cases where a satellite is unavailable for tasking over a particular location at a given point in time.

Analyzing and processing acquired imagery is another limitation, only mitigated by procurement and interpreters' skills. Some orbital sensors such as near-band infrared or synthetic aperture radar require additional techniques and systems to accurately interpret due to their unique features. Access to the data contained within some imagery types can depend on the amount of money an analyst is willing to spend on processing or interpretation software.

Chinese Shipbuilding in Imagery

In analyzing Chinese military shipbuilding, satellite imagery has numerous uses. Most significant is a method of verifying the number and frequency of hulls being produced. Infrastructure upgrades, potential indicators of future activity, may be tracked and studied.

China's shipbuilding industry as a whole is constrained by a series of bottlenecks restricting its ability to rapidly produce modern systems. Various bottlenecks common to civilian shipbuilding affect China's ability to produce modern warships as well. A major bottleneck with commercial shipbuilding involves overcapacity coupled with declining demand. The reduced demand stems from a high percentage of lower-tech products; demand for high-tech products is present but is unmet due to other production bottlenecks.[1] One solution is moving commercial shipbuilding to an external location such as Indonesia.[2]

A production bottleneck directly impacting warship production could stem from the lack of sufficient equipment and expertise dealing with modern high-tech manufacturing techniques. For example, China previously had difficulty manufacturing large marine crankshafts.[3] Dalian Huarui Heavy Industry Group Co., Ltd., now produces 150 crankshafts per year, demonstrating that China does have the ability to recognize and address such issues.[4]

Since late 2013/early 2014, at least one Type 052D destroyer hull has remained within Jiangnan's interior harbor. Continued residence at a berth associated with fitting out post-launch suggests the possibility of an additional bottleneck concerning production and availability of critical components, such as weapons system elements, electrical fittings, or other items. This could indicate a general shortage of such components within China's manufacturing establishment as a whole, or it could be due to the diversion of certain materials or components to higher-priority programs. For example, the Type 052D employs the HHQ-9 surface-to-air missile (SAM) system, a naval variant of the land-based HQ-9 mobile strategic SAM system. Similar components or systems found in both versions may be directed to land-based missile production should it be perceived as a higher priority. Alternatively, China's naval shipbuilding programs may simply be a victim of a bottleneck found within many other modern navies, including the U.S. Navy, where fitting out is typically an involved and time-consuming process due to the large quantity of systems, components, electrical fittings, and the like necessary in modern warships.

Analysis of satellite imagery, combined with study of the technical characteristics of Chinese shipyards, reveals an absence of bottlenecks in the areas of raw material availability, equipment, and production capacity. Shipyards employed in the production of Chinese naval vessels enjoy a surplus of gantry cranes, drydock space, workshops, workforce numbers, and overall space to meet production requirements, in part due to the overcapacity issues addressed previously.[5] Further research on industry bottlenecks should thus focus on previously articulated bottlenecks rather than on whether shipyards possess the space or equipment required to produce modern warships.

Modular Shipbuilding

Within Chinese shipbuilding as a whole and naval shipbuilding in particular, modular construction is being increasingly exploited as the technology matures.[6] Modular construction provides numerous advantages, including ease of modification and an ability to stockpile assembled sections while awaiting room in an assembly hall or drydock.

Modular warship construction is a multistage process. Construction of individual modules begins with cutting metal to create the module's materials. Depending on the shipyard, individual modules may be assembled inside a covered assembly hall or externally at pierside. Assembled modules are then transported to a drydock or other suitable berth where they are arranged and attached to form a warship's hull.

Observing modular warship construction in imagery is easiest during the external module construction or drydock assembly stages. At Jiangnan, assembly of individual warship modules was observed as early as August 2010. Completed modules are then transported into an assembly hall for joining. In contrast, modules are joined in a drydock at Liaoning Shipyard.

Jiangnan

Jiangnan Shipyard (Jiangnan Changxing) is one of China's newest modern shipyards. Jiangnan produces both civilian and military vessels, the latter primarily surface combatants. Current warships recently produced at Jiangnan are the Type 052D destroyer, the Type 726 air-cushioned landing craft (LCAC), and the Haijing 2901 and Haijing 3901 offshore patrol vessels.[7] Jiangnan also performs refit and repair of previously produced surface combatants such as the Type 052C destroyer.

In April 2015, satellite imagery of Jiangnan showed three 052D destroyers, two Type 726 LCACs, and the two large offshore patrol vessels within the interior harbor. At a pier outside the shipyard's perimeter, two additional Type 052D guided-missile destroyers were berthed, along with a Type 052C destroyer. The former, in differing stages of completion, represented new or recently produced hulls undergoing sea trials, while the latter was likely present for post-refit trials.

Also present in April 2015 was a *Yuan*-class Type 039B conventionally powered submarine. Yuans have been produced intermittently at Jiangnan, ostensibly to alleviate the workload at Wuhan. That particular Yuan may therefore have represented a new Jiangnan-built hull, or it may have been present for refit and repair there. To date, available imagery does not reveal which was the case.

Dalian

Dalian Shipyard is perhaps most famous for its association with China's deck aviation program, having performed refit, repair, and outfitting work on the ex-Soviet *Varyag* aircraft carrier *Liaoning*, and now building an indigenous carrier. However, Dalian also produces additional surface combatants, albeit much less frequently than Jiangnan.

Previous surface combatants produced at Dalian include the Type 051B and Type 051C destroyers. Currently, Dalian produces a small number of Type 052D destroyer hulls. The second and third Dalian-produced hulls are currently undergoing construction, while the first hull is pierside for final fitting-out and initial sea trials. Interestingly, comparison of imagery captured in March and June 2015 suggests that the Type 052D hull is not being assembled modularly. The incomplete hull visible in March 2015 was composed of segments collectively less complete than hull modules seen stored pierside at Jiangnan in previous years. Dalian's limited production of People's Liberation Army Navy (PLAN) surface combatants may alleviate the requirement for modular assembly. Also, a lack of modular assembly may suggest that Dalian's workshops are not yet outfitted to assemble individual hull modules of the type seen at Jiangnan.

Construction of China's first domestically produced aircraft carrier began in February 2015 with the arrangement of necessary support structures within the drydock previously associated with repair and refit of *Liaoning*. Throughout 2015, initial construction work resulted in the creation of a hull section similar to that seen during the construction of *Admiral Kuznetsov* at Nikolayev shipyard in Ukraine. Estimates based on construction progress as of September 2015 revealed a hull with a length of 240 meters and beam of 35 meters, matching the waterline measurements for *Liaoning* save for the incomplete bow section.

Characteristics of the hull under construction in 2015 indicated a military vessel if not an aircraft carrier. The hull featured interior compartmentalization and was constructed at a rate significantly slower than commercial hulls previously built within the drydock. In May 2016, satellite imagery revealed the installation of an angled stern section and flight deck overhangs, allowing the hull to be conclusively identified as an aircraft carrier under construction. By July 2016, the bulk of the new hull's flight deck was installed, notable absences being the ski-jump bow section and the superstructure.

While the new aircraft carrier did not initially exploit modular assembly, later hull sections and flight deck overhangs were built pierside underneath moveable assembly halls before installation within the drydock. The experience gained with modular design and assembly will permit Dalian or Jiangnan to pre-build components for follow-on aircraft carrier hulls.

Huludao

Huludao holds special significance for Chinese shipbuilding. To date, it is the only facility outfitted to produce nuclear-powered vessels. While China currently only uses nuclear power for nuclear-powered submarines (SSNs) and ballistic missile submarines (SSBNs), current expansion at Huludao may suggest an expansion of its use. Exhibit 6-1 details Huludao's configuration and recent growth.

Exhibit 6-1. Configuration and Growth of China's Huludao Shipyard

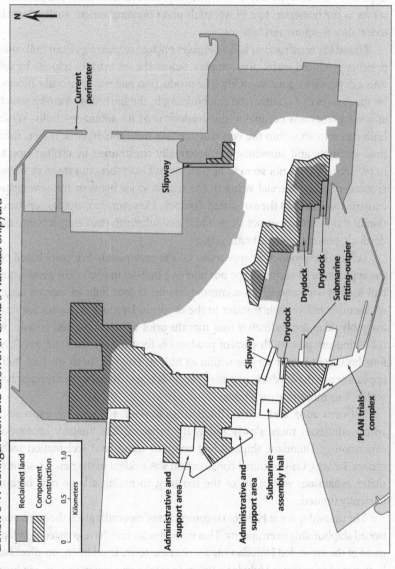

Huludao's main military purpose is the production of China's nuclear submarine fleet. All Chinese nuclear-powered submarines are produced here in a construction hall. There is no evidence that future submarines such as the Type 095 SSN or Type 096 SSBN will be produced elsewhere. Huludao also serves as the homeport to a PLAN trials unit operating various surface vessels to test new weapons and systems.

Huludao's construction hall assembles nuclear submarines from hull components produced within the complex, before the submarines relocate by rail into a drydock for final assembly. The production rate was previously affected by the presence of commercial shipbuilding in the immediate vicinity, which at some points was occupying the drydock used for submarine hulls. While hulls can remain within the construction hall until the drydock is free, their final assembly and launching are potentially constrained by civilian operations. Security does not seem to be a factor, as December 2014 imagery shows sections of a commercial vessel in the transit space between the submarine construction hall and the associated drydock. However, commercial construction of this fashion does not allow additional submarine hull transfers into the drydock, preventing their launching.

Submarine production appears to take approximately five years based on the appearance of various Type 093 and 094 hulls in imagery. The production hall itself is wide enough to accommodate up to four hulls in various stages of assembly before their transfer to the drydock. Drydock residence for final assembly takes approximately four months prior to launching and transfer to the fitting-out pier. With current production focusing on the Type 095 SSN, four hulls could enter service within as little as one year from the first hull's appearance in the drydock, provided the hulls began assembly in the main hall within four months of each other.

Between 2007 and 2009, Huludao underwent a significant expansion, which continues more slowly today. By 2009, satellite imagery confirmed expansion of Huludao's shipbuilding complex using land reclamation techniques. By 2015, only minimal construction was evident in the new, 7.5-square-meter expansion, with most of the territory, including a large new harbor, currently unused.

The unused space at Huludao is conspicuous, especially given the aforementioned shipbuilding overcapacity. That overcapacity may have arrested development of the expanded Huludao site for the near term. In addition, no effort has been noted to increase Huludao's ability to intake raw materials (e.g., via local rail spurs), a logical progression should the shipyard plan to expand its production capacity. Also, the reclaimed land features two new drydocks opening into the original harbor, currently in use for commercial shipbuilding. Relocation of commercial activities away from the submarine construction hall may free up the adjacent drydock and associated transit area for submarine production, removing a previous restriction on the production rate. Importantly, however, core nuclear submarine construction activities require an extremely level, firm foundation; not all reclamation provides suitable support.

Additional Locations of Interest

Various other locations should inform a study of Chinese military shipbuilding. Apart from numerous other shipyards engaging in military work, such as Hudong-Zhonghua producing Type 071 amphibious transport docks, numerous support facilities can provide insight into future Chinese naval developments.

One area of interest is Xiaopingdao, China's submarine-launched ballistic missile (SLBM) test facility. There, a single Type 032 conventional missile submarine (SSB) performs test firings of SLBMs and evaluates additional technologies related to various Chinese submarine programs. Additionally, Type 094 SSBNs are often spotted at Xiaopingdao, particularly early in their service lives during sea trials and weapons integration or loading. Xiaopingdao thus remains an area of interest for observation in imagery, as the presence of Type 094 SSBN hulls could suggest preparation for a JL-2 SLBM firing. In addition, Xiaopingdao represents a possible location to sight the forthcoming Type 096 SSBN should it go unnoticed during fitting out at Huludao due to a lack of suitable imagery.

Another area of interest is south of Wuhan. A lakeside complex contains a 1:1 scale mockup of *Liaoning*, possibly used for flight deck crew training, as evidenced by the presence of a J-15 mockup. In 2013, satellite imagery indicated an expansion was under way, which resulted in the construction of a superstructure mockup. This mockup is related to the forthcoming Type 055 guided-missile cruiser program, providing insight into possible sensor and weapons layouts.

Wuhan is also home to the Wuchang Shipyard, which produces conventionally powered submarines and Type 056 corvettes, including examples of the latter intended for export. The experimental Type 032 SSB is also a Wuchang product.

A further construction hall of interest is located at Guangzhou. This 450-meter facility produces the Type 054 and 056 frigates and is the license production facility for the Project 1232.2 *Zubr*-class LCACs.

Conclusion

While China's navy continues modernization and development of power-projection capabilities, various facets of the Chinese shipbuilding program will remain important focus areas for analysts and researchers. The effective fusing of open source research methodologies, including satellite imagery analysis, will remain essential to producing a more complete assessment, allowing more accurate forecasts of future capabilities and trends.

Notes

1. "金融新政难改造船业低迷态势 资金瓶颈待解" ["New Financial Policies Have Difficulty Transforming Shipbuilding Industry Depression, Capital Bottleneck Unresolved"], 新浪财经 [*Sina Finance*], May 6, 2015, http://finance.sina.com.cn/roll/20150506/203522120531.shtml; "金融支持船舶业意见出台 江苏船企盼银行帮忙" ["Financial Support Shipping Industry Idea Launches, Jiangsu Ship Expects Bank Help"], 人民网 [*People's Daily Online*], April 10, 2015, http://js.xhby.net/system/2015/04/10/024306191.shtml; "曾对2014年12大市场的猜想" ["12 Big Market Speculations from 2014"], 中国海事服务网 [*China Shipping Service Network*], January 19, 2015, http://www.cnss.com.cn/html/newspecial/2015/0119/shippingreport/index.html.

2. "印尼新政府大力发展造船业， 为中国企业带来新机遇" ["Indonesia's New Government to Develop Shipbuilding, New Opportunities for Chinese Enterprises"], 中华人民共和国驻印度尼西亚共和国大使馆经济商务参赞处 [Economic and Commercial Counsellor's Office of the Embassy of the People's Republic of China in the Republic of Indonesia], December 8, 2014, http://id.mofcom.gov.cn/article/bankbx/201412/20141200832664.shtml.

3. 胡嘉禄 [Hu Jialu], "我国造船业突破瓶颈步入快速发展轨道" ["China's Shipbuilding Industry Enters Rapid Development Track to Break Bottleneck"], 中国知识产权报 [*China Intellectual Property Rights Network News*], February 28, 2008, http://www.cipnews.com.cn/showArticle.asp?Articleid=7338.

4. "大型船用曲轴" ["Large Marine Crankshaft"], State-Owned Assets Supervision and Administration Commission of the People's Government of Dalian, November 4, 2014, http://www.gzw.dl.gov.cn/corpExhibitionProductForeView_4498.html.

5. Assessments based on shipyard facilities information provided at "Production Capacity," China Shipbuilding Industry Company Ltd.; Bohai Shipbuilding Heavy Industry Co. Ltd., http://www.bsic.com.cn/Home/Production%20Capacity/; "Bohai Shipbuilding Heavy Industry Co. Ltd. (BSHIC)," *Ship2Yard.com*, 2015, http://www.bshic.ship2yard.com/; "Jiangnan Shipyard Co., Ltd.," *Ship2Yard.com*, 2015, http://www.jiangnan.ship2yard.com/; "Dalian Shipbuilding Heavy Industry Co., Ltd. (CSIC)," *Ship2Yard.com*, May 3, 2015, http://www.ship2yard.com/yard.php?idy=8458; "外媒: 中国航母组建准备就绪 欲发展核动力航母" ["Foreign Media: China Prepared for Development of Nuclear-Powered Aircraft Carrier"], *South China Morning Post*,

October 21, 2014, http://www.nanzao.com/sc/national/14c316828688od5/wai-mei-zhong-guo-hang-mu-zu-jian-zhun-bei-jiu-xu-yu-fa-zhan-he-dong-li-hang-mu; "台媒曝中国国产航母万事俱备 一技术获欧洲认可" ["Taiwan Media Exposes Chinese Aircraft Carrier, One Technology Is European-Approved"], 环球网 [*Global Network*], October 21, 2015, http://mil.huanqiu.com/observation/2014-10/5173306.html.

6. "航母催生中国海军大舰时代 模块化造舰助'下饺子'" ["Carrier Spawns China's Large Naval Warship Era: Modular Construction Assists in Making Warship 'Dumplings'"], 中国新闻网 [*China News Service*], April 22, 2015, http://www.chinanews.com/m/mil/2015/04-22/7225330.shtml.

7. At twelve thousand tons each, these two large patrol vessels are ideally suited for "non-military" patrol of China's maritime frontier, such as remote claimed jurisdictional waters around South China Sea installations.

Daniel Alderman and Rush Doshi

Civil-Military Integration Potential in Chinese Shipbuilding

IN 2007, HU JINTAO, then General Secretary of the Chinese Communist Party (CCP), included the phrase "military-civilian fusion" (MCF) in his annual CCP Work Report.[1] Hu's use of the phrase was a major landmark in the continued development of China's civil-military integration (CMI), a broader term of art used to describe the Chinese government's continued attempts to strike the optimal balance between civilian and defense economies and their overlapping ecosystems.

MCF is frequently presented as a groundbreaking achievement in current general secretary and paramount leader Xi Jinping's plans for the future of the Chinese defense industry and economy. It is a constant presence in Chinese science and technology policies, defense industrial documents, and even China's most important planning document, the Eighteenth Party Congress Third Plenum announcement. However, this most recent push for an improved balance between civilian and military resources is only one phase in a multidecade campaign. Every Chinese leader has promoted his own version of improved CMI, dating back to Mao Zedong himself, who in 1956 stated the importance of better focusing on "handling military and civilian affairs together" (军民兼顾).[2]

This chapter addresses China's plans for and implementation of CMI in the shipbuilding industry. It analyzes how contributions from and interaction with the civilian/commercial shipbuilding industry are regarded by Chinese sources, and, where possible, how they actually stimulate or inhibit China's naval shipbuilding modernization.[3] The chapter is divided into two sections: the first focuses on central-level policy on CMI in shipbuilding, and the second on diffusion of infrastructure, methods, and technology from the civilian to the military sector.

With respect to central policy, we note that China's leading defense shipbuilders rely on the commercial sector for as much as 90 percent of their revenue. With the shipbuilding industry in the doldrums and capacity utilization at 50 percent (down from 75 percent five years ago), the government has issued a new shipbuilding plan to rescue the industry. This plan relies significantly on CMI. An analysis of its guidelines suggests two policy elements: the government views civilian shipbuilding as essential to and intertwined with military shipbuilding, and therefore is willing to support it; and it expects shipyard infrastructure, manufacturing processes, and technology to flow from the civilian to the military sectors (and vice versa). We also note that China has "white-listed" sixty of the country's several hundred shipyards for public support. An analysis of these white-listed yards shows that nearly all of China's military shipyards, its newest and most advanced yards, and its China State Shipbuilding Corporation (CSSC) and China Shipbuilding Industry Corporation (CSIC) yards made the list.

The second section focuses on diffusion from the commercial to the military shipbuilding sectors in three areas: shipyards and relevant infrastructure, ship design and production, and subcomponents and systems integration. Chinese CMI arguably has the least potential in shipyard infrastructure.[4] Although advanced civilian moving equipment and docks are dual-use, collocation of civilian and military production is challenging and, depending on its implementation, could even hamstring China's military shipbuilding industry. Diffusion has been moderately successful in ship design and advanced production methods, where some technologies and engineering knowledge used in civilian production can transfer to the military side, though specific applications often differ. We demonstrate this in part by surveying civil-military computer-aided design/computer-aided manufacturing (CAD/CAM) technology diffusion and modular construction methods.[5] Finally, diffusion has been least successful in systems integration and subcomponent design, in part because domestic Chinese civilian companies lack sufficient technological know-how and access to formal People's Liberation Army defense technology requirements information. Across all domains, we note continued dependence on foreign technology acquisition, despite policy pressures emphasizing domestic enterprises, especially in subcomponent manufacturing.

CMI and China's Shipbuilding Industry

Chinese Views of CMI

Chinese policymakers currently apply CMI in manifold sectors through a sprawling set of policies. At the highest level, CMI can be divided into two broad subgroups: commercial sector support to the defense economy, and defense industry support to the civilian ecosystem. In Western defense writings, CMI often emphasizes technology flows, focusing on spin-on (civil-military) and spin-off (military-civil) technology.

Chinese analysts take a far broader definition of CMI than simple bidirectional technology flows, instead loading this concept with a wide umbrella of meanings that transcend a sole focus on technology. This chapter focuses primarily on naval modernization–relevant CMI, with less emphasis on commercial spin-offs.

China's Shipbuilding Industry

The People's Liberation Army Navy (PLAN) largely relies on two state-owned enterprises (SOEs) to supply its surface vessels, submarines, and other maritime defense equipment. Until their ongoing merger, CSSC and CSIC were two of China's ten state-owned defense conglomerates, responsible for researching, developing, and manufacturing the vast majority of the Chinese military's equipment.[6] However, despite their stated primary responsibility of supplying defense equipment, previous CMI efforts have led to each firm receiving the vast majority of its financing from commercial activity. For instance, in recent years CSIC has stated that over 80 percent of its revenues are derived from commercial sector work,[7] and some independent estimates put the figure at over 90 percent.[8]

The division of defense work between the two firms was also heavily imbalanced, with CSIC claiming to supply over 80 percent of PLAN equipment.[9] Part of this imbalance might have stemmed from the imprecise split of these two firms in 1998, which was largely geographically, not functionally, based. Because of this imbalance and the false "competition" and infighting rumored between these two giants, there has been speculation of a re-merger between them in order to better synchronize their assets and to create unified national champions able to better serve the military and compete in the global commercial market. The CCP-owned *People's Daily*'s recognition of an impending round of mergers between all of China's SOEs, reducing their number from 112 to 40, all but guaranteed the recently reported CSSC-CSIC merger.[10] Moreover, although the firms continue to publicly deny such speculation, officials within these firms privately suggest the merger will proceed.[11] Most mergers to date have occurred within each conglomerate and between geographically proximate subsidiaries. Since CSSC and CSIC have different geographic regions, their merger will probably not result in many—or any—mergers between their respective shipyards. Its chief benefits are to reduce competition between shipyards, to eliminate redundant capacity across the two conglomerates, and perhaps to better integrate design and production since CSIC is believed to have better design capabilities.[12] Mergers across subsidiaries, however, do have direct impacts for CMI, as will be discussed later.

Implications of the Commercial Shipbuilding Downturn for Military Shipbuilding

Since the 2008 financial crisis, several commercial shipbuilders worldwide have encountered significant financial pressure, facing years of surplus capacity and diminishing orders. China's own shipbuilders have not been immune. By one measure, China's shipyard utilization rate plunged from 75 percent in 2010 to 50 percent in 2015—below that of other major shipbuilding countries.[13] Orders at Chinese shipyards have fallen for years, including by 77 percent in the first quarter of 2015 over the previous year. The head of China's largest private shipbuilder, Yangzijiang, expects the industry to contract sharply over the next three years, with perhaps half of all yards halting activity.[14] Rongsheng, once China's largest private shipbuilder, suspended operations and sold off most of its assets after teetering on the brink of bankruptcy for years.[15]

What are the implications of the downturn in commercial shipbuilding for military industry? As discussed previously, China's two main military shipbuilders—CSSC and CSIC—long derived the majority of their revenue from the very commercial sector that is now facing its most difficult years. Even as they merge, they will likely push for government support and more military projects to offset declining commercial sales. CSSC chief executive officer Hu Wenming argues that his company can only survive the global shipbuilding slump by building more advanced ships, including "high-tech ships such as naval vessels and maritime law enforcement ships."[16] This logic may be financially sound: according to some estimates, "one aircraft-carrier order could likely generate as much work for a shipyard as ten bulk carriers or supertankers."[17]

CMI in China's Shipbuilding Industry: The 2013–15 Plan

China's recent efforts at bolstering CMI in shipbuilding should be understood within the larger industry-wide downturn. Only one month after what was then the nation's largest shipyard—Rongsheng—sought government support,

China's State Council (SC) issued a three-year industry aid plan stipulating greater government support of shipbuilding, additional lending, mergers between subsidiaries, restrictions on capacity expansion, greater innovation, and scrapping older ships to bolster domestic demand.[18] Notably, CMI is also an important part of these efforts. As one document from SC researchers notes, China needs to "expand plans for the war industry . . . to digest the [surplus] production capacity through integrating the military technology with the civilian technology."[19] As an added benefit, greater CMI could enable China to hide increased military expenditure within the civilian shipbuilding budget.

An entire section of China's three-year shipbuilding plan is in fact devoted to greater CMI.[20] While the plan is prospective, many components resemble longstanding policy. The guidelines state that in order "to promote the development of military and civilian integration" in shipbuilding, China would have to:

- promote military-use and civilian-use research
- promote sharing of resources and results
- promote civilian and military ship design interoperability
- promote cooperative advanced manufacturing technology development
- strengthen military-use and civilian-use basic technology
- strengthen coordination and integration
- promote interoperability of military and civilian standards
- guide shipbuilding enterprises to give full play to technological advantages and actively develop a particular, dedicated shipping market
- base the industry in the civilian shipbuilding industrial base, rely on major civilian research projects, and thereby breach military industry capacity-building bottlenecks in key products, materials, manufacturing equipment, and so forth.[21]

Much is notable about this list. For example, it explicitly claims that China's military shipbuilding industry must be rooted in the civilian shipbuilding industrial base, rely on civilian projects, and use civilian industry to overcome military industry bottlenecks. Moreover, the document stresses the importance of shared ship design and manufacturing technologies between the civilian and military shipbuilding industries. This suggests two policy elements: China's government views civilian shipbuilding as essential to and intertwined with military shipbuilding, and therefore is willing to support it; and it expects shipyard infrastructure, manufacturing processes, and technology to flow from the civilian to military sectors, and vice versa.

There is no doubt that civil-military industrial spillover has been important to both CSSC and CSIC. For example, while the bulk of CSSC's revenue comes from the commercial shipbuilding industry, its leader worked in the "military engineering industry for several decades." Hu Wenming, CSSC's chief executive officer, is explicit about CSSC's military orientation, arguing that "military products" will be CSSC's "number one priority." He has pledged CSSC to contribute to "strengthening the military," noting that "CSSC's cadres and workers are deeply encouraged and inspired to take on the responsibility of using 'ships to serve the country.'"[22] These are significant statements. Hu held high-level positions in multiple military mega-conglomerates, including Aviation Industry Corporation of China and China North Industries Corporation, suggesting that while CSSC may have copious civilian business, it is nonetheless considered important for military purposes. Similarly, in a discussion of CSIC's priorities for the next Five-Year Guideline (2016–20), company president Sun Bo suggested that CSIC will focus on ten areas of CMI, most notably power systems, electronic information, electrical equipment, underwater defense systems, and new materials.[23] There may well be synergies between the company's focus on high-value vessels and its naval programs, with its subsidiary Dalian Shipbuilding constructing China's first indigenously built aircraft carrier.

Commercial-Military Diffusion

What aspects of commercial shipbuilding might translate into military shipbuilding? Given the military shipbuilding sector's unique requirements, commercial capacity does not always readily translate into military capacity. What shipbuilding process elements, then, most effectively support CMI? Although military advances have likely benefited the civilian sector in some areas, our primary focus is on how developments in the civilian sector have spread to the military sector.

Accordingly, we focus on three broad areas with potential synergies: shipyards and relevant infrastructure, ship design and advanced production methods, and systems integration and subcomponent design. The potential for diffusion in these areas does not mean China's government has been equally successful across them. Investments in civilian shipyard infrastructure may have military implications; however, collocation of civilian and military production is nonetheless challenging if not counterproductive. Diffusion has been moderately successful in ship design and advanced production methods, where some civil technologies and engineering knowledge can transfer to the military side, though specific applications often differ. Finally, diffusion has been least successful in systems integration and subcomponent design, in part because domestic Chinese civilian companies lack sufficient technological know-how and access to the defense industry in order to work effectively with defense mega-conglomerates.

Shipyards and Relevant Infrastructure

CMI has the greatest potential in shipyard infrastructure. As a report from the U.S. Office of Technology Assessment concluded, "Shipbuilding facilities appear to have considerable defense and commercial overlap. . . . [C]ostly, fixed shipbuilding facilities can be used for military or civilian work."[24] In China's case, before the mid-1990s, the country lacked building docks that could accommodate large commercial ships, such as very large crude carriers.[25] Today, it has dozens, many of which could accommodate the construction of large vessels, such as aircraft carriers.

China's newest, most modern shipyards are nearly as technologically sophisticated as those of Japan and South Korea. This effectively means that they have the infrastructure and technological expertise to engage in advanced naval ship production and manufacturing methods, even if their primary purpose has been civilian. For example, modular construction techniques involving independent construction of large pieces of the final vessel require unique transportation and movement equipment. This equipment, perhaps acquired for or financed by commercial shipbuilding, is unambiguously dual-use.

The dual-use potential of commercial shipbuilding technology helps explain why the central government is explicitly favoring some shipyards over others during the industry downturn. Of several hundred Chinese shipyards, roughly sixty have been deemed worthy of "support" and placed on an SC "white list."[26] The Ministry of Industry and Information Technology (MIIT) has issued the "Shipbuilding Industry Standards" (船舶行业规范条件) to determine which yards will receive support, based on factors such as safety, environmental record, and emissions.[27] In reality, these guidelines do not seem material in determining which yards make the list. Examining the white-listed shipyards reveals three patterns. First, nearly all of China's major shipyards involved in military production are included. Second, nearly all of China's newest and most advanced shipyards make the cut. Finally, nearly every CSIC and CSSC shipyard—roughly twenty in total—was white-listed.

This suggests that the Chinese government wanted to support those shipyards that are important to the country's military base and those advanced yards that, because of the dual-use potential of shipyard infrastructure, can clearly contribute to it (see exhibit 7-1).

Exhibit 7-1. China's White-Listed Shipyards

White-Listed Shipyards with Major Military Construction	White-Listed Shipyards that Rank among China's Newest and Most Advanced
• Jiangnan Shipyard Group • Hudong-Zhonghua Shipbuilding Group • Dalian Shipbuilding Industry Group • Bohai Shipbuilding Heavy (includes Huludao) • Huangpu Wenchong Shipbuilding Co. • Guangzhou Shipyard International (now CSSC Offshore and Marine Engineering [Group] Company Limited/COMEC) • Shanghai Jiangnan Changxing Heavy Industry Co. • Wuchang Shipbuilding Industry Group	• Shanghai Waigaoqiao • Guangzhou Longxue[1] • Changxingdao • Dalian Shipyard No. 2[2]

1. Its immediate owner, Guangzhou Shipbuilding Industry, was white-listed. Guangzhou Longxue was acquired in June 2014 by Guangzhou Shipyard International, which in May 2015 was renamed CSSC Offshore and Marine Engineering (Group) Company Limited.

2. Its immediate parent company was white-listed.

Although Chinese sources perceive dual-use potential in shipyard infrastructure, that does not mean that coproduction of military and commercial vessels at the same facility is efficient. As Gabriel Collins and Michael Grubb observe, "When coproduction is undertaken, delays in military production often negatively affect commercial efficiency (especially if the delay ties up a critical production point, such as a building dock)."[28] In the commercial sector, such delays can be extremely costly and can lead buyers to refuse to take ownership of the produced vessel. For this reason, with respect to shipyard utilization, there is a conflict between commercial and military interests in shipbuilding.

Despite these challenges, China is nevertheless choosing to collocate some military and civilian production. Given the industry's fiscal troubles, China's shipyards have been pursuing an unprecedented wave of mergers pushed by the SC, whose shipbuilding industry plan explicitly seeks to address excess capacity without losing hard-fought acquisition of the infrastructure necessary for high-tech shipbuilding. As a result, parent companies have forced geographically proximate shipyards to merge. In many of these cases, they have paired military and commercial shipyards so that the latter, facing thin order books, can benefit from the fiscal strength of the former, which enjoy lucrative government contracts. The result is often collocation of civil and naval shipbuilding. For example, the former Guangzhou Shipyard International (GSI), known since May 2015 as CSSC Offshore and Marine Engineering (Group) Company Limited (COMEC), bought Huangpu Wenchong Shipbuilding Company because its order book includes several military vessels.[29] Similarly, Hudong-Zhonghua is in a strong financial position because it builds both naval warships and liquefied natural gas (LNG) carriers and was asked to merge with Shanghai Shipyard, which builds commercial vessels, by their mutual parent company, CSSC. Several other financial arrangements are also pushing military and civilian shipbuilding to the same shipyards. Hudong-Zhonghua swapped shares with Shanghai Jiangnan Changxing—itself boasting military contracts—so that it could construct LNG carriers on some of Changxing's open platforms.[30] Rather than a compartmentalization of military and commercial shipbuilding, the emerging trend seems to be toward greater integration to ensure high-capacity utilization and improved finances. Additionally, among the larger subsidiaries formed from these mergers, almost all have both military and civilian shipbuilding, which strengthens the likelihood of civil-military diffusion.

Moreover, as Collins and Grubb noted in 2008, an important indicator that would signal "a shift in PRC [People's Republic of China] strategic shipbuilding priorities" would be "the introduction of significant military production at any of China's newest greenfield shipyards." This would demonstrate a desire to make the most of advanced dual-use technologies and "a willingness to forgo the optimal commercial efficiencies of these new yards."[31] Such coproduction has in fact occurred at some of China's newest, most advanced shipyards. For example, CSSC's new shipyard on Changxing Island builds LNG carriers,[32] will build the latest Type 055 cruiser, and appears involved in producing modules for China's second aircraft carrier.[33] Guangzhou Longxue, another of China's newest shipyards, was recently acquired by COMEC, which plans to expand it further and will be closing at least two other shipbuilding sites to relocate production to Longxue—already one of China's largest shipyards.[34] It seems plausible that at least some of this relocated production will be military since COMEC is "the most important production and support facility of military ships and special supporting ships of the PRC navy in southern China"[35] and boasts "the leading position in the PRC in terms of military ships, public service ships, [and] over 1,000 ton maritime police ship[s]."[36] This suggests that these yards may come to resemble several of China's largest, which build both civilian and military vessels. These include Hudong-Zhonghua, Huangpu, Dalian, and Huludao.

Such collocation of commercial and military production likely will prove inefficient, but it is possible that the inefficiencies will be manageable. First, the risk of coproduction resulting in bottlenecks still exists but is smaller given low capacity utilization and shipyard modernization. As discussed previously, China's shipyard utilization rate has fallen from 75 percent in 2010 to perhaps as low as 50 percent in 2015, with one-third to one-half of individual shipyards threatened with bankruptcy.[37] Meanwhile, the proliferation and improvement of modular construction techniques expand capacity, increasing the number of ships that can be constructed at a given yard and allowing "a ship to be built on solid land without the use of expensive dry-dock space."[38] Such techniques as "skid launches" allowed Korea's Jinhae Yard to increase capacity sixfold from 2004 to 2010 and are being applied to Chinese shipyards, such as COMEC's Guangzhou Longxue. Second, collocation of civilian and naval production is often problematic because vessels are constructed in accordance with different technical standards. In June 2015, however, the Chinese government began requiring civilian ships to be built in accordance with certain military specifications for use in wartime.[39] If the harmonization of commercial and naval technical standards is implemented more widely and prudently, it could increase the efficiency of collocation.

Shipyard infrastructure is clearly dual-use. This is why China's promotion and protection of advanced civilian facilities are likely related to its military goals. In the wake of recent mergers, collocation of commercial and naval production is increasing, though the inefficiencies of this process may be mitigated by outstanding slack capacity and standards harmonization.

Ship Design and Production

Civilian design and ship production methods have clearly diffused from commercial shipbuilding to military shipbuilding. Today's advanced shipbuilding techniques differ markedly from past practices, whereby a ship's entire hull would be built together. Hull-block construction entails building individual modules—sometimes at different building docks—that are later joined using heavy cranes and other moving equipment. An advantage of this production method is that it can minimize the impact of bottlenecks on the production process, allow greater customizability, and enable specialization within or across yards. China's largest and most advanced yards can support modular construction. According to *Introduction to Ship Technology and Design*, as a result of modular construction, "The pre-assembly rates of new types of naval and merchant ships have increased sharply, and time required to build ships has been sharply reduced."[40]

Foreign assistance enabled China's transition to these advanced ship production techniques. The government's contemporary shipbuilding efforts explicitly rely on importing foreign expertise. As two SC researchers note, China has developed the industry by "digesting and absorbing introduced technology" and must continue to "*strengthen international interaction* [emphasis added] to increase the core capacity for building high-tech vessels."[41] Chinese companies have imported key equipment and entire production lines and solicited engineering and technical assistance through joint ventures and cooperation agreements with Japanese, Korean, and European yards.[42] In many cases, "the government also requires Sino-foreign joint ventures to set up technical centres to absorb and disseminate technologies transferred by foreign investors."[43] Beyond these technical hubs, almost all Chinese shipbuilders have their own independent research institutes that employ thousands of engineers. Many of these research centers focus on both civilian and military research. In this way, technical knowledge and new manufacturing methods can diffuse within large conglomerates and across the civil-military divide.

One useful illustration of such diffusion is provided by a review of China's adoption of CAD/CAM technology roughly two decades ago. Although no longer cutting-edge today, that technology was a prerequisite for China to adopt advanced production techniques in modular construction and naval architecture. In the early 1990s, China had virtually no CAD/CAM experience. Later that decade, however, China received foreign assistance with CAD/CAM software in the civilian sector through joint ventures with Japanese, Korean, and European firms.

By the late 1990s China had begun to develop its own CAD/CAM software in independent research centers, though domestic software was often inferior to foreign imports.[44] For example, China's Qiuxin Shipyard and the Hudong Shipbuilding Heavy Industry Company—both military and civilian vessel producers—developed indigenous CAD/CAM software. Nevertheless, on the military side, as one Chinese author notes, the use of CAD/CAM in China's warship design "lagged advanced shipbuilding countries" by several years. CAD/CAM, he stresses, was extremely important for commercial shipbuilding and subsequently spread to military shipbuilding: "In the commercial shipbuilding industry, the research and development of CAD/CAM" within CSSC produced advances, but the "most important result" was its impact "in the field of military shipbuilding," especially surface warships and submarines.[45] Perhaps the clearest demonstration of these developments was that China began to develop its own military-specific CAD/CAM software. It is clear that the flow of CAD/CAM expertise was from foreign commercial shipbuilders to China's commercial shipbuilders and then finally to China's military shipbuilding enterprises.[46] In this way, China's shipbuilders "gradually absorbed and adopted a more progressive international shipbuilding model."[47]

Aside from software, significant infrastructure is needed to pursue modular construction: large cranes, moving equipment, special berths, skid barges, and other equipment. This equipment, while common at most major shipyards, is also dual-use. Modular construction methods long applied to the military sector are becoming increasingly advanced, allowing for fabrication of even heavier modules, including of carrier models. Interestingly, as shipyards expand and modernize their facilities, they are increasingly investing in better infrastructure for modular construction. For example, COMEC's Guangzhou Longxue, one of China's most advanced shipyards, is planning a rare expansion intended to facilitate modular shipbuilding just as Beijing discourages expansion. As one shipyard executive noted, "We can start building ships in the new facilities from [2016]. . . . [W]e will construct them on solid land without the use of a drydock."[48] These efforts can increase the efficiency of modular construction methods.[49]

CMI in Shipbuilding Subcomponents

Chinese leaders clearly seek significant improvements in the quality of domestically produced subcomponents and system integration designs for China's future naval equipment. The future capabilities of China's naval subcomponents, including radar, communications, navigation, fire control systems, and other automation equipment, will be key determinants of the future capability of Chinese naval assets. Their improvement and modernization would dramatically assist China's shipbuilding industry to undertake the rapid modernization it so fervently seeks. CMI is therefore seen as a critical path to overcoming bottlenecks and gaps in key technologies and subcomponents, drawing leading domestic and foreign commercial subcomponents into the largely monopolized, SOE-dominated naval shipbuilding industry.

In 2009 the CCP's leading policy journal *Seeking Truth* published an article by top CSSC executive Tan Zuojun exhorting China's shipbuilding industry to spur indigenous innovation by "introducing, digesting, absorbing, and re-innovating" (IDAR) foreign technology.[50] This concept is directly drawn from China's 2006 "National Medium- and Long-term Program for Science and Technology Development (2006–2020)" (MLP),[51] which has been criticized by Western analysts as a "blueprint for technology theft on a scale the world has never seen before."[52] Tan's call for IDAR eschews industrial espionage but does focus on open cooperation with international leaders in maritime subcomponent technology. Specifically, Tan notes that China's shipbuilding industries' indigenization effort should focus on automation controls for engines and navigation, in addition to more broadly closing the subcomponent technology gap between China and other unnamed foreign countries.[53]

Beyond previous calls for IDAR of foreign technologies, more recent complaints and policies indicate that China's shipbuilding leadership and consumers remain displeased with the technological level of China's indigenous subcomponent technologies and consequent dependence on foreign technologies. As an official 2013 CSIC report stated, a country's domestic production of subcomponent equipment is a key indicator of its level of success. The CSIC report's authors note that developed nations indigenously produce 80–90 percent of their subcomponent technologies, while CSIC is only able to produce 60 percent of subcomponent technologies domestically.[54] As another Chinese analysis notes, "Although we have the advantages in steel structures, assembly and the manufacturing link, that is . . . in 'building the empty shells,' we basically use foreign products inside the ships, including the propulsion system, the communication system and the navigation system with high added value and high technical contents."[55]

CSIC and other Chinese shipbuilders' dependence on foreign subcomponent technologies is cited as one driver for the 2013 release of the shipbuilding policy "Notice of the State Council on Issuing the Implementation Plans on Accelerating Structural Adjustment and Promoting Transformation and Upgrading of the Shipbuilding Industry (2013–2015)" ("船舶工业加快结构调整促进转型升级实施方案 [2013~2015年]") discussed above.[56] This document and its recommended policies are unique in that they offer a mid–Five Year Plan course correction for the industry that directly cites the 2006 MLP as its strategic direction and includes the IDAR concept as a recommended policy.[57] This off-cycle publication therefore underscores not only the concern surrounding China's shipbuilding industry's financial state, but also the assessed need for expanded CMI efforts and more rapid indigenization of subcomponent technologies.

Beyond the possibility of engaging in industrial espionage to achieve China's goals, official shipbuilding reports often tout official cooperative agreements with key foreign subcomponent suppliers. For example, CSSC's annual CMI report in the defense industry's official journal *Defence Science and Technology Industry* brags about key strategic cooperation agreements with leading global subcomponent firms such as General Electric, Fincantieri, and MTU Friedrichshafen.[58] Furthermore, Chinese regulators such as the defense industry's official administrator, the State Administration for Science, Technology, and Industry for National Defense (SASTIND/国家国防科技工业局), frequently publicize SOEs when they achieve domestic breakthroughs in critical technologies. For example, SASTIND recently noted that the CSSC 712th Research Institute successfully "smashed the foreign monopoly" (破国外垄断) on electric propulsion platform supply vessels.[59] Such announcements, combined with the official policies noted above, indicate continued efforts—however embellished in their public characterization—to indigenize key subcomponents.

Beyond foreign technology transfer, Chinese leaders also stipulate deepening CMI to include Chinese commercial subcomponent firms' expanded defense industry participation. This concept often appears in Chinese as "civilian participating in defense" (民参军). The effort's origins can be traced to 2010 with the release of the official policy "Locating Military Potential in Civilian Capabilities' Weapons Research and Production System" ("关于建立和完善军民结合寓军于民武器装备科研生产体系的若干意见"), commonly referred to in Chinese defense literature as Number 37 (37号).[60] This document sparked numerous efforts to better facilitate Chinese commercially focused SOEs and privately owned firms' inclusion in the traditionally monopolized state-owned defense industry.

As an example of this plan in action, the Beijing Highlander Digital Technology Co., Ltd. (北京海兰信数据科技股份有限公司) perfectly demonstrates the Chinese leadership's hope that leading producers of civilian maritime subcomponents will also supply Chinese naval shipbuilding. This company researches and develops a wide range of subcomponents related to "marine intelligence and ocean information technology" in partnership with more than thirty countries worldwide, including the United States.[61] It proudly boasts of its active contribution to the shipbuilding industry's policy of "civilians participating in defense" (民参军) and specifically cites its transfer of Integrated Navigation Systems, Small Target Detection Radars, and Vessel Management Systems as its greatest accomplishments in transferring civilian subcomponents to defense use. The company summarizes its goal in this area as "rapidly pushing mature civilian products toward transformation into defense use."[62]

Within this effort there is little chance in the foreseeable future that a major naval shipbuilding effort would be designed, researched, or manufactured by a private corporation, much less a nondefense SOE. However, propaganda advocating increased private and commercial participation in the defense industry gushes forth. To date, this effort appears to have had only minimal impact. As of 2015, news accounts and China's official 2014 CMI yearbook were still citing a 2013 statistic that only five hundred commercial companies possessed the necessary certifications to fully participate in the defense industry.[63] These limited figures provide little insight into the current state or exact figures for the shipbuilding industry, but all indications suggest lower participation rates than policymakers demand.

The reasons for low participation from private and other civilian companies in naval subcomponent design and integration are multifold. First, it is extremely difficult for nondefense firms to receive the three certificates needed to directly participate in the defense industry. As noted in previous research, efforts are afoot to help ease this process, but the basic difficulties in completing these arduous steps remain.[64] Such a high barrier to entry may explain why many commercial firms decline direct participation in research, design, and manufacturing with naval shipbuilders and instead hope for limited off-the-shelf sales to defense end users.

In addition to certification barriers, the shipbuilding industry's traditional culture of secrecy and desire to hide technological gaps and weaknesses also prohibit commercial civilian firms from learning how their subcomponents could be meaningfully adapted and integrated into the larger naval shipbuilding industry. There are limited signs that policymakers are serious about better coordinating communication between defense and civilian firms. First, there are now limited official forums that allow civilian firms to directly discuss their technologies with defense industry officials.[65] Second, science and technology policy guidance is now issued that details specific commercial technologies sought by the defense industry. For instance, in 2015 the Beijing Municipal Science and Technology Commission released a list of over one hundred technologies specifically sought by the defense industry. Two key shipbuilding subcomponents were specifically listed: diesel engine technology and advanced naval communications technologies.[66]

Additionally, MIIT has now opened a subordinate CMI Promotion Office (军民结合推进司) dedicated to facilitating better coordination between defense and commercial firms. Regarding subcomponents, recent efforts to promote leading commercial firms' inclusion seem somewhat pathetic, consisting of asking commercial companies to download and fill out a simple form stating their "technological breakthroughs." These firms are then asked to email the completed form back to the CMI Promotion Office, seemingly blind to defense industry needs.[67] These traditional Chinese bureaucratic offerings, combined with the unveiling of a defense bidding and procurement website, offer limited evidence of a serious effort to overcome the lack of participation by commercial subcomponent companies.[68]

One final barrier to deeper integration of civilian and military research, development, and manufacturing is the continued civilian-military standards gap. Lack of dual-use standards in the defense industry continues to be a major impediment to deeper CMI at the subcomponent level. Industry experts recognize that China currently has more than 26,000 national standards, with more than 11,000 additional military standards (*Guojia Junyong Biaozhun*, or GJBs).[69] Not only should these standards be better integrated with the dramatic rise of dual-use technologies, but industry experts have also noted that many GJBs are lagging in new high-tech technologies ("高新技术") of most importance to the defense industry, whereas commercial standards are frequently more advanced.[70] Small efforts at integration are evident, such as CSIC "unilaterally" implementing a program to standardize its regulations across its commercial and defense subsidiaries.[71] More serious efforts currently appear limited, however.

Notes

1. "胡锦涛在党的十七大上的报告" ["Hu Jintao's Work Report at the Chinese Communist Party 17th National People's Congress"], *Xinhua*, September 5, 2010, http://news.xinhuanet.com/newscenter/2007-10/24/content_6938568.htm.

2. Ling Shengyin, Peng Aihua, and Zou Shimeng, "Retrospect and Enlightenment of the Development of Military and Civil Integration Concept," *China Military Science*, no. 1 (2009).

3. Chinese sources reflect official slogans, strategic aspirations, and public relations pitches for organizations and individuals seeking contracts and fame. Given the drawbacks they perceived with many aspects of CMI, many Western technical experts consulted were generally skeptical about the degree to which these Chinese characterizations of technical approaches reflected substance and operational reality. Nevertheless, as Michael McDevitt suggests in his chapter in this volume, China may have an unusual ability to succeed at CMI, and, in any case, it is increasingly producing advanced naval ships.

4. One Western expert who was asked to review the China Maritime Studies Institute's conference findings reasons as follows: In a Chinese environment, CMI has the least potential, and cost drivers, in shipyard infrastructure. Land and hardware such as cranes are relatively cheap. True military shipbuilding cannot occur at a regular dockyard. Collocated dockyards cannot easily be cordoned off to allow the onsite inspection that civilian customers demand, particularly through onsite supervision by a technical representative. The greatest potential for CMI is not upstream at the final assembly level, but downstream at the systems and subcomponent levels. Subcomponent areas include propulsion (e.g.; civilian diesel engine technology from German company MTU and jet engine technology from joint ventures for destroyer turbines); electric systems; fuel transfer; navigation; hull shapes; radar; fluid dynamic modeling techniques; and modeling techniques for materials and structural integrity and strength.

5. This may reflect a lag in article coverage; CAD/CAM is already one generation behind. The current state of the art includes 3-D modeling and total lifecycle modeling design tools.

6. The company's websites are www.cssc.net.cn and www.csic.com.cn.

7. "李长印：中船重工总经理做客新华网" ["Li Changyin: CSSC President a Guest on Xinhua Net"], October 22, 2010, http://www.shipol.com.cn/rwpd/158644.htm. Chinese sources generally ignore such important questions as: How do pricing mechanisms work for military ships? To what extent does China use military funding to subsidize the civilian side? How are capacity-revenue tradeoffs assessed?

8. Yimou Lee and Michael Martina, "State-backed Shipbuilding to Raise $1.4 Billion for Naval Buildup," *Reuters*, September 11, 2013, http://www.reuters.com/article/2013/09/11/us-china-shipbuilding-idUSBRE98A02L20130911.

9. "Li Changyin: CSSC President a Guest on Xinhua Net."

10. "China Exclusive: Massive M&A Expected for Chinese SOEs," *Xinhua*, April 27, 2015, http://en.people.cn/business/n/2015/0427/c90778–8884196.html.

11. Lee Hong Liang, "Merger of CSIC and CSSC May Be Completed 'In One Year,'" *Seatrade Maritime Review*, November 5, 2015, www.seatrade-maritime.com/news/asia/merger-of-csic-and-cssc-may-be-completed-in-one-year.html.

12. Bao Zhiming, "Party Carries Out Leadership Reshuffle at State-Owned Shipbuilders," *Caixin Online*, March 26, 2015, http://english.caixin.com/2015-03-26/100795048.html.

13. Kyunghee Park, "China Shipbuilding Sector Set to Contract, Yangzijiang Says," *Bloomberg*, April 30, 2015, http://www.bloomberg.com/news/articles/2015-04-30/china-shipbuilding-industry-is-set-to-contract-yangzijiang-says.

14. Ibid.

15. "Chinese Shipyards See New Orders Fall by Almost Half in 2015," *Bloomberg*, January 18, 2016, www.bloomberg.com/news/articles/2016-01-18/chinese-shipyards-see-new-orders-fall-by-almost-half-in-2015.

16. "胡问鸣: 高端破局谋发展 助力蓝色中国梦" ["Hu Wenming: Seek Development Through High-End Breakthroughs, Support the Blue China Dream"], 国防科技工业 [*Defence Science and Technology Industry*], no. 7 (2013): 30–31.

17. Andrew S. Erickson and Gabe Collins, "China Carrier Demo Module Highlights Surging Navy," *The National Interest*, August 6, 2013, http://nationalinterest.org/commentary/china-carrier-demo-module-highlights-surging-navy-8842?page=show.

18. State Development Planning Commission, "船舶工业加快结构调整促进转型升级 实施方案 (2013–2015 年)" ["Ship Industry, Accelerating Structural Adjustment, Promoting Transformation and Upgrading, Implementation Plan (2013–2015) "], 2013, http://www.sdpc.gov.cn/zcfb/zcfbqt/201308/W020130806620700307575.pdf.

19. 马淑萍、项安波 [Ma Shuping and Xiang Anbo], 国务院发展研究中心企业所 [Enterprise Research Institute, State Council Development Research Center], "发展船舶工业: 技术创新与产业转型升级亟需提高" ["Develop the Shipping Industry: It Is Urgently Necessary to Raise the Level of Technical Innovation and Industrial Restructuring and Upgrading"], 中国发展观察 [China Development Watch] via 中国经济新闻网 [China Economic News Net], September 17, 2014, http://www.cet.com.cn/wzsy/qwfb/qwfb/1313291.shtml.

20. "国务院出台首个产业升级方案: 推船舶业军民融合" ["The State Council Promulgated the First Industrial Upgrading Program: Push CMI in the Shipbuilding Industry"], Sina.com, August 5, 2013, http://finance.sina.com.cn/chanjing/cyxw/20130805/015516341266.shtml.

21. State Development Planning Commission, "Ship Industry, Accelerating Structural Adjustment, Promoting Transformation and Upgrading, Implementation Plan (2013–2015)."

22. Quotes from "Hu Wenming."

23. Zhong Nan, "Shipbuilder Plans to Integrate Civilian, Military Businesses," *China Daily*, April 28, 2016, http://www.chinadaily.com.cn/cndy/2016-04/28/content_24915974.htm.

24. U.S. Office of Technology Assessment, *Assessing the Potential for Civil-Military Integration: Selected Case Studies* (Washington, DC: U.S. Government Printing Office, September 1995), 59.

25. Gabriel Collins and Michael Grubb, *A Comprehensive Survey of China's Dynamic Shipbuilding Industry*, China Maritime Study 1 (Newport, RI: Naval War College, August 2008), 21.

26. The official document that contains the first batch of fifty-one "white-listed" shipyards: Ministry of Industry and Information Technology Equipment, 工业和信息化部装备工业司关于符合《船舶行业规范条件》企业名单（第一批）的公示 [Announcement of the Ministry of Industry and Information Technology in Accordance with "Shipbuilding Industry Standards and Conditions" List of Companies (Batch 1)], September 3, 2014, http://www.miit.gov.cn/n11293472/n111293832/n12845605/n13916913/16124956.html. The second batch comprised nine shipyards: *The Second Batch of "White List" Shipyards* (China Classification Society, January 6, 2015), http://www.ccs.org.cn/ccswzen/font/fontAction!article.do?articleId=ff8080814a70901b014abdcab6810067. Finally, seven "offshore yards" that support the offshore industry rather than the shipbuilding industry were also white-listed in late 2015.

27. 工业和信息化部 [Ministry of Industry and Information Technology], "船舶行业规范条件" ["Shipbuilding Industry Standards and Conditions"] (Ministry of Commerce, September 2014), http://images.mofcom.gov.cn/www/201402/20140212150008498.pdf.

162 SHIPYARD INFRASTRUCTURE

28. Collins and Grubb, *A Comprehensive Survey of China's Dynamic Shipbuilding Industry*, 25.

29. Clement Tan, "Guangzhou Shipyard Surges After $900 Million of Deals," *Bloomberg*, November 2, 2014, http://www.bloomberg.com/news/articles/2014-11-03/guangzhou-shipyard-surges-94-after-announcing-takeovers.

30. Irene Ang, "Market Downturn Forces Yards to Be More Flexible," *TradeWinds*, April 12, 2013, http://www.tradewindsnews.com/weekly/315341/market-downturn-forces-yards-to-be-more-flexible.

31. Collins and Grubb, *A Comprehensive Survey of China's Dynamic Shipbuilding Industry*, 42.

32. "World First 172,000cbm LNG Carrier Built by CSSC Named," 中国船舶工业集团公司 [China State Shipbuilding Corporation], February 2, 2015, http://www.cssc.net.cn/en/component_news/news_detail.php?id=7259.

33. "Identified under Construction: China's Second Aircraft Carrier," *China Defense Blog*, August 1, 2013, http://china-defense.blogspot.com/2013/08/identified-under-construction-chinas.html.

34. Irene Ang, "Longxue Swells Capacity with 'Skid Launch' System," *TradeWinds*, February 13, 2015, http://www.tradewindsnews.com/weekly/354253/longxue-swells-capacity-with-skid-launch-system.

35. CSSC Offshore and Marine Engineering (Group) Company Limited, *Annual Report 2015*, 9, 19, http://comec.cssc.net.cn/en/upload_img/E0031720160422.pdf.

36. Ibid., 10.

37. Ang, "Longxue Swells Capacity with 'Skid Launch' System."

38. "STX O&S: Technology and Innovation at Work," *Baird Maritime*, March 3, 2013, http://www.bairdmaritime.com/index.php?option=com_content&view=article&id=5754:stx-oas-technology-and-innovation-at-work&catid=69&Itemid=60.

39. "China Approves Plan for Civilian Ships to be Used by the Military," *Reuters*, June 17, 2015, http://in.reuters.com/article/2015/06/18/china-defence-shipping-idINKBN0OY08U20150618.

40. 昭开文, 马运义 [Zhao Kaiwen and Ma Yunyi], 舰船技术与设计概论, 第2版 [*Introduction to Ship Technology and Design, Second Edition*] (Beijing: National Defense University Press, 2014), 996–98.

41. Ma Shuping and Xiang Anbo, "Develop the Shipping Industry."

42. Yin-Chung Tsai, "The Shipbuilding Industry in China," *OECD Journal: General Papers* 2010/3 (2011): 450–47; Evan Medeiros et al., *A New Direction for China's Defense Industry* (Santa Monica, CA: RAND, 2005), 130, 131.

43. Tsai, "The Shipbuilding Industry in China," 49.

44. For a brief history of CAD/CAM in China, see Guangwu Liu and Xinhua Zhang, "Using CAD/CAM More Effectively in Chinese Shipyards" (Sener, 2009), http://www.senermar.es/EPORTAL_DOCS/GENERAL/SENERV2/DOC-cw4afae2aab62dd/ICCAS2009_SENER_CADTechnology.pdf; Medeiros et al., *A New Direction for China's Defense Industry*, 130–45.

45. "舰船计算机辅助设计技术" ["Computer Assisted Ship Design Technology"], in Zhao and Ma, eds., *Introduction to Ship Technology and Design*, 791.

46. In contrast, in the West, the use of CAD/CAM spread from military industry to the civilian sector.

47. Zhao and Ma, eds., *Introduction to Ship Technology and Design*, 996–98.

48. Ang, "Longxue Swells Capacity with 'Skid Launch' System."

49. "STX O&S: Technology and Innovation at Work."

50. 谭作钧 [Tan Zuojun], "自主创新是我国成为世界造船强国的根本动力" ["Indigenous Innovation Is the Foundational Force for Turning Our Country's Shipbuilding Industry into a Global Power"], 求实 [Qiushi], July 16, 2009, http://www.qstheory.cn/zxdk/2007/200720/200907/t20090707_6773.htm.

51. English overview at http://www.gov.cn/english/2006-02/09/content_183426.htm.

52. James McGregor, "China's Drive for 'Indigenous Innovation:' A Web of Industrial Policies," https://www.uschamber.com/sites/default/files/legacy/reports/100728 chinareport_0.pdf.

53. Tan, "Indigenous Innovation Is the Foundational Force for Turning Our Country's Shipbuilding Industry into a Global Power."

54. "中国船舶重工股份有限公司 2013年度报告" ["China Shipbuilding Industry Company Limited 2013 Annual Report"], http://www.csicl.com.cn/document/2014 0512141547899448.pdf.

55. Ma Shuping and Xiang Anbo, "Develop the Shipping Industry."

56. Full text at http://www.lawinfochina.com/display.aspx?id=14911&lib=law.

57. "中国船舶重工股份有限公司 2013年度报告" ["China Shipbuilding Industry Company Limited 2013 Annual Report"], http://www.csicl.com.cn/document/2014 0512141547899448.pdf.

58. "聚合军民优势 实现全面转型 推动新常态下的改革创新与动态协调发展" ["Combine Civil and Military Superiority: Realize Comprehensive Transformation, Promote New Conditions for Reform and Innovation with Coordinated Development of the Situation"], 国防科技工业 [*Defence Science and Technology Industry*], no. 3 (2015): 34–46.

59. "中船重工七一二所电推系统再破国外垄断" ["CSSC 712 Research Institutes' Electronic Propulsion System Smashes Foreign Monopoly"], April 29, 2015, http://www.sastind.gov.cn/n137/n13098/c6019341/content.html.

60. Full text at http://wenku.baidu.com/view/f71f5ad4b9f3f90f76c61b25.html.

61. Beijing Highlander Digital Technology Co.'s website is http://www.highlander.com.cn/.

62. Beijing Highlander Digital Technology Co. discusses these accomplishments in a press release on its website: http://www.highlander.com.cn/briefing/News.asp?Sort ID=14&ItemID=116.

63. For instance, 任天佑 [Ren Tiankuo], 中国军民融合发展报告2014 [*2014 CMI Development Yearbook*] (Beijing: National Defense University Press, 2014).

64. For an expanded discussion, see Tai Ming Cheung, *Fortifying China: The Struggle to Build a Modern Defense Economy* (Ithaca: Cornell University Press, 2009).

65. For example, the 中国民营企业技术与产品参与国防建设展览会 [China Privately-run Enterprise Technology and Products Participate in National Defense Building Exhibition] was held May 5–7, 2015, in Beijing.

66. The Beijing Municipal Science and Technology Commission has released documentation seeking domestic commercial technologies: http://www.bjkw.gov.cn/n8785584/n8905230/n8905260/n9932444.files/n9931255.doc.

67. MIIT's CMI Promotion Office announced this effort on its website on February 3, 2015, http://jmjhs.miit.gov.cn/n11293472/n11295193/n11298598/16438006.html.

68. China's recent foray into open bidding of defense subcomponents has been widely publicized in state run media, including "PLA Organizes Open Bidding for Military Weaponry Procurement," *Global Times*, March 19, 2015, http://www.globaltimes.cn/content/913021.shtml.

69. "推动国防科技工业军民融合深度发展--访国防科工局发展计划司司长龙红山" ["Promote the Defense Industry's Advanced Development of Civil Military Fusion—Interview with SASTIND's Development Plan's Department, Department Head Chang Longshan"], 国防科技工业 [*Defence Science and Technology Industry*], no. 2 (2015): 13–18.

70. Ibid.

71. "聚合军民优势   实现全面转型   推动新常态下的改革创新与动态协调发展" ["Combine Civil and Military Superiority: Realize Comprehensive Transformation, Promote New Conditions for Reform and Innovation with Coordinated Development of the Situation"], 国防科技工业 [*Defence Science and Technology Industry*], no. 3 (2015): 34–46.

PART III

Naval Architecture and Design

Mark Metcalf

PLAN Warship Construction and Standardization

SINCE THE 1970S, the People's Republic of China (PRC) has been energetically developing and publishing a broad range of national and industrial technical standards with the goal of improving its industrial capabilities and growing its economy. This effort has also included the development of technical standards that would improve People's Liberation Army (PLA) capabilities.

There are four broad categories of PRC standards that are relevant to warship construction and comprise various types of specialized standards, including:

- National: PRC National Standards (GB and PRC National Military Standards [GJB])[1]

- Military: PLA Navy (PLAN) Standards (HJB)

- Industry: Shipbuilding Industry Standards (CB), Machine Industry Standards (JB), Aerospace Industry Standards (QJ), and Electronics Industry Standards (SJ)

- China Classification Society (CCS): Rules and Guidelines.

This chapter will discuss the historical development of GJBs and highlight those that address warship design, construction, and testing.

PRC National Military Standards

Guojia Junyong Biaozhun (GJB) are the overarching source of guidance for technical requirements for the various branches of the PLA.[2] They are the most influential type of standard associated with the design, construction, and testing of PLAN surface ships and submarines, serving a role that is analogous to that of U.S. military standards. As indicated in exhibit 8-1, GJBs provide several types of technical guidance.

Exhibit 8-1. Types of GJBs (*Guojia Junyong Biaozhun*, PRC National Military Standards)

Type	Number	Title (in English)[1]
Design	GJB 5155-2002	*Submarine Propeller Design Calculation Method*
Requirements	GJB 3182-98	*Accuracy Requirements of Hull Construction for Naval Surface Ships*
Specification	GJB 3154-98	*General Specification for Shipborne GPS Satellite Navigators*
Test Methods	GJB 913A-2005	*Test Methods for Shipboard Electrical Distribution and Control Equipment*

1. English language titles provided for standards, journal articles, or other Chinese sources are cited verbatim.

GJBs are highly structured documents, in terms of both format and content. Like all military standards, they provide technical guidance that is intended to satisfy specific military requirements concerning a particular topic. Of particular interest concerning GJBs, however, is their inclusion of ancillary nontechnical information that can yield significant insights into the PRC warship construction process.

The development of PLAN warship standards began during the 1950s with the publication of PRC shipbuilding standards, based primarily on those of the Soviet Union. PRC writers explain that this was a deliberate approach designed to gradually transition from "imitative" to "self-determined" development.[3] This approach continued into the 1970s when the PRC shipbuilding industry began to produce indigenous standards for both joint civilian/military use and "special use" standards for the military. During the 1980s, the China Shipbuilding Industry Department published a total of 261 GJBs and HJBs, over 1,300 standards that addressed both civilian and military requirements, and translations of 1,500 warship-related U.S. military standards.[4]

Foreign standards were "assimilated" and "transformed" to produce the first-generation GJBs. As a result, many of these GJBs contain figures, tables, and large sections of text that are simply "assimilated" translations of U.S. military standards. Where warranted, U.S. technical parameters were "transformed" to conform to PRC standards (e.g., from a 60 Hertz frequency standard to 50 Hertz). Exhibit 8-2, an excerpt from a PRC textbook, identifies

Exhibit 8-2. Electromagnetic Compatibility—GJBs and MIL-STDs

GJB Number	GJB Title (in English)	Source U.S. Reference	U.S. Title
GJB 72-85	Terminology for Electromagnetic Interference and Electromagnetic Compatibility	MIL-STD-463A (June 1, 1977)	Definitions and System of Units, Electromagnetic Interference and Electromagnetic Compatibility Technology
GJB 151A-97	Electromagnetic Emission and Susceptibility Requirements for Military Equipment and Subsystems	MIL-STD-461D (August 1, 1968)	Requirements for the Control of Electromagnetic Interference Emissions and Susceptibility
GJB 786-89	Preclusion of Ordnance Hazards in Electromagnetic Fields, General Requirements for	MIL-STD-1385A (August 1, 1986)	Preclusion of Ordnance Hazards in Electromagnetic Fields, General Requirements for
GJB 1449-92	Procedures of Conducting a Shipboard Electromagnetic Interference Survey for Surface Ships	MIL-STD-1605 (April 23, 1973)	Procedures for Conducting a Shipboard Electromagnetic Interference (EMI) Survey (Surface Ships)

electromagnetic compatibility GJBs and their U.S. military standards sources.[5] A major milestone in warship standardization occurred in 2000 with the publication of GJB 4000–2000, General Specifications for Naval Ships, described as "the flagship second generation system for warship equipment."[6] The contents of this GJB, providing the overarching standards for PLAN warship construction, are described in a subsequent section.

While the PLA General Armament Department continues to publish new GJBs, in recent years there have been concerns that many decades-old GJBs are inadequate for providing technical guidance. Some suggest that this situation could be mitigated with closer coordination of standardization efforts among the PLAN, the shipbuilding industry, and the CCS.

Warship Construction Standards

GJBs

While there are several hundred GJBs that address all aspects of warship construction, the following standards are particularly useful for obtaining a system-level understanding of the PLAN approach to warship construction.

GJB 4000–2000, *General Specifications for Naval Ships*, is the most comprehensive standard on warship requirements. Comprising over 2,000 pages of text and citing 902 references, this GJB is the result of over 7 years of work by 700 named contributors from 86 research institutes, factories, and other organizations.[7] The GJB is frequently cited in graduate theses and technical journal articles that address ship design and construction.

This GJB, pertaining to all surface ships and submarines, is applicable to new construction warships and may also be used as a reference for warships undergoing significant capability or structural modifications. Curiously, the standard directs that while the testing of auxiliary warships is to be conducted in accordance with relevant GJBs and HJBs, their design and construction shall conform to CCS rules.[8]

GJB 4000–2000 comprises ten volumes, which address subject areas and contents as delineated below (see exhibit 8-3). Each volume is marked with an "internal use" classification. The GJB also includes an unnumbered "general volume" that presents a high-level overview of the GJB and its scope, delineates all 587 work items in each part of the GJB, and contains lists of references, organizations, and authors that contributed to the standard.

The sections within each GJB 4000–2000 volume are numbered according to the work breakdown structure (WBS) defined in GJB 2258–94.[9] This WBS numbering scheme closely corresponds to U.S. Naval Sea Systems Command's 1977 Ship Work Breakdown Structure. At the lowest level, each section provides the individual specifications for a particular topic. For example, Section 124, "Submarine Internal Tank," includes an overview and definitions, which are followed by subsections that address design, material, construction, and acceptance testing requirements, as well as technical references.

GJB 4000–2000 is arguably the single most useful GJB for understanding PRC warship development requirements and priorities. Not only does its WBS-based structure make it a very accessible standard, but its propensity for thoroughly citing external technical sources also makes it an excellent source of information on the significance of various standards that are used throughout the entire warship construction enterprise.

Exhibit 8-3. GJB 4000-2000 Subject Areas

Volume	Title	Contents
0	Ship overall characteristics and management	General requirements for comprehensive effectiveness and systems engineering management
1	Hull structure	
2	Propulsion systems	
3	Power systems	
4	Electronic information systems	System effectiveness requirements that each warship system must achieve to satisfy comprehensive effectiveness
5	Auxiliary systems	
6	Hull fittings and compartment facilities	
7	Weapon launchers and supporting systems	
8	Synthesis and engineering	Requirements for essential engineering work items, assurance work items, and management engineering work items during warship design, construction, and acceptance testing
9	Construction and supporting systems	

Several other GJB series that address warship testing and interface requirements provide information about warship development requirements and priorities. These include GJB 1446–1992, *Interface Requirements for Shipboard Systems Interfaces* (29 parts), GJB 6850–2009, *Code for Mooring and Sea Trials of Surface Combatant Ships* (227 parts), and GJB 5205.11–2003, *Land-based Integration Test Specifications for Subsystems of Ship Combat Systems* (11 parts).

HJBs

HJBs are technical standards that are published by the PLAN and its subordinate elements. While there is considerable overlap between HJB and naval GJB topics, this is probably because the HJBs are written to express related requirements from a uniquely PLAN perspective or to address topics that are more appropriately handled by PLAN elements.[10] Of the 82 HJB references in GJB 4000–2000, for example, 75 address PLAN-specified testing procedures by topic. Like GJBs, many HJBs are based on information obtained from U.S. military standards.[11]

CBs

CBs, written by shipbuilding industry organizations (e.g., shipyards, research institutes, etc.), provide guidance for the construction of both civilian and military ships. CBs that are applicable to both commercial and warship construction are routinely cited in GJBs and HJBs. There are also several hundred CBs that specifically address warship construction requirements.

The China Classification Society

The CCS is responsible for the assessment and certification of the technical condition of all types of commercial ships built in the PRC.[12] The results of CCS assessments are used to determine insurance premiums, cargo capacity, or even the price of a vessel. CCS publishes a series of rules and guidelines that provide technical requirements regarding the design, construction, and evaluation of ships. The CCS also coordinates its activities with other national classification societies, participating in the twelve-member International Association of Classification Societies, Ltd.[13]

In 1998 Lloyd's Register, the United Kingdom's classification society, published the first set of classification rules for warships. In spite of differences in operational requirements that limit the applicability of commercial rules to warship production, such rules have proven beneficial. Accordingly, several classification societies have published their own warship classification rules that have been incorporated in their national warship production processes. While the CCS has not yet published warship classification rules, as previously discussed, PLAN auxiliary warship designs must conform to the CCS "Rules and Regulations for the Construction and Classification of Seagoing Steel Ships."

The successes of foreign warship classification rules have not gone unnoticed by PRC shipbuilding industry and PLAN authors. Citing the achievements of foreign navies, they have argued that China could also benefit from CCS warship classification rules. In particular, writers emphasize the potential for reducing construction costs, improving manufacturing efficiencies, and providing access to advanced foreign technologies.[14]

Meanwhile, China's shipbuilding industry is gaining practical experience in this area. In August 2014 the China State Shipbuilding Corporation (CSSC) launched an Algerian navy C-28A frigate that, for the first time at CSSC, was "designed, built, and classified" using "famous international warship classification rules."[15] Given the inherent complexities of the PLAN warship construction enterprise and the myriad political, military, and bureaucratic interests that must be addressed before a warship classification process can be implemented, perhaps the CSSC tactics will provide an unobtrusive yet pragmatic way for the PLAN to benefit from foreign warship classification rules.

There is also ongoing interaction among PLAN, CSSC, and CCS elements regarding national defense mobilization technical requirements for commercial vessels. In June 2015 the PLA announced the publication of a "Technical Standard for the Implementation of National Defense Requirements Aboard New Construction Civilian Ships" (reportedly issued as a GJB) that was the result of a five-year collaborative effort by these organizations.[16]

Observations

One of the most striking aspects of PRC technical writings about warship construction is the regularity with which they cite U.S. military standards and other technical sources. Many of these citations are undoubtedly the result of the oft-repeated refrain that the PRC trails the West in "advanced technologies" and, accordingly, it is incumbent on Chinese technologists to become familiar with Western technical developments that are relevant to their research. It is interesting to observe, however, the changes that have occurred to the *way* that foreign sources have been cited over the years. Prior to 2000, articles that cited U.S. military standards primarily focused on explaining the technical content and significance of such documents. With the new millennium the emphasis began to shift to explaining U.S. military standards in the context of GJBs and, in some cases, comparing the relative merits of each. A decade later there was another shift toward comparing U.S. military standards, GJBs, and the rules of the CCS and foreign classification societies. Some documents have even used the existing foreign and PRC standards as a baseline for proposing new technical approaches that purport to provide performance improvements.

The reason for mentioning this evolution is to highlight the observation that the technical approach that is being used by the PRC warship enterprise has changed over the past four decades. PRC warship technology is no longer merely a compilation of recycled Western or Soviet technology. While

PRC engineers and scientists continue to use foreign technologies in warship production, they are also incorporating technical improvements that are the result of domestic research and development. The unprecedented public acknowledgment of recent collaboration among PLAN, CSSC, and CCS elements offers the potential for exploiting synergies that could accelerate the development of new indigenous capabilities for improving the PRC warship enterprise. The impact of this reality is quite obvious. In order to understand PRC warship production, we need to comprehend warship production on the PRC's terms. And, while not a panacea, having both a quantitative ("what?") and qualitative ("why?") appreciation of the technical standards used in warship production is a crucial element in obtaining such an understanding.

There are two primary challenges to accomplishing this. The first challenge is language. Nearly all standards that address PLAN warship construction are highly technical documents written in Chinese. While it is not difficult to find proficient Chinese translators, it can be problematic to find Chinese translators with sufficient engineering, scientific, and/or naval expertise to accurately translate the contents of such specialized documents into English. When considering the role of such translations in subsequent analyses, it is not possible to overemphasize the tremendous importance of both accurately portraying the technical content of standards and using the appropriate specialist terminology in the translations of technical standards.

The second challenge is obtaining the warship-related standards. It is currently possible to indiscriminately download hundreds of GJBs and CBs from PRC websites, but a relatively small percentage of such documents pertain to warship production. In order to obtain a comprehensive and accurate understanding of PLAN warship production, all pertinent standards must eventually be identified, acquired, translated, and analyzed. In the meantime, engaging in an effort to translate and analyze available standards (such as GJB 4000-2000) would undoubtedly add to our understanding of the PLAN warship construction enterprise.

While these challenges may seem daunting, the fact remains that national, military, and industry standards can be a lucrative source of information about the PRC warship construction enterprise. The better that we understand such standards, the better we will comprehend the countless factors that influence the process by which the PLAN transforms a warship from a concept to a delivery. On the other hand, if we continue to avoid dealing with these key components of the enterprise, we will continue to knowingly perpetuate an incomplete understanding of the PLAN warship construction process.

Notes

1. Most standards can be identified by a digraph or trigraph derived from the *pinyin* romanized name of the type of standard. For example, GJB is derived from *Guojia Junyong Biaozhun* (国家军用标准).

2. Observations presented in this section are based on a review of more than five hundred GJBs. While this chapter addresses naval-associated GJBs, there are also GJBs that address ground force, air force, and missile force requirements and PLA-wide standards (e.g., procurement, logistics, documentation, etc.).

3. 余林刚, 丰利军 [Yu Lingang and Feng Lijun], "加强舰船辅助机电设备标准化工作的研究" ["Research on Reinforcing Assistant Machine (Auxiliary Machinery) and Electrical Devices Standardization of Warship"], 船舶标准化工程师 [*Ship Standardization Engineer*] (May 2013), 18.

4. "当代中国" 丛书编辑部编辑 ["Contemporary China" Editorial Staff], 当代中国的标准化 [*Contemporary China Standardization*] (Beijing: China Social Sciences Publishing, 1986), 254.

5. 中国船舶重工集团公司 [China Shipbuilding Industry Corporation], 海军武器装备与海战场环境概论 [*Introduction to Naval Weapons Equipment and the Maritime Battlefield Environment*] (Beijing: Ocean Publishing, 2007), 258–9.

6. GJB 4000–2000, 舰船通用规范 [*General Specifications for Naval Ships*]; Yu and Feng, "Research on Reinforcing," 18.

7. Between 2003 and 2008 the General Armament Department published six brief "revision sheets" to GJB 4000–2000.

8. GJB 4000–2000, "General volume," 5.6.

9. GJB 2258–94, 舰船工作分解结构 [*Ships Work Breakdown Structure*].

10. For example, HJB 37A-2000, 舰艇色彩标准 [*Standard for Color of Naval Ships*], delineates colors to be used for hulls, external/internal structures, and equipment on board various types of naval warships.

11. HJB 66–91, 海军订购(研制)飞机和直升机 采用的标准和技术资料要求 [*Specifications and Data of Contract Requirements for Naval Aircraft and Helicopters*] cites 153 U.S. military standards but only 2 HJBs.

12. China Classification Society English-language website: http://www.ccs.org.cn/ccs wzen/.

13. International Association of Classification Societies, Ltd., website: http://www.iacs.org .uk/.

14. 齐晓丰 [Qi Xiaofeng], "军民深度融合推动军船入级" ["The Military and Civilians Profoundly Converged Promote Warship Classification"], 中国船检 [*China Ship Survey*] (October 2014): 58–60.

15. "中船集团又一舰船出口项目首舰下水" ["CSSC Launches Another New Class of Export Warship"], August 19, 2014, http://www.cssc.net.cn/component_news/news_ detail.php?id=17730. Probably Lloyd's "Rules and Regulations for the Classification of Naval Ships," as a Lloyd's representative attended the launch.

16. "新造民船贯彻国防要求技术标准' 颁布实施" ["Technical Standard for the Implementation of National Defense Requirements Aboard New Construction Civilian Ships," Published and Implemented], June 6, 2015, http://news.mod.gov.cn/headlines/2015-06/06/content_4588640.htm.

Kevin Pollpeter and Mark Stokes

China's Military Shipbuilding Research, Development, and Acquisition System

CHINA'S SHIPBUILDING INDUSTRY is improving its ability to design and produce increasingly sophisticated surface combatants and submarines. Since 1979 it has narrowed the gap with its foreign competition through the accumulation of foreign technology and knowledge, but it also recognizes that it must move beyond copying and reengineering if it is to provide increasing value to its customers. This chapter examines China's shipbuilding research, development, and acquisition (RDA) system through the lens of the Chinese concept of integrated innovation as practiced by the China Shipbuilding Industry Corporation (CSIC), the primary builder of surface ships and submarines for the People's Liberation Army Navy (PLAN). We argue that integrated innovation facilitates technology learning and research and development (R&D) through systems engineering and explicit linkages between market demand and product development and organizational structure and technology development. In using integrated innovation, an enterprise seeks to add value by managing the entire process of product development rather than focusing on component development.

We find that Chinese analysts are dissatisfied with the level of modern shipbuilding practices adopted by the industry. Although the development of individual technologies remains important, analysts cite organizational stovepiping, the inadequate use of systems engineering, and inefficient RDA processes as the main factors retarding the ability of the industry to produce world-class products. In sum, the industry must move from component innovation to product innovation where it manages a process designed to foster innovation overall. In doing so, the industry recognizes that organizational and process innovations can be just as important as technological innovation.

Indigenous Innovation

Indigenous innovation was first introduced during the Fifth Plenum of the Chinese Communist Party held in October 2005, where it was called the strategic starting point of the development of science and technology and the restructuring of industry.[1] Chinese defense enterprises approach indigenous innovation in three ways: original innovation (原始创新), integrated innovation (集成创新), and technology transfer, or what the Chinese call "introduction, digestion, absorption, and re-innovation" (引进消化吸收再创新/IDAR).[2] Original innovation, in which an invention is created and developed into a novel product, is the most difficult. The easiest of the three types of innovation is technology transfer. This method is attractive to developing countries as it enables them to bypass generations of technology development to more quickly reach world levels. China's emphasis on "re-innovation," however, is designed not to produce exact copies of foreign technologies, but rather to improve upon them and adapt them to the China market. During the introduction stage of the IDAR process, as indicated in exhibit 9-1, foreign technologies are studied and selected based on their technological sophistication and availability. During the digestion and absorption stages, the technology is reverse-engineered using Chinese components. During the re-innovation stage, the technology is then modified to better suit Chinese market conditions and/or improved upon.[3]

Exhibit 9-1. China's IDAR Technology Innovation Process

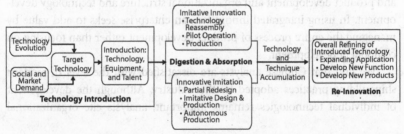

Of the three types of innovation that comprise indigenous innovation, integrated innovation is the most important for the shipbuilding industry.[4] While the IDAR process is acknowledged to be an important measure to speed science and technology development, it has its own pitfalls.[5] Chinese companies cannot simply rely on reengineering foreign technologies if they want to move to the forefront of technology innovation.[6] The focus on integrated innovation by Chinese companies is based on the belief that Chinese industry must move beyond copying and reengineering foreign technologies to achieve more value-added innovation. However, they lack the skills to engage in original innovation. Integrated innovation is thus a necessary second stage of development in the evolutionary process of China's innovation strategy.[7]

Integrated innovation is important when dealing with large projects, such as ships, and is a method to merge existing technologies with new technologies and domestic technologies with foreign technologies, as well as to facilitate collaboration between numerous organizations and personnel. Integrated innovation recognizes that complex products will comprise a combination of domestic and foreign technologies with different software and interfacing requirements that must be accounted for during the planning and design stages of the R&D process. In conducting integrated innovation, companies are required to not only develop new technologies, but also establish an organizational structure that facilitates technology development, create and retain the knowledge to successfully take products from the lab to the production line, and develop a business strategy that gets them to market.[8]

Chinese researchers view integrated innovation as a way in which the shipbuilding industry can link market demand with product development, organizational structure with the RDA process, and foreign and domestic technologies into a complete system. They argue that Chinese industry must move from relying on the copying and reengineering of foreign technologies to a role as a systems integrator where their value-added is more on the design and research of products rather than on the manufacturing.[9] This focus on systems integration is especially important for naval vessels, which can involve a wide range of systems, including propulsion, equipment, electronics, navigation, communication, environmental, reconnaissance, fire control, missile, gun, torpedo, and aircraft systems that must all be integrated.[10]

From Imitation to Integration: A Case Study

The process of moving from copying technology to integrated innovation is reflected in the experience of Dalian Vessel Heavy Industry Group Company Limited (DVHI) as it moved from building unsophisticated bulk carriers to manufacturing very large crude carriers (VLCCs). Beginning in the early 1980s, DVHI gained access to advanced foreign technology and with the help of low-cost labor and land caught up with and eventually challenged foreign competitors at the low end of the market. Advancements made by DVHI, in many cases using foreign technology and techniques, resulted in foreign shipbuilders becoming more reluctant to transfer technology. Beginning in the 1990s, when DVHI sought to move beyond the low-end market to manufacture more advanced types of ships such as VLCCs, these restrictions prohibited the large-scale introduction of foreign technologies signaling that DVHI needed to adopt more advanced forms of innovation. When developing its VLCC, DVHI elected to design the ship with the assistance of a Korean R&D services firm and selected both domestic and foreign technologies to be used on the ship. In so doing, however, DVHI maintained overall control of product development and retained critical system development capabilities.

The Military Shipbuilding RDA System

China's military shipbuilding R&D process is separated into seven stages from concept development to retirement.[11] Exhibit 9-2 details activities in the first five stages.

- Pre-research (预先研究阶段) entails initial exploration of ship requirements and basic technological research.

- During validation (总体系统立项论证阶段), the military takes the lead in assessing feasibility, drafts "R&D General Requirements" and feasibility reports, and submits the project for approval.

- Planning (总体系统方案研究设计阶段) involves preliminary design, production design, critical technology research, and new technology and equipment development. After approval, R&D units contact the military and other relevant departments to begin planning and preliminary design. They conduct research on subsystems, prototypes, and preliminary testing.

- Engineering and R&D (总体系统工程研制阶段) involve workflow design, production design, construction, launch and sea trials, equipment installation, and testing and acceptance. Based on "General R&D Requirements" and the contract, general design and scientific research testing begin. After final testing, a finalized design is submitted.

- Testing and batch production (总体系统试验定型量产阶段) involves overall testing, design finalization, and production finalization. A Product Design Finalization Committee is established to review the design. If the committee approves, production starts. When the required number of ships is constructed, production is complete.

- During employment (总体系统使用), ships are supported, crews trained, and operations conducted.

- For retirement (退役阶段), ships are removed from service.

Of the preapproval stages, pre-research and validation consume the majority of the time, while the engineering and R&D stage represents the most time-consuming period of the post-approval process. Exhibit 9-3 depicts the primary organizations involved in each of the respective seven stages.

Exhibit 9-2. First Five Stages in Military Shipbuilding Research and Development Process

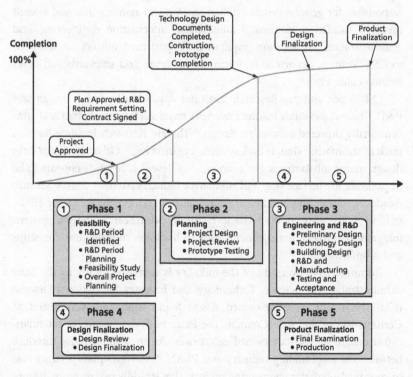

As for shipbuilding-specific procedures, the RDA process begins with the PLAN drafting detailed operational requirements documentation based upon short- (five-year) to long-term (fifteen-plus-year) force planning guidance. These requirements are then used by the Navy Equipment Department, expert groups under the General Armament Department Science and Technology Committee, the Naval Engineering Academy, and shipbuilding research institutes to determine specific ship concepts during the pre-research stage. The Navy Equipment Department also oversees feasibility studies, conceptual design, and program validation with assistance from these organizations. Approval authority for major programs likely resides with the Central Military Commission (CMC) and Central Special Committee, an ad hoc organization bridging the CMC and State Council.[12]

Under CMC and senior navy leaders' direction, the Navy Equipment Department is responsible for overseeing acquisition and sustainment of naval systems conducted by the Navy Equipment Academy. The academy consists of research institutes that support PLAN leadership in determining strategic requirements and managing acquisition programs. These institutes are responsible for general systems design, *operational systems*, ship and aircraft program validation, command automation, information engineering, and standardization. In addition, Equipment Department officers are assigned to CSIC centers, departments, institutes, factories, and shipyards and other defense enterprises.[13]

CSIC's 701 and 719 Research Institutes appear to lead ship design and R&D. The 701 Research Institute oversees naval surface combatant and conventionally powered submarine design.[14] The 719 Research Institute handles nuclear submarine design and systems engineering.[15] Other institutes help design major sub-systems. For example, 713 Research Institute appears to be responsible for surface ship and submarine launch systems.[16] CSIC's Seventh Academy, China Shipbuilding Research and Development Academy (中国 舰船研究院), also conducts basic research, pre-research, design, systems integration, project management, and technology coordination for ships and submarines.[17]

Administrative oversight of the industry is exercised jointly by the State Administration for Science, Technology, and Industry for National Defense (SASTIND) and the State-owned Assets Supervision and Administration Commission of the State Council. The latter body is responsible for financial oversight for all state-owned enterprises. As an administrative interface between the shipbuilding industry and PLAN, SASTIND plays a larger role in coordinating major engineering projects that straddle two or more defense

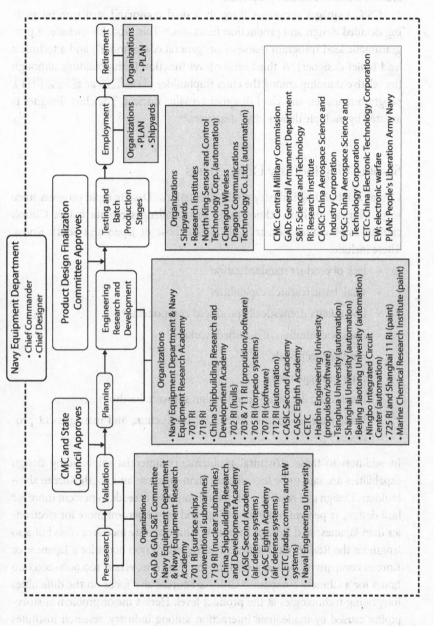

Exhibit 9-3. Primary Organizations Involved in China's Military Shipbuilding

industrial enterprises, such as the aircraft carrier and nuclear submarine-launched ballistic missile programs.[18]

CSIC manages programs through a dual command structure integrating detailed design and production functions.[19] This probably includes a programmatic lead (program manager or "general commander") and a technical lead (chief designer). A third senior-level function is shipbuilding, although the relative standing among the chief shipbuilder (总建造师 or 建造总指挥), program manager, and chief designer remains unclear. The chief designer is assisted by multiple deputy chief designers.[20]

Shipbuilding Industry Deficiencies

China's shipbuilding industry retains limitations. Despite rapid progress since 1979, Chinese analysts acknowledge that challenges remain before China's civilian shipbuilding industry will match those of Japan and South Korea. These include:

- lack of product standardization
- weak basic research capabilities
- low-quality domestically produced components[21]
- low concentration of qualified workers[22]
- outdated shipyards
- micromanagement
- insufficient use of advanced design software/hardware
- inadequate integration of design, production, and management processes.[23]

In addition to these structural problems, commercial shipbuilding design capabilities are said to be less efficient than Japanese and South Korean shipbuilders. Design as a relative cost of total ship cost exceeds 10 percent more for hull design, 12 percent more for piping, and 25–30 percent more for electronics than Japanese and Korean shipyards. This not only increases costs but also lengthens the R&D cycle. It takes an average of 50,000 hours for a Japanese or Korean company to design a ship for the first time, versus 100,000–200,000 hours for a Chinese company.[24] Chinese sources also focus on the difficulties integrating technologies at the product level. Here a major problem is stovepiping caused by inadequate interaction among industry, research institutes and academies, and academia.[25]

Conclusion

China's shipbuilding industry has made impressive progress since 1979. Yet assessments by Chinese analysts describe an industry requiring further reform. Still needed are an additional focus on systems engineering, the linking of actions to specific R&D stages, and coordination among design, R&D, and manufacturing entities. To resolve these issues, China's shipbuilding industry has turned to integrated innovation with its emphasis on systems integration, organizational coordination, and integrated manufacturing processes. Although Chinese analysts understand that the main way for China's shipbuilding industry to develop individual technologies remains the IDAR process, they also realize that the shipbuilding industry must move up the value-added chain by focusing on systems integration and process improvements. With this emphasis, China's shipbuilding industry aspires to put more stress on design and R&D stages in order to achieve product-level innovation.

Although this chapter has focused on civilian shipbuilding due to the paucity of sources on naval shipbuilding, significant differences exist between naval and commercial shipbuilding. Whereas China's commercial shipbuilding has traditionally focused on simpler bulk carriers and oil tankers where price is the most important factor, naval shipbuilding places more emphasis on performance. This requirement is especially important for a navy that seeks to compete with the world-class navies of the United States and Japan. Naval shipbuilding requires technologies not used in the civilian field, such as weapons systems and their supporting subsystems, and even shared technologies such as propulsion systems can be more complex for naval vessels. Naval vessels must also conform to military standards and meet secrecy requirements and be built to withstand the rigors of combat. As Julian Snelder documents in his chapter in this volume, however, China's shipbuilding industry has confronted these challenges by assigning its best engineers to naval programs. As a result, some of the workforce quality and cost concerns cited by commercial shipbuilders may be less applicable to naval shipbuilding. The overall move toward treating R&D as a system rather than a linear process through integrated innovation remains applicable, however, as the military moves to reduce its reliance on foreign technologies.

The implication for the U.S. Navy is that as China's shipbuilding industry continues to learn and apply modern shipbuilding techniques and technologies, it will become less reliant on foreign technologies and more capable of not only building naval vessels on its own, but also building naval vessels of increasingly higher performance to its own standards and requirements. As of

August 2015, China's navy had 303 combatant ships, including 79 large combatants and 64 submarines.[26] The U.S. Navy, on the other hand, had 273 combat ships but hopes to increase this number to 308, to include 99 large combatant ships and 60 submarines.[27] Even if the U.S. Navy is able to maintain an overall numerical advantage, however, its global commitments most likely mean that the PLAN will be able to deploy more ships in a conflict closer to its shores. Under this scenario, even a Chinese navy that is "good enough" may pose a formidable foe if present in sufficient numbers.

Notes

The authors thank Hou-ying Li for gathering sources and assembling graphic inputs.

1. "中共中央关于制定'十一五'规划的建议(全文)" ["Full Text of Chinese Communist Party Suggestions on the 11th Five-year Plan"], http://cpc.people.com.cn/GB/64162/64168/64569/65414/4429220.html.

2. For elaboration on IDAR, see Tai Ming Cheung, "The Role of Foreign Technology Transfers in China's Defense Research, Development, and Acquisition Process," *SITC Policy Brief* 5 (January 2014), http://escholarship.org/uc/item/4dp213kd.

3. Zhao Jinlou, Ke Lixia, and Wang Yingzhao, "基于过程的企业技术引创能力评价指标体系的构建" ["The Construction of Evaluation Index System for Process-based Enterprise Technology Importing and Innovative Ability"], 商业研究 [*Commercial Research*] 377, no. 9 (2008): 99.

4. "船舶科技发展'十一五'规划纲要" ["The Outline for the 11th Five-year Plan for Science and Technology Development"], http://www.msckobe.com/links/china/c9.htm.

5. Zhao, Ke, and Wang, "The Construction of Evaluation Index System," 98.

6. Gan Zhixia and Lu Haijun, "我国国防科技工业自主创新能力的现状及制约因素分析" ["The Present Situation of Our Country's National Defense Science and Technology Industry Indigenous Innovation Capability and Its Limiting Factor"], 科技管理研究 [*Science and Technology Management*], no. 3 (2008): 3–4; "加强国防科技工业自主创新 院士提出五条建议" ["Strengthen National Defense Science and Technology Indigenous Innovation, Academicians Make Five Suggestions"], 人民网 [*People's Net*], March 30, 2006, http://politics.people.com.cn/GB/1027/4252705.html.

7. Zhang Weifeng, "我国船舶制造企业技术创新模式研究" ["Research on Our Country's Shipbuilding Enterprise Innovation Model"], Ph.D. dissertation, Harbin Engineering University (2013), 34.

8. Yaguang Li, Xi Zhao, and Jianmin Qi, "The Integrated Model of Management Accounting Tools Based on Integrated Innovation Theory," *2010 International Conference on Future Information Technology and Management Engineering* (New York: Springer, 2010), 140–41; He Weiping and Liu Yulong, "集成创新理论的研究现状评析" ["Appraisal of the Present Research Situation of the Theory of Integrated Innovation"], 改革战略 [*Reformation and Strategy*] 27, no. 3 (2011): 186.

9. Wang Zhongtuo, "大力发展系统集成创新加速自主创新步伐" ["Greatly Develop System Integrated Innovation to Speed Up the Pace of Indigenous Innovation"], 管理工程学报 [*Journal of Industrial Engineering/Engineering Management*] 24 (2010), Supplement, 8.

10. You Ziping, "舰船总体系统工程的数字化思考" ["Thinking on Digitized Integrated Naval Ship System Engineering"], 舰船科学技术 [*Ship Science and Technology*], no. 2 (2008): 27.

11. Ibid.

12. See Tai Ming Cheung, "The Chinese Defense Economy's Long March from Imitation to Innovation," *Journal of Strategic Studies* 34, no. 3 (June 2011): 345.

13. Xie Wenying, "汪玉: 舰船仿真专家的两个目标" ["Wang Yu: The Two Goals of Ship Simulation"], 检查日报 [*Procuratorial Daily*], http://www.jcrb.com/n1/jcrb842/ca405657.htm.

14. See, for example, "国产新型导弹驱逐舰总师: 我们比美日有差距" ["Chief Engineer for a New Type of Domestically Developed Destroyer: There is a Gap Between Us and the United States and Japan"], *Xinhua*, August 1, 2009, http://news.xinhuanet.com/mil/2009-01/08/content_10622186.htm; "朱英富 舰船大师的航母情怀" ["Zhu Yingfu—An Important Engineer's Feelings on the Aircraft Carrier"], *Character Journal*, April 10, 2014, http://www.rweek.cn/Weeklyx.asp?id=2052.

15. "我国核动力船舶技术已经正式立项" ["Our Country's Ship Nuclear Propulsion Technology Has Formally Begun"], *Research Network*, February 20, 2013, http://m.guancha.cn/Science/2013_02_20_127532.

16. "中船重工集团713所赵世平研究员应邀作国外潜载导弹发射技术前沿报告" ["CSIC 713 Institute's Researcher Zhao Shiping Invited to Write Report on Foreign Missile Launch Technologies"], Beijing Institute of Technology website, January 26, 2015, http://sae.bit.edu.cn/xyxw/55719.htm.

17. China Shipbuilding Research and Development Academy website, May 28, 2014, http://www.csrda.cn.net/MainPage_New/Index.aspx.

18. "中船重工召开第十六次工作会议" ["CSIC Convenes Seventh Work Meeting"], CSIC website, January 28, 2015, http://www.csic.com.cn/zgxwzx/csic_jtxw/304614.htm.

19. "树立装备建设的科学质量观" ["Establish Equipment Building Scientific Quality Concept"], SASTIND website, October 14, 2013, http://www.sastind.gov.cn/n127/n219/c57484/content.html.

20. "中国海军两代驱逐舰总设计师访谈 (1)" ["An Interview with the Chief Engineer of the Chinese Navy's Second Generation Destroyer"], February 27, 2007, http://military.china.com/zh_cn/top01/11053250/20070227/13956164.html.

21. Wan Shuisheng, "着力新船型研发创新做强船舶工业" ["Focus on New Shipbuilding R&D Innovation to Strengthen the Shipbuilding Industry"], 上海造船 [*Shanghai Shipbuilding*], no. 3 (2010): 99.

22. Huang Huaming, "中国船舶工业企业技术创新系统模式研究" ["China Shipbuilding Industry Enterprise Technology Innovation System Model Research"], master's thesis, Harbin Engineering University (2004), 18.

23. Meng Mei, 船舶工业概论 [*Introduction to the Shipbuilding Industry*] (Beijing: Tsinghua University Press, 2013), 151.

24. Ibid., 120.

25. Gan and Lu, "The Present Situation of Our Country's National Defense Science and Technology Industry Indigenous Innovation Capability and Its Limiting Factor, 3–4; "Strengthen National Defense Science and Technology Indigenous Innovation, Academicians Make Five Suggestions"; Wan, "Focus on New Shipbuilding R&D Innovation to Strengthen the Shipbuilding Industry," 99; Zhang, "Research on Our Country's Shipbuilding Enterprise Innovation Model," 35.

26. U.S. Department of Defense, "Asia-Pacific Maritime Security Strategy," August 2015, 12.

27. Ronald O'Rourke, *China Naval Modernization: Implications for U.S. Navy Capabilities—Background and Issues for Congress* (Washington, DC: Congressional Research Service, June 17, 2016), RL33153, 63, http://www.fas.org/sgp/crs/row/RL33153.pdf.

Julian Snelder

China's Civilian Shipbuilding in Competitive Context
An Asian Industrial Perspective

A STUDY OF CHINA's civil shipbuilding industry might appear to be of limited relevance in assessing its naval capabilities. Civil shipbuilding is a commercial enterprise, serving economically motivated customers. Profit is a paramount goal. Navies obviously have different missions and deploy very different technologies. However, there are strong strategic motives to develop civilian industries to undergird the defense sector. This is especially true in East Asia, home to the world's three largest shipbuilding nations. This chapter will show that Chinese privately owned shipyards remain weak compared to their South Korean and Japanese counterparts, so China's large state-owned enterprises (SOEs) will likely spearhead Beijing's maritime strategic-industrial policy. Policymakers seek "spillover" benefits to the military sector too. If China is able to continue its ascent into high-complexity civil products, it will command the technical, economic, and material resources to field a very formidable navy.

The chapter is divided into three parts. First, the phenomenal rise of China's merchant marine industry is briefly analyzed with reference to the latest global shipping cycle. The conduct of customers, shipyards, and financiers is examined along with the role of the Chinese government, in first fostering and then consolidating an industry that is close to crisis once more. The second section is an examination of capabilities. China is enormous, but is it "good" qualitatively? The chapter attempts to address China's capabilities using analytical metrics where possible. The third part will examine the implications of China's trajectory, from both a commercial and a geopolitical perspective.

Background: The World Shipping Cycle

Asia's rise—first Japan, then South Korea, recently China—was long in the making. For a century, the shipbuilding industry has been characterized by long, deep cyclical waves. Each cycle—under British and then American leadership in the first half of the period and Asian in the second—was accompanied by devastating deindustrialization, as successive incumbent leaders failed to adapt to emerging new technologies and cost competition. After 1945 British yards, reliant on riveting techniques and troubled by labor disputes, lost initiative to European rivals deploying welding and immigrant labor. By 1960 Japan emerged as the leader, benefiting from large cranes, a disciplined workforce, improved welding techniques, government export promotion, and new modular techniques of construction in lean *kaizen* mode. Japanese yards could deliver in just 180 days, three times faster than British yards.[1] Catalyzed by the Suez Canal's temporary closure, tremendous expansion of large-ship construction occurred from 1960 to 1975. This boom collapsed in the mid-1970s after the first oil shock. Japan reduced its exposure to shipbuilding between the first and second oil crises, cutting its workforce nearly two-thirds over a decade.[2] By then South Korea was methodically entering the industry.[3]

Hyundai Heavy Industries, starting with basic foreign-purchased templates, adapted designs and internalized engineering know-how therein. Hyundai and its local rivals were quick to recognize growing demand for customization and containerization. Liquefied natural gas carriers (LNGCs) emerged as an important niche, and the South Koreans later pioneered membrane technology while their Japanese counterparts retained Moss-type spherical tanks. By the 1990s South Korea was closing in on Japan in aggregate deliveries. Recognition of quality came a decade later when used South Korean vessels traded at parity with Japanese counterparts in the second-hand market. During the 2000s South Korean yards were well positioned for the revived shipping cycle. They were also moving into offshore oil exploration systems, which they now dominate.

In the last decade, however, by far the most dynamic actor has been China. It is often said that Japan and South Korea, respectively, rode the last two great waves in shipbuilding, and that China's turn has come. This chapter focuses on four major conventional classes (dry bulkships/bulkers, oil/chemical product tankers, container ships, and LNGCs) where most global tonnage is deployed, and three major categories of offshore marine systems (jack-up rigs, deepwater semisubmersible rigs, and drillships). The big three Asian countries combined have around 90 percent of the market thus defined. At its peak, in 2007, they booked almost US$300 billion in orders, up tenfold in a decade. This industry, delivering on average 1,500 large ships, can be envisaged as a pyramid. At its apex are a few dozen high-value specialized systems such as drillships, advanced LNGCs, and floating production/storage/offloading (FPSO) units. China's presence remains limited there, but at the base of the pyramid it is now a global force, delivering hundreds of low- to mid-complexity bulkers, tankers, and container ships each year.

Complexity

Warships are far more complicated and specialized than civilian vessels. A simple bulk tanker may have a compensated gross tonnage (CGT) factor (the ratio of compensated gross tonnage to gross tonnage, an Organisation for Economic Co-operation and Development [OECD] measure of complexity[4]) of 0.3, while a naval combatant could range from ten (a frigate) to an order of magnitude higher (a nuclear submarine).[5] For the last twenty years an average of 100 million deadweight tonnes (dwt) of merchant tonnage has been delivered each year, corresponding to approximately 40 million CGT[6]—that is, roughly an average complexity of 0.4. Prices also reflect complexity. Among the largest civil vessels afloat is the *Valemax*-class bulker, 360 meters long and 400,000 dwt capacity, selling for US$110 million. The largest cruise ships, of similar length, cost ten times more. U.S. aircraft carriers are 333 meters long and cost about ten times more again. Few civilian projects approach such financial magnitude.[7] Clearly the technologies involved in civil and naval building are very different.

Still, lessons can be drawn from studying the civilian sector. There are dual-use transfers of technology. China's large SOEs are active in both civil and naval building. They adopt efficient civil techniques for naval projects.[8] Progress in one field might infer capabilities in another. More profoundly, Chinese leaders understand that "comprehensive national power" emanates from competitive market enterprises across all industries. They know that a Russian-style economy—strong in armaments and resources but weak in consumer products and business services—will ill serve their national development goals. While profit maximization is hardly their principal concern, their economic reforms emphasize market-driven principles. SOEs are instructed to "go out" and make money like their private counterparts. So the emergence of financially successful Chinese enterprises in the shipbuilding sector, both state and private, would provide validation and evidence of the country's continuing economic and technological progress.

Hiding in Plain Sight

Many Asian shipyards discussed in this chapter are publicly listed, so there appears to be plenty of financial information available to dissect performance. Alas, while financial statements do matter, they reveal little about underlying operational performance. Listed companies guard their commercial secrets jealously despite—or perhaps because of—their financial disclosure to the public. In the case of China's mixed civil-military SOE complexes (the main two groups, China Shipbuilding Industry Corporation [CSIC] and China State Shipbuilding Corporation [CSSC], are of particular interest), they are very opaque. Their most sensitive assets, such as their research institutes, are held in unlisted parent entities reporting directly to the State Council.

Some of the information sourced for this chapter is from nonclassified but also nonpublic sources. Commercial and technical knowledge within the civilian sector is available, albeit behind "paywalls." This includes databases published by such sources as IHS and Clarkson. Financial analysts also research the sector, but their reports are seldom distributed. The maritime industry fields many seasoned experts, acting as sole operators or working in consultancy firms, who sell know-how. It is not uncommon to see senior South Korean and Japanese engineers working in China, for instance, or for their senior Chinese SOE counterparts to be moonlighting as advisers to local private shipyards. Significant technology transfer must arise from such free agency. Furthermore, shipping liners often transfer designs from one yard to another.

Methodology

Where possible, public sources are disclosed, but this chapter also exploits research where underlying data is proprietary. Additionally, a series of detailed interviews were conducted with ten analysts and experts: four from South Korea, two from China, two from Japan, one from Singapore, and one from Europe. Although some parochial views were aired, there was general consistency of opinions amongst them, particularly regarding the relative proficiency of Chinese, South Korean, and Japanese commercial yards. They will be quoted directly but anonymously.

The Rise of China's Civil Shipbuilding Industry

Chinese industry responded to the recent global shipping boom with unprecedented expansion of shipbuilding activity. But as demand now recedes, China faces a glut of capacity, exacerbated by subsidies and financial stimulus measures. A crisis is unfolding that will severely challenge the viability of hundreds of Chinese yards.

The "Interrupted" Super Cycle, 2002–13

Merchant shipbuilding exhibits long, brutal cyclicality. Supply-side reasons are obvious: long order lead-times, high fixed costs, and high exit barriers. But the industry is also hostage to ship owners' demand-side behavior. Starting from around 2002, shipping lines underwent staggering expansion as China prepared for World Trade Organization accession. Container ship capacity more than quadrupled from 4 million to 17 million twenty-foot equivalent units (teu) from 1996 to 2013.[9] Liners correctly anticipated an increase in global trade but overshot, creating surplus capacity.

Shipyards embraced the boom, taking orders with gusto. Cresting just before the 2008 financial crisis, South Korean yards had an order backlog of 4.8 years—50 percent of then-current fleet, a level unprecedented in peacetime.[10] Even more striking was China's arrival. Senior leaders from 2002 declared the national aspiration to be a shipbuilding "great power," later formalized in state plans.[11] CSSC announced its "531" goal to become the world's leading shipbuilder by 2015.[12] In 2004 China had only one yard in the world's top fifteen; it has six today. Once a minor player in the large-vessel market, China took half of all new global CGT orders in 2009. In 2005 China had fewer than 20 large docks; by 2012, it had 130.

Today China still sits on nearly 40 percent of global CGT backlog,[13] compared to 30 percent for South Korea and 17 percent for Japan. But this orderbook now is dwindling. 2007 marked the cycle's peak, when more than US$250 billion was ordered across the seven subject vessel types. Yards were booking 10 million CGT in good months. Subsequently came two smaller "echo" cycles. The first arrived in 2009 as easier financing and China's investment stimulus spurred bulker ordering and then tanker buying by European owners and China's own SOE miners and oil companies. The second mini-cycle, starting in

2012, was oil-driven, with increased offshore petroleum activity and the advent of very large, efficient container ships.[14] As oil prices collapsed, remaining support for demand faded. Even as liners launch new 10,000-plus-teu megaships, average recorded container ship speeds have been dialed back from 13 knots to 9.5 knots since 2009.[15] Although this is partly due to regulatory pressure to reduce emissions, slow steaming also reflects an oversupply problem. Most affected is dry bulk. Bulk rates are one-third the level of running costs, and more than ten thousand ships, mostly bulkers, are reported on the resale market today.[16]

Cheap Money and Its Consequences

A catalyst for the revival in demand after the 2008 crisis was the increasingly aggressive use of financing to reactivate customer interest. Fleet owners order ships for many reasons, including freight rates, newbuild prices, and oil price. Another key factor is funding supply. As China's yards faced emptying backlogs but abundant liquidity, they offered aggressive "heavy tail" financing schemes allowing buyers to pay only 10 percent (and even 2 percent) deposit installments with the balance due on delivery.[17] This was a damaging break from the traditional "5 by 20" rule, in which equal 20 percent payments are made at the contract signing, steel-cutting, keel-laying, launching, and delivery stages. Other competitors, especially in South Korea, followed.

The heavy-tail orders were facilitated by low-rate debt financing after 2009 and the entrance of new players such as private equity firms and Chinese institutions.[18] Ship financing traditionally was dominated by European banks, but their shipping loan market share fell from 70 percent to 40 percent in the last decade.[19] Chinese banks' share rose from just 2 percent to 18 percent by 2012; in that year alone Bank of China doubled its exposure to US$24 billion.[20] China became the second largest ship financier (Germany remains larger) and highly supportive of Greek orders at Chinese yards.[21] Eighty-four percent of recent Greek bulker orders went to China.[22]

When China buys, it also "buys from itself."[23] In recent years Chinese domestic buyers have become a bigger customer of Chinese yards than Singapore, Greece, Germany, and Norway (the next four) combined.[24] Seventy percent of Chinese very large crude carrier (VLCC) orders and most of its own high-complexity types such as LNGCs and large container ships are domestic. SOE yards rely on domestic business—especially CSIC, whose backlog is majority local and military.[25] Local experts believe 80 percent of state civil orders go to SOE yards; "private yards just get the crumbs." Like Japan, China may prioritize domestic ordering for its merchant and offshore fleet. Whereas

South Korean yards take orders almost exclusively from international shipping lines and oil companies, 27 percent of Japanese shipyard orders are from Japan. More significantly, 74 percent of Japanese orders go to national yards.[26] If China follows such preferential buying, it may exacerbate overcapacity and prolong rationalization of domestic industry.

Overcapacity and easy money resulted in cutthroat pricing over low-quality, speculative orders.[27] By 2009 it was already apparent that many Chinese shipyards had no backlog beyond 2012 and little prospect of new business, spurring an emergency June 2009 stimulus plan.[28] Chinese completions peaked in 2012 and then plummeted, with utilization already under 50 percent by 2013.[29] Dozens of Chinese private yards today are suspended, with partially completed products, unable to meet specifications or find ongoing working capital.[30] Very few acquired core engineering capability. In the words of one analyst, "No one really knows whether they buy, steal or copy designs . . . but they won't be able to modify them without outside help." Another notes, "CSSC and CSIC use their research institutes for reverse engineering. Privates are their 'little brothers.' SOEs sell them designs for as little as US$150,000, but the drawings will be incomplete." The proliferation of private players during the 2000s is now a major headache for the localities that host them.[31]

A Chinese state research agency notes that the "capacity of top 10 shipbuilding enterprises as a percentage of total capacity declined from 68 percent in 2006 to 38 percent in 2011. In Japan and South Korea, [this figure] was 58 percent and 94 percent respectively. Low concentration has resulted in irrational industrial structure."[32] According to the official industry chamber, "The number of shipyards had fallen to about 1,600 from more than 3,000 in 2012," half with blue-water capacity, of which only 80 received orders in 2013 and only 60 rewarded state export finance.[33] Further consolidation is expected. In September 2014, China's Ministry of Industry and Information Technology announced a "white list" of fifty-one shipyards, twenty-three of them SOEs, that will be targeted for preferential policy treatment.[34] The chief executive officer of Yangzijiang, a private player, predicts "only 20–30 yards are needed. . . . It will take three to five years to get there."

Rongsheng Heavy's Salutary Tale

An ambitious upstart with four drydocks, thirty thousand employees, and over two million CGT of orders on hand in 2012, Rongsheng was then the largest Chinese player and appeared formidable. The author was jokingly told by a South Korean executive in 2010 that he would swap the Hyundai Heavy Industries shipyard at Ulsan for Rongsheng's facility due to its space, layout, large cranes, and subsidies. Although Rongsheng's founder blames "blind expansion" and "a policy U-turn by the government," in reality the company failed in execution.[35] "All of our problems are tied to difficulties with delivering ships," a manager admitted.[36] There have been numerous reports of poor workmanship and of large blocks being reworked or scrapped. Customers lost confidence and canceled orders, and then banks pulled funding lines, forcing the company toward bankruptcy.[37] It is rumored that potential buyers, including CSSC, have considered a rescue for Rongsheng.

What part, if any, the SOEs will play in the roll-up of other defunct private competitors is unclear. However, it seems unlikely that a world-class facility such as Rongsheng will be shuttered.[38] Continuing government support for this "strategic" sector will continue, running the gamut of research and development assistance, financing, materials supply, land, and fiscal and other concessions.[39] Indeed, it has been estimated[40] that while Chinese ships sell at a 7 percent price discount, China's government since 2006 systematically "intervened in its shipbuilding industry and reduced shipyard costs by 15–20 percent."[41] This specific estimate is debatable, but the following broader assertion is substantiated by the multitude of struggling private shipbuilders throughout the country: "China's subsidies amplified the boom and bust in shipping investment in the last decade. Indeed, without its massive increase in shipbuilding capital infrastructure, the backlog would not have increased as dramatically and as a consequence would not have crashed as bad[ly] in the 2008 crisis."

The larger question is whether Rongsheng's predicament will become emblematic of China's national aspiration. As a Chinese interviewee remarked, "We have no shortage of capital, labor, land, steel, ambition . . . or grand plans," but "what looked to be an easy industry turned out to be much more difficult than many imagined." Even as shipyards close, orders had fallen by three-quarters in early 2015, and capacity utilization at the surviving yards is just 60 percent, forcing many to seek government support.[42] If Chinese industry remains reliant on subsidies, it will be highly disruptive and will impose economic burdens globally. Nonetheless, China will continue to be a major player—probably the largest supplier—in the world market.

China's Evolving Civil Shipbuilding Capabilities

Theoretically, it should be easy to gauge a marine supplier's capabilities by how much money it makes. Unfortunately, profits have become a rare luxury. Even the most capable firms, South Korea's top three "heavies," long accustomed to

5–10 percent margins, are struggling to break even today. They make money only in advanced products. Weaker South Korean rivals are under creditor receivership and may be merged.[43] Strong currency and execution problems have not helped, but the principal challenges are overcapacity and competition—especially from China—depressing prices. Still, as noted, there are price differences in the market, reflecting perceptions of quality. Subsidies probably do lower Chinese costs, so financial metrics may not reflect true competence. However, underlying operational metrics should reveal actual skill levels. Both price and cost data are analyzed here. The product offerings of China, Japan, and South Korea are examined to assess where their frontier technologies are positioned. Experts' qualitative views of capabilities are also summarized.

Analytical Measures

New Ship Pricing

Newbuild prices have fallen overall by roughly a third from their 2007 peak, with dry bulkers falling 40–48 percent, a reflection of their simplicity. This segment is where China most directly competes with Japan, with the latter enjoying a substantial quality/reliability margin; both nations have over half of their backlog value in bulkers. According to the experts interviewed, those from China are listed within 5 percent of Japanese products, although customers still prefer smaller Japanese "handies." Chinese tankers are offered at only 3 percent below South Korean and Japanese peers. Container ships sell at 8 to 15 percent less, the gap widening with vessel size.[44] On more complex vessels, Chinese yards must offer a 20 percent discount or more. A South Korean agency estimates that the country can continue to sell advanced types at a 12 to 35 percent premium over China.[45]

Used Ship Pricing

Resale price has fallen even harder than newbuild, reflecting industry stress. The generic secondhand-to-new price ratio fell from 90 percent in 2007 to 60 percent in 2015. Chinese used vessels reportedly are discounted still further, by 20–30 percent versus the generic benchmark.[46] "The real cost of ownership comes when you sell the boat," one expert explains. "You might get a new Chinese ship cheap, but the resale discount will be even steeper." Used price may reflect actual quality better than newbuild prices, which are negotiated ex ante. The preferences of crews for certain brands of ship become more important, because duty performance (reliability, safety, handling, efficiency, etc.) is known. As shipbrokers say, "The market doesn't lie."

Facility Productivity

According to a 2014 South Korean study, Chinese yard productivity still lags.[47] Examining twelve Chinese and six South Korean facilities, this study found a wide dispersion in Chinese completion performance, in vessel/dock, CGT/dock, and CGT/area. The top end of the Chinese range is roughly the average of the South Korean range. Top South Korean yards are about 50–100 percent more productive than top Chinese yards across all three measures. A Worldyards study in 2006 found that "the productivity of the best Chinese yards is roughly one third of the best South Korean and Japanese yards" in CGT/area.[48]

Delivery and Drydock Time

Days-in-drydock is a critical cycle-time in the entire delivery process because the berth is a bottleneck. Shipyards can quicken output by reducing the number of blocks from dozens to just a few "mega-blocks" up to 3,000 tonnes (the limit of most goliath gantry cranes). A Chinese expert reckoned that the fastest docks, such as CSSC's Waigaoqiao, can assemble a hull every forty-five days, versus thirty-five to forty days in South Korea, while less productive Chinese yards take sixty days or longer. Dock cycle signifies asset productivity. Actually, outfitting and commissioning take longer and thus matter more to delivery time. A slower work rate raises amortized fixed cost. For low-complexity ships, Chinese yards can deliver promptly. But for container ships, fleet owners typically budget for 2 years' delivery from South Korea, 2.5 years from Japan, and 3 years for China, on same-ship basis, according to interviews. And for higher complexity classes, the delivery gap is more pronounced.

Direct Labor Cost

Wages vary greatly with currency and across skill levels and sites. South Korean average wages are reckoned at about US$40 an hour—higher than those in Japan at $35, although these likely include overheads. Chinese entry-level hourly wages are much lower at $4 but climb rapidly to $8–$10 with experience. China does have higher general wage inflation in heavy industry, but its labor costs are still only one-quarter of those of its peers. China's real problem, according to industry experts, is that frontline staff turnover can reach 40 percent, even for some SOE yards. This degrades consistency and quality. "Korean workers have been at their jobs for 15 years, but we change all the time," a Chinese specialist complained. Automation is not seen as a panacea: "Few tasks are replicated exactly. [Success] is in design, skill, experience, and general standardization." Where welding automation is applied, "it is *not* for labor saving, but quality, scale and cutting waste. Welds may be 3–4 percent of total steel weight but ten times more [than that] in cost."

Labor Productivity

Direct labor costs (i.e., excluding overheads) for a low-complexity Chinese ship are lower overall (e.g., 10–15 percent versus 20 percent for South Korea), because Chinese yards employ only 20–40 percent more man-hours at one-quarter the wage rate. Chinese success in bulkers and tankers is therefore unsurprising. As complexity rises and experience become more decisive, the productivity gap widens. A semisubmersible rig, which is labor-intensive, takes a competent Chinese yard 8 million work-hours, whereas Singapore takes 5 million and South Korea 2.5 million.[49] Thus for high-complexity types, China's inferior labor productivity offsets its lower wage costs. The importance of learning-curve effects was emphasized in interviews. "It takes 10–20 repeats to halve man-hours" was a widely shared view, and "even the best yard usually makes losses on the first few ships, so taking a series of same-ship orders is very important. . . . margins only rise later." One executive questioned why "China is spreading orders across many yards. . . . they'll have a critical mass problem."

Work-Hours per CGT

An OECD-derived analysis reveals that China was making steady market gains in the 2000s mainly due to a structurally lower unit labor cost per CGT.[50] This edge likely has eroded as China's wage inflation has outpaced productivity gains. Relative currency devaluation by Japan and South Korea has also improved their competitiveness by 30 percent since 2008.[51] Notably, Japan continues to excel in small bulkers and tankers and remains the benchmark for labor efficiency in these types. If South Korea has mastered complexity, Japan has "perfected simplicity." One commonly cited benchmark for productivity is work-hours per CGT. The Chinese government's 2006 plan targeted 15 hours in 2015, a level South Korea achieved in 2007 and Japan even earlier (due to simpler mix). The leanest facility in the world today, Hyundai's Mipo tanker yard, deploys 5 hours (excluding subcontractors), Japan about 6–8, and South Korea targets 7 overall within 5 years. On the other hand, Chinese journals[52] lament that the nation's average remains at about 40–50 work-hours per CGT, although some yards far surpass this and are believed to already meet the 15–20 range.

Use of Subcontractors

An analytical problem in comparing productivity levels is that China's private shipbuilders tend to use contractors more extensively. South Korea's "Big 3" limit contracting to a maximum of about 25–30 percent of work, and Japan allows less, but in China's private yards outsourcing can reach 50 percent during activity peaks.[53] This helps to manage costs but creates high staff turnover, eroding experience, skill levels, and productivity. Chinese SOEs seldom send work outside.

Steel

Steel's contribution to total cost varies with complexity: it can be 30 percent of a double-hulled VLCC's cost but just 5 percent for drillships.[54] China's vast steel industry is oversupplied, and domestic plate price has collapsed to US$400/ton, yet steel is not viewed as a major source of Chinese advantage. Asian nations buy and sell steel plate among themselves, resulting in efficient arbitrage. Because Japanese plate is regarded as superior quality, it is priced at a 5 to 10 percent premium and is often used for external hulls where surface finish is critical. Chinese mild steel is cheaper for internal sections. China still must import specialty alloys, specifically high-tensile steel for jack-up legs, and nickel steels for petrochemical and cryogenic liquefied natural gas (LNG) tanks.

Components

Major subsystems comprise 40 percent of the total cost of even a simple vessel. The global market is highly concentrated, with European companies such as GTT and Alfa-Laval dominating LNG membrane containment and auxiliary systems respectively. European leadership is most notable in main engines (10–15 percent of total cost). MAN commands three-quarters of the low-speed reciprocating market, Wärtsilä most of the rest. The pair pursue a licensing strategy in Asia, with Chinese and South Korean original equipment manufacturers typically employing designs from both vendors. Only Hyundai, Mitsubishi, and Kawasaki have seriously attempted to self-develop engine technology. "Self-developed" Chinese engines are emerging at the low end of the bulker/tanker market, but foreign buyers seldom select them. In recent years, five Chinese builders—the CSIC shipyards at Dalian, Qingdao, and Yichang and the CSSC yard at Hudong and CSSC-Mitsui—have become significant players in marine engines, climbing from a 20 percent global market share in 2010[55] to almost 40 percent by 2013,[56] challenging South Korea's Hyundai, Doosan, and STX trio. They have benefited from the proliferation of Wärtsilä and MAN facilities onshore and attractive licensing terms.

Today Chinese factories can produce Wärtsilä RT-series engines with cylinder bore of 900 millimeters (mm), up from 600mm five years ago. China once imported 70 percent of its engines from South Korea. Now customers increasingly choose a European-licensed engine built in China at a 20 percent lower price and satisfactory quality and efficiency.

Still, China's government worries about dependence on imported technology. Its 2006 plan projected having 80 percent domestic content by 2015. A South Korean survey assesses Chinese industry as being 55 percent localized, versus 80 percent for South Korea and 90 percent in Japan.[57] Official Chinese assessments concur, with an estimate in 2010 of "60 percent, significantly lower than 85 percent of Japan and South Korea." Moreover, except for deck machinery, outfitting, and engines (which, as noted, are licensed), where localization rates surpassed 50 percent, the "localization rate of other ship equipment was low . . . electrical and electronic equipment at 13 percent, cabin equipment at 19 percent and communication, navigation and automation at only 2 percent. China's marine products lack competitiveness in the market."[58] A State Council paper criticizes the industry for "building empty shells."[59] There is widespread recognition that Chinese vessels are sturdy but also relatively noisy, dirty, and inefficient. Some Chinese authors perceive a "technology blockade" from advanced competitors,[60] and several interviewees agreed with one that "environmental and safety regulations led by Europe, the United States and IMO [International Maritime Organization] might be used to thwart the challenge of Chinese shipbuilding and shipping." Moving up the technology curve therefore is a national priority.

Product Range and Upgrading

Chinese industry aims to escape its current confinement to low- and mid-complexity systems. State leaders declare that technological upgrading is imperative "to meet intense and cruel competition in the future."[61] While Chinese industry explores premium niches such as cruise ships,[62] its capability would best be demonstrated over three mainstream types: large efficient container ships, LNGCs, and drillships.

Large Efficient Container Ships

The Panama Canal's expansion, new environmental measures,[63] and aggressive ordering by Maersk triggered a trend from 2011 toward ultra large container ships (ULCs). Today it is common to see 20,000 teu ULCs ordered, with even larger ones on the horizon.[64] Substantial fuel savings are claimed; bunker fuel comprises the majority of operating costs, although most of the fuel conservation actually results from lower steaming speed.[65] But technical differences do matter. The numerous, capacious internal holds of ULCs require more, and better, welding than a bulker or tanker. South Koreans claim a 6–10 percent fuel saving over Chinese counterparts in propulsion efficiency, and another 4–8 percent in hydrodynamic efficiency.[66] South Korea commands this "eco-ship" segment, with the forty largest ULCs contracted today all at South Korean–operated yards. But increasingly China will compete here. Yangzijiang surprised the market in 2011, sharing Seaspan's order for 10,000 teu ULCs.[67] Its execution impressed some observers, although others criticize the series' design for underperforming international standards. CSSC is building three 18,000 and five 14,500 teu ships (all for Chinese SOE customers). China Ocean Shipping Company (COSCO) recently tendered for eleven 20,000 teu ships at four local SOE yards.[68] Yangzijiang was not invited; to date it has not won any ULC orders since 2011. Japan's Imabari is also constructing a new drydock expressly targeting the class.[69]

LNG Carriers

Gas carriers, too, are upsizing. Previous generations were limited to 150,000 cubic meters; now top South Korean yards can deliver in the 266,000-cubic-meter class. Only one Chinese yard, CSSC-Hudong, is constructing large LNGCs today, and its delivery commitment is five years, twice the South Korean schedule. But CSSC has high ambitions in this category. Its chief designer claims, "In future, our output will outstrip Japan and Korea."[70] A surprising feature of China's LNG initiative is that Japan is actively assisting it. Hudong's 2011 anchor customers included Mitsui OSK Line, possibly for "political reasons."[71] Japanese technical expertise was offered. Kawasaki will shift LNGC construction to its Nantong COSCO KHI Ship Engineering Co., Ltd., joint-venture yard in China where it claims costs are 20 percent lower than in Japan.[72] The technological art in LNGCs is to maximize insulation of the cooled gas and to utilize any "boil-off" vapor for main engine fuel. South Korean firms command the insulated panel market. First with Wärtsilä's dual-fuel and now MAN's ME-GI technology, South Korea's Daewoo led the use of efficient reciprocating engines (rather than steam turbines) to harness LNG as a clean fuel.[73] The alloy containment tanks in LNGCs must be welded with exceptional integrity. Some interviewees believe Hudong is struggling with the process and uses only female welders, who are reputedly more patient. South Korean yards use robotic welders for flat sections; this is one reason membrane tanks are cheaper than Moss spheres.

Drillships

China's SOE yards have scooped recent jack-up rig orders, supposedly by offering low prices and easy financing to speculative drilling debutantes,[74] and they are already fairly capable in semisubmersibles. But drillships present a daunting technological challenge.[75] CSSC-Shanghai took two orders from a local company in 2012; the first was delivered in late 2014.[76] Its specifications are modest in terms of water depth and displacement, and its rumored US$200–$300 million price is far below South Korean billings. Little is known about the proficiency of this vessel, which CSSC claims is built entirely with Chinese know-how.[77] However, ABB is providing the dynamic propulsion system, and Cameron and other vendors supply critical plant. Even in South Korea, which has built 80 percent of all drillships ordered, around 70 percent of the ship's value is imported equipment. Integrating these components into a compact hull is complex by civil standards. Most interviewees expressed skepticism about CSSC's profitability in this line. According to customers, Samsung today requires 1.5 million hours[78] and targets 1.1 million. Singaporeans need 3 million for their Brazil ships, and CSSC might need 4 million. Singapore and South Korea remain confident of their offshore edge.[79] Chinese assessments acknowledge that, despite some breakthroughs in marine engineering equipment, "China's core technologies are weak and [remain] severely reliant on overseas countries."[80]

Qualitative Expert Assessment: Design Capability, Talent, and Planning Are Decisive

Industry experts interviewed all concur that the key ingredient for civil shipbuilding success is not cheap inputs, but intelligent planning of complex workflows and procedures. This requires an experienced critical mass of engineering design capability, able to quickly modify core design elements in-house. South Korea's Big 3 each has around 3,000 such experts. Interviewees agreed that Chinese industry probably has no more than this number, dispersed across many sites.

"Everything starts with production design and planning. Private yards don't have detailed design capability. Only the SOEs do, but the Navy gets priority," was a typical statement, and "Global customers probably aren't seeing what China's real skill levels are." Several experts shared the sentiment that "critical mass is 500 engineers capable of site inspection. CSIC and CSSC have maybe 1,000 each, but their best talent is allocated to the military." Another thought was, "Don't compare civils welding 20mm plate with Dalian welding

60mm armor plate. CSIC might still run largely on Soviet lines, but that's why Dalian is competent in offshore [platforms]." However, SOE talent is also thought to be poorly allocated: "SOEs have their engineers located centrally in research institutes, sometimes literally in the middle of China. The Koreans are sitting dockside, a huge advantage."

There is a consensus that China will catch up in some segments; indeed, at the low end it already has. But opinions vary over its potential in high-complexity types. Some interlocutors consider Chinese claims to be ambitious, even overreaching: "CSSC-Waigaoqiao first advertised FPSOs fifteen years ago. They have sold just three." However, others warn that "Koreans overestimate their lead. China can't do high-end segments yet but they will master most within a decade."

Exhibit 10-1. Experts' Assessment of China Capability Gap versus Class Leader

Category	Leader	How far behind is China's capability as of today? Static assessment (years as of 2015)	How long will it take China to catch up? Dynamic assessment (years as of 2015)
Bulker	Japan	0–2	0–3
Tanker	Japan/Korea	1–4	2–5
Containership	Korea	2–5	3–7
Liquefied natural gas carrier	Korea	4–8	5–15
Jack-up rig	Singapore	2–5	3–7
Semisubmersible rig	Korea	3–6	5–10
Drillship	Korea	6–10	10–20

Source: Expert interviews, 2015.

Conclusions and Implications: Will China Rule the Waves?

Chinese leaders study carefully, and self-consciously, the historical rise and fall of great powers.[81] They are well aware of the role of sea power and likely entertain greater global maritime ambitions than did, say, the Soviet Union, which recognized its own condition as "the largest continental state in the world" and accordingly constrained its vision of sea dominance to only those oceanic areas "vital to the assertion of Soviet interests."[82] China, by contrast, is the world's leading mercantile trader. State command of wealth stems from national savings at historically unprecedented rates,[83] heavy tax exaction,[84] and an apparently robust fiscal position.[85] Financial abundance ultimately may be curbed by slowing growth, demographic aging, and rising levels of indebtedness, but for the next decade or two the central government will have vast economic resources at its disposal. China's gross domestic savings are almost double those of the United States at current market prices.[86] On a purchasing power parity basis, the gap is starker still.

Even so, China, like its peers, will face the inexorable escalation in the unit costs of naval combatant systems—and therefore will experience material constraints to relative naval power—that Philip Pugh observed from the Napoleonic era onward: "While budgets are rising, the cost of military equipment is rising faster still. . . . Navies will continue to exist with each being the size and strength commensurate with the ability of their national economies to pay for them."[87]

The dynamic in merchant shipping is different (unit freight rates fall as ships expand) but as China militarizes its presence on the seas, it must also submit to the naval cost spiral problem that arises from security competition. The microeconomic effectiveness of its shipbuilding industry thus becomes instrumental to its strategic aims.

China's industry now stands at a threshold. Beijing must simultaneously undertake a major shakeout of overcapacity while enlarging a few groups into internationally competitive enterprises. This is likely to be a state-led restructuring process in which SOE "national champions" will play a major role. However, it is not certain that such firms will become truly viable or trusted in the global market. Protectionism and subsidies may increase, generating geopolitical friction. Some of the technological limitations evident in China's civilian industry may also hamper its naval efforts.

Too Much, Too Soon?

The industry has grown tremendously. But today it is fundamentally challenged by overcapacity and remains constrained in low- and mid-complexity segments. It arrived late, but in full force, to the last shipping boom. Now it suffers a hangover.

Chinese shipbuilding faces several dilemmas. The industry is simultaneously too large and too small. It remains highly fragmented, but with the playing field still tilting heavily toward gigantic SOEs. Its most capable engineering resources are bureaucratized and centralized in SOE research institutes far from actual shipyard construction and shielded from market pressure. Exuberant expansion has become a major problem as the shipping cycle retreats, with few positive catalysts in the near future. "China blew its bull market on low-end ships," noted a European specialist, but "didn't benefit from learning-curve effects on advanced projects." If this prognosis holds, Chinese industry may peak prematurely, facing a long wait until the next global super-cycle. China's booming "new economy" is already luring staff from this "sunset" industry. This could impede formation of a stable, experienced, skilled workforce. A local expert criticizes China's "agricultural mentality" and asserts that the country needs "loyalty, precision and discipline to continually improve our quality." Meanwhile, rivals in South Korea continue to invest heavily in technology, and Japan is rebuilding capability with a comprehensive rejuvenation program.

Japan and South Korea demonstrate the importance of human capital development and retention. South Korea has cultivated 120,000 skilled staff in its industry.[88] By contrast, Japan's workforce has dwindled to about one-third that number.[89] A decade ago, half of Japan's shipyard workforce was over fifty years old, a proportion surely higher today. China's workforce is relatively youthful but, as noted, it is mobile. To replicate Japan and South Korea's merchant marine development success, China would need to foster multiple enterprises each with thousands of experienced marine engineers capable of top-to-bottom design and production engineering, overseeing tens of thousands of skilled tradespeople. Considering its 480,000-member shipbuilding workforce, this sounds feasible, but the key challenge will be the cultivation of a stable corps of expert design engineers. South Korea graduates around 1,800 each year from over 54 separate institutions (roughly 2,800 admissions).[90] China, with a much larger population, enrolls 2,500–3,000 undergraduates annually in naval architecture and ocean engineering degree programs.[91] Its scale is advantageous, but not decisively so.

Serving the Nation

South Korean and Japanese specialists dismiss Chinese private shipyards, viewing them as speculative financial endeavors. So far, the Chinese private yards have manifestly failed—lacking the scale, capabilities, patience, and motivation—to match their foreign counterparts. Increasingly, Chinese policymakers also may doubt whether the nation can or should rely on its private sector to undertake consolidation and innovation. "We need our own Lockheed Martins," says the entrepreneur who acquired China's first aircraft carrier.[92] Yet while the state officially welcomes private firms into the defense market, today the reverse seems more likely: Beijing will lean on SOEs to drive civil shipbuilding development.[93] Industrial policies have always been at this sector's forefront, with five major guidelines announced since 2012 alone. In addition to subsidies and customer financing to support local shipbuilders, numerous other programs, such as scrapping incentives, have been introduced.[94] Two other potential policy measures would be especially significant: SOE restructuring and national fleet purchases.

SOE Restructuring

In the last few months there has been increasing speculation, to repeated denials, that CSSC and CSIC are to be re-merged.[95] The supposed rationale for their complementary integration is that the northern-based CSIC remains stronger in research and military systems while the southern-central CSSC is commercially savvier and has built an attractive suite of component factories. Whatever transpires ultimately, the two companies are pursuing internal reforms to concentrate control while exposing themselves to the capital markets.[96] One possibility is that the CSIC and CSSC research and design institutes are injected into the listed entities to improve their commercialization. Only 45 percent of these two groups, by assets and profits, is listed today.[97] The trend is toward public financing or "mixed ownership"—and possibly more transparency—for naval yards.[98] Beijing prioritizes "national champions" once again. In shipbuilding the champions are much more likely to be listed SOEs than private companies.

China's "strategic sectors" will remain nationalized. Reforms are intended to make SOEs more efficient, commercially responsive, and profitable. Meanwhile, policymakers argue for Chinese shipbuilders to "intensify, diversify and integrate," and note approvingly the conglomerated nature of South Korean and Japanese firms.[99] The high-profile "Made in China 2025" plan further aims to pursue advanced sectors, including "maritime engineering and high-tech vessel manufacturing."[100] This will be a costly undertaking. The compatibility of these aims remains questionable. Moreover, CSIC and CSSC both straddle the civil and military sectors in a way few foreign firms successfully achieve. To be sure, South Korean and Japanese firms do participate in defense projects, but their primary focus is the commercial sector, where procurement is very different. Chinese leaders probably aspire for CSIC and CSSC to evolve into true world-class hybrids—Samsung Heavy plus General Dynamics, say—in the state's grasp.

Yet the best Chinese companies—notably in information and communications technology—have been private, emerging in the shadows of giant SOEs. State capitalism typically excels at concentrating resources but struggles to handle innovation and competition that arise organically in the marketplace. It is hard to see how Beijing can foster competition and "market-based pricing" in naval procurement when, for example, CSIC's 701 Institute in Wuhan has produced all China's recent frigate, destroyer, and conventional submarine designs.[101] There is obviously tension between market-oriented objectives and re-merger of monopoly SOEs in nuclear engineering and locomotives. Systematic policies to create national champions have occasionally yielded success elsewhere (e.g., Airbus)—but only rarely. Shipbuilding is a notoriously difficult business. Both private and foreign shipbuilders, including South Korean firms, have struggled in China. The interviewees' unanimous verdict: "It is exceedingly tough to make money in this industry, especially in China, even for the best companies."

Expanding Sovereign Shipping Lines

Beijing may also expand self-buying, aimed at increasing the national fleet using locally produced ships, following Tokyo's postwar industrial policy. A recent State Council opinion paper recommends exactly this course.[102] China relies much more on foreign lines for vital sea imports than Japan: 65 percent versus 20 percent in crude oil, and 90 percent versus 32 percent in iron ore.[103] Central planners believe a sovereign fleet mitigates supply risks. China is the world's largest merchandise exporter; its policymakers ask why its two container liners are ranked only sixth and seventh globally, and may conclude they need greater "economies of scale."[104] However, China Shipping Container Lines and COSCO, laboring under debt/equity burdens of 100 percent and 200 percent respectively,[105] already depend on subsidies.[106] China's government can invest through alternative channels, of course. Rather than purchase cheap second-hand vessels, Beijing would fund newbuild orders to its own shipyards. The result would be more capacity into an already glutted shipping and shipbuilding market. This will not be welcomed. State-directed ordering of new VLCCs starting in 2011 was criticized abroad as "wholly irresponsible and unnecessary."[107]

A Maritime and Naval Power

A Great White Fleet

Beyond trade friction, an aggressive shipbuilding policy might indirectly heighten tensions. A recent mandate requires new Chinese merchant ships to be interoperable with the People's Liberation Army Navy in case of emergency mobilization.[108] With government encouragement, Chinese ventures plan giant factory-ships for fishing waters as distant as Antarctica.[109] Beijing may deem that these fleets require "rights protection" escort support. China has recently consolidated its paramilitary and constabulary maritime services, and the new China Coast Guard fleet is likely to be both prolific and vigorous,[110] with 25 percent quantitative growth forecast even as older, less advanced ships continue to be replaced by improved models.[111] State Council researchers explicitly recommend military and paramilitary expansion as a means to "digest capacity" and to integrate military and civil techniques.[112] Many Chinese shipyards can build light patrol craft, large trawlers, barges, and dredgers. They would welcome new orders to build up China's strategically emphasized "maritime economy." Extending this concept, researchers at the aforementioned 701 Institute even propose floating seabases to demarcate and secure China's "maritime space."[113] Because the actors in Chinese maritime endeavors are diverse,[114] including state-sponsored fishing enterprises, oil companies, and local governments, Beijing can spread the financial costs of coordinated oceanic activities to such agencies' ample budgets, allowing the central government budget to focus on "hard" naval capabilities.

Good Enough for Export

Another consequence of a determined shipbuilding policy could be an increased Chinese presence in the low end of the arms export market, where offering "good-enough" products at low prices would help to keep berths busy. Examples include corvettes made at Hudong for Algeria's navy.[115] Lloyd's Register supervised the various CSSC design bureaus and applied international naval classification standards. While this is a military design built in a military yard, some interviewees contend that such practice conceivably could be extended to civil yards in China, supporting a building boom in light naval ships both for China and export.

Civil Shipbuilding as a Gauge of China's Naval Prowess

Although most defense sectors pursue the concept of civil-military integration, in reality technologies differ substantially. Nevertheless, there are civilian observations to read-across to the naval side. To begin with, although Asian experts are highly critical of general U.S. shipbuilding practices and productivity ("three times too expensive" was their common assessment), they acknowledge American leadership in certain complex subsystems such as offshore oil drilling equipment. Notably, lightweight gas turbine engines are essential for some naval craft. China relies mainly on Russia for military turbine sets, and it is nearly absent from the industrial utility segment, where GE commands half the market and Siemens and Mitsubishi-Hitachi most of the rest.[116] The development of competitive gas turbines for marine and aviation applications represents a key test for China's defense complex.

Chinese merchant ships are praised as "rugged" and have avoided the embarrassing structural failures recently experienced by Japanese[117] and South Korean[118] peers. "China has its own standards, and they seem to work," one consultant said. But as this chapter has documented, Chinese vessels are still perceived as inferior in quality and efficiency, and also in noise, vibration, and hydrodynamic performance. The latter problems stem from various possible causes (e.g., engine bearings, propeller design, hull detail) and result in an enlarged acoustic profile. That would be a serious concern for a naval shipbuilder. In auxiliary systems too—thrusters, ballast, pumping, cooling, desalination, navigation, and so forth—China is not self-sufficient. Individually, these subsystems may not be "strategic," but collectively, they determine whether vessels and platforms can stay at sea for long voyages or operational missions and whether they can safely visit foreign ports.

Chinese industry recognizes all these limitations. Chinese economic reformers also acknowledge that it will not be easy (nor even desirable) for the country to achieve capitalist outcomes within institutions that primarily serve the party-military-state complex. For example, China's large civil airliner enterprise (Commercial Aircraft Corporation of China, or COMAC) was deliberately separated from its parent SOE (Aviation Industry Corporation of China, or AVIC), precisely because the requisite skills and organizational culture were thought very different from serving the People's Liberation Army, which prioritizes other requirements. Yet it is possible that AVIC could become a more effective competitor in defense than COMAC can be in the commercial segment. In other words, civil and military markets are different; success or failure in one may not necessarily impinge on the other. It is not clear to this author whether, or to what degree, problems experienced in the civil industry extend to China's naval shipbuilding realm. What is obvious is China's attempt to shift toward more market-oriented performance but with greater centralized oversight, and this will be a difficult balancing act. Interviewees noted that CSIC and CSSC allocate their best engineers to navy projects; probably this applies to their entire workforce. Staff allocated there certainly have higher status or prestige and likely work under a different regimen from their civil counterparts and especially from those in private yards. The Japanese and later the South Korean "heavies" succeeded with a military culture of discipline. Perhaps the Chinese draw this as their conclusion.

Notes

1. Teruhiko Nishimura, "Widening Gap between Japanese and South Korean Shipbuilders," Credit Suisse, August 31, 2007.

2. Shipbuilders' Association of Japan (SAJ), http://www.sajn.or.jp/e/.

3. Lars Bruno and Stig Tenold, "The Basis for South Korea's Ascent in the Shipbuilding Industry, 1970–90," Norwegian School of Economics and Business Administration, http://www.ebha.org/ebha2010/code/media_168359_en.pdf.

4. Organisation for Economic Co-operation and Development (OECD), "Compensated Gross Ton (CGT) System," 2007, http://www.oecd.org/industry/ind/37655301.pdf.

5. Bulkers and tankers are usually specified in dwt units, container ships in teu, and LNGCs in cubic meters, so CGT is often used as normalizing baseline. Analysts assume a rough CGT/dwt factor of 0.6 for South Korean yards. Department of Defense (DoD), *Global Shipbuilding Industrial Base Benchmarking Study—Part I: Major Shipyards* (Washington, DC: DoD, May 2005), http://www.nsrp.org/5-ad_hoc/benchmarking/fmi-global_industrial_benchmarking-major_yards-navy-rpt.pdf.

6. This ready rule is not identical to OECD's calculation, which indexes gross tonnage, actually a volume measure: http://www.worldyards.com/notesoncgt.php.

7. LNG-FPSO platform *Prelude*, 488 meters long and displacing 600,000 tonnes under full load, cost Shell US$10 billion–$12 billion including installation setup. See "Shell's Record-Breaking *Prelude* Takes to the Water," *BBC*, December 4, 2013, http://www.bbc.com/news/technology-25213845.

8. Morgan Clemens, Gabe Collins, and Kristen Gunness, "The Type 054/054A Frigate Series: China's Most Produced and Deployed Large Modern Surface Combatant," *China SignPost*™ 93, August 2, 2015, http://www.chinasignpost.com/2015/08/02/the-type-054054a-frigate-series-chinas-most-produced-and-deployed-large-modern-surface-combatant/.

9. Aaron Ibbotson, "Navigating a Boomless Recovery," Goldman Sachs, October 10, 2013.

10. Sangkyoo Park, "Order Book Years to Decline Sharply," Morgan Stanley, September 22, 2008.

11. COSTIND, "Long and Medium Term Plan for Shipbuilding Industry (2006)," http://www.beinet.net.cn/zcfg/gh/qggh/200802/P020080423597953846572.pdf.

12. CSSC, "中国船舶工业集团公司发展综述" ["Summary of the Development of CSIC"], July 5, 2005, http://www.gov.cn/test/2005-07/05/content_12081.htm.

13. About 30 percent by value, reflecting its lower mix.

14. "South Korea Shipbuilders Harness Much-Needed Tailwind," *Financial Times*, October 21, 2013, http://www.ft.com/intl/cms/s/0/afbf7bfe-37e0-11e3-8668-00144feab7de.html#axzz3Vw6FJJlU.

15. Bloomberg Energy data series.

16. "Shipowner Warns Private Equity," *Financial Times*, March 30, 2015, http://www.ft.com/intl/cms/s/0/92b08e0e-d48d-11e4-8be8-00144feab7de.html#axzz3Vw6FJJlU.

17. "China Shipyards Hurt by Low Down Payments," *Bloomberg*, July 22, 2013, http://www.bloomberg.com/news/articles/2013-07-21/china-shipyards-squeezed-by-low-down-payments-amid-credit-crunch.

18. "Shipowners Anchor Themselves," *Financial Times*, April 1, 2015, http://www.ft.com/intl/cms/s/0/78588538-d498-11e4-9bfe-00144feab7de.html#axzz3Vw6FJJlU.

19. Yong-suk Son, "Asian Shipbuilders," UBS, February 2014.

20. "China's Exim Bank to Lend More," *Wall Street Journal*, June 3, 2014, http://www.wsj.com/articles/chinas-exim-bank-to-lend-more-to-greek-shipowners-1401796164.

21. "China Attracts Greek Shipping Giants," *Wall Street Journal*, October 1, 2013, http://www.wsj.com/articles/SB10001424052702303918804579106732244443344.

22. Sokje Lee, "Debt Crisis of Greece a Problem for Shipbuilding?" JP Morgan, April 20, 2015.

23. "China's State Shipyards," *Bloomberg*, August 6, 2013, http://www.bloomberg.com/news/articles/2013-08-06/china-s-state-shipyards-help-widen-lead-over-korea-in-orders.

24. Terence Park, "Asian Shipbuilding," CLSA, October 4, 2013.

25. Ibid.

26. Yong-suk Son, "Asian Shipbuilders."

27. "China's Shipbuilders See Wave of New Orders but Profitability Is Low," *Caixin*, November 3, 2014, http://english.caixin.com/2014-11-03/100746130.html.

28. Ministry of Industry and Information Technology, 船舶工业调整和振兴规划 [Shipbuilding Industry Restructuring and Revitalization Plan], June 9, 2009, http://www.gov.cn/zwgk/2009-06/09/content_1335839.htm.

29. "China's Young, Burly Shipyards Sinking Fast," *Caixin*, May 10, 2012, http://english.caixin.com/2012-05-10/100388707.html.

30. "Shipyards in China Are Risk," *Reuters*, April 6, 2014, http://www.reuters.com/article/2014/04/06/us-china-shipping-refunds-insight-idUSBREA350MZ20140406.

31. "China Vows to Turn Tide on Flood of Ships," *Financial Times*, November 4, 2011, http://www.ft.com/intl/cms/s/0/0021452c-0611-11e1-adoe-00144feabdco.html#axzz3Vw6FJJlU.

32. 陈朔帆 [Chen Shuofan], "中国船舶工业的产业链重构" ["Restructuring China's Shipbuilding Industry Chain"], 中国船检 [*China Ship Survey*], no. 6 (June 2014): 57–59.

33. "China's Shipbuilding Industry Faces Further Consolidation," *South China Morning Post*, February 27, 2015, http://www.scmp.com/business/china-business/article/1725245/chinas-shipbuilding-industry-faces-further-consolidation.

34. "Yards Picked for Special Treatment," *South China Morning Post*, September 5, 2014, http://www.scmp.com/business/china-business/article/1585459/china-picks-shipyards-special-treatment.

35. "Rongsheng Boss: Problems Linked to Blind Expansion, Gov't Policies," *Caixin*, March 12, 2015, http://english.caixin.com/2015-03-12/100790700.html.

36. "Ghost Ship," *Caixin*, March 11, 2015, http://english.caixin.com/2015-03-11/100790192.html.

37. "Rongsheng Reports Negative Revenues," *Bloomberg*, March 31, 2015, http://www
.bloomberg.com/news/articles/2015-03-31/china-rongsheng-reports-negative-sales
-on-order-cancellations.

38. "Is Rongsheng Too Big to Fail?" *Reuters*, July 7, 2013, http://www.reuters.com/arti
cle/2013/07/07/us-rongsheng-government-idUSBRE9660IB20130707.

39. Yin-Chung Tsai, "The Shipbuilding Industry in China," *OECD Papers* 3, no. 16 (2010):
37–69, http://www.oecd-ilibrary.org/economics/the-shipbuilding-industry-in-china_
gen_papers-2010-5kg6z7tg5w5l.

40. "Tilted Marine," *Economist*, August 9, 2014, http://www.economist.com/news/
finance-and-economics/21611109-new-techniques-show-damage-done-subsidies
-heart-global.

41. Myrto Kalouptsidi, "Detection and Impact of Industrial Subsidies: The Case of World
Shipbuilding," Department of Economics, Princeton University, March 2014, http://
sites.utexas.edu/harrington-io-conference/files/2014/03/Paper-10-March-2014.pdf.

42. "China Shipbuilding Sector Set to Contract," *Bloomberg*, April 30, 2015, http://www
.bloomberg.com/news/articles/2015-04-30/china-shipbuilding-industry-is-set-to
-contract-yangzijiang-says.

43. "Lenders Set to Create Korean Yard Leviathan," *Tradewinds News*, March 6, 2015,
http://www.tradewindsnews.com/weekly/355464/lenders-set-to-create-korean-yard
-leviathan.

44. Additional discounts often are conceded on list prices.

45. Korea Export-Import Bank (KEXIM).

46. Five-year-old bulker/tanker, ten-year-old container ship.

47. Yong-suk Son, "Asian Shipbuilders"; KEXIM.

48. Gao Zhangpeng and Matthew Flynn, *Lloyd's Shipping Economist*, June 2006.

49. Terence Park and Saurabh Chugh, "Docking in China," CLSA, October 4, 2013.

50. Liping Jiang and Siri Strandenes, "Assessing the Cost Competitiveness of China's
Shipbuilding Industry," September 2011, University of Southern Denmark, https://
ideas.repec.org/p/sdk/wpaper/111.html.

51. Sokje Lee, "Asian Shipbuilding Industries," JP Morgan, November 25, 2014.

52. 满颖 [Man Ying], "高成本时代的中国造船" ["The High Cost Era in Chinese
Shipbuilding"], 中国船检 [*China Ship Survey*], no. 2 (February 2011): 40–42, http://
www.shipol.com.cn/jszl/lwbg/177086.htm.

53. Cheryl Lee, "Comparing Shipyards," UBS, September 6, 2012.

54. Sangkyoo Park, "South Korean Yards Have Shifted Focus," Morgan Stanley, December
12, 2013.

55. Interview with Youngsoo Han, financial analyst, Samsung Securities.

56. Japan Institute of Marine Engineers, http://www.mesj.or.jp/e/publication/yearbook/
yb/pdf08/YB08_2.pdf.

57. Korea Offshore and Shipbuilding Association (KOSHIPA).

58. Man, "The High Cost Era in Chinese Shipbuilding."

59. 马淑萍、项安波 [Ma Shuping and Xiang Anbo], 国务院发展研究中心企业所 [Enterprise Research Institute, State Council Development Research Center], "发展船舶工业: 技术创新与产业转型升级亟需提高" ["Develop the Shipping Industry: It Is Urgently Necessary to Raise the Level of Technical Innovation and Industrial Restructuring and Upgrading"], 中国发展观察 [China Development Watch] via 中国经济新闻网 [China Economic News Net], September 17, 2014, http://www.cet.com.cn/wzsy/qwfb/qwfb/1313291.shtml.

60. 张为峰, 吕开东 [Zhang Feng and Liu Kaidong], "中国船舶工业发展趋势及企业生产经营建议" ["Proposals on the Development Trend of Shipbuilding Manufacture and Management in China"], 船舶工程 [Ship Engineering] 33, no. 2 (2013): 1–5.

61. "China's Shipbuilders Need Technology to Keep Edge," South China Morning Post, November 10, 2011, http://www.scmp.com/article/984425/chinas-shipbuilders-need-technology-keep-edge.

62. "Chinese Shipbuilder Joins Carnival Cruise Venture," Financial Times, October 15, 2014, http://www.ft.com/intl/cms/s/0/2543c0b6-5427-11e4-84c6-00144feab7de.html#axzz3Vw6FJJlU.

63. International Maritime Organization (IMO), Global Maritime Energy Efficiency Protocol GLOMEEP, http://glomeep.imo.org.

64. "24,000 TEU Ships on the Way," Shipping Watch, October 16, 2014, http://shippingwatch.com/carriers/Container/article7115808.ece.

65. Marine Environment Protection Committee, 62nd session, July 11–15, 2011, IMO, http://www.imo.org/en/MediaCentre/MeetingSummaries/MEPC/Pages/MEPC-62nd-session.aspx.

66. Jinmook Kim, "Korean Yards 10% Ahead of Chinese Yards in Fuel Efficiency," Goldman Sachs, April 7, 2014.

67. "Yangzijiang Wins $700 Million Box Ship Order," Bloomberg, June 9, 2011, http://www.bloomberg.com/news/articles/2011-06-09/yangzijiang-wins-700-million-box-ship-order-from-seaspan-1-.

68. "Chinese Giant Is Only Talking to Domestic Yards," Tradewinds News, March 27, 2015, http://www.tradewindsnews.com/weekly/356886/cky-duo-cosco-and-yang-ming-plot-mega-boxship-orders-blitz.

69. "Manufacturing Called Back Home," Nikkei, January 30, 2015, http://asia.nikkei.com/Business/Companies/Imabari-to-build-giant-dock-in-Japan.

70. "China to Build More LNG Tankers in High-Tech Push," Reuters, August 5, 2014, http://in.reuters.com/article/2014/08/05/china-lng-ships-idINL3N0O838P20140805.

71. "LNG Tanker Builders Vie for Market Share," Wall Street Journal, December 20, 2013, http://www.wsj.com/articles/SB10001424052702304866904579269290895618508.

72. "Kawasaki to Construct LNG Tankers in China," Bloomberg, June 25, 2014, http://www.bloomberg.com/news/articles/2014-06-24/kawasaki-to-build-lng-tankers-in-china-to-take-on-korean-rivals.

73. "DSME Tops 2014 Orders Table for LNG Ships," Tradewinds News, December 12, 2014, http://www.tradewindsnews.com/weekly/350598/DSME-tops-2014-orders-table-for-LNG-ships.

74. "China Shipyards to Spark Rig Price War," *Bloomberg*, January 10, 2013, http://www .bloomberg.com/news/articles/2013-01-09/china-shipyards-set-to-spark-price-war -among-rigmakers.

75. Gerald Wong, "China as the Next Leading Rigbuilder?" Credit Suisse, October 11, 2013, https://doc.research-and-analytics.csfb.com/docView?language=ENG&source=ulg&f ormat=PDF&document_id=1023681401&serialid=24TKAWPDAZwq%2BoisQz2%2B GovDDl5bTirYAKoT90%2BuFNQ%3D.

76. "Opus Offshore's First Drillship Christened," *Offshore Energy*, November 12, 2014, http://www.offshoreenergytoday.com/opus-offshores-first-drillship-christened-in -china/.

77. "CSSC to Build Two Drillships," *World Maritime News*, January 16, 2013, http://world maritimenews.com/archives/73384/china-cssc-to-build-two-drillships-for-reign wood-group/.

78. "Pride's First New Drillship," *Rigzone*, February 23, 2010, http://www.rig zone.com/news/oil_gas/a/88228/Prides_First_Newbuild_Drillship_Rolls_Off_ the_Line_at_Samsung; "Pacific Drilling Claims Four Drillships Completed in 6.35mn Hours," SEC filing, January 2012, http://www.sec.gov/Archives/edgar/ data/1517342/000119312512013837/d274690dex991.htm.

79. "The Deeper the Better," *Economist*, November 23, 2013, http://www.economist.com/ news/business/21590496-korean-and-singaporean-yards-have-adapted-well-chinas -challenge-deeper-better.

80. "我国海洋工程装备产业发展形势与对策" ["Development Situation and Counter-measures of China's Marine Engineering Equipment Industry"], 船海工程 [*Ship and Ocean Engineering*], no. 1 (February 2014).

81. "China, Shy Giant," *New York Times*, December 9, 2006, http://www.nytimes .com/2006/12/09/world/asia/09china.html.

82. In George Modelski and William Thompson, *Seapower in Global Politics, 1494–1993* (Seattle: University of Washington, 1988), 11.

83. Dennis Tao Yang et al., "Why Are Savings Rates So High in China?" NBER Working Paper no. 16771 (February 2011), http://www.nber.org/papers/w16771.

84. Stein Ringen, "The High Cost of China's Heavy Tax Burden," *South China Morning Post*, May 4, 2015, http://www.scmp.com/comment/insight-opinion/article/1783301/ high-cost-chinas-heavy-tax-burden.

85. Yuanyan Sophia Zhang and Steven Barnett, "Fiscal Vulnerabilities and Risks from Local Government Finance in China," IMF Working Paper, January 2014, http://www .imf.org/external/pubs/ft/wp/2014/wp1404.pdf.

86. World Bank, "Gross Domestic Savings (% of GDP)," http://data.worldbank.org/indica tor/NY.GDS.TOTL.ZS.

87. Philip Pugh, *The Cost of Seapower: The Influence of Money on Naval Affairs from 1815 to the Present Day* (London: Conway Maritime Press, 1986), 31, 388.

88. "Peer Review of the Korean Shipbuilding Industry and Related Government Policies," OECD, January 13, 2015, http://www.oecd.org/officialdocuments/publicdisplaydocum entpdf/?cote=c/wp6(2014)10/final&doclanguage=en; KOSHIPA.

89. SAJ, "Shipbuilding Statistics," September 2014, http://www.sajn.or.jp/e/statistics/Shipbuilding_Statistics_Sep2014e.pdf.

90. KOSHIPA.

91. China Higher Education Student Information and Career Center, http://gaokao.chsi.com.cn/zyk/zybk/specialityDetail.action?specialityId=73384672.

92. "Foster Private Defense Firms," *South China Morning Post*, April 29, 2015, http://www.scmp.com/news/china/diplomacy-defence/article/1780006/man-who-bought-chinas-first-aircraft-carrier-now-wants.

93. "China Poised to Gain Control," *Bloomberg*, August 12, 2013, http://www.bloomberg.com/news/articles/2013-08-11/china-poised-to-gain-control-as-shipyard-shakeout-looms-freight.

94. "China Raises Ship-Scrapping Subsidy," *Bloomberg*, December 9, 2013, http://www.bloomberg.com/news/articles/2013-12-10/china-raises-ship-scrapping-subsidy-50-to-trim-glut-of-vessels.

95. "Shipbuilders Deny Merger Rumor," *Global Times*, March 26, 2015, http://www.globaltimes.cn/content/914203.shtml.

96. "造船业的健美重塑" ["Reshaping China's Shipbuilding"], 中国船检 [*China Ship Survey*], no. 1 (January 2014): 13–15, 108–9.

97. Jin Zhang and Wenzhuo Du, "Ride the Tide of Reform," CICC, July 25, 2014.

98. "CSSC to Raise $1.4 Billion for Naval Buildup," *Reuters*, September 11, 2013, http://www.reuters.com/article/2013/09/11/us-china-shipbuilding-idUSBRE98A02L20130911.

99. 张为峰, 吕开东 [Zhang Weifeng and Lu Kaidong], "中国船舶工业发展趋势及企业生产经营建议" ["Proposals on the Development Trend of Shipbuilding Manufacture and Management in China"], 船舶工程 [*Ship Engineering*] 33, no. 2 (2013): 1–5.

100. "Premier Li Pushes Forward 'Made-in-China 2025' at State Council Meeting," PRC State Council, March 25, 2015, http://english.gov.cn/premier/news/2015/03/25/content_281475077518617.htm.

101. 海军舰艇大全 [*Navy Warship Encyclopedia*], http://www.haijun360.com/.

102. "State Council Issues Guidelines," *South China Morning Post*, September 4, 2014, http://www.scmp.com/business/china-business/article/1584738/state-council-issues-guidelines-reform-shipping-industry.

103. Sky Hong, "China to Re-Shape Global Shipping," Deutsche Bank, March 5, 2015.

104. "China Liners May Merge," *Marine Link*, April 9, 2015, http://www.marinelink.com/news/shipbuilders-afloat-merge389568.aspx.

105. Fiscal year 2014 financial statements for listed entities (not parents).

106. "Beijing Aid Keeps China Shipping Lines in Profit," *Reuters*, March 25, 2015, http://www.reuters.com/article/2015/03/25/china-shipping-results-idUSL6N0WL1YS20150325.

107. "China Ship Order Fuels Market Glut Fears," *Financial Times*, December 8, 2011, http://www.ft.com/intl/cms/s/0/c7c59190-21ba-11e1-a19f-00144feabdc0.html#axzz3WKD436tQ.

108. "China Approves Plan for Civilian Ships to Be Used by Military," *Reuters*, June 17, 2015, http://www.reuters.com/article/2015/06/18/us-china-defence-shipping-idUSKBN0 OY08N20150618.

109. "Country Steps Up Operations in Antarctic," *China Daily*, March 4, 2015, http://usa .chinadaily.com.cn/epaper/2015–03/04/content_19716649.htm.

110. Nong Hong, "China's Maritime Law Enforcement Reform and its Implication on the Regional Maritime Disputes," Asia Maritime Transparency Initiative, April 1, 2015, http://amti.csis.org/chinas-maritime-law-enforcement-reform-and-its-implication -on-the-regional-maritime-disputes/.

111. DoD (2014), 38, http://www.defense.gov/pubs/2014_DoD_China_Report.pdf.

112. Ma and Xiang, "Develop the Shipping Industry."

113. 陆超 [Lu Chao], "浅析我国海洋发展战略及未来船舶发展趋势" ["Analysis of Our Marine Strategies and Future Trends"], 船海工程 [*Ship and Ocean Engineering*], no. 3 (June 2013).

114. Linda Jakobson, *China's Unpredictable Maritime Security Actors* (Sydney: Lowy Institute, December 11, 2014), http://www.lowyinstitute.org/publications/chinas-un predictable-maritime-security-actors.

115. "First Algerian C28A Corvette Launched," IHS *Janes*, August 20, 2014, http://www .janes.com/article/42238/first-algerian-c28a-corvette-launched-in-china.

116. "A Bull Market for Gas Turbines," *McCoy Power Reports*, June 17, 2014, http://www .power-eng.com/articles/print/volume-118/issue-6/features/a-bull-market-for-gas-tur bines.html.

117. "*MOL Comfort* Casualty Report," Royal Institute of Naval Architects, http://www.rina .org.uk/mol_comfort_accident.html.

118. Tom Leander, "*Vale Beijing* Moved for Repairs," *Lloyd's List*, December 7, 2011, http:// www.lloydslist.com/ll/sector/dry-cargo/article385908.ece.

PART IV

Remaining Shipbuilding Challenges

Leigh Ann Ragland-Luce and John Costello

PLA Shipboard Electronics
Impeding China's Naval Modernization

CHINA'S AMBITION TO BUILD a blue-water navy capable of conducting maritime expeditionary operations requires not only logistics support such as overseas basing and supply chains, but also an improved command, control, communications, computers, intelligence, surveillance, and reconnaissance (C4ISR) infrastructure. Like the People's Liberation Army's (PLA's) other services and branches, the PLA Navy (PLAN) has faced multiple challenges in its efforts to accomplish what Chinese military officials describe as "simultaneous mechanization and informatization."

The PLAN's informatization requires a defense industry capable of producing numerous varieties of military-grade products and shipborne equipment, preferably with minimal reliance on foreign components and supply chains.[1] Several key PLAN technologies are difficult to import, such as radiation-hardened terminals for satellite communications and specialized software for naval weapons platforms.

This chapter analyzes China's defense shipboard electronics research, development, and acquisition (RDA) ecosystem and the role of these electronics in fulfilling the PLAN's strategic requirements. Particular attention is given to the organizational dynamics involved in the shipboard electronics industry, including military-civilian and public-private integration. This chapter also scrutinizes the interplay between military and civilian actors regarding relevant People's Republic of China (PRC) technical standards, since these documents are important rubrics for PLAN shipboard electronics development and thus a potential indicator of changes in its RDA ecosystem.

Evolving Naval Ambitions: Matching Grasp with Reach

China's 2015 Defense White Paper (DWP) focusing on national security strategy reflects recent and important shifts in approach on several fronts for the PLA and its role in China's international affairs. The PLAN in particular is expected to "gradually shift its focus from near seas defense" to a combination of "near seas defense" and "far seas protection."[2] The DWP illustrates the importance of the naval domain to China's future and asserts that China must be able to "develop a modern military force structure" to protect "sovereignty and maritime rights and interests" and the "security of strategic Sea Lines of Communication [SLOCs] and overseas interests."

This evolution of the PLAN's core missions is also reflected in authoritative PLA writings such as the 2013 edition of *Science of Military Strategy* (SMS), which describes the PLAN as being in its "third phase" of existence. In this view, the PLAN previously evolved from "coastal and in-shore" defense to a second phase of "near seas defense," and since 2004 it has been in the process of moving toward "near seas defense and blue-water defense,"[3] which the 2015 DWP then broadened to include "far seas protection."[4] SMS further argues that the PLAN must be able to integrate with other forces and conduct information operations in its domain in order to fulfill essential duties such as securing key SLOCs.[5] As the authors explain, China's economic development and expanding global interests have generated greater reliance on SLOCs, which require new capabilities to secure: "These navigation routes and waterways already have become the 'lifelines' of our socioeconomic development, and although in overall terms they are kept unimpeded, they are nonetheless not owned by us, nor are they controlled by us. Once a crisis or war at sea occurs, our sea transport may be severed."[6]

Accordingly, outlining in the PLAN's strategic requirements for "near seas and blue-water defense," the SMS authors call on the navy to raise the informatization level of its personnel and to be able to conduct military operations other than war.

SMS specifically cites U.S. power projection capability as a model for Chinese leaders deciding how best to develop the PLA's C4ISR assets strategically, and asserts that information technologies are at the center of naval dominance. The PLAN needs to be able to fuse intelligence across tactical, operational, and strategic levels and among air, surface, and subsurface domains. This makes technologies such as shore- and ship-based long-range radar, overhead reconnaissance platforms, satellite communications, and precision-targeting fire control crucial to the PLAN's development.[7]

PLA leaders thus understand that China must modernize and expand the RDA ecosystem for its maritime and space-based C4ISR infrastructure if it hopes to maintain a sustainable force operating overseas. This requirement is not confined to any particular capability alone; rather, it necessitates comprehensive, systemic development capability coupled with deep institutional reform in areas such as procurement, deployment, and command. Intelligence must be collected, transmitted, processed, fused, and disseminated expeditiously, avoiding institutional or physical bottlenecks that could slow the speed and effectiveness of command decisionmaking. Until modern defense electronics systems are produced and utilized widely by the PLAN, allowing vessels to operate capably even when overseas, China's maritime reach will continue to exceed its grasp.

As a result of this reliance on defense electronics, the PLAN's modernization initiatives are intimately linked to reform efforts in China's defense industrial base. China is attempting to shift its domestic industry from merely producing advanced marine electronics based on established foreign models to actively designing them through independent innovation. However, inefficiency in the large state-owned enterprises (SOEs) that dominate China's defense industry, stovepiping, lack of competition, and poor performance have severely hampered PLAN modernization and represent key challenges in shipboard electronics innovation. Further complicating matters, Chinese investments in marine electronics are spread between two major industries: the defense electronics industry, dominated by China Electronic Technology Corporation (CETC), and the shipbuilding industry, through major SOEs such as China State Shipbuilding Corporation (CSSC) and China Shipbuilding Industry Corporation (CSIC).

Shipboard electronics systems that constitute the full suite of military capabilities can be divided by intended purpose and function into roughly seven different classifications:

- communications systems—utilized for external communication and reception as well as facilitating communication within the ship itself
- radar, sonar, and detection systems—dealing primarily with domain sensing and awareness, threat detection, and threat identification

- navigation and control systems—for domain sensing and awareness using global satellite navigation systems, radio, radar, and ship control and guidance systems

- combat and fire control systems—enabling missile, projectile, or kinetic weapon targeting, launch, guidance, and/or battlefield damage assessment

- electronic countermeasure systems—enabling specific emitter targeting and identification under electronic support measures and enabling electronic attack or physical defensive electronic defense (chaff, decoys, etc.)

- maintenance, damage control, and repair systems—all automated or electronic systems used in standard or emergency maintenance, repair, and damage control

- engine power control and monitoring systems—industrial electronic control for generators, engines, or propulsion and electronics systems used to manage, distribute, meter, and apportion power supply to different vessel sections, systems, and components.

These systems are distinguished from each other not only by their intended purpose, function, and type of electrical engineering required, but also by the different industrial control or information systems networked into their operation.

As electronics systems in an informatized navy are, by definition, networked with other electrical systems, various dependencies exist among systems and subsystems in a complex web of interrelated capabilities. To operate in an "informatized" manner, the PLAN will have to focus its energies on systemic upgrades rather than piecemeal solutions. Accordingly, change for the PLAN will happen incrementally and unevenly, as entire systems are upgraded or replaced altogether.

Industrial Reform Targeting Shipboard Electronics

PLA modernization requirements (and their PLAN subset) are one of several key drivers in China's long-term efforts to push its leading enterprises, largely defense industry SOEs, toward independent research, development, and manufacturing capabilities and international competitiveness. This trend is accelerated by the State-owned Assets Supervision and Administration Commission's (SASAC's) recent announcement that it intends to comprehensively overhaul

SOEs, most of which are dedicated to defense industries. This reform's results will have major implications on China's naval shipbuilding industry.[8]

In 2005 the State Council approved a Shipbuilding National Medium- and Long-term Plan (2006–15), which was formulated by the National Development and Reform Commission and, notably, the Commission of Science, Technology, and Industry for National Defense (COSTIND).[9] Goals included spurring greater technical innovation in the marine equipment industry, encouraging foreign investment and Sino-foreign joint ventures, increasing output of locally produced ship equipment by more than 60 percent by 2015, and focusing on systematic planning to identify and remove barriers to industrial development. This plan was also designed to bolster the ability of China's civilian defense industrial base to supply shipboard electronics to the PLAN.

Unsurprisingly, China's eleventh Five-Year Guideline (2006–10) echoed these goals.[10] While increasing the technological level of marine equipment was a major goal of this plan, targets were also emphasized for shipboard electronics. Although specific military technology requirements are not discussed but rather are echoed in these plans, COSTIND's goals for the period are revealing. Specifically, COSTIND set a goal of producing 60 percent of all subcomponents on Chinese-built commercial ships by 2010 and 80 percent by 2015. Also in this plan, marine electronics emerged as a new national economy growth area, as a by-product of the shipbuilding industry.

However, before the end of the Five-Year Guideline, the "Plan on the Adjustment and Revitalization of the Shipbuilding Industry (2009)" was released, its timing suggesting considerable urgency.[11] This plan acknowledged redundancies and inefficiencies in the bloated shipbuilding industry, calling for restructuring of enterprises and mergers and acquisitions. Relatedly, the plan reemphasized the importance of raising the level of technological capacity by encouraging indigenous innovation and research and development (R&D) and investing more in high-tech and high-value-added technologies such as environment-saving and energy-efficient shipbuilding, maritime equipment projects, and critical internal equipment within ships.[12] Reading further into the plan's purpose and timing, it appears that China's commercial and military shipbuilding industry was struggling to produce the type of ships—and internal equipment, or electronics—required to compete internationally, on an economic level and potentially even on a military level.

Shipboard electronics are further stressed in China's Shipbuilding Twelfth Five-Year Plan (2011–15). This plan shows a continued emphasis on increasing

R&D and design capabilities in maritime electronics.[13] The Five-Year Plan also stipulated industry-wide restructuring aimed at achieving these broad goals and emphasized the role of technology clusters in innovation.

Despite the fact that China's central government targeted raising marine equipment capabilities as a strategic national defense and national economic interest in 2006, and the central planning and guidance that continued to target this field together with subsequent government support, available criticism suggests that the overall level of marine technology achieved remains relatively low.[14] PLAN vessels remain dependent on foreign electronics imports or foreign shipboard electronics designs.[15] The level of "indigenous innovation," which largely consists of reverse-engineering foreign shipboard electronics equipment and localization for China's military and civilian use, has been criticized within the industry as substandard.

Composition of the PLAN's Shipboard Electronics Industrial Base

The industrial base for military shipboard electronics base appears fractured and inefficient in places. If so, this would serve as an impediment to the modernization required by PLAN goals. At the highest level of the defense industry, the resources and capabilities logically required to develop military-use shipboard electronics appear to be divided between two backbones: the electronics and information technology industry, and the shipbuilding industry. Within each respective industry, talent, resources, and investment are further divided among SOE subordinate entities.

China's shipbuilding industry largely consists of 117 government-owned and supervised state-owned shipbuilding enterprises administered directly by SASAC under the State Council. They divide shipyards and businesses geographically, with CSIC responsible for northern shipyards and businesses and CSSC responsible for southern ones. After over a decade of doing business as separate companies, CSIC and CSSC are in the process of re-merging. On September 13, 2015, the Communist Party of China Central Committee and State Council jointly released "Guiding Opinion on Deepening the Reform of State Owned Enterprises," which officially issued the next round of SOE reforms calling for conglomerate mergers. Following this, CSIC and CSSC swapped leadership, which led to speculation that both may formally announce draft merger plans in the future.[16] As this volume went to press, both companies were still denying this speculation.[17] In any case, such consolidation would have little immediate effect on shipboard electronics–focused research institutes, which already are concentrated under CSIC (see exhibit 11-1).

Within industry, shipboard electronics manufacturing naturally overlaps occasionally with other areas of electronics manufacturing, particularly the commercial industry category of marine navigation and other equipment manufacturing (including navigation, meteorological, and oceanographic special equipment manufacturing). Shipbuilding industry guiding documents indicate that the industry organizes shipbuilding activities into three major sub-industries and leverages specific classification codes defined in the recommended National Economic Industry Standard (GB/T 4754–2011). Its shipbuilding activities are thus broadly classified under category 373 (vessels and related equipment manufacturing), while other activities have been placed into categories 341, 343, 344, 345, 402, and 403.[18]

Shipboard Electronics

Outside the traditional shipbuilding industry, a portion of economic activities relevant to military shipboard electronics occurs in the electronics and information technology industry, specifically at CETC.[19]

CETC plays a perhaps surprisingly active role in the production of China's military shipboard electronics, given the existence of shipbuilding research institutes that specialize in comparable areas. CETC's role becomes very obvious after evaluating the partial body of full-text Chinese military standards relevant to shipboard electronics openly shared on commercial Chinese websites, consisting of both open documents as well as restricted internal-use documents.

Several of CETC's fifty-five directly subordinate research institutes are involved in military standardization work related to military shipboard electronics, including the CETC 14th, 20th, 32nd, 38th, and 54th Research Institutes.[20] CETC participated in relevant standards work for both national military standards (GJBs) and for civilian technology standards—both codified for military use under *Classification for Military Standardization Documents* (军用标准文件分类; GJB 832–2005) or its predecessor.[21] Notably, little integration between CETC and shipbuilding research institutes, in the form of partnerships or joint ventures, appears in the commercial sector.

Perhaps CETC's relative success in participating in joint ventures, which would result in technology transfer, explains its redundant role in the shipbuilding industry. CETC's strategy leverages foreign ventures and foreign technology procurement, as well as civilian products, to develop systems for the

Exhibit 11-1. Key Shipbuilding Organizations Specializing in Shipboard Electronics

Organization Name	Description
704 Research Institute (704研究所/七〇四研究所) Shanghai Marine Equipment Research Institute (上海船舶设备研究所)[1]	electronics systems for physical transport, logistical, maintenance, and heavy-lift deck and shipboard equipment power distribution equipment auxiliary propulsion control
709 Research Institute (709研究所/七〇九研究所) Wuhan Digital Engineering Research Institute (武汉数字工程研究所)[2]	command and control systems general information infrastructure systems computer software engineering
716 Research Institute (716研究所/七一六研究所) Jiangsu Automation Research Institute (江苏自动化研究所)[3]	control systems engineering operational command and control systems automated control devices system modeling and control[4]
722 Research Institute (722研究所/七二二研究所)[5] Wuhan Ship Communications Research Institute (武汉船舶通信研究所)	ship integrated communication systems[6]
724 Research Institute (724研究所/七二四研究所) Nanjing Ship Radar Research Institute (南京船舶雷达研究所)	threat detection systems domain/battlespace awareness sensors (e.g., radar)[7]

1. 中船重工704研究所 [CSIC 704 Research Institute], 第七0四研究所 [704 Research Institute], 2010, http://www.smeri.com.cn/p_665.html?_id=61.
2. 武汉数字工程研究所 [Wuhan Digital Engineering Research Institute], 百度百科 [Baidu Baike], http://baike.baidu.com/view/7014690.htm; Wuhan Digital Engineering Research Institute, 中国高等学校学生信息网 [China Higher Education Student Information Network], http://yz.chsi.com.cn/sch/schoolInfo-schId-368336.dhtml.
3. 杰瑞科技集团有限责任公司 [Jierui Science and Technology LLC], 杰瑞科技集团有限责任公司 [JARI], http://www.716.com.cn/Portal/Index.aspx#.
4. 江苏自动化研究所 [Jiangsu Automation Research Institute], 百度百科 [Baidu Baike], http://baike.baidu.com/view/4124393.htm.
5. 武汉船舶通信研究所 [Wuhan Institute of Marine Communication], 中国电动车网 [China Electric Vehicle Network], http://whchuanbo.ddc.net.cn.
6. Ibid.; 武汉船舶通信研究所_院校信息_中国研究生招生信息网 [Wuhan Institute of Marine Communication School Information China Research Information Network], 中国高等学校学生信息网 [China Higher Education Student Information Network], http://yz.chsi.com.cn/sch/schoolInfo--schId-368343.dhtml.
7. 舰载雷达情报系统通用规范 [General Requirements for Shipborne *Radar Information Systems], GJB* 2226-1994, marked FL 1285; 舰载雷达通用规范 [*General Specification for Shipborne Radars*], GJB 403A-98, marked FL5840; 中国船舶重工集团第七二四研究所 [China Shipbuilding Industry Corporation 724 Research Institute], http://www.china724.com/.

PLA, while simultaneously leveraging military-use technology to develop products for the civilian market. CETC describes this behavior in its "3-3-3 Transform and Ascend Strategy" (三三三转型升级战略) advocating a proactive approach to the development of CETC's three core markets simultaneously: military, civilian, and foreign.[22]

RDA Process for PLAN 054A Frigate Electronics Suite: Combat Control System

The electronics systems fielded on the 054A frigate represent the types of electronics systems required and currently operational in PLAN far seas operations.[23] At this time, the assorted electronics systems reported to exist on the ship hail from a variety of imports, suggesting that the electrical components were designed not holistically, but individually.[24] The resulting miscellany may indicate that electronics systems were integrated fairly late in the construction process. A closer look at the RDA process for the combat control systems in particular emphasizes the role that foreign technology transfer plays within PLAN shipboard electronics components and integrated systems.

The development path for modern PLAN combat control systems— particularly the ZKJ-5 and H/ZBJ-1—accelerated from the 709th Research Institute's release of their ancestor in 1979.[25] The early system, the ZKJ-1, was fielded on 051 Dalian and Hefei model destroyers.[26] By some Chinese media accounts, the 723rd Research Institute assisted in the R&D.[27] However, Chinese sources indicate that this early model suffered significant technical problems, including "poor stability" and "low computing power," and due to these factors was not produced en masse.[28]

Due to the technical issues encountered by the ZKJ-1, unsurprisingly the next series of combat command systems integrated an indeterminate level of foreign technology, which has sparked debate between Chinese and foreign analysts.[29] According to some Chinese media sources, the next series of combat command systems released in ZKJ-3 and ZKJ-4 integrated technology from the French TAVITAC system with indigenously developed technology.[30] However, other Western and Japanese sources claim that these systems are in fact the TAVITAC system.[31] It appears possible that some element of truth exists in both statements; Chinese sources often use concepts of "indigenous" content more loosely than their Western counterparts. Moreover, as Kevin Pollpeter and Mark Stokes document in their chapter in this volume, China's "introduction, digestion, absorption, and re-innovation" (IDAR) strategy prioritizes precisely such hybrid approaches.

In a classic example of IDAR, Chinese media articles on the develop-ment of Chinese combat command systems discussed the role that the 723rd Research Institute played in the "reverse mapping imitation" (逆向测绘仿制) of foreign products and shared the outcomes of this process with the 709th Research Institute, along with the 722nd, 716th, and 724th Research Institutes.[32] The 723rd Research Institute received credit for this as allowing for the "local-ization" (国产化) of advanced foreign electronics. Given that Chinese media sources do not refute similarities between TAVITAC and the later ZKJ series, perhaps the system should be characterized as a reverse-engineered TAVITAC or similar system that may have some modifications to allow for localization.[33] The same logic would apply to the later ZKJ-5 combat command system.

Still, little authoritative information exists on the development process for the H/ZBJ-1 automated command system or ZKJ-5 combat command sys-tems reportedly fielded in key PLAN vessels, including the 054A frigate, the carrier Liaoning, and the 052 destroyer.[34] After the relative failures to produce indigenous systems seen with the earliest ZJK-1, ZJK-3, and ZJK-4, it remains possible, although unlikely, that this development project was moved outside the 709th Research Institute's primary control. Regardless of which organiza-tion leads this project, the continued reliance on foreign electronics systems in the 054A in particular indicates that the industry still lacks the capability to have independently designed the H/ZBJ-1 system. Although Chinese sources may argue that the system, like the mid-ZKJ series combat systems, was devel-oped indigenously, these claims should be viewed with skepticism unless new authoritative evidence indicates otherwise.

Far Seas Sustainment Infrastructure: Physical and Virtual Dimensions

A dominant component in far seas power projection capability is an estab-lished support infrastructure for both logistics and communications. China has undertaken diplomatic agreements and ground-based infrastructure investments to secure overseas logistical support for a forward-deployed fleet. Space-based C4ISR infrastructure investment must proceed in lockstep with ground-based assets.

PLAN strategic deployments' increasing reliance on space infrastructure has vast implications for combat capability. Space infrastructure should be seen as a key indicator of PLAN intent and overall informatization capabil-ity. Investment in space-based infrastructure that supports future operations in strategic areas should be viewed in the same context and with the same scrutiny as foreign port agreements, foreign bases, and overseas interests. All are extensions of, and inextricable from, naval power. Mark Stokes underscores the role of space infrastructure as a bellwether for PLA overseas interest: "The PLA is investing in a diverse set of increasingly sophisticated electro-optical (EO), synthetic aperture radar (SAR), and electronic reconnaissance assets. . . . Satellite communications also offer a survivable means of linking sensors to strike systems, and will become particularly relevant as PLA interests expand further from PRC borders."[35]

For instance, China's burgeoning satellite positioning, navigation, and timing system, Beidou, is rapidly expanding its regional capabilities to be able to provide service globally. This would free the PLAN from having to rely on systems, infrastructure, and ultimately information tools over which it has little to no control, thereby further securing its information supply line. Beidou is slated for near-global coverage by 2020.[36]

China's planned civilian overseas satellite communications infrastructure promises to simultaneously increase the PLAN's potential communications infrastructure, given that PLA literature indicates that it already relies on civilian satellite infrastructure to supplement the gaps in its military satellite coverage.[37] However, large-scale international projects present unique opportunities. In March 2015 China announced its intention to develop its "One Belt, One Road" (OBOR) economic corridors, both of which require substantial investment and maintenance. In extension of that economic aim, on April 25, 2015, China announced that it would launch multiple satellites in the next few years to ensure communications coverage and Internet access for areas within and along the OBOR corridors.[38] This would mean that China would expand its space-based telecommunications network to include a land-based region stretching from central Asia to the Baltic and a maritime corridor stretching from Indonesia through the Suez to the Mediterranean.[39]

This satellite deployment follows China's averred strategic interests. It also has the advantage of establishing a ready-made, dual-use communications network available for China's armed forces that happens to strategically serve the areas most vital to its national security. In crises, the PLAN will benefit dramatically from having a well-developed space-based telecommunications infrastructure and will undoubtedly have equipment to utilize and exploit it. These investments in the information realm dovetail nicely with the physical and diplomatic investments China has made in the same region. In a remarkably coordinated strategy, China is laboring on all fronts to secure physical, economic, and information footholds in areas over which it desires greater influence and even, in some cases, control.

Conclusion

PLA and PLAN policy documents continually emphasize the need for "informatization," which, in the naval domain at least, represents the full spectrum of C4ISR capabilities: domain awareness, radar sensing, satellite downlink, and so forth. These individual capabilities do not exist in a vacuum, nor are they simple plug-and-play components. They are remarkably complex capabilities and have to be considered as constituent parts in an overall whole.

Civilian and military-use shipboard electronics are an area where China's central government aims to increase investment and high-technology output, both to boost the sagging shipbuilding industry's capabilities to produce modern ships for export, and to produce advanced military vessels for modern war. Multiple civilian enterprises, largely SOEs, within China's electronics industry and shipbuilding industry appear to actively coordinate with the PLA to develop technology standards, and ultimately electronics, for PLAN vessels. There also appears to be coordination among relevant civilian and military standards, suggesting emphasis on producing dual-use technology. Despite this strategic investment in this industry since 2006, and limited collaborative activities between civilian and military sectors, the industry still appears weak as a whole, and there are indications that technical capabilities are redundantly organized and unevenly distributed.

Although electronics industry units and shipbuilding industry units have coordinated on some high-level general military standards, such as GJB 4000-2000, *General Shipbuilding Standards*, there appears to be little coordination across the two industries at times, suggesting limited horizontal integration and redundant capabilities. Normally, market competition would reduce such inefficiencies, suggesting that government subsidies (or potentially even corruption) support multiple enterprises in this field artificially.

The fractured nature of China's defense industry, particularly between naval shipbuilding and electronics firms, may stand as an obstacle to progressive change and substantial improvement in PLAN shipboard electronics as well as civilian-use electronics. CSIC and CSSC's re-merger will not immediately address these issues, as the bulk of shipboard electronics research institutes are already concentrated within CSIC. While civilian shipbuilding is doubtless hampered by the same industry limitations, it has the luxury of using off-the-shelf components or publicly available technologies, which, while lacking military systems' reliability and security, are fairly reliable and available with ready-built infrastructure. This is adequate for civilian use; military applications can benefit from these technologies for redundancy and backup.

Military systems need to be ruggedized, secure, encrypted, surge-proof, and wholly reliable.

It is clear that China is making incremental improvements in its ability to utilize maritime expeditionary forces in operational deployments, as seen with the 054A frigate. However, reviewing PLAN shipboard electronics systems reveals continuing reliance on foreign technology. The 054A's primary satellite communications systems, electronic warfare suites, and combat data systems are largely foreign, with China's own indigenously produced systems serving in a subordinate or redundant role. These off-the-shelf or foreign systems have distinct advantages in that they can be bought relatively cheaply or licensed for manufacture—allowing China to reverse-engineer them—and have infrastructure in place for upgrading, maintenance, and support. The downside is that this is by nature a compartmentalized, piecemeal solution. These technologies are not standardized laterally across the companies and borders from which they derive and certainly are not tested for electromagnetic compatibility. The PLAN's failure to design and acquire components from a top-down systemic design represents a serious flaw.

Aside from highlighting areas where electronics systems are reliant on foreign technology, the 054A shipboard electronics case study also highlights a development trend that may affect other PLAN vessels: the ship does not appear to be designed with a centralized system in mind. This may indicate that electronics systems integration does not proceed organically; rather, it is affected on an ad hoc basis as various systems are installed. If true, this piecemeal approach would suggest China's defense industry still lacks the ability to not only design indigenous electronic system components, but also independently design domestic integrated control systems. Taken together, the shipboard electronics the PLAN relies on for far seas operations represent the work of a defense shipboard electronics production base that remains very much in transition.

Appendix A: Classification for Military Standardization Documents

First published by the General Armament Department in 1990 and revised in 2005, GJB 832-2005, *Classification for Military Standardization Documents* (军用标准文件分类), outlines the separate categorization system for military documents. Here, *FL* denotes military use category code, and the 4 digits that follow indicate the topic (2 digits) and sub-topic (2 digits) categorization, spanning from 099–9900.[40]

Sub-categories relevant to shipboard electronics from within GJB 832A-2005 include:

- Those within electronics system standards (12): integrated (1200 综合标准), radar system (1211 雷达系统标准), communications system (1221 通信系统标准), command automation system (1241 指挥自动化系统标准), radio management (1271 无线电管理标准), and other (1290 其他标准) standards.

- Within the ship systems standards (15): electrical system (1515 电气系统标准), weapons system (1520 武器系统标准), auxiliary system (1521 辅助系统标准), and potentially also system testing and evaluation (1580 系统试验与评定标准) standards.

- Naval defense engineering standards (5430 海防工程标准), which include naval command automation communications engineering.

For documents published prior to 2005, the classification code guidelines described in GJB 832-1990 apply.

GJB 832-1990, *Major Categories Relevant to Shipboard Electronics*, are as follows:

- 12 Fire Control Equipment (火力指控设备)

- 19 Warship, Landing Stage, and Dry Dock (舰艇、趸船和浮船坞)

- 20 Warship Equipment (舰艇设备)

- 58 Communications, Survey, and Related Radiation Emitting Equipment (通信、探测和相干辐射设备)

- 59 Electricity and Electric-Powered Components (电气和电子用设备元器件)

- 61 Electrical Wire, Electric Power, and Power Distribution Equipment (电线、电力和配电设备)

- 66 Instrumentation and Testing Equipment (仪器仪表和实验室设备)
- 70 Common-Use Automated Data Processing Equipment, Software, Auxiliary Equipment, and Products (通用自动数据处理设备、软件、辅助设备和用品).

Notes

1. Committee on Materials for High-Temperature Semiconductor Devices, Commission on Engineering and Technical Systems, National Research Council, *Materials for High-Temperature Semiconductor Devices* (Washington, DC: National Academies of Sciences, 1995), http://www.nap.edu/openbook.php?record_id=5023&page=10.

2. Andrew S. Erickson, "China's Blueprint for Sea Power," Jamestown *China Brief* 16.11 (July 6, 2016): 3–7, http://www.jamestown.org/single/?tx_ttnews%5Btt_news%5D=45570&no_cache=1&mc_cid=c426a575fi&mc_eid=28225bedb2.

3. Shou Xiasong, ed., 战略科学 [*Science of Military Strategy*] (Beijing: Military Science Press, 2013), 206–08.

4. 中国的军事战略 [*China's Military Strategy*] (Beijing: 中华人民共和国国务院新闻办公室 [State Council Information Office, PRC], May 2015), http://www.81.cn/dblj/2015-05/26/content_6507373.htm.

5. *Science of Military Strategy*, 208.

6. Ibid., 209.

7. Ibid., 213–16.

8. "中共中央国务院印发《关于深化国有企业改革的指导意见" ["CPC Central Committee and State Council Issue 'Guidelines on Deepening the Reform of State-Owned Enterprises'"], 新华网 [*Xinhuanet*], September 13, 2015, http://news.xinhua net.com/politics/2015-09/13/c_1116547080.htm.

9. "船舶工业中长期发展规划2006–2015 年" ["Shipbuilding National Medium- and Long-Term Plan 2006–15"], http://wenku.baidu.com/view/35a0bcc4bb4cf7ec4afed091.

10. "船舶配套业发展"十一五"规划纲要" ["Shipbuilding Industry Develops 11th Five Year Plan"], http://www.chinabaike.com/law/zy/bw/gw/gfk/1340588.html, http://www.msckobe.com/links/china/145.htm.

11. "物联网"十二五"发展规划" [Physical Network 12th Five Year Plan Development Program], 工业和信息化部 [Ministry of Industry and Information Technology/MIIT], http://www.miit.gov.cn/n11293472/n11293832/n11294072/n11302450/12402840.htm.

12. Yang Mu, "China's Shipbuilding Industry: An Update," EAI Background Brief 592, January 13, 2011, http://www.eai.nus.edu.sg/BB592.pdf.

13. "船舶工业'十二五'发展规划" ["Shipbuilding Industry 12th Development Plan"], MIIT, March 12, 2012, http://ghs.miit.gov.cn/n11293472/n11294974/n11296797/n11449 2503.files/n14492477.doc.

14. "泰州重点行业运行情况调研之船舶产业篇" ["Shipping Industry Writings on the State of Key Trades in Taizhou"], 泰州市统计局 [Taizhou Statistics Bureau], http://tjj .taizhou.gov.cn/art/2013/6/8/art_2445_211479.html.

15. Morgan Clemens, Gabe Collins, and Kristen Gunness, "The Type 054/054A Frigate Series: China's Most Produced and Deployed Large Modern Surface Combatant," *China SignPost*™ 93 (August 2, 2015), http://www.chinasignpost .com/2015/08/02/the-type-054054a-frigate-series-chinas-most-produced-and-deployed-large-modern-surface-combatant/. Identified foreign technology transfer supporting systems used on Type 052/Type 054, covering technology originating in Italy, Russia, France, and domestic development activities at the CETC 724 Research Institute, 712 Research Institute, and 20 Research Institute specifically.

16. "機械類: 國務院印發混改意見, 鋼構、風帆延期複牌" ["Mechanical Securities: State Council Issues Opinion on Mixed-ownership Reform, Resumption of Trading for Steel and Sailing Securities is Postponed"], 中信建投證券 [*China Securities*], October 1, 2015, http://www.cnyes.com/report/rsh_article.aspx?id=199549. The article's title paraphrases a recently issued State Council opinion on developing mixed-ownership in state-owned enterprises. "Reform on Developing Mixed-Ownership in SOEs" ("国有企业发展混合所有制改革") is substantially shortened to "混合改革," or simply "混改."

17. "Shipbuilders CCSC, CSIC, Deny Merger Rumor," *Global Times*, March 26, 2015, http://www.globaltimes.cn/content/914203.shtml.

18. "工业和信息化部关于船舶工业2011年统计年报和2012年定期统计报表工作的通知" ["Notice on MIIT Shipbuilding Industry 2011 and 2012 Statistical Yearbooks Period Statistical Work Report"], MIIT, http://www.miit.gov.cn/n11293472/n11293832/n12845605/n13916973/14417679.html.

19. "电子信息产业(行业)分类注释" ["Electronic Information Industry Classification Annotations"], *China Intellectual Property Net*, http://www.cnipr.com/news/hyqy/dz/dzjbzs/201004/t20100414_111306.html?COLLCC=2272108385&.

20. 舰载GPS卫星导航仪通用规范 [*Shipborne GPS Satellite Navigation Apparatus General Specification*], GJB 3154–1998, marked FL 5825; 舰载雷达通用规范 [*General Specification for Shipborne Radars*], GJB 403A-98, marked FL 5840; 军用声纳数据记录设备通用规范 [*Military Sonar Data Recording Equipment General Specification*], SJ 20968–2007, marked FL 1200; 舰船通用规范总册 [*General Shipbuilding Standards*], GJB 4000–2000, marked FL 0199; 舰载雷达通用规范 [*General Specification for Shipborne Radars*], GJB 403A-1998, marked FL 5840. Here, *FL* denotes military-use category code, and the 4 digits that follow indicate the topic (2 digits) and sub-topic (2 digits) categorization, spanning from 099–9900.

21. First published by the General Armament Department in 1990 and revised in 2005, GJB 832-2005, *Classification for Military Standardization Documents* (军用标准文件分类), outlines the separate categorization system for military documents. 军用标准文件分类 [*Classification for Military Standardization Documents*], GJB 20832A-2005; 船用电子设备环境试验条件和方法　总则 [*General Provisions Shipboard Electronic Equipment Environmental Testing Conditions and Methods*], SC/T 7002.1–1992; 船用电子设备环境试验条件和方法 总则 [*Marine Low-Voltage Electrical Product Quality Grading*], JB/T 56120–1999; 船用对称式通信电缆 一般规定 [*Shipboard Cables with Symmetrical Conductors General*], GJB 9333.1–1988.

22. "中国电科2010年社会责任报告" ["CETC 2010 Social Responsibility Report"], 中国电子科技集团公司 [China Electronic Technology Corporation], 4, http://www.cetc .com.cn/WebSite/cetc/Upload/File/201111/20111116155744312500.pdf.

23. Clemens, Collins, and Gunness, "The Type 054/054A Frigate Series."

24. Ibid.

25. 安风 [An Feng], "日媒紧盯我海军'中华神盾'作战系统" ["The Japanese Media Has Focused Its Attention on Our Navy's 'Chinese Aegis' Combat System"], 中国国防报 [China National Defense Report], March 7, 2014, http://www.81.cn/jmy wyl/2014–03/07/content_5799936.htm.

26. Ibid.

27. "中国军舰"神经系统"不输美日宙斯盾" ["Chinese Warship 'Nervous System' Did Not Steal U.S. or Japanese Aegis"], 昆仑军事网 [Kunlun Military Network], http://www.kunlun.com/wqzb/2015/28448.shtml.

28. Ibid.

29. James Bussert, "China Copies Russian Ship Technology for Use and Profit," *Signal Magazine* (June 2008), http://www.afcea.org/content/?q=china-copies-russian-ship-technology-use-and-profit.

30. 安然 [An Ran], "日刊: 中国舰艇'大脑'日趋进步" ["Japanese Media: Chinese Warship 'Great Brain' Has Been Developing Apace"], 中青在线 [*China Youth Online*], April 2, 2014, http://qnck.cyol.com/html/2014–04/02/nw.D110000 qnck_20140402_2-19.htm.

31. "深度: 中国国产指挥系统用于我航母助其避成攻击目标" ["Deepening: Chinese Indigenous Command System Used in Our Carrier Aids in Concealing Attack Targets"], 新浪军事 [*Sina Military*], June 11, 2015, http://mil.news.sina.com.cn/2015 -06-11/1145832879.html.

32. An Feng, "The Japanese Media Has Focused Its Attention on Our Navy's 'Chinese Aegis' Combat System."

33. Ibid.

34. Ibid.

35. Mark Stokes, testimony at hearing on the "Implications of China's Military and Civil Space Programs," U.S.-China Economic and Security Review Commission, May 11, 2011, http://www.uscc.gov/sites/default/files/5.11.11Stokes.pdf.

36. Yang Jinghao, "China's Beidou to Rival GPS," *Global Times*, http://www.globaltimes .cn/content/690206.shtml.

37. 朱义勇[Zhu Yiyong],"融合民用卫星通信加强我海军通信能力的思考"[Thoughts on How Integrating Civilian-Use Satellite Communications Strengthens Our Navy's Communications Capabilities," 海军工程大学学报 (综合版) [Journal of Naval University of Engineering (Comprehensive Edition)], No.1 (2016): 50.

38. 索寒雪 [Suo Hanxue], "一带一路通信信号2018年或全覆盖 将发射多颗卫星" ["One Belt, One Road Communications Signal to Have Full Coverage in 2018, Launching More Satellites"], 科学网 [*Science Net*], April 25, 2015, http://news.scien cenet.cn/htmlnews/2015/4/317620.shtm.

39. "China Planning New Satellites to Back Its Belt and Road Initiative," *Want China Times*, April 29, 2015, http://www.wantchinatimes.com/news-subclass-cnt.aspx?id=20 150429000131&cid=1102.

40. 军用标准文件分类 [*Classification for Military Standardization Documents*], GJB 20832A-2005.

Andrew S. Erickson, Jonathan Ray, and Robert T. Forte

Underpowered
Chinese Conventional and Nuclear Naval Power and Propulsion

UNDERSTANDING CHINA'S TRAJECTORY in naval power and propulsion is critical to understanding its future at sea. Propulsion determines how fast and far a ship can go; overall power determines what it can accomplish in a given location. The density of water (829 times greater than air) imposes an unforgiving reality on these dynamics: the cubic relationship between power and speed. For a ship to go three times faster, twenty-seven times the power is needed. Furthermore, modern advanced weapons systems require high and growing amounts of power to operate. For all these reasons, an ambitious nation such as China would prefer to power its navy using the most advanced sources available. Propulsion has been one of the greatest weaknesses for China's navy and for its military in general, however. The main question is how quickly and effectively it can master the relevant technologies.

The chapter begins by briefly reviewing conventional propulsion requirements and Chinese capabilities in this regard. Given the disproportionate potential of nuclear propulsion and continued Chinese limitations in that regard, the majority of the chapter focuses on that subject. A conclusion then reviews China's remaining challenges and prospects for overcoming them.

Conventional Power

Diesel/Gas Turbines

Foreign-derived turbines continue to power the majority of China's surface fleet. China has drawn in particular on engines from Germany's MTU, France's SEMT Pielstick, Finland's Wärtsilä, and various Ukrainian manufacturers. In some cases, China has developed its own versions of these engines.[1]

Air-Independent Power

For submarines, the next best thing to nuclear power is an advanced variant of conventional power. One approach that advanced navies, including the PLAN's *Yuan*-class submarines with their Stirling engines, have adopted is air-independent power (AIP). Beginning in March 2015, a *Yuan* conducted a protracted Indian Ocean patrol that included the PLAN's first submarine call on Karachi, Pakistan, at the end of May.[2]

This method greatly extends the time a submarine can cruise at low speed without draining its battery and risking detection in recharging it by raising an air intake and an exhaust tube (for perhaps as long as two weeks). It also allows saving Main Storage Battery energy accumulated for relatively fast evasive maneuvers (for perhaps as long as two hours).[3] AIP's biggest advantage is that it provides tactical flexibility to the submarine commanding officer. He now has both more leeway to choose when he recharges his batteries and the ability to use higher speeds if the tactical situation warrants.

Air-independent power is not quite as big a game changer as some advocates claim, however. AIP systems use liquid oxygen as the oxidizer, necessitating large tanks and cumbersome, dangerous processes. AIP cannot be drawn down quickly. Nor does it add to the time a boat can operate at a "burst" speed; the rate at which it can convert stored energy to power is small. Even with AIP, a commanding officer still only has several hours at flank from the Main Storage Battery, and little additional coverage. In sum, an AIP submarine has far too little power or stored energy to resemble a "baby nuke."

Advanced Batteries

For conventional submarine propulsion, lithium-ion (Li-ion) batteries (锂离子电池) appear to be the wave of the future. They have great power density and weigh much less than their lead acid predecessors, but they have a problem with thermal runaway that occasionally causes them to combust.

Chinese specialists are scrutinizing these developments carefully and seek to parlay China's substantial if still limited Li-ion battery industry into submarine applications. Four Chinese-language technical articles lay out a natural progression. Two 2011 articles survey foreign journals on Li-ion technology and discuss the possibilities of using Li-ion batteries in submarines in the future.[4] These articles are a stronger indicator of keen interest in using Li-ion batteries in conventional submarines than in concrete demonstration of actual progress in that regard.

Yet China appears to be working hard to make concrete progress even in this cutting-edge area. The third article (2013) discusses actual funding and the goal of putting the batteries on submarines soon. The author, from China Ship Design and Development Center (CSDDC) in Wuhan, predicts that during the next Five-Year Guideline, they "will carry out modeled land-based experiments and experiments installed on ships at sea. The new generation of non-nuclear powered submarines will be equipped with these new types of Li-ion batteries."[5] The last article (2014) shows steps being taken in that direction. These authors, also from CSDDC, claim to have developed a simulation testing platform that can evaluate the properties of three different array connection configurations for Li-ion battery modules as well as scanning for constant power discharge. If this platform works as claimed, it will allow analysis of various Li-ion battery array connections to determine which type is best suited to their boats.[6] These four articles thus suggest a logical progression: from hoping, to funding, to testing and analysis. The next step is installation in Chinese submarines, a process the authors hope to finish in the 2015–20 time frame.

Nuclear Power

Nuclear power is the ultimate gold standard in submarine power. It is essential for long-term, long-range, high-performance operations. While conventional power or a small (~300 kilowatts) nuclear reactor may be adequate for slow, stealthy anti-access operations close to home waters, full-scale nuclear power is needed for high-speed, high-performance, long-range submerged operations. Demanding arctic or tropical environments only increase the disparity. For example, submarines must typically reduce speed in warm-water environments such as the Persian Gulf.

That said, deploying nuclear naval power requires overcoming major engineering challenges, developing comprehensive infrastructure, and training crews to operate sophisticated, sensitive, dangerous equipment. Nuclear-powered submarines require two fundamental characteristics: extremely high power density (for an advantageous power-to-volume ratio) and long core life for economic and operational efficiency. China entered this club long ago, but has yet to emerge in the top tier inhabited by the United States, Russia, France, and the United Kingdom.

Civilian nuclear industry is not an indicator of naval nuclear competence because the technologies and skill sets are so different. High-temperature gas-cooled reactors, for instance, while exhibiting significant promise for civil land applications and studied widely in China, cannot be taken to sea because they lack requisite energy density.

These factors represent the state of the art and pose key questions regarding China's pursuit of these standards, such as:

- To what extent is China transitioning from Soviet technology, and what countries or designs influence its current design choices?

- How would China develop or acquire such advanced designs? What foreign technologies is China drawing upon in its efforts to improve?

- Finally, given the lack of transparency on China's military technology development and nuclear propulsion, how can analysts answer these questions?

The authors surveyed Chinese views on relevant subjects to answer these questions and help elucidate the extent to which China is taking a Western versus a Russian approach regarding key naval reactor design aspects, and how realistic its approach is in practice.

Current State of China's Nuclear Propulsion

The role of China's nuclear-powered navy is growing and will be critical for China's strategic missions and securing growing interests abroad. From December 13, 2013, to February 12, 2014, a *Shang*-class (Type 093) nuclear-powered attack submarine navigated near Sri Lanka and into the Persian Gulf, transiting the Strait of Malacca on the way to and from its homeport on Hainan Island.[7] For "more than two months," until returning to Qingdao on April 22, 2015, an updated *Han*-class (Type 091) supported antipiracy patrols in the Gulf of Aden, escorting two ships and a supply vessel.[8] This is the latest in China's incremental approach to increasing out of area operations, and demonstrates the importance of nuclear propulsion to a blue-water navy. Compared to conventional powered submarines, these nuclear attack submarines are more capable of operating farther from China, conducting intelligence, surveillance, and reconnaissance and antisurface warfare missions. According to the U.S. Office of Naval Intelligence (ONI), Type 094 *Jin*-class ballistic missile submarines (SSBNs) will soon assume a central role in Beijing's nuclear deterrent as they conduct China's first SSBN patrols with submarine-launched ballistic missiles.[9] The Pentagon forecasts the first deterrent patrol to occur by the end of 2016.[10]

Current Priorities

China is prioritizing advanced designs and reactors for an improved variant of its 093 *Shang*-class attack submarine (SSN). Initial production halted after only two hulls were launched in 2002 and 2003;[11] they entered service in 2006 and 2007 after lengthy trials.[12] A Chinese news article circulating in online forums claims the 093 is comparable to later second-generation designs by the United States and Russia.[13] China launched in 2012 and 2013, and commissioned in 2015 and 2016, two hulls of a hydrodynamically improved variant, the 093A. Two more are expected by 2020, for a total of six *Shang*s, before China transitions to producing the Type 095 SSN.[14]

For the future Type 095, Chinese media coverage indicates new technologies needed.[15] An article lists a new pump jet propulsion system, high-strength steel, mixed single- and dual-hulled structure, new comprehensive shock absorption rafting system, possibly improved vertical launch tubes for cruise missiles, and a third-generation submarine reactor.[16] For the reactor, priorities include the reactor design, natural circulation, and the reactor's loops (there is no mention of prioritizing the primary or secondary loop).[17] It is important to treat this media coverage with caution, although numerous Chinese websites host it.[18]

Russian Technology

Russia has been, and continues to be, a major source for Chinese naval nuclear power technology. Lacking access to much other foreign knowledge, China based its first- and second-generation submarines largely on early Soviet reactor designs. The 1960s and '70s first-generation design drew from nuclear reactors installed on the Soviet icebreaker *Lenin*, a decision based more on information availability and bureaucratic politics than technological merit, and it posed enormous challenges in noise levels and containment design.[19] Since the end of the Cold War, China has obtained significant Russian technology and even technicians for direct work.[20] Russian resource constraints likely exacerbated this trend. Chinese researchers with China Shipbuilding Industry Corporation's (CSIC's) 719 Research Institute (RI), a lead design institute for China's nuclear submarines, commented in 2008 that Russia's development of fourth-generation nuclear submarines had encountered financial difficulties and outflows of personnel, trends that hindered the submarines' development.[21]

Consequently, Russian conglomerates have been willing to sell China nearly all their products and some technologies, although it is unclear if nuclear reactors represent a bridge too far. In the submarine sphere specifically, the *Song*'s seven-bladed skewed screw suggests that China acquired and implemented technology associated with the twelve *Kilos* it purchased from Russia. China designed the Type 093 in conjunction with Russian experts.[22] Regarding nuclear reactor designs China may target, in 2009 professors at Harbin Institute of Technology stated that the natural circulation abilities of France's nuclear submarine equipment CAS-48 and K-15 integrated pressurized water reactor (PWR) could reach 80 percent natural circulation, while the ABV-6Y under research in Russia can realize 100 percent natural circulation.[23]

Aside from Russian technology, China also monitors U.S. designs. A senior engineer from the Navy 991 Engineering Office credits natural circulation reactors as a key factor in the quietness of U.S. submarines.[24] According to his analysis, the S5G reactor natural circulation PWR begun in 1959 was a key starting point. The S9G in the *Virginia*-class is both the most advanced and the model for the next generation of U.S. nuclear submarines. The next generation would turn the S9G into a transformational technology core (TTC). The first TTC design was started in 2004 and delivered in 2014. The analysis also states nuclear propulsion will be the basis of any future all-electric-propulsion U.S. submarines.

Chinese Nuclear Reactor Development and Training

Chinese nuclear submarines must be supported by an effective research, development, and acquisition process that handles the "growing pains" for which Soviet submarines were notorious. An overall Chinese priority for nuclear submarine and propulsion design is better modularization. Modular designs facilitate more efficient construction and allow new technologies to be inserted into a submarine without an expensive redesign.[25] Beginning in 1990, China emphasized improvements not only for the submarines themselves, but also for mass production capabilities.[26] According to online accounts, during the tenth Five-Year Plan (2001–5), China began a new generation of submarine and nuclear propulsion development research and development, a focus of which was greater modularity.[27]

In 2014 Chinese media covered work by Liu Chunlin at CSIC's 719 RI on China's new generation of submarine nuclear propulsion.[28] Liu joined the institute in 1998 after graduating from Harbin Institute of Technology, and in 2005 he was made assistant designer in charge of an unnamed system, which many speculated involved the propulsion system for the 093 SSN and 094 SSBN. Liu's team focused on technologies relevant to the secondary loop of a reactor, including integrated secondary loop system technology, emergency cooling, and secondary side passive residual heat removal technology for steam generators. He also led teams on numerous priority projects for national defense, although specifics were not provided.

Aircraft Carrier

In 2012 China commissioned its first aircraft carrier, *Liaoning*, which employs conventional propulsion. It is currently building its first indigenous carrier in Dalian. Many analysts believe China is also interested in additional aircraft carriers that use nuclear propulsion. In 2013 the Ministry of Science and Technology "formally launched Project 863 to research key technologies for nuclear-powered vessels" and "S&T [science and technology] support project for small-scale nuclear reactor technology and its demonstrated applications."[29] Key objectives for the plan include developing core technologies and safety studies for nuclear-powered ships and technical support for small nuclear reactors. One article notes, "Industry insiders [suggested the original CSIC announcement] signified China could be setting out to research a nuclear-powered aircraft carrier or similarly large aircraft."[30] An analyst pointed out that it made sense strategically for China to "work toward a nuclear-powered one after the technology was mature."[31]

Bringing It All Together: Integrated Electric Propulsion?

One of China's fundamental challenges is that even as it seeks to close the gap with the state of the art, that frontier continues to advance. Integrated electric propulsion (IEP) is one major trend in naval power, though thus far only the U.S. *Zumwalt*-class destroyer has fully adopted it. China may seek to pursue this approach for future aircraft carriers, though it currently lacks IEP experience almost completely. China's scientific survey[32] and coast guard ships[33] are initial adopters of IEP.

Conclusion

Power, including both propulsion and the powering of onboard systems, is of vital importance to any navy. It is an indicator of overall capability and blue-water progress. As such, it is a field in which China must make major achievements in order to realize the great power navy that it seeks.

The complexity and demanding performance parameters of naval propulsion make this a difficult field to master. Piecing together foreign and indigenous technologies of civil and military origin has served China relatively well in some other areas, but does not work so well here given the degree to which components must work together as a sophisticated system-of-systems. Some types of propulsion, particularly nuclear, are guarded zealously by leading foreign powers such as the United States and Russia. For these reasons, propulsion remains an area of enduring weakness across China's military, and the navy is no exception.

Yet Beijing is determined to succeed here, and it continues to progress. It has developed its own versions of foreign diesel and gas turbines. It has deployed AIP on its most advanced conventional submarines and is working to progress to next-generation Li-ion batteries. Of greatest significance for China's long-term naval capabilities and scope will be its mastery of naval nuclear power. Here China continues to suffer major weakness in performance and quieting. It still lacks experience with nuclear power for aircraft carriers, having only one hull in service with gas turbines. But China is making a broad-based effort to improve, and it should not be underestimated in the long run. In the nearer term, the degree of Russian assistance that China is able to obtain will be a key variable influencing its rate of progress.

Notes

The authors thank CAPT Christopher P. Carlson, USNR (Ret.), CAPT James H. Patton Jr., USN (Ret.), and an anonymous reviewer for invaluable inputs.

1. For claims of substantial progress in gas turbine development, including validation during Gulf of Aden antipiracy deployments, see "国产燃气轮机取得进展 造舰高潮开始" ["Domestic Gas Turbines Make Progress—Shipbuilding High Tides Begin"], September 18, 2010, http://bbs.tiexue.net/post2_4492258_1.html.

2. Department of Defense, *Annual Report to Congress: Military and Security Developments Involving the People's Republic of China, 2016* (Washington, DC: Department of Defense, 2016), 22 (hereafter, DoD [2016]); James Hardy and Sean O'Connor, "IMINT Confirms Type 041 [*sic*] Visit to Karachi," *Jane's Defence Weekly*, July 8, 2015.

3. Edward Whitman, "Air-Independent Propulsion," *Undersea Warfare*, http://www .navy.mil/navydata/cno/n87/usw/issue_13/propulsion.htm.

4. 陈新传 [Chen Xinzhuan], 宋强 [Song Qiang], and 吕昊 [Lü Hao], "国内外锂离子动力电池发展概况及启示" ["International and Domestic Development Trends and Reviews on Lithium-Ion Batteries"], 船电技术 [*Marine Electric and Electronic Engineering*] 31, no. 4 (2011): 7; 陈新传 [Chen Xinzhuan], 宋强 [Song Qiang], 吕昊 [Lu Hao], and 王路 [Wang Lu], "锂离子电池应用于潜艇动力可行性分析" ["Feasibility Analysis of Using Lithium-Ion Batteries in Submarine Power Systems"], 船电技术 [*Marine Electric and Electronic Engineering*] 31, no. 6 (2011): 20, 28.

5. 崔为耀 [Cui Weiyao], "锂离子蓄电池在非核动力潜艇上的应用研究" ["Application of Lithium-Ion Batteries in Conventional Submarine Propulsion Systems"], 船电技术 [*Ship Electronic Technology*] 33, no. 5 (2013): 55–58.

6. 邢剑 [Xing Jian], 任思敏 [Ren Simin], 邹永铸 [Zou Yongzhu], and 王云鹤 [Wang Yunhe], "锂离子动力电池装艇适用性研究" ["Applications for Lithium-Ion Batteries in Submarines"], 船电技术 [*Marine Electric and Electronic Engineering*] 34, no. 11 (2014): 59–63.

7. Dong Zhaohui, ed., "PLA Navy Submarine Visits Sir Lanka," China Military Online, September 24, 2014, http://eng.chinamil.com.cn/news-channels/china-military-news/ 2014-09/24/content_6152669.htm.

8. CCTV-7 report, as documented frame-by-frame in "官媒首曝海军091改型核攻击潜艇巡航亚丁湾画面" ["First Official Media Exposure of Modified PLAN Type 091 Nuclear-Powered Attack Submarine in Gulf of Aden"], *Xinhua*, April 27, 2015, http:// news.xinhuanet.com/mil/2015-04/27/c_127736846.htm.

9. Office of Naval Intelligence (ONI), *The PLA Navy: New Capabilities and Missions for the 21st Century* (Suitland, MD: ONI, 2015), 5, 11.

10. DoD (2016), 26.

11. ONI, *The PLA Navy*, 16.

12. Ronald O'Rourke, *China Naval Modernization: Implications for U.S. Navy Capabilities—Background and Issues for Congress* (Washington, DC: Congressional Research Service, June 17, 2016), RL33153, 17, http://www.fas.org/sgp/crs/row/RL33153.pdf.

13. "深度: 095核潜艇将首用6项新技术战力已接近美军" ["In Depth: The 095 Nuclear Submarine Will for the First Time Use 6 New Technologies Whose Combat Abilities Approach Those of the U.S. Military"], 新浪军事 [Sina Military Affairs], December 27, 2013.

14. DoD (2016), 26.

15. "In Depth: The 095 Nuclear Submarine Will for the First Time Use 6 New Technologies Whose Combat Abilities Approach Those of the U.S. Military."

16. Ibid.

17. Ibid.

18. Ibid.

19. John Lewis and Xue Litai, *China's Strategic Seapower: The Politics of Force Modernization in the Nuclear Age* (Stanford, CA: Stanford University Press, 1994), 31–32.

20. The authors have searched Chinese- and Russian-language sources but have not found evidence of open collaboration between 719 RI and any Russian counterpart.

21. 陈虹 [Chen Hong] and 冷文军 [Leng Wenjun], "美、俄核潜艇技术发展述评" ["Comments on the Nuclear Submarine Technology Development of the U.S. and Russia"], 舰船科学技术 [*Ship Science and Technology*] 30, no. 2 (April 2008): 38–44.

22. "*Shang* class (Type 093/093A)," *Jane's Fighting Ships*.

23. 田兆斐 [Tian Zhaofei] et al., "自然循环与强迫循环转换过渡过程研究" ["Study on Transient Characteristics of Transition Between Natural Circulation and Forced Circulation"], 哈尔滨工程大学学报 [*Journal of Harbin Engineering University*] 31, no. 10 (October 2010): 1398–1404.

24. 王汉刚 [Wang Hangang], "美国核潜艇推进系统减振降噪技术发展分析" ["Study of Vibration Isolation and Noise Reduction Technology in U.S. Nuclear Submarine Propulsion System"], 船舶科学技术 [*Ship Science and Technology*] 35, no. 7 (July 2013): 149–53.

25. "Future Submarine Force: Modular Design & Technology Insertion," Chief of Naval Operations, Submarine Warfare Division, http://www.navy.mil/navydata/cno/n87/future/modular.html.

26. Yang Lianxing, "The 'Four Stages' of the Innovation and Development of China's Nuclear Submarines ("中国核潜艇创业发展的"四个阶段"), *China Nuclear Industry* (中国核工业), no. 11 (2013).

27. "船舶工业的"尖兵"—记中船重工集团第七一九所高级工程师刘春林"   ["The Ship Industry's 'Ultimate Soldier'—Remembering CSIC 719 RI's Senior Engineer Liu Chunlin"], 武汉科技报 [*Wuhan Science and Technology Weekly*], December 27, 2010, http://tianjiangxiangruilike.lofter.com/post/2f508a_1331153.

28. Original announcement from SASTIND, "中船重工刘春林获"中国青年五四奖章" ["CSIC Liu Chunlin Receives 'China Youth May Fourth Prize'"], press release by国家国防科技工业局 [State Administration of Science, Technology, and Industry for Defense], May 6, 2014, http://www.sastind.gov.cn/n112/n117/c323172/content.html.

29. "七一九所科技产业化工作再创佳绩" ["719 RI's Work in Science and Industrialization Again Creates Success"], CSIC press release, February 19, 2013, http://www.laohucaijing.com/news/15277.html.

30. "中国着手造核动力航母 五年内建两个航母战斗群" ["China Sets Out to Build Nuclear-Powered Aircraft Carrier, Building Two in Next Five Years"], 中国网 [China Internet Information Center], February 22, 2013, http://www.cs.com.cn/xwzx/cj/201302/t20130222_3868760.html.

31. Ibid.

32. 祁亮 [Qi Liang], 刘亮清 [Liu Liangqing], 邱爱华 [Qiu Aihua], 赵同宾 [Zhao Tongbin], and童宗鹏 [Tong Zongpeng], CSIC 711 RI, "海洋科学考察船动力系统现状及发展趋势概述" ["Overview of the Status and Development Trends of Power Plant Systems for Ocean Scientific Research Ships"], 船舶工程 [*Ship Engineering*] 36, no. 6 (2014): 1–4.

33. The first China Coast Guard (CCG) ship to have IEP was the 3,000-ton CMS 83 (now CCG 3383), commissioned in 2005. All new 3,000-ton CCG ships, of which many were launched/commissioned in 2014, appear equipped with IEP. These systems are

apparently foreign imports; China is just figuring out how to build them. Unlike any PLAN vessels to date, many also have azipods, fixed-pitch propellers mounted on steerable gondolas containing the propeller's drive motor. This gives them greater efficiency and far greater maneuverability than ships with standard shaft/propeller and rudder fits. See "Chinese Shipbuilders Develop Integrated Electric Propulsion Technology," *Next Big Future*, August 26, 2013, http://nextbigfuture.com/2013/08/chinese-shipbuilders-develop-integrated.html. Regarding CMS 83, see 苏涛 郝冬 [Su Tao and Hao Dong], "中国海监装备建设系列报道之—船舶篇—卫海疆 '剑' 出鞘" ["Report in Series on the Construction of China Marine Surveillance Equipment—Part on Ships—The 'Sword' Guarding Territorial Seas Comes out of its Scabbard"], 中国海洋报 [China Ocean News], March 15, 2011, A5, http://epaper.oceanol.com/shtml/zghyb/20110315/29507.shtml. Regarding CCG 1306, a new three-thousand-ton cutter with IEP, see "中国最先进海警执法船入列: 原地调头可横走(图)" ["China's Most Advanced Coast Guard Law Enforcement Vessel is Commissioned: Can Move Laterally, Turn Around in Place (Photos)"], CCTV via 凤凰网资讯 [Phoenix Network News], October 16, 2014, http://news.ifeng.com/a/20141016/42221643_0.shtml. Thanks to Ryan Martinson for these sources.

*Andrew Scobell, Michael E. McMahon,
Cortez A. Cooper III, and Arthur Chan*

China's Aircraft Carrier Program
Drivers, Developments, Implications

ONE OF THE MOST eye-catching episodes in the defense buildup of the People's Republic of China (PRC) was the September 25, 2012, commissioning of its first aircraft carrier. The 65,000-ton *Liaoning* launched with much fanfare, underscoring both the remarkable advances in the PRC's shipbuilding and the significant limitations that remain.

One Chinese security analyst proclaimed the launch on par in strategic significance with China's acquisition of the "two bombs [nuclear and hydrogen] and one satellite." Others sought to downplay the event, such as retired admiral Yin Zhuo, who stressed it was only a first step.[1] No matter how modest the beginnings, there are indications that China has ambitious plans: *Liaoning* is likely to be the first of as many as five carriers that the People's Liberation Army Navy (PLAN) intends to commission.[2]

That said, a number of questions remain over China's carrier program. Aviation development is a particularly important area: whether China chooses to pursue, for example, ski jump versus flat top flight decks or nuclear versus conventional propulsion will impact the range of operations that future carriers can undertake. The kinds and number of key technologies that China has mastered, is in the process of mastering, and has not yet mastered will also strongly impact how quickly the program advances. There are, additionally, a number of hurdles in technical and operational know-how that will similarly affect the pace of development.

In light of this, we examine the drivers, the operational capabilities, and the potential future trajectory of China's carrier program. Finally, we evaluate the implications of the carrier program for the balance of power in the western Pacific and beyond.

Drivers over the Decades

The earliest posited explanation for China's maritime ambitions was that of bureaucratic interests, which were identified with the South China Sea and suggested as the key driver for the carrier program.[3] The emergence of a program suggested the growing influence of the PLAN. Nevertheless, the dominant service in the People's Liberation Army (PLA) continues to be the ground force,[4] while the program's key champion appears to have been an individual rather than a bureaucracy.

A second explanation is that the carrier program is driven primarily by nationalism.[5] Most Chinese would likely agree with Major General Zhang Shiping's insistence that "for China to become a major world power without an aircraft carrier is completely unthinkable." The general, an Academy of Military Sciences researcher, insisted that "acquiring a carrier was an historical necessity" for China.[6]

A third possible driver of China's carrier program is an evolving overarching strategic logic or coherent maritime strategy.[7] Accordingly, China is pursuing a grand strategic vision by which the PLAN gradually extends its reach outward into the Pacific Ocean in three phases. By 2000, it extended its area of operations in the near seas out as far as the First Island Chain. By 2020, it will extend to the Second Island Chain. By 2050, China will become a global sea power.

This road map for the development of China's sea power grew in significance as China experienced rapid economic expansion, including in seaborne trade, during the 1980s and 1990s. China's maritime strategy gained further traction in the twenty-first century as it perceived itself as being under growing threat from the United States. We suggest that an evolving overarching strategic logic has propelled China's carrier program forward, while the program's lengthy gestation is attributable to the absence of a strategic imperative until quite recently.

China's Carrier Program Foundation

1970s: One Man's Dream

China's carrier program languished because of a lack of strategic imperative, but it persisted because of a key PLAN leader, Liu Huaqing, who rose to the Central Military Commission (CMC) vice chairmanship in 1989. As early as 1970, Liu floated to his military superiors a proposal that China begin preparations to acquire a carrier, but he did not receive much support.[8] This is unsurprising, since China's main threat was Soviet overland attack. Neither did the most logical maritime scenario—conflict involving Taiwan—receive any serious attention.

1980s: A Vision

Following Mao Zedong's death, a carrier seemed more plausible. As China embraced foreign investment and expanded international trade, Beijing began to attach greater weight to maritime matters. Territorial claims in the South China Sea and Taiwan provided added impetus for PLAN modernization.

A PRC company's purchase in 1985 of the decommissioned Australian carrier *Melbourne* signaled Beijing's growing interest in a carrier program. Liu also contributed by commissioning a study on the feasibility of carriers in 1982 and directing Guangzhou Naval Academy to initiate a training course for carrier commanders in 1985.

1990s: Serious Debate

By the mid-1990s, maritime challenges had moved to the forefront of Beijing's security concerns due to the increasing importance of the near seas and China's growing dependence on the sea lines of communication (SLOCs) extending beyond the First Island Chain. Accordingly, from 1998 to 2000, Chinese entities bought three Soviet-era carriers. By the end of the decade, CMC chair Jiang Zemin had reportedly given the green light to begin designing a carrier.

2000s: A Decision Is Made

In the new century, the maritime domain loomed ever larger in strategic significance for Beijing. The result was a "paradigmatic change" in naval thinking from the near seas to the "far seas."[9] The CMC reportedly made the decision to proceed with the construction of a carrier in August 2004, almost certainly in conjunction with CMC chairman Hu Jintao's announcement of revised military strategic guidelines. Addressing the CMC on December 24, 2004, Hu outlined what became known as the "New Historic Missions," two of which were protecting China's "national interests" and safeguarding "world peace."[10] Reportedly, Hu subsequently endorsed the concept of "far sea operations."

Together, these developments put in place the strategic and doctrinal logic for naval force modernization and for acquiring carriers. Extensive work was under way throughout the mid-2000s to complete *Varyag*, and in March 2009, PRC minister of national defense General Liang Guanglie declared that the PLAN was preparing to build its own carriers.[11]

2010s: Commissioning a Carrier

In this decade, tensions emerged with the United States and China's near seas neighbors that underscored the growing importance of sea power to China. The evolution of a strategic logic became more apparent: a carrier was needed to cope with China's expanding maritime interests. Against this backdrop, in late September 2012 the former *Varyag* was commissioned as *Liaoning*, although experts contend that it will not become fully employable for several more years.

Trajectory: A Hybrid Navy

For the next two to four years, *Liaoning* will serve primarily as a training platform, operating mostly within the First and Second Island Chains. Time will be needed for its air wing to become operationally competent and for the ship itself to conduct proficiency training with destroyers, frigates, and submarines. China will not achieve a true aircraft carrier capability until an organized and trained air component and a fully tested, fleet-configured carrier have been coupled. Incorporation of fully trained and organized, mission-capable, fleet tactical air wings is unlikely until 2018 or later.

In December 2015 an anonymous military source suggested that it would be logical to have Dalian Shipyard handle the construction of both China's first and second indigenous carriers, as the technical specialists there could capitalize on the experience and skills gained from their involvement in the construction of *Liaoning*. PLAN Research Institute specialist Senior Captain (Ret.) Li Jie maintained that it normally takes four to five years to construct a carrier in order to "ensure quality and quantity."[12] Later in March 2016, in response to a question about whether the carrier was very close to entering service, Ministry of National Defense spokesperson Yang Yujun stated that it was still undergoing construction.[13] IHS *Jane's* analysts, for their part, have estimated that

China's first domestic carrier will enter into service in 2025, with a second one following by around 2030.[14] In July 2016, satellite imagery analysis of Dalian suggested that most of the flight deck had been installed on China's first indigenous aircraft carrier hull, but the superstructure has yet to be assembled and many internals still need to be inserted.[15]

To gauge the timeline for the commissioning of China's second carrier, it makes sense to monitor the development of air component training and organization and also full production of the J-15 aircraft, and perhaps the development of the J-31. These timelines will run concurrently with the design of any indigenous carrier.

Additional carriers will probably come on line over the next two decades. The longer this is delayed, the likelier the design will be to adopt a larger deck format and increased capabilities. Also, the most modern computer-assisted design tools, construction practices, and facilities that China's shipbuilding industry has to offer will be available for the project. Major technological innovations in shipbuilding already exist, such as digitization—otherwise known as virtual manufacturing—which acts as a "factory inside the computer" to create virtual product models that allow people to foresee potential problems and outcomes ahead of actual manufacturing.[16] There is also mass customization, which continues to evolve to achieve the lowest cost for the most individualized degree of customization for ship components.[17] Over the next two decades, these technologies will continue to evolve, to the great benefit of the carrier program. The large scope of the design work involved in *Liaoning*'s conversion is also likely to provide a "walking start" for a more modern carrier.

The PLAN does not appear to be building a future force with carriers at its core, according to current doctrine and naval modernization. Nevertheless, as Yin Zhuo observes, the introduction of carriers demands a major change in PLAN thinking and requires in the near term a modified "grouping format" of escort vessels with *Liaoning* at the center.[18] Therefore, China's navy appears to have adopted a hybrid approach encompassing both carrier and surface-action groups for mission-specific operations and the projection of influence.

Operational Demands

China's growing maritime interests expand the operational demands on the PLAN. Meanwhile, the most pressing operational logic for aircraft carriers relates to the value they add in wartime. Today, carriers offer the PLAN extended blue-water capability and an improved capacity for antisubmarine warfare (ASW) and airborne early warning (AEW). At present, however, ASW and AEW vulnerabilities remain too great for *Liaoning* to be successfully employed in high-intensity maritime combat.

What difference would carriers make in a contingency inside the First Island Chain? In a South China Sea clash, *Liaoning* would provide extra air-power projection against opposing combatants. One or two carriers would offer little in an East China Sea battle, however. As for a Taiwan contingency, carrier air would not contribute much in the fight. The use of a carrier would further complicate the PLA's current doctrinal approach—missile-centric fire-power strike and counterintervention operations, supported by advanced information warfare.

The choice to retain the Soviet-era short take-off but arrested recovery (STOBAR) design suggests that *Liaoning*'s missions will be limited. A ski jump bow and the absence of catapults restrict the size and weight of an aircraft that can take off from the deck (and the payload and amount of fuel it can carry). Thus, the on-board air wing will focus on air defense. Finally, *Liaoning* is con-ventionally powered, limiting its range and necessitating regular refueling.

Noncombat Operations

Additional demands include expected contributions to peacetime operations. Since at least 2008 the PLA has emphasized military operations other than war (MOOTW) as a doctrinal component. MOOTW "with Chinese charac-teristics" includes substantial maritime and overseas elements, and the PLAN appears poised to play a central role in the doctrine, including in support of SLOC protection, humanitarian assistance, and disaster relief.

Program Prospects

Given that aircraft training on *Liaoning* has utilized J-15 carrier-based fighter aircraft in the current STOBAR design arrangements, the observed pace of other tactical aircraft development, and potential sea-based aircraft hosted missions, one can assume that any follow-on carrier designs will be a large angled deck design for either STOBAR aircraft operations (initially) or trend-ing toward a larger ship in displacement and size with catapult-assisted takeoff and a multimission air component in subsequent ships.

It is reasonable to believe that an indigenously designed and constructed carrier program may follow an evolutionary design path. There are several reasons why this may occur and why it may be expected that the PLAN's first follow-on carrier might be a large deck, STOBAR derivative of the *Liaoning* or a derived hull form with some initial technology insertion. First, the technology maturity from development through production is likely not available for key future desired systems.

Second, a pathway to a different propulsion scheme with a (necessary) substantial increase in electrical power generation will require a large ship design and component development effort. However, there is no evidence that this is occurring at an advanced developmental state. China's military research, development, testing, and evaluation (RDT&E) activities would likely utilize highly capable design product model tools. Such efforts for the eventual desired platform may be ongoing concurrent to design and early construction of ship modules for the first indigenous carrier. More recently, there has been added impetus for these efforts—stemming not only from the significant limitations to what *Liaoning* can do but also from the maritime ambitions of India. In early May 2015, the government of India announced the approval of the IAC-2 aircraft carrier program, which is focused to deliver a large 65,000-ton aircraft carrier with catapults and potentially nuclear propulsion. In light of this, China may choose this same path in order to keep pace with this potential rival in the Indian Ocean.

Mastering Key Technologies

Development of next-generation sea-based tactical aircraft and engine technology will be among the greatest challenges for China's military RDT&E system. There is little doubt that China could construct a large angled deck carrier. Catapult and arresting gear technology is derivable from existing technology, but transition to electromagnetic launch systems is likely years away in development. Similarly, transition to alternate carrier propulsion schemes would be a considerable developmental step. As Andrew Erickson, Jonathan Ray, and Robert Forte note in their chapter in this volume, integrated electric propulsion (IEP) and nuclear power are two promising alternative approaches that China might choose to pursue for future carriers. It is true that "it currently lacks IEP experience almost completely" and "still lacks experience with nuclear power with aircraft carriers." However, these options could become feasible given sufficient time. Moreover, if China's shipbuilding industry can master such new energy technologies as biofuels, photovoltaic/wind energy, and others, it will lead to the PLAN operating at a lower cost and "improve the ability of the Chinese navy to perform independent and sustained combat operations."[19]

Overcoming Principal Hurdles

Two key areas for future system development are likely to be the manufacturing technology in aircraft engines and the manufacturing technology and system design in power electronics. Another substantial hurdle will probably be pilot and flight deck crew proficiency for carrier flight operations. China's military RDT&E system is likely to have substantial information on carrier-based technologies for many of the key systems discussed by acquiring unclassified information. Much of this has come and continues to come from Russia through open purchase of a wide range of advanced technologies and systems as well as obtaining Russian assistance in reverse-engineering them. China also closely monitors developments in U.S. naval technology and seeks to emulate them, as the PLA Naval University of Engineering is now doing with the Electromagnetic Aircraft Launch Systems. However, difficulties arise when it comes to pulling all of this information together to create not just individual systems but a unified system-of-systems. Moreover, although China is a prolific shipbuilder, it has a shortage of experts—that is, engineers with sufficient levels of technical know-how—creating another potential bottleneck. Acquiring and mastering new generations of tactical aircraft development and training will also prove difficult.

Conclusion

An overarching strategic logic and still-evolving national maritime strategy powered China's carrier program to initial realization. This growing strategic logic and the emerging operational demands for a carrier in the twenty-first century corresponds to an extension of PLA thinking beyond a Taiwan Strait scenario. Moreover, the strategic and operational value of a carrier increases as the PLAN expands its horizons beyond the First and Second Island Chains.

Liaoning remains far from fully operational. Significant hurdles also remain in terms of aviation development and Chinese mastery of the key technologies needed to increase the operational flexibility of future carriers. Meanwhile, the PLAN remains years away from projecting and sustaining significant naval power out of area. In China, however, *Liaoning* has captured imaginations, and Beijing is intent on playing a greater role in patrolling SLOCs. China's first aircraft carrier is also a visible symbol of the country's growing naval prowess and is useful in noncombat missions. But in an era of precision-guided munitions and enhanced over-the-horizon surveillance and reconnaissance, in wartime *Liaoning* becomes vulnerable, especially against a highly capable adversary.

Therefore, China's aircraft carrier program by itself does not merit alarm in the Pentagon. Carriers will extend the range of Chinese airpower and further complicate an already complex operating environment in the near seas, but one or more PLAN carriers will not fundamentally transform the balance of power in the western Pacific. In the near and medium term, for example, if U.S. forces needed to intervene in the South China Sea and directly confront Chinese forces, the latter would inevitably be at a disadvantage. Moreover, by the time China possesses multiple carriers and becomes adept at operating them, carriers may be almost irrelevant.[20] Perhaps the greatest impact of China's carrier program will be the stimulus it provides to the naval shipbuilding industry. For example, focusing on the engineering challenges associated with carriers might produce technological innovations that could have wider applications. Moreover, the carrier program might inspire a generation of Chinese engineers to pursue a career path they otherwise would never have considered if not for incentives such as scholarships, research grants, and the chance to design and build powerful symbols of China's great power status.

Notes

1. 曲延涛 [Qu Yantao], "专家: 中国航母入列犹如核武将降低战争概率" [Experts: Chinese Carrier Enters Service—Like Nuclear Weapon, Will Reduce Frequency of War], 环球时报 [Global Times], September 7, 2012, http://mil.huanqiu.com/observ ation/2012-09/3152679.html.

2. For a more detailed analysis with full citations, see Andrew Scobell, Michael McMahon, and Cortez A. Cooper III, "China Carrier Program: Drivers, Developments, Implications," *Naval War College Review* 68, no. 4 (Autumn 2015).

3. See, for example, John W. Garver, "China's Push through the South China Sea: The Interaction of Bureaucratic and National Interests," *China Quarterly*, no. 132 (December 1992): 999–1028.

4. See Andrew Scobell and Andrew J. Nathan, "China's Overstretched Military," *Washington Quarterly* 35, no. 4 (Fall 2012): 135–48.

5. See, for example, Robert S. Ross, "China's Naval Nationalism: Sources, Prospects, and the U.S. Response," *International Security* 34, no. 2 (Fall 2009): 46–81.

6. Zhang Shiping, 中国海权 [*China's Sea Power*] (Beijing: People's Daily Press, 2009), 2.

7. See, for example, Bernard D. Cole, *The Great Wall at Sea: China's Navy in the Twenty-First Century,* second ed. (Annapolis, MD: Naval Institute Press, 2010).

8. Liu Huaqing, 刘华清回忆录 [*Memoirs of Liu Huaqing*] (Beijing: PLA Press, 2004), 477.

9. Tang Fuquan and Han Yi, "人民海军沿着党指引的航向破浪前进" ["People's Navy Advances Along the Course Set by (the) Party"], 中国军事科学 [*China Military Science*], no. 4 (2009): 14.

10. The text of Hu Jintao's speech has not been made public but has been widely cited. For a concise overview, see Daniel Hartnett, "China Military and Security Activities," Hearings before the U.S.-China Economic and Security Review Commission, 111 Cong., 1st sess., March 4, 2009 (Washington, DC: U.S. Government Printing Office, April 2009), 45–55.

11. Cole, *Great Wall at Sea*, 88–90.

12. Zhang Yichi, "专家: 中国造航母有自己的节奏 前两艘或都大连造" ["Expert: China Has Own Pace for Making Carriers, First Two May Be Made at Dalian"], 环球时报 [*Global Times*], December 8, 2015, http://mil.huanqiu.com/observation/2015-12/8124361.html.

13. Qiu Yue, "国产航母距离下水不远了? 国防部: 建造过程当中" ["Indigenous Carrier Not Far from Launch? MND: Still Undergoing Construction"], 人民网 [*People's Daily* online], March 31, 2016, http://military.people.com.cn/n1/2016/0331/c1011-28242395.html.

14. Alex Pape and Take Nurkin, paper presented at "China's Naval Shipbuilding: Progress and Challenges" conference, China Maritimes Studies Institute, May 19, 2015, 7.

15. Sean O'Connor, "Flight Deck of China's First Indigenous Carrier Almost Complete," *Jane's Defence Weekly*, July 20, 2016.

16. Zhao Kaiwen and Ma Yunyi, 舰船技术与设计概论, 第2版 [*Introduction to Technology and Ship Design, Second Edition*] (Beijing: National Defense University Press, 2014), 1004.

17. Ibid., 1001.

18. Qu, Zhou, and Cai, 解放军报, 4.

19. Xie Wei and Lu Chao, "浅析我国海洋发展战略及未来船舶发展趋势" ["An Analysis of China's Maritime Development Strategy and Trends in Ship Development"], *Ship and Ocean Engineering* 42, no. 3 (June 2013): 16.

20. For a U.S. perspective, see Robert C. Rubel, "The Future of Aircraft Carriers," *Naval War College Review* 64, no. 4 (Autumn 2011): 13–27.

PART V

Conclusions and Alternative Futures

James E. Fanell and Scott Cheney-Peters

Maximal Scenario
Expansive Naval Trajectory to "China's Naval Dream"

IN 2013, AS PRESIDENT Xi Jinping unveiled his "China Dream" in a speech to the People's Republic of China's (PRC's) National People's Congress, China Central Television aired the week-long series "Shaping Tomorrow's China," exploring what Chinese people think about the China Dream. What is noteworthy is that the network began the series with the story of a People's Liberation Army Navy (PLAN) East Sea Fleet–based executive officer just returned from his third escort mission in the Gulf of Aden. Lieutenant Commander Shi Lei related that when he joined the PLAN a decade prior, he had never envisioned sailing so far from land, but he now believed the PLAN would one day have a "blue-water navy whose sailors can take on any mission on the open sea."[1]

China's Maritime Dream

Significantly, this episode explains China's shift in maritime strategy over the past decade, from solely capabilities for a "near seas active defense" strategy to a national maritime strategy based on responsibilities and presence across the global maritime domain. Not surprisingly, it aligned President Xi's call for

China to become "a strong maritime power" with former President Hu Jintao's direction to "resolutely safeguard China's maritime rights and interests, and build China into a maritime power."[2] Since the end of the Ninth Five-Year Plan in 2000, the PRC has embarked on an ambitious naval construction program that has dramatically increased the PLAN's and China Coast Guard's (CCG's) blue-water operations within the First and Second Island Chains while substantially increasing far seas deployments around much of the globe. With the realization of the "China Dream" firmly linked to a global naval capability, this chapter contends that China's leaders have not yet achieved their goals; however, they have both the will and the means to push for rapid increases in the PLAN's order of battle by 2030 in support of an expanding set of missions to fulfill their "China Dream" of national restoration and rejuvenation. Undergirding this thesis are China's present and future naval construction capabilities and capacity, successful ongoing expansion of naval operations, and official advocacy for a modern, global naval force—one that is already posing a challenge for its neighbors and the U.S. Navy.

Our projections are based on several assumptions. First, regardless of potential domestic political or economic difficulties, China's leaders will continue investment "in the Navy, Coast Guard, and maritime industries to more actively and effectively assert its security and economic interests in the coming decades."[3] Second, China will continue to enjoy a military shipbuilding cost advantage over rivals.[4] And third, China will master the technical advances required to overcome issues arising from the production and incorporation of advanced naval systems—from phased array radars to nuclear reactors.

Shipbuilding Capability and Capacity[5]

Since the 1990s, Chinese naval shipyards evolved from an era of very limited high-end production (i.e., building only three destroyers in the 1990s) to one of rapid mass production, with a single shipyard simultaneously producing seven Type 052D Luyang III-class guided missile destroyers (DDGs).[6] The past fifteen years of Chinese naval shipbuilding were transformative, exhibiting several trends affecting capabilities and capacity. First, naval construction in China focused on platform modernization over fleet expansion. Second, both the preference for and quality of indigenous ship design increased. And third, shipbuilding itself became more advanced and efficient in China.

During 2005–12, the growth in Chinese naval shipbuilding supported "modernization and replacement, not rapid expansion," with China's combatant fleet growing only "slowly."[7] The Office of Naval Intelligence (ONI) also noted China's modernization "concentrated on improving the quality of its force, rather than its size."[8] This was the case despite an increase in average production of major surface combatants (destroyers and frigates) from 1.6 per year in 2000–04 to 4.2 per year in 2010–14.[9]

Meanwhile, the unified CCG that emerged in 2013 inherited and continued a "major modernization, increasing both the sizes of its ships and their overall capability." Over the past decade, nearly one hundred new vessels joined the fleet, while the 2012–15 phase of construction alone is expected to increase the CCG's force level by 25 percent.[10]

Simultaneously, Chinese shipbuilders have relied less on foreign expertise in the design of vessels and their systems, underwritten by a growth in technical expertise across the shipbuilding enterprise.[11] By 2010, thanks in part to "China's rapid technological advancement in naval design," surface ship production shifted largely to Chinese designs, while warships' weapons and sensor systems likewise became indigenous.[12]

Moreover, the technological capability of production has itself increased, boosting shipbuilding efficiency.[13] For example, Chinese shipyards have adopted modular construction techniques for warship production, allowing integration of dispersed centers of technical excellence and production.[14] Meanwhile, advances at individual shipyards are likely to be shared due to collaboration by the two state-owned naval vessel producers—China State Shipbuilding Corporation (CSSC) and China Shipbuilding Industry Corporation (CSIC).[15]

Future Naval Shipbuilding Trends

Increased Capacity

According to ONI, "In 2013 and 2014, China launched more naval ships than any other country."[16] Developments indicate this trend will hold for the next fifteen years and provide a capacity for more marked fleet expansion and greater technical capabilities.

Regarding capacity, CSSC's and CSIC's shipyards boast some of the newest, "quite good" infrastructure, so investment can be dedicated to expansion rather than upgrades.[17] The PLAN has been similarly modernized, as China's policy of rapidly replacing legacy combatants updated much of the fleet.[18] By conservative estimates, 74 percent of PLAN nonamphibious surface vessels are "modern."[19] While many of these consist of small missile craft designed for near seas operations, new far seas vessels will augment, not replace, their coastal counterparts. Although a portion of current and future shipyard capacity must still be devoted to recapitalizing current vessels, thanks to the PLAN's modernization, a greater share can be turned to fleet expansion.

China can also exploit nonmilitary shipyard capacity. CCG modernization and a boom in commercial shipbuilding expanded capacity and developed workforce skills. However, a downturn has roughly halved China's commercial delivery tonnage, creating a large amount of slack capacity and a struggling sector that could be buoyed through naval shipbuilding orders, although so using these yards would be costly.[20] Beyond unfamiliarity with naval systems, many of these struggling private shipyards would require infrastructure upgrades to meet technological standards and increasingly stringent Chinese shipbuilding regulations.[21] Instead, state yards' commercial subsidiaries might be the beneficiaries as experts predict that "with commercial shipbuilding in the doldrums," CSSC and CSIC "are likely to" lobby "hard for fleet expansion."[22]

Another source of capacity is the growth of China's naval exports. Increased Chinese technical capabilities are likely to bolster China's standing as "a serious export competitor in the corvette, frigate and diesel-submarine markets," which in turn increases the capacity of its naval shipyards, cost advantage, and workers.[23] While China has mostly focused on selling smaller surface vessels, its buyers' list has grown, and orders have increased in complexity. The capacity required to support this business and the vessels under contract could, as in past conflicts, be turned to domestic use.

Increased Capability

In technical capability, too, several trends indicate an increasing Chinese ability to support an expansive naval trajectory, with many having the added benefit of increasing production efficiency—an area still ripe for gains in Chinese shipyards.

At one end of the labor spectrum, Chinese shipyards could seek productivity gains by adopting increased automation. In one South Korean shipyard, robots execute tasks "from cutting and grinding steel to polishing freshly assembled hulls," having automated 68 percent of welding work.[24] Samsung has even developed a "spider automatic welding robot" with reported productivity gains of 400 percent.[25] At the other end of the spectrum, exoskeletons combine experienced human shipyard workers' expertise and judgment with increased strength and endurance. This approach provides a range of benefits for shipyards, including reduced labor costs and increased productivity, quality, and retention of a skilled labor pool.[26]

Another advance with major impacts to shipyards is the increasing sophistication of additive manufacturing (AM), more commonly known as three-dimensional (3D) printing. AM can aid shipbuilders by reducing the time and costs of prototyping, increasing the efficiency of naval ship systems and their construction, and increasing large-scale automation and rapid customization.[27] At Norfolk Naval Shipyard, for example, workers have gained experience using AM in direct applications for ship overhauls and refits with techniques that can readily apply to ship construction.[28]

Chinese officials and researchers are actively exploring how technology will allow them to "bolster their defense industry and play a leading role in the next technological revolution."[29] The PLAN demonstrated its willingness to adopt AM operationally when the *Luyang III*-class DDG *Harbin* suffered an engine bearing casualty while on antipiracy patrol in the Gulf of Aden and used its onboard 3D printer to create a replacement part.[30] It also appears that a CSIC subsidiary has used AM for rapid prototyping of naval systems.[31] Although China's shipyards have not yet fully implemented AM, they are adopting many of the underlying concepts driving its potential, including digitization of naval vessel system designs for use in planning, prototyping, construction, and digital parts files.

These trends—opportunities for increased capacity, maturing technical capabilities, and a willingness to engage with new technologies that can drive capacity and capability further—support the underpinnings of a growing PLAN. Even granted this chapter's assumptions, PLAN modernization and growth challenges remain—from systems integration to continued reluctance for collaboration at the research stage—yet none are insurmountable. Despite additional recapitalization, the PLAN will retain considerable capacity for fleet expansion thanks in part to completed modernization and capacity developed for other purposes—should PRC decisionmakers choose to pursue the option.

The Demand Signal

What, then, are the requirements of the PLAN and CCG in support of China's "rejuvenation," and how do they influence shipbuilding demand? Lacking a detailed Chinese shipbuilding plan, our analysis examined external evidence to extrapolate the numbers of ships and submarines needed by 2030 to achieve internal goals. The following requirements are assessed as most important for China's future expansive naval trajectory:

- nears seas active defense operations
- far seas operations
- goodwill deployments
- surge operations
- the "Maritime Silk Road"
- carrier strike groups (CSGs)
- amphibious assault groups
- submarine-launched ballistic missile (SLBM) patrols.

Near Seas Active Defense Operations

The near seas active defense strategy was introduced in 1993, and the PLAN embarked on a naval modernization program aimed at preventing the U.S. Navy from aiding Taiwan and impeding an opposing naval force by establishing a layered defense in and around the First Island Chain.[32] In 2014, Admiral Wu Shengli noted China must "actively expand [its] strategic defensive depth in the maritime direction."[33] With reunification with Taiwan remaining a "core national interest" for China, the near seas active defense strategy will remain a primary requirement for the PLAN into the foreseeable future.

Far Seas Operations

China's maritime strategy has evolved to support "far seas protection," with the main purpose of "defending China's expanding national interests."[34] Concurrent with China's growing global interests, over the course of the past decade the world witnessed the PLAN's expanded operations. Admiral Wu has remarked that "China needs to take a broad view of the world, become globalized, and extend the perspective of strategic management of the sea from the doorstep of our territorial seas and exclusive economic zones to the far seas."[35]

An examination of previous PLAN operations and emerging missions indicates an upward-pointing trajectory. Researching PLAN development from 2004 to 2014, Christopher Sharman concluded that China is "likely to gradually increase" the frequency of deployments "to the far seas over the next 5 to 7 years," strongly suggesting the past decade is a harbinger of a new normalization for far seas operations.[36] PLAN transformation will thus require a new force structure, mandating increases in naval platforms' number and type.

Goodwill Deployments

PLAN combatants are also venturing further afield in goodwill deployments to "show the flag" and demonstrate the nation's great power capability. For instance, the PLAN's eighteenth antipiracy task force conducted an unprecedented visit to northern Europe while aiming to enhance rapport with the overseas Chinese communities in each of the visited countries.[37] PLAN diplomacy deployments have expanded to include exercises with foreign navies. In the Mediterranean exercise Joint Sea 2015-I, three PRC ships exercised the "protection of navigation safety in the far seas" with six ships from Russia.[38]

By "facilitating real-time interagency coordination," PLAN sailors and officers learn how to face unscripted situations at sea and gain unprecedented operational training, unquestionably boosting China's confidence.[39] Beijing understands that PLAN "show the flag" deployments can be a valuable instrument of foreign policy and will ensure it has the ships to conduct them.

Surge Operations

The PLAN also demonstrated the capability to conduct rapid, surge far seas deployments in 2014, when China dispatched multiple PLAN, CCG, and even Maritime Militia vessels to the Indian Ocean to search for the lost Malaysian airliner MH370. While the Chinese are proud of providing the largest number of naval forces and resources for this search, more importantly PLAN leaders learned first-hand the value of being able to surge a naval force at the time and place of their choosing. Yet this kind of rapid reaction capability is not something the PRC can sustain within existing force structure, as it learned when forced to redirect vessels from the antipiracy operation in the Gulf of Aden to noncombatant evacuation operations in Aden, Yemen, in 2015.

"Maritime Silk Road"

President Xi Jinping's new "Silk Road Economic Belt and 21st Century Maritime Silk Road" initiative will also influence PLAN shipbuilding. An essential part of the "China Dream," the "One Belt, One Road" is intended "to better connect" China's "economy with the rest of Asia, Africa, the Middle East, and Europe."[40] While the "blueprint" for the belt and road continues to evolve, it increases the demand for more combatants to protect this global initiative.

Carrier Strike Groups

The development of CSGs will also have a profound impact on China's shipbuilding program, with estimates of at least four total aircraft carriers, matching an historic U.S. Navy four-to-one force structure for operations.[41] The associated strike group for each carrier protects it against air, surface, and subsurface threats. Additionally, carriers and their huge crews and embarked air wings need ships providing logistics support for far seas operations. Although some suggest these requirements could be resourced by diverting ships from the PLAN's three fleets ad hoc, "leading figures in the PLA" argue "that carriers are envisioned as 'forming maritime operations systems.'" As *People's Navy* notes, "Without the large-scale comprehensive operations power of an aircraft carrier group, it is difficult for [China's] ocean forces to form overall organic operations."[42]

PLAN leaders have not published the exact disposition of the CSG; however, a *PLA Daily* article stated it will include "four to six guided missile destroyers and guided missile frigates, one to two nuclear attack submarines or new-type conventional submarines and one comprehensive supply ship."[43] By including a logistics ship and escort submarines, the potential exists that each Chinese carrier strike group could be as large as ten combatants, while "large amphibious warfare ships . . . will also be included in the formation."[44]

Amphibious Assault Groups

A large-scale invasion capability remains a PLAN primary requirement.[45] While conducting a large-scale amphibious assault on Taiwan would generate its own force requirements, given the PRC's actions in the East and South China Seas, it is also now likely PLAN leadership will pursue the development of credible amphibious assault forces for these contingencies over the next fifteen years.

PLAN leadership has been testing various amphibious designs and has chosen the *Yuzhao*-class Type 071 amphibious transport dock for serial production. China is likely to combine these with new support forces into several groups of amphibious assault forces. Additionally, the PLAN is expected to produce a complementary Type 081 landing helicopter dock amphibious assault ship.

SLBM Patrols

ONI's most recent assessment suggested that to "maintain a continuous peacetime presence, the PLAN would likely require a minimum of five *Jin*-class SSBNs [ballistic missile submarines]"; four are currently in service.[46] Yet a single *Jin*-class SLBM patrol provides neither serious survivability nor credible second-strike deterrence capability. China's leaders would plausibly pursue multiple SSBNs on patrol by 2030, necessarily requiring increased numbers of SSBNs. Congressional testimony by then-U.S. Pacific Command commander Admiral Samuel Locklear, USN (Ret.), supports this hypothesis, stating China might have eight *Jin*-class SSBNs by the end of the decade.[47]

Future PRC Naval Force Estimate

What does this mean for Chinese naval construction over the next fifteen years? The bottom line is that Beijing has demonstrated it has the shipbuilding capacity and capabilities, untapped productivity gains, and global requirements to drive a transformational period of growth in Chinese naval construction and combat capability by 2030 to meet an expanded mission set.

ONI's most recent study (see exhibit 14-1) reports the PLAN consists of over 330 surface vessels and a total of 66 submarines.[48]

Exhibit 14-1. PLAN—Platform Inventory in 2015

Platform	Inventory
Destroyers	26 (21 modern)
Frigates	52 (35 modern)
Corvettes	20 (all modern)
Missile patrol craft	85 (60 modern)
Amphibious ships	56
Mine-warfare ships	42 (30 modern)
Major auxiliaries	50+
Total surface combatants	331+
Nuclear-powered attack submarines	5
Ballistic missile submarines	4
Submarines	57
Total submarines	66

Source: Office of Naval Intelligence, *The PLA Navy: New Capabilities and Missions for the 21st Century* (Suitland, MD: Office of Naval Intelligence, 2015).

Given the increasing PRC shipbuilding capacity and capabilities outlined above, it is likely that by 2030 the PLAN surface force could approach 450 hulls and over 99 total submarines (see exhibit 14-2), a growth rate of 30 percent and over 50 percent respectively, compared to approximately 15 percent for over-all 2000–15 PLAN growth.[49] This expected force would satisfy the requirements for fleet expansion to meet Beijing's "goal of rejuvenation of the Chinese Nation."[50]

Exhibit 14-2. PLAN 2030—Forecast Platform Inventory

Platform	Inventory
Destroyers	34
Frigates	68
Corvettes	26
Missile patrol craft	111
Amphibious ships	73
Mine-warfare ships	55
Major auxiliaries	65+
Total surface combatants	432+
Nuclear-powered attack submarines	12
Ballistic missile submarines	12
Conventionally powered submarines	75
Total submarines	99

Source: Authors' calculations.

In order to achieve the "China Dream," the PLAN of 2030 will not resemble the PLAN of 2015. Rather, it will enjoy a global presence characterized by multiple strike groups, a credible SLBM capability, and an ever-present network of ships at sea. Thanks to the strength of its naval shipbuilding capacity and its commitment to national rejuvenation, the PLAN will present an expansive and formidable challenge, one the United States can ill afford to underestimate or ignore.

Notes

1. Han Bin, "Shaping Tomorrow's China: PLA Navy Modernization," China Central Television, May 1, 2013, http://english.cntv.cn/program/newshour/20130501/102999.shtml.

2. "Full Text of Hu Jintao's Report at the 18th Party Congress," *Xinhua*, November 17, 2012, www.china-embassy.org/eng/zt/18th_CPC_National_Congress_Eng/t992917.htm.

3. Office of Naval Intelligence (ONI), *The PLA Navy: New Capabilities and Missions for the 21st Century* (Suitland, MD: ONI, April 2015), 5.

4. Gabe Collins and Andrew Erickson, "U.S. Navy Take Notice: China Is Becoming a World-Class Military Shipbuilder," *Diplomat*, November 1, 2012, http://thediplomat.com/2012/11/u-s-navy-take-notice-china-is-becoming-a-world-class-military-shipbuilder/.

5. Although we differentiate naval and commercial shipbuilding wherever possible, we consider CCG vessels with the former due to the comparable resources and complexity required.

6. "Seven Type 052D Destroyers Being Built in Shanghai Port," *Want China Times*, May 2, 2015, http://www.wantchinatimes.com/news-subclass-cnt.aspx?cid=1101&MainCatID=11&id=20150502000003.

7. Collins and Erickson, "U.S. Navy Take Notice."

8. ONI, *The PLA Navy*, 4.

9. Ronald O'Rourke, "China Naval Modernization: Implications for U.S. Navy Capabilities—Background and Issues for Congress," Congressional Research Service, July 28, 2015, 28, 30.

10. ONI, *The PLA Navy*, 42.

11. For example, by 2008, China produced 1,500 marine engineers and naval architects per year, roughly seven times the graduates from U.S. institutions. Gabe Collins and Michael Grubb, "A Comprehensive Survey of China's Dynamic Shipbuilding Industry," China Maritime Studies 1 (Newport, RI: U.S. Naval War College, August 2008), 2.

12. Ibid., 12, 15.

13. ONI, *The PLA Navy*, 9.

14. Gabe Collins and Andrew Erickson, "China Carrier Demo Module Highlights Surging Navy," *National Interest*, August 6, 2013, http://nationalinterest.org/commentary/china-carrier-demo-module-highlights-surging-navy-8842.

15. Office of the Secretary of Defense (OSD), *Annual Report to Congress: Military and Security Developments Involving the People's Republic of China 2016* (Washington, DC: Office of the Secretary of Defense, April 2015), 80.

16. ONI, *The PLA Navy*, 12.

17. Collins and Erickson, "China Carrier Demo."

18. ONI, *The PLA Navy*, 10.

19. Based on data available in ONI, *The PLA Navy*, 12, 15.

20. Kyunghee Park, "China Loses Shipbuilding Crown to South Korea: Chart of the Day," *Bloomberg News*, December 9, 2014, http://www.bloomberg.com/news/arti cles/2014-12-09/china-loses-shipbuilding-crown-to-south-korea-chart-of-the-day.

21. "Deconstructing China's Shipbuilding Industry," *Naval Architect* (February 2014), http://www.rina.org.uk/article1335.html.

22. Collins and Erickson, "China Carrier Demo."

23. Ibid.

24. Hal Hodson, "Robotic Suit Gives Shipyard Workers Super Strength," *New Scientist*, August 4, 2014, http://www.newscientist.com/article/mg22329803.900-robotic-suit -gives-shipyard-workers-super-strength.html.

25. "Spider Automatic Welding Robot," Samsung Heavy Industries, https://www.shi.sam sung.co.kr/Eng/product/tech_prd02.aspx.

26. Andrew Herr and Scott Cheney-Peters, "Between Iron Man and Aqua Man: Exosuit Opportunities and Maritime Operations," Center for a New American Security, January 2015, 13.

27. Scott Cheney-Peters and Matt Hipple, "Print Me a Cruiser!" U.S. Naval Institute *Proceedings* 139, no. 4 (April 2013).

28. Michael Brayshaw, "Process Improvement: How 3D Printing is Changing Norfolk Naval Shipyard," *CHIPS*, April 16, 2014, http://www.doncio.navy.mil/CHIPS/ ArticleDetails.aspx?id=5071.

29. Eric Anderson, "Additive Manufacturing in China: Aviation and Aerospace Applications—Part 2," *IGCC SITC Bulletin Analysis*, May 2013, http://igcc.ucsd.edu/ assets/001/504640.pdf.

30. Sarah Anderson, "China's PLA Navy Deploys 3D Printers Onboard Warships to Replace Small Parts," *3Dprint.com*, January 8, 2015, http://3dprint.com/3598l/china -pla-navy-3d-printing.

31. "Ship Components Made by SLA Laser Light Curving Process," *Shining 3D*, November 25, 2014, http://en.shining3d.com/support_detail-4311.html.

32. Christopher Sharman, "China Moves Out: Stepping Stones Toward a New Maritime Strategy," China Strategic Perspectives 9 (Washington, DC: National Defense University Press, November 2014), 4, http://ndupress.ndu.edu/Portals/68/Documents/ stratperspective/china/ChinaPerspectives-9.pdf.

33. Wu Shengli, "Learn Profound Historical Lessons from the Sino-Japanese War of 1894– 1895 and Unswervingly Take the Path of Planning and Managing Maritime Affairs, Safeguarding Maritime Rights and Interests, and Building a Powerful Navy," *China Military Science* (April 2014): 1–4.

34. Office of Naval Intelligence, *The People's Liberation Army Navy: A Modern Navy with Chinese Characteristics* (Suitland, MD: ONI, 2013), 7.

35. Wu, "Learn Profound Historical Lessons," 2.

36. Sharman, "China Moves Out," 1–2.

37. "Remarks by H. E. Ambassador Liu Xiaoming at Reception for Chinese Naval Escort Group (Portsmouth, 12 January 2015)," Embassy of the People's Republic of China in the United Kingdom of Great Britain and Northern Ireland, January 13, 2015, http://www.chinese-embassy.org.uk/eng/EmbassyNews/t1227628.htm.

38. "Defense Ministry's Regular Press Conference on April 30, 2015," Ministry of National Defense, The People's Republic of China, http://eng.mod.gov.cn/TopNews/2015-04/30/content_4582748.htm.

39. Andrew Erickson and Austin Strange, "No Substitute for Experience: Chinese Antipiracy Operations in the Gulf of Aden," China Maritime Studies 10 (Newport, RI: U.S. Naval War College, November 2013), 2–3, http://www.usnwc.edu/Research-Gaming/China-Maritime-Studies-Institute/Publications.aspx.

40. "Blueprint Set for Belt, Road," *Global Times*, March 30, 2015, http://www.ecns.cn/2015/03-30/159822.shtml.

41. Admiral Gary Roughead, USN (Ret.), "No to a Smaller Navy," *New York Times*, March 13, 2015, http://www.nytimes.com/2015/03/14/opinion/no-to-a-smaller-navy.html?_r=0.

42. 左立平 [Zuo Liping], 航母舰队—驰骋海战场的大国重剑 ["Carrier Group Is the Fencing Foil of a Great Nation, Plays a Major Part on Sea Battlefields"], 人民海军 [*People's Navy*], December 3, 2014, 4; op. cit. Andrew Erickson, "A Work in Progress: China's Development of Carrier Strike," *Jane's Navy International*, June 19, 2014, 3.

43. "PLA Navy Makes Preparations for Aircraft Carrier Formation," *PLA Daily*, December 13, 2012, http://eng.chinamil.com.cn/news-channels/china-military-news/2012-12/13/content_5140986.htm.

44. Ibid.

45. Phillip Saunders, Christopher Yung, Michael Swaine, and Andrew Nien-Dzu Yang, eds., *The Chinese Navy: Expanding Capabilities, Evolving Roles* (Washington, DC: National Defense University Press, 2011), 50, 53.

46. ONI, *The PLA Navy*, 20.

47. "Demystifying Nuclear Subs a Welcome Move," *Global Times*, October 29, 2013, http://www.globaltimes.cn/content/820956.shtml.

48. ONI, *The PLA Navy*, 15, 19.

49. Craig Murray, Andrew Berglund, and Kimberly Hsu, "China's Naval Modernization and Implications for the United States," U.S.-China Economic Security Review Commission Staff Research Backgrounder, August 26, 2013, 7.

50. Xi Jinping, "Achieving Rejuvenation Is the Dream of Chinese People," *The Governance of China* (Beijing: Foreign Languages Press, 2014), 38.

Michael McDevitt

Medium Scenario
World's Second "Far Seas" Navy by 2020

CHINA'S SHIPPING CAPACITY growth over the past decade has been phenomenal. Many assume this growth greatly facilitates the expansion of the People's Liberation Army Navy (PLAN) and that China's shipbuilding capacity will be able to satisfy PLAN growth objectives—whatever they may be. Is this assumption correct, or will limitations on China's warship building capacity restrict PLAN growth, forcing the service to pace its developmental objectives to the ability of Chinese shipbuilders to produce complex warships?

Unfortunately, since the building objectives for the PLAN are not publicly available, a definitive answer is not possible—at least using open sources. Unlike every other country with a major naval establishment, China is unique in that it does not reveal how many ships and submarines of each class it intends to build. In all other sea powers, this information is available: building warships is expensive and involves seeking funds from legislative bodies. This process naturally involves public information specifying what a government actually intends to buy.

Because of this lack of Chinese transparency, reaching judgments about future PLAN size and composition requires an iterative approach that combines informed speculation by experienced PLAN watchers, semi-authoritative comments from Chinese specialists, open-source space- and ground-based photos of Chinese shipyards, commentary from official U.S. government sources such as the recent Office of Naval Intelligence (ONI) report on the PLAN[1] and the annual reports to Congress on the People's Liberation Army (PLA) from the Department of Defense,[2] and a working understanding of China's shipbuilding industry. This chapter will focus on this last aspect of PLAN building and will extrapolate from previous chapters to reach subjective judgements on what sort of PLAN will ply the seas in the early 2020s. In doing so, it will offer a near-term forecast on the nexus of Chinese shipbuilding and the increasingly important mission of "far seas protection." I begin by address-ing the shipbuilding industry's ability to satisfy the demand signal created in 2012 when Beijing embraced the goal of becoming a "maritime power."

Demand Signal

Any consideration of the PLAN's future must start with statements of intent or ambition made public by the Chinese party-state. In this regard, Beijing has been remarkably transparent in disclosing its maritime ambitions, which rest on the foundation of a strong PLAN.

At both the Communist Party Congress in November 2012 and the National People's Congress in March 2013, leaders called for China to become a maritime power. In his swan-song work report to the Eighteenth Party Congress, then-President Hu Jintao urged that China "should enhance our capacity for exploiting marine resources, develop the marine economy, pro-tect the marine ecological environment, *resolutely safeguard China's mari-time rights and interests, and build China into a maritime power*" (emphasis added).[3]

Hu's work report also asserted that "building strong national defense *and powerful armed forces that are commensurate with China's international standing* and meet the needs of its security and development interests is a stra-tegic task of China's modernization drive. . . . We should attach great *impor-tance to maritime*, space and cyberspace security. We should make active planning for the use of military forces in peacetime, expand and intensify mil-itary preparedness, and enhance the capability to accomplish a wide range of military tasks, the most important of which is to win local war in an informa-tion age" (emphasis added).[4]

These two points were repeated in the 2012 Defense White Paper, which was not released until April 2013, after Xi Jinping had assumed party and national leadership. According to the white paper: "China is a major maritime as well as land country. The seas and oceans provide immense space and abundant resources for China's sustainable development, and thus are of vital importance to the people's wellbeing and China's future. It is an essential national development strategy to exploit, utilize and protect the seas and oceans, *and build China into a maritime power. It is an important duty for the PLA to resolutely safeguard China's maritime rights and interests*" (emphasis added).[5] Becoming a recognized "maritime power" will be a major addition to what China calls its comprehensive national power and one more step toward becoming the undisputed power in East Asia. Given American security obligations and strategic friendships with many of the nations in the region, this is also an issue of interest for the United States.

Four years after Hu's departing exhortations, it is clear that the emphasis on maritime power was not simply one among a long list of aspirational national objectives. Beijing is very serious about this objective, as evidenced in the latest (2015) Chinese Defense White Paper entitled *China's Military Strategy*.[6] In a document devoted to an overall explication of national military strategy, a striking amount of emphasis is placed on maritime issues. The following are four specific excerpts from the white paper that directly relate to the national objective of becoming a maritime power and corresponding expansion of the PLAN's mission set:

With the growth of China's national interests . . . the security of overseas interests concerning energy and resources, strategic sea lines of communication (SLOCs), as well as institutions, personnel and assets abroad, has become an imminent issue.

China's armed forces mainly shoulder the following strategic tasks:

- To deal with a wide range of emergencies and military threats, and effectively safeguard the sovereignty and security of China's territorial land, air and sea;
- To resolutely safeguard the unification of the motherland;
- To safeguard China's security and interests in new domains;
- To safeguard the security of China's overseas interests;
- To maintain strategic deterrence and carry out nuclear counterattack;
- To participate in regional and international security cooperation and maintain regional and world peace;
- To strengthen efforts in operations against infiltration, separatism and terrorism so as to maintain China's political security and social stability; and

- To perform such tasks as emergency rescue and disaster relief, rights and interests protection, guard duties, and support for national economic and social development.

In line with the strategic requirement of near seas defense and far seas protection, the PLA Navy (PLAN) will gradually shift its focus from "near seas defense" to the combination of "near seas defense" with "far seas protection," and build a combined, multi-functional and efficient marine combat force structure. The PLAN will enhance its capabilities for strategic deterrence and counterattack, maritime maneuvers, joint operations at sea, comprehensive defense and comprehensive support.

The seas and oceans bear on the enduring peace, lasting stability and sustainable development of China. *The traditional mentality that land outweighs sea must be abandoned, and great importance has to be attached to managing the seas and oceans and protecting maritime rights and interests* [emphasis added].

It is necessary for China to develop a modern maritime military force structure commensurate with its national security and development interests, safeguard its national sovereignty and maritime rights and interests, protect the security of strategic SLOCs and overseas interests, and participate in international maritime cooperation, so as to provide strategic support for building itself into a maritime power.[7]

In sum, China's leaders have clearly set a very ambitious maritime agenda for themselves, the fulfillment of which requires China's shipbuilding industry to meet the needs of multifarious maritime actors, including the merchant marine, the fishing industry, the coast guard, and—most importantly—the PLAN.

China's Shipbuilding Takeoff

China achieved first place in terms of merchant shipbuilding production in 2010 and has subsequently retained this leading position. China has viewed shipbuilding in strategic rather than commercial terms and has developed the industry to ensure it was self-sufficient in sea trade. This strategic perspective endures; Beijing still wants its imports of raw materials and food, as well as its exports, to the extent possible, to be undertaken by Chinese-built or -owned ships. But beyond building for self-sufficiency, the global demand for new ships sparked by the globalization of trade turned China's shipbuilding sector into a money-maker. It quickly expanded to include building ships for export when global demand for ships made it possible for China to compete internationally because of low labor costs and rapidly improving quality.[8]

China grew into a leading shipbuilder as hundreds of private yards opened to compete with state-run companies. The number of shipyards in China swelled to as many as 1,647.[9] Starting with the 2008 global economic crisis, however, all Asian shipbuilders—including China's—were hit by a sharp decline in demand for new ships. Not only did new orders evaporate, but many existing orders were canceled as well. Having peaked in 2012, China now faces the reality it must shed builders and exploit economies of scale by consolidating and creating megayards.

China's Shipbuilding Future: Consolidation, Complexity, Size

As Sue Hall and Audrye Wong explain in their chapter in this volume, efficiency can increase with size. Certainly, state-owned Chinese shipyards under the China State Shipbuilding Corporation (CSSC) and the China Shipbuilding Industry Corporation (CSIC), which have larger total throughputs, may gain some economies of scale. But much of the overhead function, and hence cost, of the operation is generated by the shipyard itself, and therefore groups of yards are generally not as cost-efficient as a single large yard of the same capacity. Economies of scale can also generate significant purchasing economies or efficiencies for high-volume shipyards and individual yard members of large shipbuilding groups.

For China to stabilize its shipbuilding after its decade-long expansion, fully one-third to one-half of the yards will probably have to disappear through acquisitions and closings. State-run companies enjoy easier access to credit to pay workers, buy raw materials, and provide financing for clients. CSSC, CSIC, and other government-backed companies won three-quarters of all orders in the first half of 2014. There have already been bankruptcies and closures among private yards, while many others have vanished with even fewer traces.

Meanwhile, major consolidation in both CSSC and CSIC is under way, alongside relocation of established yards to modern, larger-capacity newly developed shipyards. The goal is to be able to move up the complexity chain and challenge South Korea and Japan by building high-value complex ships such as liquefied natural gas tankers. Heretofore, China has focused on building simpler, less complex break-bulk raw material carriers and container ships.

Both CSSC and CSIC have merged and integrated some of their older ship-yards, with CSSC constructing four new megayards. The Chinese government is also helping its flagship yards through military workloads. According to its website, "CSIC has a very clear strategy, namely to become China's leading pro-vider of warships and related equipment and systems."[10] Hu Wenming, CSSC's chief executive officer, argues that the company must deal with the global ship-building slump by building more advanced ships, including "high-tech ships such as naval vessels and maritime law enforcement ships."[11]

Civil-Military Integration: Industry Consolidation with Chinese Characteristics[12]

New megayards emerging from recent relocations will almost certainly form a secure core of state-owned shipbuilding capacity. Accordingly, in 2013 China's State Council issued a three-year plan to aid the industry. The document called for greater government support of shipbuilding, additional lending, mergers between subsidiaries, restrictions on capacity expansion, greater innovation, and the scrapping of older ships to bolster domestic demand.[13]

The vast majority of shipbuilding industry experts maintain that during peacetime, naval and merchant shipbuilding do not mix well. Yet civil-mili-tary integration is an important part of Beijing's plan to bolster the indus-try. As one document from State Council researchers notes, China needs to "expand plans for the war industry . . . to digest the [surplus] production capacity through integrating the military technology with the civilian tech-nology."[14] An entire section of China's three-year shipbuilding plan is in fact devoted to greater civil-military integration in shipbuilding.[15] The plan explic-itly argues that China's military shipbuilding industry must be rooted in the civilian shipbuilding industrial base, rely on civilian projects, and use civilian industry to overcome military industry bottlenecks. Moreover, the document stresses the importance of shared ship design and manufacturing technologies between the civilian and military shipbuilding industries. This suggests two elements of China's policy: first, that the government views civilian shipbuild-ing as essential to and intertwined with military shipbuilding, and second, that the government expects shipyard infrastructure, manufacturing processes, and technology to flow between the civilian and military sectors.

Connecting Shipbuilding and PLAN Development

China seems to be an exception to the general observation that there is a lack of "natural synergy" between naval and merchant shipbuilding activities. In fact, in China there is clearly an increasing level of integration between the two, actively encouraged by governmental policy. However surprising to commercial specialists, evidence for this claim is found in the water—the PLAN's present hardware. Multiple official U.S. government sources, particularly ONI's 2015 PLAN report and the last few years of the Department of Defense's Annual Report to Congress,[16] recognize Chinese shipyards' ability to deliver modern, well-armed warships and submarines. Significantly, these reports do not infer that Chinese-built ships and submarines are inferior or substandard. To the contrary, except for weakness in antisubmarine warfare (ASW), the reports speak to impressive capabilities. Chinese shipyards are not turning out junk for the PLAN.

Perhaps the best indicator of quality is the remarkable reliability of the engineering plants of Chinese ships on antipiracy patrols—there are only a very few reported instances of PLAN ships having to linger in port awaiting parts and specialized technical assistance. Much of this is undoubtedly due to the German diesel engines built under license in China and the Russian and French combat systems that have been copied and produced in China. Beijing itself must have great confidence in the reliability of its combat systems and weapons, given the number being marketed at weapons expos around the world. According to one expert, the Chinese approach has been to procure a wide variety of systems from advanced weapons makers: "They poured considerable resources into reproducing these technologies by absorbing key foreign weapons technologies while investing heavily in indigenous weapons research and development programs. The result was the ability to produce technologies that, while perhaps not cutting-edge, were considerably more advanced than what they could have produced just a few years earlier. . . . And while they're not better than Russian or U.S. alternatives, they are often good enough."[17]

How is it, then, that while China has had difficulty in moving up the complexity chain in terms of the classes of merchant ships it wants to build, it is able to produce well-regarded complex warships? It is not that China cannot build complex ships, but rather that it has not yet mastered the ability to build complex ships at a commercially competitive price like South Korean shipyards can. PLAN warships and submarines do not have to be commercially competitive in price, although even in this case there are exceptions; an export variant of the Type 054A *Jiangkai II* frigate has been offered during arms shows and is priced attractively enough to be considered for purchase by several foreign nations. Additionally, China's military shipyards appear to have access to the nation's best financial, technical, and human resources, a critical advantage over their commercial counterparts.

Building Warships for What?

The latest Defense White Paper on China's military strategy states clearly what the Chinese party-state expects its navy to be able to accomplish: "In line with the strategic requirement of near seas defense and far seas protection, the PLA Navy (PLAN) will gradually shift its focus from 'near seas defense' to the combination of 'near seas defense' with 'far seas protection,' *and build a combined, multi-functional and efficient marine combat force structure*" (emphasis added).[18]

The PLAN has two primary missions. First and most important is near seas defense of the area between China's coastline and the Second Island Chain, including the Philippine Sea and the northern three-quarters of the South China Sea.[19] It is the more important of the PLAN's primary missions because it involves defending China proper and its island and maritime claims.

The concept China uses to accomplish this mission is "active defense." China intends to do this through a joint combined arms campaign involving the PLAN, the People's Liberation Army Air Force (PLAAF), and the PLA Rocket Force (PLARF). This joint operational concept has been known in the West as anti-access/area denial (A2/AD). This Pentagon-created term encapsulates the idea that China wants to keep approaching hostile forces at bay by attacking them far from China (anti-access) or, if that fails and hostile forces are already within striking range of China (as much of the U.S. 7th Fleet would likely be in case of conflict), attempt to deny them freedom of operational and tactical action (area denial). From the perspective of an opposing naval force, what China's A2/AD means in practical terms is that it will have to *fight to gain* "sea control" that is essential to conduct operations and will have to *fight to sustain* "sea control" if the naval campaign is envisioned as anything longer than a hit-and-run raid.

The fact that China wants to be able to control, or at least deny control of, the proximate near seas is hardly surprising: this is what China essentially said it planned on doing a decade ago. It is worth recalling that in its 2004 Defense White Paper, Beijing already discussed achieving command of the sea: "While continuing to attach importance to the building of the Army, the PLA gives priority to the building of the Navy, Air Force and [Rocket] force to seek balanced development of the combat force structure, in order to strengthen the capabilities for *winning both command of the sea and command of the air, and conducting strategic counter strikes*" (emphasis added).[20]

The PLAN's main contributions to the defense of China and its outstanding claims against an attack from the sea are its submarine force and land-based naval air forces. These units would operate in concert with the PLARF's missiles, especially the DF-21D antiship ballistic missile, which carries a maneuverable warhead that purportedly can hit a moving ship. The PLAAF also plays a crucial role in A2/AD. Aircraft launched from land bases carrying long-range antiship cruise missiles (ASCMs) are a potent threat, particularly as the PLAAF continues to improve its overwater operational skill and the missiles' range and sophistication.

But beyond capable platforms crewed by competent submariners and airmen, Chinese A2/AD operational success depends on the ability to find ships on the high seas. In short, China must be able to maintain an up-to-date surveillance picture of the thousands of square miles of the Pacific Ocean that constitute China's seaward approaches. Surveillance is absolutely essential for finding hostile warships and then targeting ballistic missiles and providing slower-moving aircraft and submarines an attack vector to intercept approaching naval striking forces.

The PLAN's surface warships lack a major offensive role in such a campaign: once they venture out beyond Chinese land-based air cover, perhaps 200–300 nautical miles, they become vulnerable to hostile air attack. They do have a role in providing close-in antisubmarine protection, and possibly as seaward extensions of China's mainland air defenses, in the waters very near to China—specifically the East China Sea and in the vicinity of important Chinese bases in the northern portions of the South China Sea. They are also vulnerable to hostile submarine attack, especially should they move west from the relatively shallow waters of most of the East China Sea. The PLAN surface navy does have an important role, of course, if the conflict involves invasion of Taiwan. It would be charged with handling Taiwan's navy, transporting Chinese ground forces to Taiwan, and resupplying them.

Unprecedented: A Wartime Far Seas Mission for the PLAN

Where the PLAN surface force really comes into its own is in the mission that Beijing terms far seas protection. The relevant portion of the 2015 white paper (quoted above) removes any doubt that China intends that its navy become more than a regional force. As the white paper indicates, protecting

China's interests in the far seas will receive progressively greater attention. If the white paper verbiage is to be taken seriously, far seas protection is evolving toward being a co-equal primary mission for the PLA Navy. Specifically, "It is necessary for China to develop a modern maritime military force structure commensurate with its national security and development interests . . . [and] *protect the security of strategic SLOCs and overseas interests*" (emphasis added).[21]

It is important to appreciate that far seas protection did not materialize instantaneously; it rather represents the latest iteration in Chinese thinking about how to use the PLAN beyond China's seaward approaches. It can be traced in official pronouncements to 2004, when the PLA was for the first time assigned responsibilities well beyond China and proximate waters.[22] This was official recognition that China's national interests now extended beyond its borders and that the PLA's missions were to be based on those expanding interests, not just geography. These missions have been characterized as "far seas," an area Western observers frequently call "distant seas" or "blue water."[23] However, from the beginning, top-down guidance was focused on the *peacetime* uses of the navy. The PLA borrowed an old U.S. military acronym—MOOTW (military operations other than war).[24] China's 2008 Defense White Paper described MOOTW as playing an important role for China's armed forces and noted that the PLA is developing MOOTW capabilities.[25]

What is new is that in the 2015 white paper, the enumeration of peacetime MOOTW missions no longer includes any reference to sea lanes on which China relies. These are addressed in separate sections within the context of "protection," which strongly suggests that thinking regarding far seas has shifted from conceptually framing those operations as strictly peacetime to a broader framework that takes into account having to protect "strategic SLOCs" in wartime. This has obvious long-term implications for PLAN force structure—protecting crucial sea lanes that originate at the Indian Ocean's far western reaches requires a mix of ships, aircraft, and submarines that can credibly accomplish such a mission thousands of miles from Chinese territory.

The far seas protection mission also makes sense within the context of Xi's much-ballyhooed "21st-Century Maritime Silk Road" initiative extending from China's major ports through the Indonesian Straits, then along the Indian Ocean's northern littoral, grazing eastern Africa, before transiting the Red Sea and Suez Canal into the eastern Mediterranean. Finally, sea lane defense's upgrading to a potential wartime mission has also undoubtedly been encouraged by some Western writers who assert that in time of conflict, the way to bring China to its knees is to cut its sea lanes.[26]

The PLA Navy Far Seas Protection Force

China does not need a far seas navy to execute an A2/AD strategy, but when it comes to far seas protection, the primary focus shifts from land-based air defenses and submarines to surface ships. (Recent PLAN submarine deployments to the Indian Ocean do indicate that submarines, especially nuclear-powered attack submarines [SSNs] and modern air-independent power [AIP]–equipped conventional submarines also factor into PLAN calculations regarding far seas protection.[27]) Whether for surface ships or submarines, far seas protection requires a different mix of naval capabilities than the wartime near seas defense. Far seas operations demand multiproduct logistics support ships, amphibious ships with helicopter facilities, larger multimission destroyers and frigates with better endurance, reliable propulsion systems, helicopter facilities, improved antisubmarine systems, and especially longer-range air defenses.

Lacking land-based air cover, a credible far seas navy must be able to defend itself from air attack. Destroyers with long-range surface-to-air missiles (SAMs) can accomplish this where the air threat is limited, but most of China's most important SLOCs—for example, over the northern Arabian Sea—face a more substantial air threat. I believe this was a very important (although not the only) factor in the China's decision to build a modest aircraft carrier force.[28] Despite the ski-jump takeoff used on the *Liaoning* that imposes weight penalties on the type and amount of ordnance the aircraft can launch with, carrier-based aircraft can at a minimum provide PLAN far seas operations with air cover. Looking ahead, all indications are that by around 2020–22, the PLAN will likely operate two *Liaoning*-style aircraft carriers.

The air wing is, of course, an aircraft carrier's raison d'être. Details regarding the composition of *Liaoning*'s air wing remain sketchy, probably because the PLAN itself has not finalized them. Informed speculation suggests the air wing will include twenty-four J-15 fighters, four to six ASW helicopters, four helicopters dedicated to airborne early warning (putting an air-search radar in the sky), and two helicopters dedicated to pilot rescue during flight operations ("plane guard" in U.S. Navy [USN]-speak).[29]

The backbone of these far seas forces will be the multi mission Type 052C and 052D *Luyang II/III*-class destroyers. These ships have phased array radars and a long-range SAM system that provides the PLAN with its first credible area air-defense capability (the ability to defend more than just one-self). Because these ships are fitted with a multipurpose sixty-four-cell vertical launching system (VLS), they will also be able to load land-attack cruise missiles. On paper, at least, these are state-of-the-art multimission warships; the phased array radar, also known as the active electronically scanned array, is similar in technical approach to the radar in the USN-developed Aegis combat system. When combined with long-range surface-to-air missiles housed in vertical launch cells, this radar system provides the ship with tremendous anti-air firepower—the ability to engage multiple targets simultaneously. These are expensive to build; only a few navies in the world can afford them. For example, Japan has six and by 2020 will have eight, whereas today China already has eight, and by 2020 will have eighteen to twenty.

If the Type 052D is intended as the backbone, the Type 054A guided-missile frigate has for the past seven-plus years been the workhorse of PLAN far seas antipiracy operations in the Gulf of Aden and follow-on presence operations spanning the Indian Ocean littoral, eastern Mediterranean, and Black Sea. At 4,100 tons, this large frigate is well armed with long-range ASCMs, a 32-cell VLS launcher with medium-range SAMs, and a helicopter with hangar. Their ASW suite is likely to be improved with the addition of a towed array and variable-depth sonar that is already being fitted on China's Type 56 corvettes.[30] China operates seventeen of these ships today, and by 2020 is expected to have approximately twenty-four Type 54A and around six of an improved Type 054B frigate in commission.

The PLAN has mastered the logistics of sustaining small task groups on distant stations. With the China Ocean Shipping Company, a state-owned enterprise providing global logistics services, Beijing enjoys built-in shore-based support structure at virtually all the major ports along the Pacific and Indian Oceans. When combined with its modern multiproduct replenishment ships that have developed significant sea support skill, this has become a successful approach to logistic sustainment halfway around the world from Chinese bases. One of the main lessons the PLAN has learned from its antipiracy deployments is the absolute importance of having enough multipurpose replenishment ships. American experts have long opined that the most important indication of PLAN out-of-area ambitions would be construction of replenishment ships. That is exactly what China is doing. PLAN inventory of 23,400-plus-ton *Fuchi*-class replenishment ships (AORs) has increased to eight today,[31] with as many as ten major replenishment ships probably operating by 2020, more than enough to support continuous far seas operations in addition to the antipiracy patrols.[32]

For years, analysis of PLAN amphibious shipping has focused on assessing the PLA's ability to invade Taiwan. While that contingency requires continued attention, the PLAN is in the process of assembling an impressive far seas expeditionary capability. It now has four 20,000-ton amphibious ships clas-sified as landing platform/docks (Type 071). Each ship can embark between 800 and 1,000 marines or soldiers, four air-cushioned landing craft, and sev-eral helicopters. Forecasts suggest even more of these ships as well as perhaps a larger amphibious assault–type ship will be built.[33] By 2020, China will have the world's second-largest modern amphibious capability (after the United States) and could potentially embark 5,500–6,500 marines for operations any-where in the world. When combined with modern destroyers and an aircraft carrier to provide air defense, China will have far seas power projection capa-bility for the first time since Admiral Zheng He's last voyage (1431–33).[34]

China's submarine force has correctly been seen as primarily focused on near seas defense. Because of their endurance, SSNs have been considered the most suitable type of submarine for long-range, long-endurance missions nor-mally associated with out-of-area operations for any navy. The PLAN has long had a small SSN force, but in the past few years China has created a mod-ern SSN force of six Shang-class (Type 093) boats and is expected to introduce a new Type 095 class that could result in a 2020 inventory of seven to eight, which would exceed the British and French SSN forces and place China third globally, behind the United States and Russia.

China is also expanding its ballistic missile submarine (SSBN) force. While not designed for the far seas protection mission as it is properly understood, that is exactly what this element of China's strategic nuclear deterrent force will be doing. The approximately four thousand-nautical-mile range of its JL-2 submarine-launched ballistic missile (SLBM) dictates the operating theater somewhere in the Eastern Pacific for its missiles to hold targets throughout the United States at risk.[35] The PLAN has four SSBNs in service and least two more are expected by 2020, a larger SSBN force than that of either France or the United Kingdom.

The PLAN's most modern conventionally powered submarine is the AIP-equipped Yuan-class (Type 039A/B).[36] It has been in series production since 2004, with as many as twenty expected by 2020. Conventionally pow-ered submarines would not normally be considered in the category of capa-bilities associated with far seas protection missions except for the fact that this large conventional submarine was sent to the Indian Ocean, calling at Karachi, Pakistan, in April 2015. This was the third submarine the PLAN has deployed to the Indian Ocean in the past two years; the earlier deployments were by a Type 093 SSN and a Type 039 Song-class conventional boat, much to Indian observers' dismay.[37]

It is important to emphasize how essential over seven years of uninterrupted antipiracy operations in the Arabian Sea have been in teaching the PLAN how to conduct distant seas operations. One reason they have learned so quickly is because the antipiracy patrols are a real-world battle laboratory. All of the classes of ships mentioned, except for the carrier, the SSBN, and the new Type 052D destroyers, have been deployed on antipiracy operations. Not only has this been a chance to "shake down" new ship classes and to determine what equipment performed best, it has also provided an opportunity to observe most of the world's great navies' daily operations and absorb best practices.[38]

Looking Ahead: World's Second Far Seas Navy by 2020

To understand the magnitude of PLAN far seas protection capabilities development, it is useful to compare them to the other "great" navies of the world. Exhibit 15-1 is a forecast that attempts to compare the PLAN classes of ships discussed in the proceeding section with ships of similar capabilities from other navies routinely operating in far seas. This comparison is not an overall order of battle inventory of ships but rather an attempt to compare "far seas apples to apples" around 2020.

For perspective, exhibit 15-2 also compares the PLAN classes that have been discussed with similar classes in the U.S. Navy. It shows that while the PLAN's far seas capabilities are very impressive when measured against the rest of the world, there is still no comparison when measured against U.S. far seas naval forces.

Preliminary Judgments

China's shipbuilding industry has unquestionably demonstrated the ability to produce modern warships and submarines, while at the same time continuing to lead the world in total shipbuilding output. Since the vast majority of China's warships and submarines are built in state-owned yards, it is unlikely that the contraction of China's shipbuilding industry—especially private yards—will harm the ability to deliver warships and submarines at the rate observed over the past decade.

This yields the observation that almost all of the ships discussed in preceding paragraphs have been commissioned over the last decade; the obvious conclusion is that China's far seas protection mission will be executed by

Exhibit 15-1. Far Seas Navies' Major Ships, circa 2020

	PLA Navy	United Kingdom	France	Japan	India	Russia
Carriers	2	2	1	0	2	1
Aegis-like destroyer*	18–20	6–8	2	8	5–6	0
Frigates	30–32	1–2	1	4	3–10	9–11
Large amphibious	6–8	6	3	3	0–3	0
Auxiliary oiler and replenishment	8–10	3	4	5	0–3	4 (very old)
Nuclear submarines, air-independent power submarines	6–7 / 20	7	6	0 / 22	1–2 / 6	8–9 + 6 cruise missile submarines / 9–11
Ballistic missile submarines	5–6	4	4	0	1–2	10–12

*Aegis-like destroyers include the United Kingdom Type 045 *Daring* class, the Japanese *Kongo* and *Atago* classes, and the Indian *Kolkata* and *Visakhapatnam* classes.

Exhibit 15-2. Major Far Seas Ships, PLAN versus U.S. Navy, circa 2020

	PLAN Far Seas	U.S. Navy Overall
Carriers	2	11
Aegis-like destroyer	18–20	88
Frigate	30–32	0
Large amphibious	6–8	33
Auxiliary oiler and replenishment (far sea replenishment)	8–10	30
Nuclear submarines, air-independent power submarines	6–7	48 + 4 cruise missile submarines
	20	0
Ballistic missile submarines	5–6	14

a new, modern force. This force, clearly well balanced in capabilities and ship classes, resembles a much smaller version of the U.S. Navy.[39] In coming years, the PLAN's far seas component will increasingly resemble a miniature version of America's navy.

The question is: Will Beijing employ this microcosm of the U.S. Navy the same way Washington uses its navy? So far, trends are moving in that direction. Like the U.S. Navy, the far seas operations the PLAN conducts are the whole range of activities associated with what is normally characterized as peacetime presence: naval diplomacy, emergency evacuations, disaster relief, and exercises with friendly navies. What has not yet been seen is traditional power projection. China's far seas navy is assembling power projection components—carrier air, land attack cruise missiles, and amphibious forces—that are very credible. In fact, it is not a stretch to argue that by 2020, China will have the second most capable far seas navy in the world. Certainly, in terms of numbers of relevant ship classes, it will be in that position. It is unlikely that China deliberately set out to achieve this position by 2020, since its ranking among the world's great navies is greatly facilitated by the fact that while the PLAN was expanding, practically all of the other traditional maritime powers were reducing major warship production. Nonetheless, intended or not, the PLAN is not only a formidable near seas challenge thanks mainly to its submarine contribution to the A2/AD concept of operations, it also is on the cusp of becoming a balanced and very capable far seas navy. Significantly, it now has an official green light to focus on a far seas protection mission that includes combat. How it trains for this mission should provide insights into how China's far seas navy will be employed.

Uncertainties

It is necessary to also address the many questions that these judgments raise. First and foremost, as any professional naval planner would ask: How good are these folks? Are PLAN operators competent? Will PLAN combat systems operate as advertised? Will China's unique consensus-based dual command system, wherein the ship's commanding officer and political officer share equal positions, work in the stress of combat, particularly since success or failure in a surface engagement has historically been dictated by who wins the "battle of the first salvo"?

The open-source answers to these questions are more conjecture than fact, but some signposts are available. Over seven years of antipiracy deployments suggest PLAN ships are very reliable during peacetime operations. Over the course of these deployments, the PLAN has learned to be remarkably adaptable; there is now a contingent of officers, including admirals, with extended deployed operational experience. We also have insights into the growing sophistication of PLAN warfare-oriented training taking place in far seas environments. Christopher Sharman has mapped the growing complexity of PLAN at-sea training, noting that "the PLA-wide emphasis on information over the last decade suggests PLAN far sea missions will operate with enhanced C4ISR [command, control, communications, computers, intelligence, surveillance, and reconnaissance] capabilities."[40]

Perhaps the biggest uncertainty is how large the far seas PLAN will become—potentially very large indeed, if one takes seriously the words in the Eighteenth Party Congress Work report: "Building strong national defense and powerful armed forces that are *commensurate with China's international standing* and meet the needs of its security and development interests is a strategic task of China's modernization drive" (emphasis added). Several years ago I asserted that China was not trying to replicate the Imperial Japanese Navy and build a force aimed at having a climactic battle for sea control somewhere in the Philippine Sea. I still believe this to be true, but the image of a regional navy as capable as the Imperial Japanese Navy was in 1941—a formidable force of 10 battleships, 12 aircraft carriers, 18 heavy cruisers, 20 light cruisers, 126 destroyers, and 68 submarines—reminds us of what a regional navy could become.[41]

Implications for the United States

Seeing Chinese warships in the Indian Ocean and the Mediterranean's far reaches will become routine. U.S. combatant commanders responsible for those regions may have different perspectives on PLAN presence than their Pacific compatriots and in some cases (e.g., antipiracy patrols) may welcome that presence. There may be more opportunities for U.S. Navy–PLAN cooperation the farther from China's sovereignty claims that naval interactions occur, but if Sino-Russian naval activities in the eastern Mediterranean and the Black Sea assume the appearance of being against American interests, that cooperation could quickly change.

Should the PLAN begin to maintain a routine naval presence in the Indian Ocean in addition to its antipiracy operations, that will become even more of a red flag to India than it already is. That will increase the incentives, certainly from Delhi's point of view, for even closer Indo-American naval relations. The pace of that relationship will naturally be dictated by the overall state of Sino-Indian relations, but it is conceivable that an increase in PLAN presence, especially submarines, could result in some sort of a combined Indo-U.S. ASW organization dedicated to tracking PLAN submarines in region.

Naturally, the potential for PLAN facilities along the Indian Ocean littoral has been an issue of sometimes heated commentary. Since the PLAN is already evolving toward a "places, not bases" approach in the Indian Ocean region, it is not farfetched to speculate that the far seas protection mission helps to rationalize Chinese logistics "outposts" in the western portion of the Indian Ocean. China has established its first overseas naval support facility in Djibouti, and Gwadar, Pakistan, is also a possibility.[42] The combination of a "place" along with future deployments of PLAN far seas forces means that U.S. authorities can no longer assume sea control off Middle Eastern and eastern African hotspots if Chinese interests are involved and differ from those of Washington.

Closer to home, keeping track of far seas–deployed PLAN submarines will create new capacity challenges for the United States—especially in U.S. exclusive economic zones. During the Cold War, a U.S. Navy at least twice the size of today's navy, with almost a third of its force structure dedicated to the primary mission of ASW, invested considerable operational effort into keeping track of Soviet submarines operating near American coasts. Will the United States be willing and able to do the same in the near future?

Finally, the image of a Chinese "global" navy could over time attenuate perceptions of American power, especially in maritime regions where only the U.S. Navy or the navies of its friends have operated freely since the end of the Cold War. As *Xinhua* reported on May 12, 2015, "This is the first time that [China] has conducted naval exercises in the Mediterranean Sea. It is a new challenge for the Chinese Navy. It also showed that [China] is expanding its national interests and security interests to waters further away from China. People should get used to seeing China's warships out in the sea."[43]

Notes

1. Office of Naval Intelligence (ONI), *The PLA Navy: New Capabilities and Missions for the 21st Century* (Suitland, MD: ONI, 2015), http://www.oni.navy.mil/Intelligence_Community/china_media/2015_PLA_NAVY_PUB_Interactive.pdf.

2. The latest such report is Department of Defense, *Annual Report to Congress: Military and Security Developments Involving the People's Republic of China, 2016* (Washington, DC: DoD, April 2016), http://www.defense.gov/Portals/1/Documents/pubs/2016%20China%20Military%20Power%20Report.pdf (hereafter DoD [2016]).

3. "Full Text of Hu Jintao's Report at the 18th Party Congress," *Xinhua*, November 17, 2012, http://news.xinhuanet.com/english/special/18cpcnc/2012-11/17/c_131981259.htm.

4. Ibid.

5. *The Diversified Employment of China's Armed Forces* (Beijing: State Council Information Office, April 2013), http://news.xinhuanet.com/english/china/2013-04/16/c_132312681.htm.

6. *China's Military Strategy* (Beijing: State Council Information Office, May 2015), http://eng.mod.gov.cn/Database/WhitePapers/index.htm. Where relevant, suboptimal phrases from the English-language version ("offshore defense," "open seas") will be replaced with the best translations of terms ("near seas," "far seas") from the Chinese version. See 中国的军事战略 [*China's Military Strategy*], http://www.81.cn/dblj/2015-05/26/content_6507373.htm.

7. Ibid. (English version), 3, 5, 8, 9.

8. Yin-Chung Tsai, "The Shipbuilding Industry in China," *OCED Journal-General Papers* 2010, no. 3 (August 2011), http://www.keepeek.com/Digital-Asset-Management/oecd/economics/the-shipbuilding-industry-in-china_gen_papers-2010-5kg6z7tg5w5l#page4.

9. Jasmine Wang and Kyunghee Park, "China Poised to Gain Control as Shipyard Shakeout Looms," *Bloomberg*, August 12, 2013, http://www.bloomberg.com/news/articles/2013-08-11/china-poised-to-gain-control-as-shipyard-shakeout-looms-freight.

10. The group is able to design and build many different types of naval ships including submarines, missile destroyers, and fleet replenishment vessels. See http://www.csic.com.cn/en/Survey.htm.

11. "胡问鸣: 高端破局谋发展 助力蓝色中国梦" ["Hu Wenming: Seek Development Through High-End Breakthroughs, Support the Blue China Dream"], 国防科技工业 [*Defence Science and Technology Industry*], no. 7 (2013): 30–31.

12. This section is based in part on Dennis Blasko, "China's Merchant Marine," paper for "China as 'Maritime Power'" conference, July 28–29, 2015, CNA Corporation, Arlington, VA, https://www.cna.org/cna_files/pdf/China-Merchant-Marine.pdf.

13. State Development Planning Commission, "船舶工业加快结构调整促进转型升级 实施方案 (2013–2015 年)" ["Ship Industry, Accelerating Structural Adjustment, Promoting Transformation and Upgrading, Implementation Plan (2013–2015)"], 2013, http://www.sdpc.gov.cn/zcfb/zcfbqt/201308/W020130806620700307575.pdf.

14. 马淑萍、项安波 [Ma Shuping and Xiang Anbo], 国务院发展研究中心企业所 [Enterprise Research Institute, State Council Development Research Center], "发展船舶工业: 技术创新与产业转型升级亟需提高" ["Develop the Shipping Industry: It Is Urgently Necessary to Raise the Level of Technical Innovation and Industrial Restructuring and Upgrading"], 中国发展观察 [China Development Watch] via 中国经济新闻网 [China Economic News Net], September 17, 2014, http://www.cet.com.cn/wzsy/qwfb/qwfb/1313291.shtml.

15. State Development Planning Commission, "Ship Industry, Accelerating Structural Adjustment, Promoting Transformation and Upgrading, Implementation Plan (2013–2015)."

16. DoD (2016), 31–42.

17. Joseph E. Lin, "China's Weapons of Mass Consumption," *Foreign Policy*, March 20, 2015, http://foreignpolicy.com/2015/03/20/chinas-weapons-of-mass-consumption/.

18. *China's Military Strategy* (2015), 8.

19. It would be a mistake to assume that near seas, or anti-access/area denial, applies only to waters inside the First Island Chain. For Chinese strategists, the issue is when the Chinese mainland will be in range of U.S. systems. Depending on which weapon one considers, that could be well over one thousand nautical miles from China. A Tomahawk land attack cruise missile has ranges, depending on the variant, of up to 1,500 nautical miles.

20. *China's National Defense in 2004* (Beijing: State Council Information Office, 2004), http://www.china.org.cn/e-white/20041227/.

21. *China's Military Strategy* (2015), 9.

22. 胡锦涛 [Hu Jintao], "认清新世纪新阶段我军历史使命" ["Understand the New Historic Missions of our Military in the New Period of the New Century"], December 24, 2004, available via 江西国防教育网 [Jiangxi Province National Defense Education Net], April 16, 2010, http://gfjy.jxnews.com.cn/system/2010/04/16/011353408.shtml.

23. For instance, the 2008 Defense White Paper states that China continues to develop its ability to conduct near seas operations *while gradually building* its ability to conduct operations in "distant seas." Emphasis added. *China's National Defense in 2008* (Beijing: State Council Information Office, 2009), http://www.china.org.cn/government/central_government/2009-01/20/content_17155577.htm.

24. Joint Publication 3–07, *Joint Doctrine for Military Operations Other than War* (Washington, DC: Joint Chiefs of Staff, June 16, 1995), http://www.bits.de/NRANEU/others/jp-doctrine/jp3_07.pdf.

25. *China's National Defense in 2008.*

26. See, for example, T. X. Hammes, "Offshore Control: A Proposed Strategy for an Unlikely Conflict," *Strategic Forum* 278 (Washington, DC: National Defense University Press, June 2012), http://www.dtic.mil/dtic/tr/fulltext/u2/a577602.pdf.

27. P. K. Ghosh, "Game Changers? Chinese Submarines in the Indian Ocean," *The Diplomat*, July 6, 2015, http://thediplomat.com/2015/07/game-changers-chinese-submarines-in-the-indian-ocean/.

28. Nan Li and Christopher Weuve, "China's Aircraft Carrier Ambitions: An Update," *Naval War College Review* 63, no. 1 (Winter 2010): 15, www.usnwc.edu/publications/Naval-War-College-Review/2010-Winter.aspx.

29. Thomas Newdick, "China's Got an Aircraft Carrier—What About the Air Wing?" *War Is Boring*, March 3, 2014, https://medium.com/war-is-boring/chinas-got-an-aircraft-carrier-what-about-the-air-wing-c95283bc0279.

30. Andrew Tate, "China Commissions Fourth ASW-Capable Type 056 Corvette," IHS *Jane's Navy International*, May 11, 2015, http://www.janes.com/article/51341/china-commissions-fourth-asw-capable-type-056-corvette.

31. "China's 7th and 8th Type 903A Fleet Replenishment Oilers Commissioned into PLAN South Sea Fleet," *Navy Recognition*, July 16, 2016, http://www.navyrecognition .com/index.php?option=com_content&task=view&id=4206.

32. Bernard Cole, "China's Navy Expands Its Replenishment-at-Sea Capability," *The Interpreter*, August 26, 2015, http://www.lowyinterpreter.org/post/2015/08/26/Chinas -Navy-Expands-Replenishment-Capability.aspx.

33. ONI, *The PLA Navy*, 18.

34. For the most accurate account of Zheng He's "power projection" voyages, see Edward Dreyer, *Zheng He: China and the Oceans in the Early Ming Dynasty, 1405–1433* (New York: Pearson, 2006).

35. DoD (2016), 9.

36. Christopher Carlson, "Essay: Inside the Design of China's *Yuan*-class Submarine," *USNI News*, August 31, 2015, http://news.usni.org/2015/08/31/essay-inside-the-design -of-chinas-yuan-class-submarine.

37. DoD (2016), 19; Rajat Pandit, "Chinese Submarine in Karachi, India Alarmed," *Times of India*, June 27, 2015, http://timesofindia.indiatimes.com/india/Chinese-submarine -in-Karachi-India-alarmed/articleshow/47845930.cms; Andrew S. Erickson and Austin Strange, *Six Years at Sea . . . and Counting: Gulf of Aden Anti-Piracy and China's Maritime Commons Presence* (Washington, DC: Jamestown Foundation, 2015), 98–102.

38. Michael McDevitt, "PLA Naval Exercises with International Partners," in *Learning by Doing: The PLA Trains at Home and Abroad*, ed. Roy Kamphausen et al. (Carlisle, PA: U.S. Army War College Press, 2012), 102, http://www.strategicstudiesinstitute .army.mil/pdffiles/pub1135.pdf.

39. This comparison is in terms of larger, more capable, longer-range ships suitable for a far seas navy. Numerous smaller craft deployed relatively close to China already give the PLAN numbers that rival those of the U.S. Navy in aggregate.

40. Christopher H. Sharman, *China Moves Out: Stepping Stones Toward a New Maritime Strategy*, China Strategic Perspectives No. 9 (Washington, DC: National Defense University Press, April 2015), 37, http://inss.ndu.edu/Portals/68/Documents/ stratperspective/china/ChinaPerspectives-9.pdf.

41. David Evans and Mark Peattie, *Kaigun: Strategy, Tactics, and Technology in the Imperial Japanese Navy, 1887–1941* (Annapolis, MD: Naval Institute Press, 1997).

42. Saibal Dasgupta, "China Gets 40-Year Management Rights on Pak's Gwadar Port, Access to Arabian Sea," *Times of India*, April 14, 2015, http://timesofindia.indi atimes.com/world/china/China-gets-40-year-management-rights-on-Paks-Gwadar -port-and-access-to-Arabian-Sea/articleshow/46923252.cms; Angela Yu, "China Leases 800 ha Land at Gwadar Port," *IHS Maritime 360*, September 9, 2015, http://www.ihs maritime360.com/article/19228/china-leases-800-ha-land-at-gwadar-port.

43. 黄子娟 [Huang Zijuan], "中俄主战舰艇聚首地中海 专家: 应习惯我军舰赴远海" ["Chinese and Russian Main Battleships Meet in the Mediterranean—Expert: Must Become Accustomed to Our Naval Ships Going to the Far Seas], 新华网 [Xinhua Net], May 12, 2015, http://news.xinhuanet.com/world/2015-05/12/c_127791919.htm.

Paul Scharre and Tyler Jost

Technological "Wild Cards" and Twenty-First-Century Naval Warfare

THE LIST OF POTENTIAL future military game changers is long and muddled, a blend of science and science fiction. How can militaries differentiate the likely, the possible, and the idle speculation?

Modern militaries invest heavily in new technologies to modernize their forces, but determining *which* technologies hold the greatest promise is more art than science. It requires militaries to think on multiple levels simultaneously. They must assess the potential utility of a new technology—how much operational or strategic value it will convey. They must weigh the maturity of the technology and the likelihood that their investments will pay off. And they must assess their investments relative to both alternative investments and potential adversary countermeasures that might negate or erode their hard-fought advantages. All of these decisions must be made under conditions of extreme uncertainty and possible enemy deception.

Furthermore, some new technologies—whether novel or proven—applied in combination with new concepts of operation, organization, training, and doctrine can lead to disruptive changes in warfare that alter the very character of how militaries fight and the metrics for what makes weapons useful. Investing in improved stirrups for horse cavalry in the 1920s would have been a poor use of resources when adversaries were developing tanks that would revolutionize land warfare.

The U.S. military is the most technologically advanced on the planet, and yet it frequently gets these assessments wrong. The list of failed "next-generation" acquisition programs is long and inglorious, and in many cases even sizable investments have proved insufficient to overcome technology limitations or developmental failures.[1] Even if military planners and engineers can accurately estimate which technologies are required to achieve a game-changing capability—say, a megawatt-class laser to shoot down incoming ballistic missiles—the engineering hurdles to achieving that capability are not always obvious beforehand.

Moreover, militaries cannot solely pursue game changers, spending the entirety of their defense research and development dollars on long-shot, potentially disruptive technologies. Disruptive change by its very nature is uncertain, and even if disruptive change in general is likely, any one given technology breakthrough is not. Therefore, militaries must also plan for business as usual, for incremental improvements in countermeasures and counter-countermeasures. After all, if the tank had not emerged, then a modest improvement in horse cavalry might have resulted in a decisive edge on the battlefield. War is a punishing environment, where even a small edge in capability can lead to dramatically different outcomes. A longer spear or a slightly longer-range missile or sensor can mean the difference between life and death.

This tension between steady-state incremental innovation and periodic disruptive innovation is particularly acute in naval warfare, where modern militaries build naval forces on extremely long time horizons. Modern ships have lifespans in decades, and a U.S. supercarrier has an operational lifespan of fifty years. Over such timescales, the odds of disruptive innovations that change the rules of the game are increasingly likely. In 2015, the U.S. Navy began laying the keel for the USS *John F. Kennedy* (CVN-79), which will remain in active service until 2070. Will the capabilities it brings to bear still be relevant more than half a century from now?

History should leave us skeptical that naval warfare will remain unchanged for so long. From galleys to ships of the line to battleships, submarines, and aircraft carriers, naval warfare has undergone many disruptive changes over the course of the three-plus millennia humans have been fighting at sea. Many of these changes have occurred in the past two hundred years. The Industrial Revolution brought sweeping changes in previously agrarian societies and similarly changed war on land and at sea and expanded war to the air and undersea. In the nineteenth and early twentieth centuries, naval warfare saw dramatic changes as steam-powered ships replaced sail and ironclads were introduced, before giving way to battleships, submarines, and aircraft carriers. In the latter half of the twentieth century, nuclear propulsion and guided missiles have continued to change naval strategy and ship design, although without the "decisive battle" that often vividly demonstrates a disruptive shift in warfare.

The recent pace of major paradigm shifts in naval warfare in the nineteenth and twentieth centuries suggests a healthy degree of hedging against disruptive change in the twenty-first century. This is further buttressed by the fact that we are living in the midst of a technological revolution that is sweeping through human societies: the information revolution.

Information technology is changing how we do business, shop, communicate, make friends, and make war. The information revolution is staggering in its scale. In 2015, global spending on information technology was expected to exceed $3.8 trillion, or double all military spending—procurement, research and development, personnel, construction—by every country on Earth.[2] The scale of this investment, along with the continued exponential growth in computing power, practically guarantees disruptive change.[3] Indeed, in the past two years the U.S. Navy has demonstrated three novel capabilities that would have been difficult if not impossible without advanced computers—landing an unmanned aircraft on a carrier, landing a tailless aircraft on a carrier, and performing automated aerial refueling with an unmanned aircraft. As the information revolution continues, in what ways might it change warfare?

The Unfolding Information Revolution

The information revolution is upending a range of industries, with applications as wide-ranging as social media, warehouse robots, and home-streaming videos. What is the nature of the information revolution? What are the underlying trends in what information technology enables, and how might these change warfare? Across the many diverse applications of information technology run three core trends: increasing transparency, connectivity, and machine intelligence.

Increasing Transparency
One of the core features of the information revolution is the "datafication" of our world—the generation of large amounts of digital data. Combined with the fact that computers make it almost costless to copy information, this has

resulted in a freer flow of information that is making the world increasingly transparent. Satellite images, once the province only of superpowers, are now available free online. Even secret government data is not as secret as it once was. Edward Snowden, a U.S. intelligence community contractor, has been reported by the U.S. government to have stolen in excess of about 1.7 million documents, the largest leak in history.[4] A leak of such scale would have been nearly impossible in a predigital era. Compare, for example, the Vietnam-era Pentagon Papers, seven thousand pages that were photocopied by hand.[5] The datafication of our world combined with the ease with which digital information can be copied and shared is leading to a world that is more transparent, with secrets harder to keep on all sides. Sifting through this massive amount of data, particularly when it is unstructured and heterogeneous, becomes a major challenge.

Increasing Connectivity

Information technology is increasing the degree of connectivity between people and things, both in terms of the number of people and things online as well as the volume and bandwidth of information exchanged. As the Internet continues to colonize the material world, more objects are increasingly networked (i.e., Internet of things), enabling remote access and information-sharing, as well as making them susceptible to hacking. Social media enables many-to-many communication, allowing any individual to share their story or report on abuses of authorities. The result is a fundamental shift in communication power dynamics, upending relationships between individuals and traditional authorities. In addition, connectivity allows crowdsourcing of problems and ideas, accelerating the pace of innovation and the velocity and volume of human communication.

Increasingly Intelligent Machines

The rapid growth in computing power is resulting in increasingly intelligent machines. When embodied in physical machines, this trend is allowing the growth of increasingly capable and autonomous robotic systems. Advanced computing also allows for the processing of large amounts of data, including gene sequencing, enabling advances in "big data," artificial intelligence, and synthetic biology. While current computing methods have limitations and face tapering growth rates,[6] possible novel computing methods—such as quantum computing, neural networks, and deep learning, or neuromorphic computing—hold potential promise for continued growth in intelligent machines.

Chinese Naval Warfare in the Information Age

The importance of the information revolution for the future of war is well recognized on both sides of the Pacific. Since at least the 2000s, China has sought to build a military capable of winning "localized wars under informatized conditions." Chinese military sources prioritize control of the information environment as a key aspect of modern military operations, particularly since the "revolution in military affairs." Chinese analysts describe a fundamental shift in the relative importance of material power vis-à-vis technological development and information systems. For example, Chinese semi-official doctrinal sources, such as *Science of Military Strategy*, state that while material power and capability remain important, information has replaced them as the "dominant factor" in modern warfare.[7]

The evolution of information technology and Beijing's expanding security interests are shaping China's military and naval development in profound ways. The 2015 Military Strategy released by the Ministry of Defense states that "the national security issues facing China encompass far more subjects, extend over a greater range, and cover a longer time span than at any time in the country's history."[8] As China's near and far seas interests expand, deterring or winning probable future conflicts requires military systems capable of quickly generating decisive and disruptive advantages early in a future campaign.

While China retains an "active defense" posture in the strategic sense, Chinese naval modernization is prioritizing capabilities that enable localized offensive operations—such as information attacks, firepower attacks, air-sea blockades, and island landings.[9] The importance of offensive-enabling capabilities seems to be recognized at multiple levels of the People's Liberation Army (PLA). For example, in a 2014 article, the commander in chief of the Chinese navy, Wu Shengli, implicitly argues for the adaptation of more offensive capabilities through highlighting the strength of the Japanese navy vis-à-vis China's in the Sino-Japanese war: "In a few short years [the Japanese navy's] power surpassed that of the Beiyang. [Japan] followed the West's example and undertook reforms, setting up joint fleets and unifying command of the navy. *They placed emphasis on offensive combat at sea, using all of their power to seize command of the sea, and taking the initiative in wartime*" (emphasis added).[10] Similarly, *Science of Military Strategy* argues, "Future naval limited warfare will depend on offensive operations to seize the initiative and secure victory."[11]

Accordingly, not only has naval modernization become a priority effort in Chinese military strategy—along with supporting air, space, and cyber capabilities—but China is also striving to achieve unique advantages enabled by information technology. For example, *Science of Military Strategy* emphasizes semi-large-scale, semi-high-intensity antisecession wars, likely linked to a conflict scenario across the Taiwan Strait. This strategic assessment has important implications for the Chinese navy, as the most likely threats are "*maritime limited military conflicts*" and the conflict scenarios for which China should focus its preparation are "semi-large-scale, semi-high-intensity limited *maritime* wars under nuclear deterrence conditions" (emphasis added).[12]

The information revolution enables and even incentivizes the Chinese military to pursue technologies that afford opportunities to overcome material asymmetries. As suggested in the 2015 Military Strategy, advanced militaries emphasize the development of "long-range, precise, smart, stealthy, and unmanned weapons."[13] China is thus pursuing breakthrough information technologies comparable to its competitors. However, China simultaneously recognizes that adversary reliance on information systems renders them uniquely vulnerable. As a result, China has prioritized the control and paralysis of key adversary information systems, both in its doctrine and in its technological development.[14]

Disruptive Technologies in Four Contests of Future War

Both the U.S. and Chinese navies are modernizing, but toward what end? Trends in information technology—greater transparency, connectivity, and increasingly intelligent machines—will change how militaries fight. Computers have enabled satellite positioning, navigation, and timing (PNT) systems and communications, precision-guided weapons, and stealth technology (possible because of computer simulations). Further advances in information technology are enabling greater autonomy, networking, robotics, cyberweapons, data fusion and processing, artificial intelligence, and synthetic biology.

First-generation information technology has enabled *reconnaissance-strike networks* consisting of sensors, command and control networks, and precision-guided weapons. These allow military forces to detect and destroy enemy forces with great precision over long distances. They represent a fundamental shift from a prior warfighting regime of unguided weapons, which depended on mass, maneuver, and volume and density of fire.[15]

As the information revolution matures, reconnaissance-strike networks will give way to *reconnaissance-strike swarms*, with larger numbers of autonomous, networked, cooperative forces on the battlefield; larger volumes of information flow; and a faster tempo of operations. As militaries continue to evolve their concepts of operation to a maturing information revolution, four contests will shape the future of warfare: hiding versus finding, understanding versus confusion, network resilience versus network degradation, and hitting versus intercepting.

While information technology is enabling greater transparency, connectivity, and more intelligent machines, war occurs in a competitive environment. Many of the same technologies that can be used to increase understanding and lethality on the battlefield can also be used to disrupt adversary operations and sow confusion. While militaries will seek dominance on both sides of these contests, technological developments may alter the inherent characteristics of future war such that they favor one side or the other of these contests.

Hiding versus Finding

One of the prominent features of information-enabled warfare to date is the development of precision-guided weapons that can strike ships, aircraft, and bases at long distances. Defensively, this has placed a premium on hiding. Nonstate groups seek to blend into civilian populations. State actors rely increasingly on mobile systems, such as mobile air defense systems and mobile missile launchers. Because of these adversary innovations in hiding, offensive operations are often limited by intelligence, surveillance, and reconnaissance (ISR) capabilities. For the past two decades, the United States has been on the offensive side of this exchange. However, adversary developments in long-range precision strike are forcing Washington to think more carefully about concealment strategies as well, including at sea.

One important asymmetry in the hiding versus finding contest is the ability to leverage increasing computer processing power to sift through noise to detect objects, including synthesizing information gained from multiple active or passive sensors. This makes it increasingly difficult for those seeking to hide because they must conceal their signature or actively deceive the enemy in multiple directions at once and potentially against multiple methods of detection. Advanced electronic warfare measures enable precision jamming and deception, but these methods require knowing the location of enemy sensors, which may be passive. Thus, a contest of hiding and finding capital assets may first depend on a preliminary contest of hiding and finding distributed sensors and jammers lurking in the battlespace. These techniques, both for distributed passive sensing and distributed precision electronic warfare, depend upon effectively networked, cooperative forces, which are intimately linked with other contests.[16]

Because precision-guided weapons can deliver a high volume of lethal firepower directly on a target, whoever gets the first salvo may decide victory, both at sea and in the air. Getting that first shot may also depend increasingly on one's ability to effectively hide, while deploying sufficient sensors to find the enemy first. The maxim "look first, shoot first, kill first" may apply not only in beyond-visual-range air-to-air combat, but in all domains of warfare as well. Technology areas that could enhance hiding include:

- adaptive and responsive jamming
- precision electronic attack
- counterspace capabilities (kinetic and nonkinetic)
- metamaterials for electromagnetic and auditory cloaking
- cyberdefenses
- low-cost autonomous decoys
- autonomous undersea vehicles (limiting factor: power)
- undersea payload modules.

Technology areas that could enhance finding include:

- sensor/data fusion
- distributed sensing
- foliage-penetrating radar
- space-based surveillance
- low-cost robotic systems, including leveraging commercial components for clandestine surveillance
- long-endurance power solutions (such as radioisotope power) to enable persistent robotic surveillance systems
- networked undersea sensors
- cyberespionage
- quantum computing (to break encryption).

In conflict scenarios between China and the United States, geographic asymmetries play an important shaping role. China possesses the advantage of proximity—a large land mass from which to project power into the near periphery. While the United States maintains forward bases in East Asia, in general it has thousands of miles of ocean to cross before fully bringing its military assets to bear. In order to exploit this geographic asymmetry, however, China requires well-developed early warning technologies to detect U.S. forces while they are still en route. Improvements in precision strike first require supporting systems that can accurately detect, identify, and target enemy assets.

China therefore is improving its ISR capabilities.[17] Chinese research and development in ISR has increased since the Gulf War and the 1995–96 Taiwan Strait crisis, corresponding with an outline published by the PLA in the early 2000s detailing the requirement for improved early warning systems.[18] ISR improvements include three key areas that, if successfully developed into a network of Chinese sensors coupled with advanced information processing, could degrade the capabilities of some U.S. systems.

First, China is improving land-based over-the-horizon backscatter (OTH-B) radars. China's first OTH-B development programs were reportedly launched in the 1960s, and Chinese academic journals discussed military application of the technology as early as the 1970s.[19] Recently, China has made investments in new technologies that provide more accurate and precise detection.[20] In particular, some suggest that sky wave and surface wave radars may provide targeting support for antiship ballistic missiles.[21] In the process, China is leveraging its civilian expertise. A 2006 State Council Directive specifies that China's defense industries are now pursuing radar development and manufacturing.[22] Since at least the early 2000s, Chinese companies such as the China National Electronics Import and Export Corporation have been developing sky wave OTH-B radar.[23] Scholars at Jiangnan University have been working on similar technology.[24]

Second, China is improving its airborne ISR capabilities. China has developed manned aircraft with early warning capabilities—namely, the KJ-200 and KJ-2000 airborne warning and control systems—using domestic companies such as Xi'an Aircraft Corporation, Sha'anxi Aircraft Corporation, and China Electronic Technology Company. China is reportedly also developing the KJ-500, which employs a similar but smaller version of the KJ-2000's fixed active phased array radar.[25] In addition, there is at least some evidence to suggest that these firms have improved the pace of development, particularly in the case of the KJ-200.[26]

Investments in manned surveillance aircraft are complemented by those in unmanned aerial vehicles (UAVs), and Chinese drone production capacity is improving. In the early 2000s, it took approximately three years to take the *Winglong/Pterodactyl 1* from project initiation to prototype display.[27] China is now reportedly building UAVs at an increasingly rapid rate—in part the result of improvements to the indigenous Beidou PNT System and high-speed data links.[28] According to the U.S. Department of Defense, China may be planning to field over 40,000 land- and sea-based unmanned platforms by

2023.[29] Chinese scholars see UAVs playing a unique role in overcoming current asymmetries between China and its rivals: "UAVs will play an important part, responsible for continuous reconnaissance, the searching out and tracking enemy fleets, simultaneously returning information, thereby making up for the weakness of easily destroyed manned reconnaissance aircraft, real-time reconnaissance satellite inadequacies, and shortcomings of over-the-horizon radars."[30] Other Chinese military analysts note the expansion of the UAV mission set, from battlefield ISR to carrier-based operations, antisubmarine warfare, antiship attack, jamming, communications interception, targeting guidance, communication relay, and air defense.[31]

Third, China is investing in its submarine fleet, whose ISR mission ranks as one of its most important. In assessing submarine developments in foreign militaries, several Chinese scholars (some affiliated with the PLA) note: "Countries of the world attach great importance to the development of underwater surveillance technology." The authors look especially to the U.S. Navy, which has "considered the information collection, access, and sharing as an important part of implementing network-centric warfare."[32] In particular, the authors argue for increased research investment in underwater acoustics and advanced reconnaissance in response to the threat caused by U.S. improvements in underwater detection systems.[33]

China is also investing in technologies that will make its submarine fleet faster, quieter, and more flexible. There is some evidence that Chinese scholars affiliated with the PLA Navy are working on magnetic bearing systems, which could dampen the high noise levels currently emitted by Chinese submarines.[34] Finally, the China Shipbuilding Industry Corporation's Wuhan Institute of Marine Electric Propulsion reportedly finalized an integrated electrical propulsion model in July 2013.[35] Integrated electrical propulsion systems provide improved flexibility to submarine commanders.[36]

China has also reportedly equipped the *Yuan*-class submarine with an air-independent power (AIP) system, which increases underwater endurance through alternative power sources while submerged.[37] While the impact of AIP on naval warfare is debatable, some Chinese analysts emphasize it. For example, an editorial from *PLA Daily* in November 2014 argued that AIP technologies would become an "important future direction of development in conventional submarines," due to their relative stealth and ability to remain submerged for long periods of time.[38] A recent *People's Daily* editorial released details regarding advancements in Chinese AIP technologies: "In the field of special propulsion systems, the Stirling [i.e., AIP] engine department of the 711 research institute of the China Ship Scientific Research Center has been around for 10 years and has independently developed a completely new engine, which is 117% more efficient than similar products overseas, which puts it in the lead worldwide. It is set to be installed in China's next generation of warships."[39] Some Chinese analysts also argue that unmanned underwater vehicles (UUVs) are an important investment to improve detection, antisubmarine capabilities, and weaponization.[40] UUVs could also serve as forward-deployed sensors to be used in conjunction with other naval platforms, such as submarines.[41] In a 2013 article in *Ship Electric Engineering*, Chinese authors argued that "Submarines, Unmanned Underwater Vehicles, and divers are playing an increasingly important role in modern warfare."[42] In 2014, researchers at Tianjin University tested the UUV *Haiyan* in the South China Sea; it was reportedly operational for twenty-one days. Some reports indicate that the *Zhishui* (智水) *III* UUV completed testing in 2000 and is already in service with the PLA Navy.[43] Presently, long endurance power solutions are a limiting factor for autonomous undersea vehicles, so breakthroughs in power could advantage either side.

Understanding versus Confusion

As the volume and pace of information (including misinformation) on the battlefield increase, turning information into *understanding* will be key. A key contest in war will be between adversary cognitive systems, both artificial and human, to process information, understand the battlespace, and decide and execute faster than the enemy. Advances in machine intelligence show great promise for increasing the ability of artificial cognitive systems to understand and react to information in intelligent, goal-oriented ways. However, machine intelligence remains "brittle." While it is possible to design machines that can outperform humans in narrow tasks, such as driving, playing chess, or answering trivia, human intelligence far outstrips machines in terms of its robustness and adaptability to a wide range of problems. For the foreseeable future, the best cognitive systems are likely to be hybrid architectures combining human and machine cognition, leveraging the advantages of each.

These technologies also offer the potential for new vulnerabilities, as militaries will attempt to thwart their enemies' ability to understand the operating environment by denying accurate information, planting misinformation, and sowing doubt in whatever information an enemy already has. Deception has been a key component of military operations for millennia and will remain so in the future, and these technologies will offer new opportunities for increasing confusion. Technology areas that could affect understanding include:

- artificial cognitive systems (advanced microprocessor design, neural networks and neuromorphic computing, data processing, artificial intelligence, and "deep learning")
- human cognitive performance enhancement and degradation (pharmaceutical enhancements, such as Adderall or Modafinil, training methods, such as transcranial direct current stimulation, and synthetic biology)
- human-machine synthesis (human factors engineering and human-machine interfaces, brain-computer interfaces, and synthetic telepathy).

Technology areas that could affect confusion include:

- cyberespionage and sabotage
- misinformation, deception, and spoofing attacks
- human performance degradation
- tailored biological weapons.

An important asymmetry between the United States and China is the uneasiness with which human enhancement technologies are viewed in the United States. While there are no legal or ethical objections per se to human enhancement, these technologies raise many legal and ethical issues that must be addressed. Experiments with cognitive-enhancing drugs and training techniques can and have been performed in military labs, meeting stringent legal and ethical requirements.[44] However, there remains a cultural prejudice in some military communities against human enhancement, even for treatments that have been shown to be both safe and effective. The U.S. Department of Defense currently lacks overarching policy guidance to the military services to articulate a path forward on human performance-enhancing technologies.[45]

Network Resilience versus Network Degradation

Networking allows military forces to fight as a coherent whole, rather than as individual, noncohesive units. For the past two decades, the U.S. military has been able to leverage the advantages of a networked force and has largely fought with freedom of maneuver in space and the electromagnetic spectrum. However, military networks will be increasingly contested by jamming, cyber-attacks, and physical attacks on communications nodes. Resilient networks that are flexible and adaptable in the face of attacks, as well as doctrine that can adapt to degraded network operations, will be key to maintaining a force that can fight through network attacks. This includes "thin line" redundant backups that may offer limited communications among distributed forces, as well as off-network solutions. While many solutions for network resilience encompass doctrine and training to fight under degraded network conditions, technological solutions are also important to maintain networks under stress. This includes not only communications, but also PNT data, which are critical for synchronized and precise global military operations.

It is now well established that China is developing network and cyberspace capabilities as part of its military strategy.[46] For at least a decade, Chinese military doctrine has prioritized the importance of information networks. More recent texts, however, have begun to designate cyberspace as a separate domain (领域) of conflict.[47] The 2015 Military Strategy clearly specifies that "cyberspace has become a new pillar of economic and social development, and a new domain of national security."[48] *Science of Military Strategy* argues that "one successful cyberattack can cause the other side's economy to collapse and paralyze their information systems."[49] Furthermore, the text argues that the technical realities of cyberspace, particularly the difficulty in avoiding software vulnerabilities and the low cost of malware, render cyberspace "easy to attack and difficult to defend" (易攻难防).[50]

Technology areas affecting network resilience include:

- protected communications, such as low probability of intercept and detection communications
- high-altitude long-endurance aircraft or airships to function as pseudo-satellites (limiting factor: power)
- software-defined radios (to allow adaptable communications)
- open-architecture communications systems (to allow rapid adaptability of hardware and software to respond to enemy jamming)
- cyberdefenses
- autonomous undersea vehicles (to protect undersea communications infrastructure)
- lower-cost space launch options
- faster responsive space launch options to replenish degraded space architectures
- global positioning system (GPS)–independent PNT.

Technology areas affecting network degradation include improved jamming techniques, cyber offensive weapons, antisatellite weapons (kinetic and nonkinetic), and high-powered microwave weapons to disrupt or destroy electronic systems.

More effective command, control, communications, computers, and intelligence capabilities remain critical to Chinese military modernization. Indeed, one of the core focus areas for the PLA in the past decade has been joint interoperability. Starting in 2003, the PLA developed a new system called the Integrated Command Platform (ICP) to address existing challenges. This has been described as a "military computing platform connecting information systems from multiple services, combat arms, and units to enable the transmission, processing, and storage of information in a shared environment."[51] The ICP reportedly utilizes Beidou to provide a common operating picture of troop positions to commanders.[52] The General Staff Department's 61st Research Institute, integrating a team of approximately eight thousand military and civilian personnel, spearheaded the six-year development of ICP.[53] The 2016 U.S. Department of Defense annual report on the Chinese military indicates that the PLA is now fielding ICP platforms to "units at lower echelons" across services and military regions.[54]

Similar efforts integrating civilian and military expertise continue in other areas as well. For example, in September 2014, the China State Shipbuilding Corporation and the China Aerospace Science and Industry Corporation (CASIC) signed an agreement to collaborate on research and development (including sharing costs and expertise and developing a framework for joint training, international business activities, and development of new products) in the areas of "information security, networking, satellite communications, UAVs, and GPS." CASIC signed a similar agreement with the China Aerospace Science and Technology Corporation in July 2014.[55]

Hitting versus Intercepting

Finding the enemy, understanding the data, and passing it to the right warfighting elements is only a precursor to achieving effects on target, frequently from missiles or torpedoes. Because guided weapons can put lethal effects directly on a target, intercepting inbound threats or diverting them with decoys is generally a more effective response than attempting to mitigate direct hits via improved armor. However, missile defense is a challenging task. Missiles are difficult to strike midflight, requiring multiple interceptors, resulting in cost-exchange ratios that favor the offense.

This phenomenon creates incentives for early employment of missiles. Specifically, *Science of Military Strategy* describes that PLA Second Artillery conventional missiles are in many ways limited, precisely because their employment may be "uneconomic" against certain targets. In certain strategic opportunities, however, conventional missiles can be used for "early strike" against enemy early warning systems, electronic warfare systems, anti-air missile positions, and air bases—as well as military-use satellites and information system nodes. The key, however, is to "fight for the strategic initiative" and "achieve strategic objectives as soon as possible."[56]

A number of possible technology breakthroughs could tilt this balance in either direction. Developments favoring hitting include:

- networked, cooperative munitions, including cooperative decoys and jammers
- hypersonic weapons
- advanced stealth, both for missiles and aircraft
- large numbers of low-cost swarming missiles or uninhabited systems to saturate enemy defenses
- airborne, undersea, or sea surface arsenal ships or "missile trucks" to cost-effectively transport missiles to the fight
- high-fidelity decoys to increase the costs to defenders
- long-endurance uninhabited aircraft to enable long-range persistence and strike.

Developments favoring intercepting include:

- low cost-per-shot electric weapons, such as high-energy lasers and electromagnetic railguns
- high-quality radars for tracking incoming rounds and guiding interceptors
- long-endurance uninhabited aircraft for forward ballistic missile defense, both for launch detection and boost phase intercept
- persistent clandestine surveillance, from space assets, stealthy uninhabited aircraft, or unattended ground sensors for early detection of ballistic missile launch and prelaunch preparation.

The U.S. military has long sought low cost-per-shot weapons such as high-energy lasers and electromagnetic railguns to upend the missile defense cost-exchange ratio. High-energy lasers have already been demonstrated against slow-moving, unhardened targets such as low-cost drones or mortars. Current operationally ready lasers are in the tens of kilowatts, however, and scaling up to sufficient power to intercept ballistic missiles would require on the order of a megawatt, more than an order of magnitude improvement.[57] While such improvements are frequently seen in computer-based technologies, laser technology, and, perhaps more importantly, key enablers such as cooling and energy storage are not improving at such a rapid pace. Electromagnetic rail-guns, on the other hand, likely show the most promise for defense against ballistic missiles. They require massive amounts of power, however, on the order of tens of megajoules, necessitating more advanced power management systems, similar to those on the DDG-1000.[58]

The Chinese have been pursuing directed energy weapons since the 1960s,[59] and the Chinese government continues to emphasize the role that these "cutting-edge" technologies might play in future conflict.[60] In 2014, China Poly Group displayed a nonlethal antipersonnel system, similar to the U.S. Active Denial System.[61] The *PLA Daily*, quoting an "expert on ships and naval armament," describes that Chinese navy ships, including those that have deployed to the Gulf of Aden, have "some kinds of directed-sound wave weapons on its ships, enabling them to shock and disperse hostile vessels."[62] Other sources indicate that Chinese universities, such as Beijing University of Aeronautics and Astronautics, Xi'an Jiaotong University, the Chinese Academy of Engineering Physics, the Harbin Institute of Technology, and the Naval Aeronautical Engineering Institute of the PLA, may be developing "antilaser materials" to deflect directed energy weapons.[63]

However, one outstanding question relating to Chinese directed energy weapons is whether new systems could be installed into existing ships and whether those vessels would possess sufficient power. New marine energy technologies might help alleviate energy shortage issues. Biofuels, photovoltaics, and wind energy could potentially reduce energy costs at sea. Yet it remains to be seen whether the existing electrical infrastructure on Chinese naval vessels could support directed energy weapons.

Conclusion: Anticipating Disruptive Change in Naval Warfare

Naval warfare underwent several major paradigm shifts in the nineteenth and twentieth centuries, and the ongoing information revolution presents many opportunities for disruptive change in the twenty-first. Hedging against disruptive change that may alter the very metrics that make warfighting assets valuable is extremely challenging in a world in which ship lifespans are measured in decades and supercarrier lifespans in half-centuries. Predicting the character of naval warfare in the 2040s or 2050s may seem like a hopeless task, but when a navy lays down the keel for a new ship, it is doing just that. Each acquisition decision represents a multi-billion-dollar bet that that asset will continue to be valuable several decades hence. Meanwhile, these investments occur in an innovation landscape in which information technology changes are measured in months.

The ideal military platform would be highly modular, with open architecture design and the ability to "plug and play" new hardware capabilities rapidly, as well as easily upgrade software. Indeed, the U.S. Navy has shifted to a paradigm of "payloads over platforms," and "software over payloads" may well be a useful addendum. Many naval assets are inherently modular. Aircraft carriers, after all, are merely enormous "trucks" for the aircraft they bring to bear. Vertical launching system cells on ships and submarines have the ability to plug and play a variety of missiles. Some disruptive technologies have the potential to stretch naval vessels beyond their modular limits, however. Size, weight, power, and cooling (SWaP-C) are limiting factors in a platform's basic design and may be extremely difficult to change once it is built. Without knowing whether any given technology will bear fruit, designers may not know how much additional SWaP-C to build into a platform and may under- or over-design it. These limitations suggest that while modular design can help a navy hedge against technological game changers, it will not solve the problem entirely, especially if technology developments favor major doctrinal shifts, such as expanding power projection from undersea.

Finally, while this chapter has focused on technology, many battlefield advantages derive from superior training, doctrine, organizations, and culture. In fact, new technologies alone generally do not accrue significant battlefield advantage if they are not used in combination with new concepts of operation, training, doctrine, and organization. From a training perspective, the U.S. military currently retains many advantages over the PLA. However, that also means the PLA has more room for improvement. When it comes to embracing new doctrinal or organizational shifts, U.S. military dominance may be a weakness, as U.S. organizations heavily invested in current ways of warfighting may be slow to adapt to disruptive changes.[64]

Ultimately, it is likely to be the ability to rapidly adapt to a changing warfighting environment that will confer the most long-term advantages. Any individual technological advantage is likely to be fleeting, particularly in a world in which secrets can be so easily copied and transmitted across borders. The ability to rapidly adjust not only the hardware and digital software comprising naval forces, but also the human software—the training, doctrine, concepts of operation, and organizations—is likely to be the most critical factor in ensuring long-term advantage. Strategic agility, above all else, should be the guiding star for naval planners.

Notes

1. Stephen Rodriguez, "The Top Ten Failed Defense Programs of the RMA Era," *War on the Rocks*, December 2, 2014, http://warontherocks.com/2014/12/top-10-failed-defense-programs-of-the-rma-era/.

2. "Gartner Says Worldwide IT Spending to Grow 2.4 Percent in 2015," *Gartner.com*, January 12, 2015, http://www.gartner.com/newsroom/id/2959717.

3. Computing power continues advancing at an exponential rate, but the pace of change has begun to decline. See "Performance Development," *Top500.org*, http://www.top500.org/statistics/perfdevel/; and Michael Feldman, "Life Beyond Moore's Law," *Top500.org*, http://www.top500.org/blog/life-beyond-moores-law/.

4. Chris Strohm and Del Quentin Wilber, "Pentagon Says Snowden Took Most U.S. Secrets Ever: Rogers," *Bloomberg.com*, January 9, 2014, http://www.bloomberg.com/news/articles/2014-01-09/pentagon-finds-snowden-took-1-7-million-files-rogers-says.

5. Douglas O. Linder, "The Pentagon Papers (Daniel Ellsberg) Trial: An Account," 2011, http://law2.umkc.edu/faculty/projects/ftrials/ellsberg/ellsbergaccount.html.

6. Feldman, "Life Beyond Moore's Law."

7. 寿晓松 [Shou Xiaosong], ed., 战略学 [*Science of Military Strategy*] (Beijing: 军事科学出版社 [Military Science Press], 2013), 91.

8. 中国的军事战略 [*China's Military Strategy*] (Beijing: State Council Information Office, May 2015), http://www.81.cn/dblj/2015-05/26/content_6507373.htm.

9. Shou, *Science of Military Strategy*, 209.

10. 吴胜利 [Wu Shengli], "深刻吸取甲午战争历史教训坚定不移走经略海洋维护海权发展海军之路" ["Learn Profound Historical Lessons from the Sino-Japanese War of 1894–1895 and Unswervingly Take the Path of Planning and Managing Maritime Affairs, Safeguarding Maritime Rights and Interests, and Building a Powerful Navy"], 中国军事科学 [*China Military Science*] (April 2014): 3.

11. Shou, *Science of Military Strategy*, 216.

12. Ibid., 100.

13. *China's Military Strategy*, 2015.

14. Shou, *Science of Military Strategy*, 92–93.

15. Robert O. Work and Shawn Brimley, "20YY: Preparing for War in the Robotic Age," Center for a New American Security, January 2014, http://www.cnas.org/sites/default/files/publications-pdf/CNAS_20YY_WorkBrimley.pdf.

16. Paul Scharre, "Robotics on the Battlefield Part II: The Coming Swarm," Center for a New American Security, October 2014, 32, http://www.cnas.org/sites/default/files/publications-pdf/CNAS_TheComingSwarm_Scharre.pdf.

17. For other advances in command, control, communications, computers, intelligence, surveillance, and reconnaissance (C4ISR) capabilities, see Shane Bilsborough, "China's Emerging C4ISR Revolution," *The Diplomat*, August 13, 2013, http://thediplomat.com/2013/08/chinas-emerging-c4isr-revolution/.

18. Kevin Pollpeter, "Towards an Integrative C4ISR System: Informationization and Joint Operations in the People's Liberation Army," in *The PLA at Home and Abroad:*

Assessing the Operational Capabilities of China's Military, ed. Roy Kamphausen and David Lai (Carlisle, PA: U.S. Army War College Press, 2010).

19. Mark A. Stokes, *China's Strategy Modernization: Implications for the United States* (Carlisle, PA: U.S. Army War College Press, 1999), 40; "什么是超视距雷达" ["What Is Over-the-Horizon Radar"], 无线电工程译文 [Wireless Electrical Engineering Translation], May 1, 1971, http://www.cnki.com.cn/Article/CJFDTOTAL-WXDG197102010.htm.

20. Department of Defense (DoD), *Annual Report to Congress: Military and Security Developments Involving the People's Republic of China 2016* (Washington, DC: DoD, 2016), 79–83 [hereafter DoD (2016)].

21. Owen R. Cote Jr., "Assessing the Undersea Balance between the U.S. and China," *SSP Working Paper Series*, February 2011, 16.

22. DoD (2016), 54.

23. "China to Test Air-Defence Radar," *Jane's Defence Weekly*, August 17, 2001.

24. Chen Baiying, "远程超视距目标无源定位与跟踪技术" ["Research on Long-Range Over-the-Horizon for the Passive Location and Tracking of Targets"], graduate thesis, Jiangnan University, March 2013, http://cdmd.cnki.com.cn/Article/CDMD-10295-1013242887.htm; and Liu Yian, "超视距雷达信息处理技术研究" ["Information Process Technology Research on Over-the-Horizon Radar"], graduate thesis, Jiangnan University, June 2014, http://cdmd.cnki.com.cn/Article/CDMD-10295-1014380585.htm.

25. James Hardy and Richard D. Fisher, "China's ADIZ Provokes Tit-for-Tat Patrols Over East China Sea," *Jane's Defence Weekly*; DoD (2016), 62.

26. "预警机总师欧阳绍修: 云—8被大胆修改了80%," July 13, 2011, http://military.china.com/05/11078235/20110713/16644851.html.

27. Andrew S. Erickson, "China's Modernization of Its Naval and Air Power Capabilities," *Strategy Asia 2012–2013: China's Military Challenge* (Washington, DC: National Bureau of Asian Research, 2012), 121.

28. "China's UAV into a Period of Fast Progress," *People's Daily Online*, February 7, 2013, http://en.people.cn/90786/8124958.html.

29. DoD (2016), 36. Even if this figure is accurate, the vast majority of these would likely be smaller, tactical UAVs.

30. Mao Zhiwen, "中日下代战机对决: 歼20导弹种类多—日心神不宁" ["Determining Victory in the Next-Generation Sino-Japanese Military Crisis: More F-20 Guided Missiles—Japan Uneasy"], 人民日报 [People's Daily], April 28, 2014, http://military.people.com.cn/n/2014/0428/c1011-24950479.html.

31. Miao Xiumei, "国外舰载无人机技术的发展动向与分析" ["Development Trend and Analysis of Foreign Ship-Based UAV Technology"], 航船电子工程 [Ship Electric Engineering] 33, no. 12 (2013): 18–19.

32. Zheng Junjie et al., "外军水下侦察技术现状与发展趋势" ["Current Situation and Development Trends in the Underwater Reconnaissance Technology of Foreign Militaries"], 航船电子工程 [Ship Electronic Engineering] 33, no. 8 (August 2013): 15.

33. Ibid., 18.

34. Kang Wang et al., "Analytical Modeling of Permanent Magnet Biased Axial Magnetic Bearing with Multiple Air Gaps," *Magnetics* 50, no. 11 (November 2014): 1–4.

35. Zhao Lei, "Chinese Shipbuilder Reveals Breakthrough Technology," *China Daily*, August 20, 2013.

36. "An Integrated Power System: The Next Step," *Undersea Warfare* 3, no. 1 (Fall 2000), http://www.navy.mil/navydata/cno/n87/usw/issue_9/power_system.html.

37. Jesse Karotkin, senior intelligence officer for China, "Trends in China's Naval Modernization," testimony before U.S.-China Economic and Security Review Commission, January 30, 2014, http://www.uscc.gov/sites/default/files/Karotkin_Testimony1.30.14.pdf.

38. "潜艇的前世今生" ["The Past and Present of Submarines"], 解放军报 [*PLA Daily*], November 15, 2014, http://jz.chinamil.com.cn/n2014/tp/content_6224643_2.htm.

39. Quoted in "Details of China's New AIP Submarine Technology Revealed," *Want China Times*, May 7, 2015, http://www.wantchinatimes.com/news-subclass-cnt.aspx?id=20150507000080&cid=1101.

40. Lu Jianxia, "2014解放军六大科技: 水下无人机护卫钻井平台" ["Six Major Technologies of the PLA in 2014: Underwater Drones Protect Drilling Platforms"], 解放军报 [*PLA Daily*], July 20, 2014, http://news.xinhuanet.com/mil/2014-07/21/c_126774520.htm.

41. Jonathan Greenert, "Navy 2025: Forward Warfighters," U.S. Naval Institute *Proceedings* 137, no. 12 (December 2011), http://www.usni.org/magazines/proceedings/2011-12/navy-2025-forward-warfighters.

42. Zheng Junjie et al., "Current Situation and Development Trends in the Underwater Reconnaissance Technology of Foreign Militaries," 15.

43. Jeffrey Lin and P. W. Singer, "Not a Shark, but a Robot: Chinese University Tests Long-Range Unmanned Mini Sub," *Popular Science*, June 4, 2014; Michael Chase et al., *Emerging Trends in China's Development of Unmanned Systems* (Santa Monica, CA: RAND, 2015), http://www.rand.org/pubs/research_reports/RR990.html.

44. See, for example, J. A. Caldwell et al., "Modafinil's Effects on Simulator Performance and Mood on Pilots During 37 H Without Sleep," *Aviation, Space, and Environmental Medicine* (September 2004): 777–84, http://www.ncbi.nlm.nih.gov/pubmed/15460629; R. A. McKinley et al., "Acceleration of Image Analyst Training with Transcranial Direct Current Stimulation," *Behavioral Neuroscience* (February 2015), http://www.ncbi.nlm.nih.gov/pubmed/24341718.

45. For an overview, see Patrick Lin et al., "Enhanced Warfighters: Risk, Ethics, and Policy," January 1, 2013, http://ethics.calpoly.edu/greenwall_report.pdf.

46. See, for example, Jon Lindsay et al., eds., *China and Cybersecurity: Espionage, Strategy, and Politics in the Digital Domain* (New York: Oxford University Press, 2015).

47. See Shou, *Science of Military Strategy*, 188–97; 肖天亮 [Xiao Tainliang], ed., 战略学 [*Science of Military Strategy*] (Beijing: 国防大学出版社 [National Defense University Press], 2015), 143–49.

48. *China's Military Strategy*, 2015.

49. Shou, *Science of Military Strategy*, 191.

50. Ibid., 193; China also claims to prioritize defensive cyberspace operations, while simultaneously giving attention to offensive cyberspace attacks, see ibid., 196.

51. Kevin Pollpeter et al., "Enabling Information-Based System of System Operations: The Research, Development, and Acquisition Process for the Integrated Command Platform," *SITC Research Briefs*, January 2014, https://escholarship.org/uc/item/6f26w11m.

52. Kevin McCauley, "Putting Precision in Operations: Beidou Satellite Navigation System," *China Brief* 14, no. 16 (August 22, 2014), http://www.jamestown.org/single/?tx_ttnews%5Btt_news%5D=42767&no_cache=1#.VeSOGbQbBos.

53. Ibid., 3.

54. DoD (2016), 63.

55. "China's CSSC and CASIC Sign Naval C4ISR Agreement," *Jane's Defence Weekly*, September 26, 2014, http://www.janes.com/article/43734/china-s-cssc-and-casic-sign-naval-c4isr-agreement.

56. Shou, *Science of Military Strategy*, 236.

57. Jason Ellis, "Directed Energy Weapons: Promise and Prospects," Center for a New American Security, April 2015, http://www.cnas.org/sites/default/files/publications-pdf/CNAS_Directed_Energy_Weapons_April-2015.pdf.

58. Office of Naval Research, "Electromagnetic Railgun," http://www.onr.navy.mil/Science-Technology/Departments/Code-35/All-Programs/air-warfare-352/Electromagnetic-Railgun.aspx; U.S. Navy, "DDG-1000 Fact Sheet," http://www.navsea.navy.mil/teamships/PEOS_DDG1000/DDG1000_factsheet.aspx.

59. For historical background, see Stokes, *China's Strategy Modernization*, 195–214; National Ground Intelligence Center, *Assessment of Chinese Radiofrequency Weapon Capabilities*, April 2001; National Ground Intelligence Center, "China: Medical Research on the Bio-Effects of Electromagnetic Pulse and High-Power Microwave Radiation, August 17, 2005.

60. "Annual Conference on World Military Situation Held in Beijing," *China Military Online*, January 12, 2015, http://english.chinamil.com.cn/news-channels/china-military-news/2015-01/12/content_6305322.htm.

61. Richard D. Fisher Jr. and James Hardy, "China's Poly Group Unveils WB-1 Directed-Energy Crowd-Control Weapon," IHS *Jane's 360*, November 27, 2014, http://www.janes.com/article/46377/china-s-poly-group-unveils-wb-1-directed-energy-crowd-control-weapon.

62. "Country Develops Nonlethal Energy Beam Weapon," *China Military Online*, December 20, 2014, http://usa.chinadaily.com.cn/china/2014-12/20/content_19131281.htm.

63. Stephen Chen, "U.S. Lasers? PLA Preparing to Raise its Deflector Shields," *South China Morning Post*, March 10, 2014, http://www.scmp.com/news/china/article/1444732/us-lasers-pla-preparing-raise-its-deflector-shields.

64. For one example, see Paul Scharre, "How to Lose the Robotics Revolution," *War on the Rocks*, July 29, 2014, http://warontherocks.com/2014/07/how-to-lose-the-robotics-revolution/.

Ronald O'Rourke

How China's Shipbuilding Output Might Affect Requirements for U.S. Navy Capabilities

CHINA'S MILITARY MARITIME modernization effort, including its shipbuilding output, has become a significant factor in public discussions on the current and future size and capabilities of the U.S. Navy. While U.S. Navy and Department of Defense (DoD) officials participate in these public discussions, DoD's formal activities for determining official requirements for U.S. military forces are conducted largely in house and are generally not discussed in detail in public. In addition, Navy and other DoD officials in their public statements for the past several years have tended to avoid singling out China by name as a determinant of U.S. military requirements or object of U.S. military planning—a practice some observers have termed the "Voldemort syndrome."[1] These two factors make it difficult for observers outside of DoD to know exactly how China's shipbuilding output or other aspects of its military maritime modernization effort have been affecting requirements for U.S. Navy capabilities. Observers are left to draw inferences from open sources.

Over a Decade of Influence

One general inference that might be drawn is that China's military maritime modernization effort (including its shipbuilding output) appears to have been affecting requirements for U.S. Navy capabilities for over a decade.

As one indication of this, observers might point to the 2004 Office of Naval Intelligence (ONI) report on worldwide maritime challenges, which contained numerous references to China;[2] it was followed by ONI reports specifically on China's navy and associated military maritime capabilities in 2007, 2009, and 2015.[3] Unlike the annual DoD report on military and security developments involving China, which is mandated by Congress, these ONI reports appear to have been prepared and released by the Navy on its own initiative. It seems unlikely that the Navy would want to repeatedly publicize the Chinese military maritime modernization efforts that are discussed in these reports unless those efforts were of at least some importance for internal Navy deliberations.

As a second indication, observers might point to DoD's direction to the Navy in the final report of the 2006 Quadrennial Defense Review (QDR) "to adjust its force posture and basing to provide at least six operationally available and sustainable carriers and 60% of its submarines in the Pacific to support engagement, presence and deterrence,"[4] and the statement in the final report on the 2014 QDR that "by 2020, 60 percent of U.S. Navy assets will be stationed in the Pacific, including enhancements to our critical naval presence in Japan."[5]

As a third indication, observers might highlight the Navy's announcement in July 2008 that it wanted to reverse its plans for procuring destroyers by truncating the *Zumwalt*-class (DDG-1000) destroyer program at two ships[6] and restarting procurement of *Arleigh Burke*-class (DDG-51) destroyers, which had ended in fiscal year (FY) 2005. In explaining this reversal—a sudden, major change in procurement plans—the Navy cited "rapidly evolving threats" and a consequent need to focus destroyer procurement henceforth on providing capabilities for countering antiship cruise missiles (ASCMs), conducting ballistic missile defense (BMD) operations, and conducting blue-water anti-submarine warfare (ASW) operations. The Navy stated that DDG-51s could provide these capabilities and would be affordable in larger numbers than additional DDG-1000s (the design of which would need to be modified to add BMD capability).[7] It is unclear exactly how significant a role China played in the Navy's stated desire for adding capability for countering ASCMs and ballistic missiles, since ASCMs are widely proliferated and countries such as North Korea and Iran have theater-range ballistic missiles, but China's ASCMs and its antiship ballistic missile (ASBM) program—mentioned in DoD's annual report for the first time in 2008[8]—seem likely to have contributed something to that concern. China's submarine force appears to have figured strongly in the Navy's stated desire for adding capability for conducting blue-water ASW operations, since China's submarine force was modernizing rapidly between 2004 and 2007, and no other potential adversary at that point was operating or projected to soon be operating a numerically large force of relatively modern attack submarines.[9]

Renewed Focus on High-End Warfare

A second general inference that might be drawn is that a principal apparent effect of China's military maritime modernization effort (including its ship-building output) on requirements for U.S. Navy capabilities over the last several years has been to refocus U.S. Navy planning back onto a goal of having capabilities for conducting "high-end" warfare in mid-ocean waters so as to defeat capable maritime anti-access/area denial (A2/AD) forces and thereby gain and maintain sea control.

Having such capabilities was a central planning focus for the U.S. Navy during the Cold War. Following the Cold War's end, the dissolution of the Soviet Union, and the collapse of Soviet/Russian military capabilities, the U.S. Navy's planning focus shifted from that goal toward one of having capabilities for operating in littoral waters and projecting power from the sea against regional adversaries that could not substantially challenge U.S. sea control. This shift was articulated in the 1992 strategy document . . . *From the Sea*.[10] Shipbuilding programs such as the *Zumwalt*-class destroyer (a multimission destroyer with an emphasis on naval surface fire support and operations in littoral waters) and the littoral combat ship (LCS) can be viewed as two reflections of this shift in planning focus. Following the October 12, 2000, boat-bomb attack on USS *Cole* (DDG-67), and the September 11, 2001, terrorist attacks, post–Cold War planning emphasis on having capabilities for operating in littoral waters and projecting power from the sea against regional adversaries that could not substantially challenge U.S. sea control was supplemented by additional focus on counterterrorism operations and irregular warfare.[11]

While the U.S. Navy remains concerned about these post–Cold War and post-9/11 areas of emphasis, it is once again also concerned about having capabilities for high-end mid-ocean warfare against an adversary that can substantially challenge U.S. sea control. Although Russia at some point might regain its status as such an adversary, for the time being only China appears clearly headed in the direction of fitting that description.

As one reflection of the U.S. Navy's renewed focus on having capabilities for conducting high-end warfare in mid-ocean waters, and of the Navy's growing willingness to suggest (gingerly) that China's military modernization effort might have something to do with this, observers might note that the October 2007 maritime strategy does not use the terms *anti-access* or *area denial*, *warfighting*, or *China/Chinese*, while the March 2015 revision uses those terms eight, eighteen, and six times, respectively.[12]

As another indication of China's apparent role in prompting the Navy's new emphasis on having capabilities for conducting high-end warfare, observers might emphasize the following Navy statements:

- "The security environment in the Indo-Asia-Pacific requires that the U.S. Navy station the most capable ships forward."[13]

- As part of the Navy's contribution to the military pillar of the U.S. strategic rebalancing, "Our most capable platforms will operate in the Western Pacific, including the newest DDGs, JHSV [joint high-speed vessel], both LCS variants, P-8A, EA-18G, upgraded F/A-18E/F, E-2D, and F-35C."[14]

- "We continue to carefully screen and send our most talented people to operate and command ships and squadrons in the Asia-Pacific."[15]

Five Unresolved Debates Concerning Strategy, Budgets, and Force Architecture

China's military modernization effort (including its shipbuilding output) and its actions to assert and defend its maritime claims have become a factor in public debates over U.S. strategy, budgets, and force architecture. To the extent that they are also a factor in internal U.S. government debates on these issues, they could affect requirements for U.S. Navy capabilities.

Preventing the Emergence of a Regional Hegemon

World events since late 2013—including China's actions in the East and South China Seas since November 2013 (actions facilitated in part by China's shipbuilding output) as well as Russia's seizure and annexation of Crimea in March 2014—have led some to conclude that the international security environment is undergoing a shift from the familiar post–Cold War era of the last twenty to twenty-five years, also known as the unipolar moment (with the United States the sole superpower), to a new strategic situation that features renewed great power competition and challenges to elements of the postwar U.S.-led international order.

Discussion of this shift has catalyzed renewed emphasis in discussions of U.S. security and foreign policy on grand strategy and geopolitics. From a U.S. perspective on these topics, it can be noted that most of the world's people, resources, and economic activity are located not in the Western Hemisphere but in Eurasia. In response to this basic feature of world geography, U.S. policymakers for the last several decades have chosen to pursue, as a key element of national strategy, a goal of preventing the emergence of a regional hegemon anywhere in Eurasia, on the grounds that such a hegemon could represent a concentration of power strong enough to threaten U.S. vital interests (e.g., by denying Washington access to some of the other hemisphere's resources and economic activity). Although U.S. policymakers have not often explicitly stated this key national strategic goal in public, U.S. military (and diplomatic) operations in recent decades—both wartime operations and day-to-day operations—can be viewed as having been conducted in support of this key goal.

The U.S. goal of preventing the emergence of a regional hegemon in one part of Eurasia or another is a major reason why the U.S. military is structured with force elements that enable it to cross broad expanses of ocean and air space and then conduct sustained, large-scale military operations upon arrival. Force elements associated with this goal include, among other things, an Air Force with significant numbers of long-range bombers, long-range surveillance aircraft, long-range airlift aircraft, and aerial refueling tankers, and a Navy with significant numbers of aircraft carriers, nuclear-powered attack submarines, large surface combatants, large amphibious ships, and underway replenishment ships.

Given China's growing economic and military might and what some observers believe to be Beijing's unacknowledged goal of becoming the dominant power in East Asia, a key question for U.S. policymakers going forward is whether to maintain a goal of preventing the emergence of a regional hegemon in one part of Eurasia or another as a key element of national strategy. Choices that policymakers make on this issue could have a profound effect on U.S. Navy capabilities requirements.

Terms of Debate over U.S. Defense Plans and Programs

A previous shift in the international security environment—from the Cold War to the post–Cold War era—prompted a broad reassessment of U.S.

defense funding levels, strategy, and missions. Many of the resulting changes were articulated in the 1993 Bottom-Up Review, a reassessment of U.S. defense plans and programs whose very name conveyed the fundamental nature of the reassessment that had occurred.[16] The review reshaped the U.S. military into a force that was smaller than the Cold War military and was oriented toward a planning scenario of being able to conduct two major regional contingencies.

A new shift in the international security environment—from the post–Cold War era/unipolar moment to a new strategic era featuring renewed great power competition—could similarly prompt reassessment of the current overall terms of debate over U.S. defense plans and programs. The current terms of debate include limits on defense spending established under the Budget Control Act (BCA) of 2011,[17] as amended, the defense strategic guidance document of January 2012,[18] and the 2014 QDR.[19] If the terms of debate largely reflect the features of the post–Cold War era, they may not be responsive to features of the new strategic situation that some observers have identified.[20]

Some observers, citing recent world events, have raised the question of whether defense spending should be increased above levels set forth in the BCA, and consequently whether the BCA should be amended or repealed.[21] If policymakers judge that a shift in strategic situations of the kind discussed here is occurring, the nature of the U.S. response to that shift could lead to defense spending levels that are higher than, lower than, or about the same as those in the BCA. Since available resources are, as a practical matter, an influence on strategy, a change in the terms of debate over U.S. defense plans and programs, including future defense spending levels, could again have a profound effect on requirements for U.S. Navy capabilities.

Division of Resources

In addition to the above question regarding the future overall DoD budget top line, there is the follow-on issue of the division of that top line between the military departments. DoD officials have steadfastly maintained that the U.S. strategic rebalancing to the Asia-Pacific region that was formally announced in the defense strategic guidance document of January 2012 is not directed toward any particular country.[22] Even so, many observers believe the strategic rebalancing was prompted in part by China's military modernization effort (including its shipbuilding output) and its actions in its near sea areas. Since the Asia-Pacific region is, for U.S. military forces, primarily a maritime and aerospace theater, the announcement of the strategic rebalancing created an argument in favor of allocating a greater share of the DoD top line in coming years to the Navy and Air Force.

That argument, however, has now been blunted by developments in Europe (Russia's seizure and annexation of Crimea, its "ambiguous warfare" operations in eastern Ukraine, and its generally more assertive posture in the region) and the Middle East (the rise of the Islamic State organization). These developments have drawn U.S. policymakers' focus back to the security needs of those two regions, where land-based U.S. forces have traditionally played a larger relative role. Consequently, whatever the DoD top line turns out to be, it is now less certain that the Navy's share will increase as much as some might have anticipated. Other things held equal, this could constrain Navy budgets more than what observers might have projected, which in turn could affect the determination of requirements for U.S. Navy capabilities, since the Navy's acquisition community has been particularly conscious in recent years about how the definition of operational requirements can affect weapons system acquisition costs.

Air-Sea Battle Concept versus Offshore Control

As they have done with the U.S. strategic rebalancing, DoD officials have steadfastly maintained that the Air-Sea Battle (ASB) concept—recently renamed the Joint Concept for Access and Maneuver in the Global Commons (JAM-GC)[23]—is not directed at any particular country. Even so, many believe it is focused to a large degree, if not principally, on countering Chinese and Iranian anti-access forces.

Some observers have criticized ASB/JAM-GC, in part because they believe it calls for attacking land targets in China. As an alternative, they have advocated an alternative military strategy, which they call Offshore Control, that would not involve attacking land targets in China.[24] Supporters of ASB/JAM-GC, in turn, have defended it (while also pointing out that it is not a strategy) and have criticized the Offshore Control strategy.[25] How the debate over the relative merits of JAM-GC versus Offshore Control plays out could affect requirements for U.S. Navy capabilities, particularly in areas such as capabilities for defeating A2/AD systems, conducting strike operations, and achieving effects at long standoff ranges.

Current versus More Highly Distributed Surface Force Architecture

Some observers, viewing the anti-access aspects of China's naval modernization effort, including ASBMs, ASCMs, and other antiship weapons, have raised the question of whether the U.S. Navy should respond by shifting over time to a more highly distributed surface force architecture featuring a reduced reliance on carriers and other large ships and an increased reliance on smaller surface ships.[26] Supporters of this option argue that such architecture could generate comparable aggregate fleet capability at lower cost and be more effective at confounding Chinese maritime anti-access capabilities. Skeptics, including supporters of the currently planned surface force architecture, question both of these arguments.

Navy officials can point out that its 308-ship force structure goal includes 62 smaller and less expensive ships (52 LCSs and 10 joint high-speed vessels). They can also point to the Navy surface community's recently introduced distributed lethality concept, which calls for placing weapons on a wider array of Navy surface ships and implementing new operational concepts for Navy surface ship formations.[27] How the debate over surface force architecture plays out could affect requirements for U.S. Navy capabilities, particularly in terms of how functions and capabilities are distributed across the force.

Capability Areas of Apparent Increased Interest

In discussions of current and future U.S. Navy capabilities, China's military maritime modernization effort (including its shipbuilding output) and the associated U.S. Navy focus on having capabilities for conducting high-end warfare in mid-ocean waters so as to defeat capable maritime A2/AD forces appear to have led to an increased interest in the following things, among others:

- procuring longer-ranged ship and aircraft weapons and longer-ranged carrier-based aircraft, so as to improve the fleet's ability to outrange Chinese weapons and operate effectively at greater standoff ranges

- achieving significant improvements in surface combatant magazine depth and cost-per-shot for air and missile defense operations, so as to improve the ability of Navy surface combatants to effectively and affordably counter large numbers of air and missile threats, including relatively inexpensive unmanned aerial vehicles, ASCMs, and ASBMs

- breaking the kill chains of enemy weapons at all possible points, including points on the "left side" of the kill chain (that is, the earlier part of the kill chain), using various kinetic and nonkinetic means, so as to both improve overall effectiveness in countering enemy weapons and (particularly through the use of nonkinetic means) reduce the cost of doing so

- procuring attack submarines, since U.S. Navy attack submarines are viewed as being able to bypass above-water A2/AD systems, avoid detection, and operate well inside an adversary's A2/AD perimeter

- increasing operational proficiency in ASW operations (particularly blue-water ASW operations) and developing and fielding new, networked approaches to ASW[28]

- placing a major new emphasis on developing capabilities for cyber-warfare and for electromagnetic maneuver warfare (EMW), which *A Cooperative Strategy for 21st Century Seapower* describes as "a relatively new concept, which blends fleet operations in space, cyberspace, and the electromagnetic spectrum with advanced non-kinetic capabilities to create warfighting advantages."[29]

Surface Combatants

A case can be made that the U.S. Navy's surface combatant community has been particularly affected by developments prompted by China's military maritime modernization effort (including its shipbuilding output):

- The Navy's 2008 reversal on destroyer procurement was mentioned earlier. Navy plans call for shifting DDG-51 procurement in FY2016 to the new Flight III design, which is to be equipped with the new Air and Missile Defense Radar, which, as its name suggests, is to improve the ship's air and missile defense capability.

- The Navy's restructuring of the LCS program in 2014, which has resulted in a Navy plan to build the final twenty ships in the program to a modified design featuring a larger amount of built-in weapons and sensors, was directed by then–Secretary of Defense Chuck Hagel, who stated, in announcing the restructuring, that "we need to closely examine whether the LCS has the independent protection and firepower to operate and survive against a more advanced military adversary and emerging new technologies, especially in the Asia Pacific."[30]

- The Navy is developing new long-range antiship and land-attack weapons for surface ships.[31]

- The Navy's desire to achieve significant improvements in surface ship magazine depth and cost-per-shot for air and missile defense operations provides much of the impetus behind the effort to develop and field solid-state lasers, the electromagnetic railgun (EMRG), and the hypervelocity projectile (the same projectile used by the EMRG, but fired from the five-inch powder guns on Navy cruisers and destroyers).

- As one reflection of the Navy's new emphasis on developing capabilities for cyberwarfare and EMW, Navy surface combatants (along with aircraft carriers, amphibious ships, and Coast Guard cutters) are to have their electronic warfare capabilities improved through the Surface Electronic Warfare Improvement Program, an evolutionary development block upgrade program for the SLQ-32 electronic warfare system.

The future of the Navy's surface combatant force, particularly in the context of capable A2/AD systems like those China is fielding, has been a matter of discussion for several years[32] and was the topic of an April 2015 hearing before the Seapower and Projection Forces subcommittee of the House Armed Services Committee.[33]

In addition to questions about how quickly efforts such as those listed above should or will be implemented, a key question relating to the future of surface combatants in the context of Chinese shipbuilding output and other aspects of China's military maritime modernization effort is whether and when procurement of large surface combatants should shift from the DDG-51 class to a new-design ship that might feature integrated electric drive (to provide robust support for electric weapons), increased growth margins, producibility features to reduce construction cost-per-ton, and features (such as those permitting a smaller crew) to reduce life-cycle operation and support costs. This question can be viewed as having been on the table since the Navy's decision, announced in 2010 in connection with the submission of its proposed FY2011 budget, to cancel the CG(X) cruiser program. The Navy's FY2016 thirty-year shipbuilding plan includes no ship identified as a cruiser and instead shows procurement of DDG-51s continuing through FY2045, the final year of the plan, with procurement shifting to a Flight IV version of the DDG-51 in FY2030.

Another (smaller-scale) question is whether Combat Logistics Force (CLF) ships such as the new TAO(X) oiler should be armed with a greater number of ship self-defense systems, like the Navy's AOE- and AOR-type multiproduct replenishment ships generally were during the final years of the Cold War, or with a smaller number of such weapons, like the Navy's CLF ships generally were during the post–Cold War era. The Navy's current concept for the TAO(X) oiler's original suite of weapons might be viewed as being closer to the latter.[34]

Aircraft Carriers and Carrier-Based Aircraft

Aircraft carriers and carrier-based aircraft are another area that has been very much at the center of discussions about the future of the Navy in the context of capable A2/AD systems such as those China is fielding. Key issues include the survivability of carriers and the effective combat radius of the carrier air wing.[35] A recent key matter of debate has been the mission orientation of the Unmanned Carrier-Launched Surveillance and Strike System aircraft, which was the focus of a July 2014 hearing before the Seapower and Projection Forces subcommittee of the House Armed Services Committee.[36] An additional recent question has been whether to procure additional EA-18G Growler electronic attack aircraft, so as to increase to seven (from a currently planned total of five) the number of such aircraft in each embarked carrier air wing.[37]

Discussions of the effective combat radius of the carrier air wing have focused largely on the operating radius of carrier-based aircraft, and to some degree on the range of their air-to-surface weapons. An additional question that by comparison has been largely overlooked is whether the Navy should develop and procure a long-range air-to-air missile for its carrier-based strike fighters. During the Cold War, Navy F-14 carrier-based fighters were equipped with a long-range air-to-air missile called the Phoenix. The F-14/Phoenix combination was viewed as key to the Navy's ability to effectively counter Soviet land-based strike aircraft equipped with long-range ASCMs that appeared designed to attack U.S. Navy aircraft carriers. A successor to the Phoenix called the Advanced Air-to-Air Missile was being developed in the late 1980s, but it was canceled as a result of the end of the Cold War. The Navy today does not have a long-range air-to-air missile, and DoD has announced no program to develop such a weapon.

Capabilities for Countering China's "Salami-Slicing" Tactics in the Near Seas

Although this discussion has focused on U.S. Navy capabilities for high-end warfare, a final matter to consider is how China's military maritime modernization effort (including its shipbuilding output) might affect requirements for U.S. Navy capabilities for countering China's "salami-slicing" tactics in nearby seas, which are designed to remain below the level of outright conflict. The issue can be viewed as particularly pertinent to this discussion, because in terms of numbers of ships produced for government agencies, two of the most active areas of Chinese shipbuilding in recent years have been production of cutters for the China Coast Guard and production of Type 056 corvettes for the PLA Navy.

Observers have made a number of suggestions for actions the United States might take as part of a strengthened strategy for countering China's salami-slicing tactics. Some of them have suggested having U.S. forces conduct more frequent surface and air patrols of these waters, which is something that could have implications for numbers, basing arrangements, or operational patterns for U.S. Navy ships and aircraft. Others have also suggested expanding or accelerating U.S. actions to improve the capabilities of the Philippines, Vietnam, and other countries in the region to maintain maritime domain awareness and to patrol their exclusive economic zones. This suggestion, if acted on, could put a focus on U.S. Navy capabilities for conducting engagement and partner capacity-building operations with the navies and coast guards of these countries.

One additional possibility that has not been mentioned much would be to equip U.S. Navy ships with more or improved less-than-lethal weapons so that they would have an improved array of options other than the use of lethal force should they find themselves in a confrontation in these waters that did not rise to the level of outright conflict.

Notes

1. See Andrew F. Krepinevich, "China's 'Finlandization' Strategy in the Pacific," *Wall Street Journal*, September 11, 2010, http://www.wsj.com/articles/SB1000142405274870 4164904575421753851404076.

2. Office of Naval Intelligence (ONI), *Worldwide Maritime Challenges* (Suitland, MD: ONI, 2004). The words "China," "China's," and "Chinese" appear in this report a total of more than sixty times, an average of more than once per page.

3. ONI, *China's Navy 2007* (Suitland, MD: ONI, 2007), https://fas.org/irp/agency/oni/ chinanavy2007.pdf; ONI, *The People's Liberation Army Navy: A Modern Navy with Chinese Characteristics* (Suitland, MD: ONI, August 2009), http://fas.org/irp/ agency/oni/pla-navy.pdf; ONI, *The PLA Navy: New Capabilities and Missions for the 21st Century* (Suitland, MD: ONI, 2015), http://www.oni.navy.mil/Intelligence_ Community/china.html.

4. U.S. Department of Defense (DoD), *Quadrennial Defense Review Report*, February 6, 2006, 47, http://archive.defense.gov/pubs/pdfs/QDR20060203.pdf.

5. DoD, *Quadrennial Defense Review Report 2014*, March 4, 2014, 34, 54, http://archive .defense.gov/pubs/2014_Quadrennial_Defense_Review.pdf.

6. A third DDG-1000 class ship was procured as part of the FY2009 budget that was being reviewed by Congress in July 2008.

7. See Statement of Vice Admiral Barry McCullough, Deputy Chief of Naval Operations for Integration of Capabilities and Resources, and Allison Stiller, Deputy Assistant Secretary of the Navy (Ship Programs), before the Subcommittee on Seapower and Expeditionary Forces of the House Armed Services Committee on Surface Combatant Requirements and Acquisition Strategies, July 31, 2008.

8. DoD, *Military Power of the People's Republic of China 2008* (Washington, DC: DoD, 2008), 2, 23, http://www.andrewerickson.com/wp-content/uploads/2015/11/DoD_China-Report_2008.pdf.

9. Data from *Jane's Fighting Ships* show that China added eighteen relatively modern attack submarines to its order of battle during 2004–06, including eight Russian-built *Kilo*-class submarines and ten submarines built in China. (Two more new submarines—an SSBN and an SSN—were added in 2007.) A chart in the 2008 DoD annual report shows the percentage of modern boats in China's submarine force increasing from 9 percent in 2003 to 40 percent in 2007. DoD, *Military Power of the People's Republic of China 2008*, 34.

10. U.S. Navy, . . . *From the Sea: Preparing the Naval Service for the 21st Century*, September 1992, http://www.comw.org/qdr/fulltext/02navyvision.pdf.

11. Years later, the Navy's focus on irregular warfare was formally set forth in U.S. Navy, *The U.S. Navy's Vision for Confronting Irregular Challenges* (January 2010), http://www.navy.mil/navydata/cno/CNO_SIGNED_NAVY_VISION_FOR_CONFRONTING_IRREGULAR_CHALLENGES_JANUARY_2010.pdf.

12. U.S. Navy, *A Cooperative Strategy for 21st Century Seapower* (October 2007), https://www.ise.gov/sites/default/files/Maritime_Strategy.pdf; U.S. Navy, *A Cooperative Strategy for 21st Century Seapower: Forward, Ready, Engaged* (March 2015), http://www.navy.mil/local/maritime/150227-CS21R-Final.pdf.

13. U.S. Pacific Fleet Public Affairs, "Navy Aircraft Carrier Moves Underscore Pacific Rebalance Strategy," *Navy News Service*, January 14, 2014, http://www.navy.mil/submit/display.asp?story_id=78601.

14. U.S. Navy, *CNO's Navigation Plan 2015–2019*, August 2014, 3, http://www.navy.mil/cno/docs/140818_CNO_Navigation_Plan.pdf.

15. Jonathan Greenert, "Sea Change: The Navy Pivots to Asia," *Foreign Policy*, November 14, 2012, http://foreignpolicy.com/2012/11/14/sea-change/.

16. DoD, *Report on the Bottom-Up Review*, October 1993.

17. S. 365/P.L. 112–25, August 2, 2011.

18. DoD, *Sustaining U.S. Global Leadership: Priorities for 21st Century Defense*, January 2012, http://archive.defense.gov/news/Defense_Strategic_Guidance.pdf.

19. DoD, *Quadrennial Defense Review Report 2014*.

20. See, for example, John Grady, "Think Tank Panel Tells House U.S. Military Faces More Challenges, Suggests Pentagon Spending Reforms," *USNI News*, February 11, 2015, http://news.usni.org/2015/02/11/think-tank-panel-tells-house-u-s-military-faces-challenges-suggests-pentagon-spending-reforms.

21. See, for example, John T. Bennett, "Could Global Threat Picture Restore U.S. Defense Increases?" *Defense News*, August 31, 2014.

22. DoD, *Sustaining U.S. Global Leadership: Priorities for 21st Century Defense*.

23. See, for example, Terry S. Morris et al., "Securing Operational Access: Evolving the Air-Sea Battle Concept," *The National Interest*, February 11, 2015, http://nationalinter est.org/feature/securing-operational-access-evolving-the-air-sea-battle-12219.

24. See, for example, T. X. Hammes and R. D. Hooker Jr., "America's Ultimate Strategy in a Clash with China," *The National Interest*, June 10, 2014, http://nationalinterest.org/ feature/americas-ultimate-strategy-clash-china-10633.

25. See, for example, Wendell Minnick, "China Threat: Air-Sea Battle vs. Offshore Control?" *Defense News*, June 23, 2014.

26. See, for example, David Gompert, *Sea Power and American Interests in the Western Pacific* (Santa Monica, CA: RAND, 2013), RR-151-OSD, http://www.rand.org/pubs/ research_reports/RR151.html.

27. See Thomas Rowden et al., "Distributed Lethality," U.S. Naval Institute *Proceedings* (January 2015): 18–23.

28. See Otto Kreisher, "As Underwater Threat Re-Emerges, Navy Renews Emphasis on ASW," *Seapower* (October 2004), 15, http://www.military.com/ NewContent/0,13190,NL_ASW_100404-P1,00.html.

29. U.S. Navy, *A Cooperative Strategy for 21st Century Seapower*, 21.

30. DoD News Transcript, "Remarks by Secretary Hagel and Gen. Dempsey on the Fiscal Year 2015 Budget Preview in the Pentagon Briefing Room," February 24, 2014, http:// www.defense.gov/transcripts/transcript.aspx?transcriptid=5377.

31. Statement of the Honorable Sean J. Stackley, Assistant Secretary of the Navy (Research, Development and Acquisition), Vice Admiral Joseph Mulloy, Deputy Chief of Naval Operations for Integration of Capabilities and Resources, and Lieutenant General Kenneth J. Glueck Jr., Deputy Commandant, Combat Development and Integration and Commanding General, Marine Corps Combat Development Command, before the Subcommittee on Seapower and Projection Forces of the House Armed Services Committee on Department of the Navy Seapower and Projection Forces Capabilities, February 25, 2015, 26.

32. See, for example, Robert Work, *Know When to Hold 'Em: Modernizing the Navy's Surface Battle Line* (Washington, DC: Center for Strategic and Budgetary Assessments, September 20, 2006).

33. See Committee on Armed Services, Subcommittee on Seapower and Projection Forces, "The Role of Surface Forces in Presence, Deterrence, and Warfighting," Washington, DC, April 15, 2015, http://docs.house.gov/Committee/Calendar/By Event.aspx?EventID=103268.

34. Navy information paper for Congressional Research Service and Congressional Budget Office on TAO(X) self-defense capabilities, April 30, 2015.

35. See, for example, U.S. Navy, *Naval Aviation Vision 2014–2015*, http://www.navy .mil/strategic/Naval_Aviation_Vision.pdf.

36. See http://armedservices.house.gov/index.cfm/hearings-display?ContentRecord_id=130 F9D60–4763–4446–966B-2981719E114B.

37. See, for example, Dave Majumdar, "Why the Navy Wants More Growlers," *USNI News*, March 12, 2014, http://news.usni.org/2014/03/12/navy-wants-growlers.

Acronyms

A2/AD	anti-access/area denial
AAW	anti-air warfare
AEW	airborne early warning
AIP	air-independent power
AM	additive manufacturing
AOR	auxiliary oiler and replenishment
ASB	Air-Sea Battle
ASBM	antiship ballistic missile
ASCM	antiship cruise missile
ASuW	antisurface warfare
ASW	antisubmarine warfare
AVIC	Aviation Industry Corporation of China
BCA	Budget Control Act
BMD	ballistic missile defense
C4ISR	command, control, communications, computers, intelligence, surveillance, and reconnaissance
CAD/CAM	computer-aided design/computer-aided manufacturing
CANSI	China Association of the National Shipbuilding Industry
CASIC	China Aerospace Science and Industry Corporation
CCG	China Coast Guard
CCP	Chinese Communist Party
CCS	China Classification Society

CETC	China Electronic Technology Corporation
CG	guided-missile cruiser
CGT	compensated gross tons
CLF	Combat Logistics Force
CMC	Central Military Commission
CMI	civil-military integration
CMSI	China Maritime Studies Institute
COMAC	Commercial Aircraft Corporation of China
COMEC	CSSC Offshore and Marine Engineering (Group) Company Limited
COSCO	China Ocean Shipping Company
COSTIND	Commission of Science, Technology, and Industry for National Defense
CSDDC	China Ship Design and Development Center
CSG	carrier strike group
CSIC	China Shipbuilding Industry Corporation
CSSC	China State Shipbuilding Corporation
DD	destroyer
DDG	guided-missile destroyer
DoD	Department of Defense
DVHI	Dalian Vessel Heavy Industry Group Company Limited
DWP	Defense White Paper
dwt	deadweight tonnes
EMRG	electromagnetic railgun
EMW	electromagnetic maneuver warfare
EU	European Union
FFG	guided-missile frigate
FPSO	floating production/storage/offloading
FY	fiscal year
GJB	*Guojia Junyong Biaozhun*
GPS	global positioning system
GSI	Guangzhou Shipyard International
ICP	Integrated Command Platform
IDAR	introduction, digestion, absorption, re-innovation
IEP	integrated electric propulsion
IOC	initial operating capability

ISR	intelligence, surveillance, and reconnaissance
JAM-GC	Joint Concept for Access and Maneuver in the Global Commons
km	kilometer
KMT	Kuomintang
LACM	land-attack cruise missile
LCAC	air-cushioned landing craft
LCS	littoral combat ship
LHD	landing helicopter dock
Li-ion	lithium ion
LNG	liquefied natural gas
LNGC	liquefied natural gas carrier
LPD	landing platform/dock
LRASM	Long-Range Antiship Missile
LSM	landing ship medium
LST	landing ship/tank
MCF	military-civilian fusion
MCMV	mine countermeasure vessel
MIIT	Ministry of Industry and Information Technology
MLP	National Medium- and Long-term Program for Science and Technology Development (2006–2020)
mm	millimeter
MOOTW	military operations other than war
NWC	Naval War College
OBOR	"One Belt, One Road"
OECD	Organisation for Economic Co-operation and Development
ONI	Office of Naval Intelligence
OPV	offshore patrol vessel
OTH-B	over-the-horizon backscatter
PC	patrol craft
PGG	patrol/missile craft
PLA	People's Liberation Army
PLAAF	PLA Air Force
PLAN	PLA Navy
PLARF	PLA Rocket Force
PNT	position, navigation, and timing
PRC	People's Republic of China

PWR	pressurized water reactor
QDR	Quadrennial Defense Review
R&D	research and development
RDA	research, development, and acquisition
RDT&E	research, development, testing, and evaluation
RI	research institute
RMB	renminbi
SAM	surface-to-air missile
SASAC	State-owned Assets Supervision and Administration Commission
SASTIND	State Administration for Science, Technology, and Industry for National Defense
SBI	shipbuilding industry
SC	State Council
SLBM	submarine-launched ballistic missile
SLOC	sea line of communication
SMS	*Science of Military Strategy*
SOE	state-owned enterprise
SSB	conventional missile submarine
SSBN	ballistic missile submarine
SSK	conventionally powered attack submarine
SSN	nuclear-powered submarine
SSP	diesel attack submarine
STOBAR	short take-off but arrested recovery
SWaP-C	size, weight, power, and cooling
teu	twenty-foot equivalent units
TTC	transformational technology core
UAV	unmanned aerial vehicle
ULC	ultra large container ship
ULCC	ultra large crude carrier
USN	U.S. Navy
USNI	U.S. Naval Institute
UUV	unmanned underwater vehicle
VDS	variable depth sonar
VLCC	very large crude carrier
VLS	vertical launching system
WBS	work breakdown structure

About the Contributors

DANIEL ALDERMAN, a deputy director at Defense Group, Inc. (DGI), is Chinese language–proficient and oversees analytic production at DGI's Center for Intelligence Research and Analysis.

ERIC ANDERSON, a Chinese-proficient research analyst, leads Sino-American sectoral innovation analysis at the University of California (UC), San Diego's Study of Innovation and Technology in China (SITC) project.

JACK BIANCHI, a research associate at DGI, employs Chinese-language sources to analyze China's defense-related science and technology development.

CAPT. CHRISTOPHER P. CARLSON, USNR (RET.), a submariner and intelligence officer, designs war games and has published a wide range of articles and books.

ARTHUR CHAN, a research associate at RAND, is proficient in Chinese.

SCOTT CHENEY-PETERS, a civil servant at the State Department and a Reserve surface warfare officer, is founder and president of the Center for International Maritime Security.

MORGAN CLEMENS, a research analyst at DGI, studies China's armed forces and defense industry using Chinese-language sources.

GABE COLLINS, a licensed Texas attorney, conducts security, commodity, and market research in Chinese, Russian, and Spanish.

LT. COL. CORTEZ A. COOPER III, USA (RET.), is a Chinese language–proficient senior policy analyst at RAND and affiliate faculty member of Pardee RAND Graduate School.

JOHN COSTELLO, a Chinese language–proficient U.S. Navy veteran with intelligence analysis and program management experience, is a research analyst at DGI.

RUSH DOSHI, a Raymond Vernon fellow in Harvard University's Ph.D. program in government, conducts research in Mandarin and Hindi.

IAN EASTON, a research fellow at the Project 2049 Institute, uses Chinese-language sources to analyze emerging Asian security issues.

CAPT. JAMES E. FANELL, USN (RET.), a naval intelligence officer specializing in Indo-Asia-Pacific security affairs for nearly three decades, runs the leading English-language listserv on Chinese military issues.

LT. COL. ROBERT T. FORTE, USMC (RET.), formerly U.S. naval attaché at U.S. Embassy Beijing, is a senior research analyst with DGI.

SUE HALL is managing director of Shipyard Economics, a firm providing specialist consulting services in the shipbuilding, ship repair, and shipyard industries worldwide.

TYLER JOST, a Chinese language–proficient former Army intelligence officer, is a Ph.D. student in Harvard University's Government program.

REAR ADM. MICHAEL MCDEVITT, USN (RET.), an analyst of China's maritime developments, formerly carrier battle group commander and commandant of the National War College, is presently a senior fellow at the CNA Corporation.

REAR ADM. MICHAEL E. MCMAHON, USN (RET.), a senior research associate at RAND with a Ph.D. in mechanical engineering, served as the U.S. Navy's fifth program executive officer for aircraft carriers.

CDR. MARK METCALF, USN (RET.), a surface warfare officer and naval cryptologist, provides systems engineering and Chinese-language research, translation, and technical analysis support to government clients.

TATE NURKIN is senior director of the Strategic Assessments and Futures Studies Center for IHS Aerospace, Defense, and Security.

SEAN O'CONNOR is the principal imagery analyst at IHS *Jane's*.

RONALD O'ROURKE, a naval analyst for the Congressional Research Service of the Library of Congress, issues constantly updated reports on China's navy.

ALEX PAPE is a principal analyst with IHS *Jane's DS Forecast* and *Defence Procurement*, which provide real-time coverage of procurement and upgrade programs worldwide.

KEVIN POLLPETER, a Chinese language–proficient research scientist at CNA, has also served as deputy director of technically focused research programs at both UC San Diego and DGI.

LEIGH ANN RAGLAND-LUCE, a research analyst at DGI, conducts Chinese-language research on China's defense electronics and information technology sectors.

JONATHAN RAY, a DGI research associate, conducts Chinese-language studies of national security, science, and technology issues.

PAUL SCHARRE, a former infantryman in the Army's 75th Ranger Regiment with multiple tours in Iraq and Afghanistan, is a senior fellow and director of the 20YY Future of Warfare Initiative at the Center for a New American Security.

ANDREW SCOBELL, proficient in Chinese, is a senior political scientist at RAND and adjunct professor of Asian studies at Georgetown's School of Foreign Service.

JULIAN SNELDER, a partner in a global investments fund, has conducted investment research from Asia for nearly a quarter-century.

LT. COL. MARK STOKES, USAF (RET.), the Chinese-proficient executive director of the Project 2049 Institute, formerly served as assistant air attaché at U.S. Embassy Beijing.

AUDRYE WONG, fluent in Chinese, is a Ph.D. student in Security Studies at Princeton's Woodrow Wilson School of Public and International Affairs.

JORDAN WILSON is a policy analyst at the U.S.-China Economic and Security Review Commission, where he conducts Chinese-language research.

About the Editor

ANDREW S. ERICKSON is Professor of Strategy in the Naval War College (NWC)'s China Maritime Studies Institute (CMSI) and a Visiting Professor in Harvard University's Department of Government. The recipient of NWC's inaugural Research Excellence Award, he runs the China studies website http://www.andrewerickson.com.

Index

All ships are Chinese except where indicated

additive manufacturing (AM), 265

Advanced Air-to-Air Missile (United States), 327

air defense: capabilities for mission, 113, 114, 284–85, 286; expansion of mission of PLAN, 9, 282; indigenous systems for, development of, 23, 32; missile-based system for, 31; Russian systems for, purchase of, 23, 32; weakness in technology for, 31

airborne early warning (AEW), 254

aircraft carriers: aircraft for, 256, 284; budget and funding for, 107–8; capabilities for operations with, 25, 252–54; carrier strike groups, 267–68; Dalian production of, 4, 12, 104, 112, 137, 138, 252–53; deck aviation design and program, 6, 137, 249, 254–55; drivers for development of, 250; flat top flight decks, 249; force strength and projected production of, xvi–xvii, 3, 112, 249, 252–53, 267–68, 284; foreign carrier purchases, 104, 112, 137, 251, 252, 256; foreign navies, comparison to, 288, 289; foreign navies mission focus for, 37; great-power status of China and, 250; indigenous design and production, 137, 138, 254–55; mission focus of, 284; naval strategy evolution and capabilities for operations with, 28; nuclear propulsion and power technologies for, 244, 255; operational lifespans of, 297; pilot and flight deck crew proficiency, 256; power projection with, 250, 254, 256–57; production of, 63; program for develop-

ment of, 6, 22, 23–24, 249–50; program foundation, 251–52; program prospects, 254–55; propulsion and power technologies for, 6, 244, 249, 255; publications on operations, principles, and technologies, 129; Russian systems purchases, 112, 137, 252, 254, 256; short take-off but arrested recovery (STOBAR) design, 254; ski jump bow configuration, 37, 138, 249, 254, 284; strike warfare mission focus of, 37; technologies for, 255–56; timeline for production and commissioning, 252–53; U.S. carriers, 318, 327

air-independent power (AIP) systems, 10, 35–36, 107, 111, 239, 245, 284, 305

Air-Sea Battle (ASB) concept, 323

Algeria, 55, 105, 125, 127, 173, 209

amphibious assault groups, 268

amphibious ships: budget and funding for, 107–8; case study of, 53–55; force strength and fleet size, 54, 60nn69–71; force strength and projected production of, 269–70, 285–86; foreign navies, comparison to, 288, 289; future requirements for, 122; Taiwan invasion, ships for potential, 53–55, 60n62, 268, 285–86

amphibious ships (LSMs), xvi–xvii, 54, 60n70, 122

amphibious ships (LSTs and LPDs): force strength and projected production of, xvi–xvii, 3, 54, 60n69, 117, 124, 125, 127, 128, 268, 285–86; foreign navies, comparison to, 288, 289; future requirements

for, 122; Hudong production of, 55, 117,
127, 128–29, 141; mission focus of, 54–55;
Wuhan production of, 124
Amur 1650 SSK, 111
anti-access/area denial (A2/AD), 13, 281–82,
284, 294n19, 319–20, 323–27
anti-air warfare (AAW): capabilities for, 21;
destroyer capabilities for, 113, 114; frigate
capabilities for, 114; naval strategy and
competency in, 20, 28, 31–32
antiship ballistic missile (ASBM) program,
319, 323, 324
antiship cruise missiles (ASCMs): A2/AD
use of, 282; adoption of use of and evolution of capabilities, 27–31; capabilities to
deploy, 8; quantity available for deployment, 13; range of, 8, 35; Russian/Soviet
systems purchases, 29, 30, 32; submarine
deployment of, 35, 109; U.S. capabilities
for countering, 318–19; U.S. Navy systems, 8, 13. See also Yingji-class missiles
antisubmarine warfare (ASW): capabilities
for, 21, 25, 253–54; corvette capabilities
for, 116, 121; Indian Ocean operations,
292; naval strategy and competency in,
20, 28, 32–34; U.S. capabilities for, 319,
325; weakness in technology for, 32, 280
antisurface warfare (ASuW), 20, 21, 27–31
Arleigh Burke-class (DDG-51) destroyers
(United States), 318, 325, 326
Asia-Pacific region: regional hegemon in,
prevention of emergence of, 320–21;
salami-slicing tactics by China in,
327–28; U.S. force posture and basing in,
318, 322–23
auxiliary ships: force strength and projected
production of, 118–20, 125, 128, 269–70;
foreign navies, comparison to, 288, 289;
future requirements for, 121; Guangzhou
production of, 105, 118–19; Hudong production of, 118–19, 125, 128; U.S. fleet, 326

ballistic missiles: ASBM program, 319,
323, 324; SLBMs, 28, 36–37, 109, 111, 141,
241–42, 286; U.S. capabilities for countering, 318–19
Bangladesh, 127, 129
batteries: advancements in, 10, 239–40;
lithium-ion batteries, 10, 239–40, 245;
main storage batteries, 239
Beidou PNT system, 231, 304, 309

Bohai Shipbuilding Heavy Industry: CSIC
ownership of, 88; mergers, integrations,
and internal consolidations at, 12; productivity and output of, 87, 88; throughput volume, 95; white-listed shipyards,
inclusion in, 151
bonds, 47, 65–66, 69
Budget Control Act (BCA), 322

capital market access and activities, 47, 62,
63, 64–67, 68–69, 89
CB standards, 167, 172, 174
Central Military Commission (CMC), 9, 22,
182, 183, 251–52
China: economic and military expansion
in, 13; economic conditions and socioeconomic development in, 43, 44, 45,
191–92, 206, 222, 267; economic growth
in, 23, 24, 251; economic risks of combat
fleet build-out trajectory, 13; foreign trade
dependence of, 23, 24; global investment
strategy of, 24–25, 251; great-power status
of, role of SBI in development of, 8, 41,
204–10, 261–62, 291; great-power status
of and carrier program, 250; land-based
threats to, 2, 20, 25, 44, 277; nuclear
industry in, 241; shipbuilding power status of, 44, 45–46, 75, 81, 193; Sino-Indian
relations and Indian Ocean patrols,
291–92; world's largest shipbuilder desig-
nation, target year for, 2, 75, 81, 277
China Aerospace Science and Industry
Corporation (CASIC), 183, 309
China Aerospace Science and Technology
Corporation, 183, 309
China Classification Society, 12, 167, 172–74
China Coast Guard (CCG), 328; capabilities
of, 209, 262, 263, 271n5; cutter production and launchings, 68, 105, 328; force
strength of, 263; future vessel require-
ments for, 121–22; IEP on ships of, 244,
247–48n33; modernization of force, 263;
ship construction for, 63, 64, 68, 262
China Dream, 6, 261, 267, 270
China Electronic Technology Corporation
(CETC), 222–23, 227, 229
China Maritime Studies Institute (CMSI),
2, 3, 14
China Ocean Shipping Company
(COSCO), 57n6, 86, 87, 88, 95, 98, 202,
208, 285

China Ship Design and Development Center (CSDDC), 240

China Shipbuilding Industry Corporation (CSIC): capital market access and activities, 63, 64–67; civil-military integration at, 149; efficiency and innovation at, barriers to, 8–9; financial resources for, 64; historical background of, 42–43; institutional culture at, 8–9; integrated innovation use at, 5, 177; merchant shipbuilding revenue earned by, 146, 149, 160n7; merger with CSSC, 5, 11, 12, 146–47, 207, 226–27, 232, 263, 278–79; mergers, integrations, and internal consolidations at, 12, 90, 99; military shipbuilding by, 145, 146–47, 149, 279, 293n10; productivity and output of, 43, 57n6, 62, 64, 84, 146; RDA system at, 182–84; shipyards owned by, 84, 85–90; split from CSSC, 62; standards implementation program at, 159; state ownership of, 43; white-listed shipyards, inclusion in, 145, 150–51

China Shipbuilding Industry Corporation (CSIC) Limited, 64–67, 69

China Shipping Group, 57n6

China State Shipbuilding Corporation (CSSC): CAD/CAM technology use by, 155; capital market access and activities, 63, 64–67; civil-military integration at, 149; efficiency and innovation at, barriers to, 8–9; financial resources for, 64; historical background of, 42–43; institutional culture at, 8–9; internal consolidation, reforms, and 1236 strategy, 12, 50–51; merchant and military ship production at, 152; merchant shipbuilding revenue earned by, 146, 149; merger with CSIC, 5, 11, 12, 146–47, 207, 226–27, 232, 263, 278–79; mergers, integrations, and internal consolidations at, 90, 99; military shipbuilding by, 145, 146–47, 149; productivity and output of, 43, 57n6, 62, 64, 84, 203; shipyards owned by, 84, 85–90; specialization and reputation building at, 55; split from CSIC, 62; state ownership of, 43; white-listed shipyards, inclusion in, 145, 150–51

China State Shipbuilding Corporation (CSSC) Holdings, Ltd., 64–67, 69

China's Naval Shipbuilding: Progress and Challenges conference, 2, 3; areas of disagreement and subsequent developments, 11–12; implications and policy recommendations, 12–13; insights from, 8–10; summary of discussion at, 7–8

Chinese Communist Party (CCP): budget and funding for PLAN, 26; coastal defense decision of, 20; consolidations and mergers, call for, 226–27; PLAN modernization, support for, 22; SBI role and requirements assigned by, 4, 8, 41, 55–56

civilian shipyards. See private shipyards

civil-military integration (CMI): barriers to, 158–59; benefits of, 52, 146–49; diffusion from commercial to military sectors, 145, 149–59, 160n4; government plan to aid industry, 147–49, 279; growth of, 4–5, 52, 104–5, 209; historical background of, 144; military-civilian fusion, 144; naval shipbuilding modernization and, 144–45, 159n3; objective of, 52, 145; standards and barrier to, 159; vessels for, 45; views of, 146

Classification for Military Standardization Documents (GJB 832-2005), 227, 234

Coast Guard, U.S., 13–14

Cold War and post–Cold War activities, 22, 292, 319–22, 329n11

combat and fire-control systems, 129, 224, 229–30

Combat Logistic Force (CLF) ships (United States), 326

command, control, communications, computers, intelligence, surveillance, and reconnaissance (C4ISR) infrastructure, 221, 222–23, 230–31, 232, 291, 309

commercial/merchant ships: challenges facing shipbuilders of, 98–99; China as largest shipbuilder of, 75, 81; complexity and size evaluation, 99–101, 102, 191–92, 211nn5–7; construction requirements to support military mobilization, 12; coproduction of military and commercial vessels, 104–5, 145, 149–53, 160n4; decline in orders for, 10, 135, 145, 147–48, 193–94, 264; dual-use civilian vessels, 53–54, 60n62, 208–9; global shipping cycle, 189–93; historical production and orderbook phasing, 81, 82–83, 106n4; integration of commercial and naval shipbuilding processes, 11, 279–80; Jiangnan production of, 137; naval shipbuilding compared to building of, 101, 103–5, 185, 189, 264; orderbooks and forward production, 80–81, 99; peak ship construction period, 10, 77, 81; prices and complexity of, 191, 211n7; prices and price volatility, 96–97, 169, 213n44, 213n46; productivity and output of, 42; quality of ship construction, 203–4, 209–10; rise of merchant marine industry, 189, 193–96; shipbuilding production trends, 75–81; throughput volumes, 93, 94–95, 99, 198; world production/output of, 75, 81

communications systems: electronics and capabilities for, 223; information technology–based systems, 51; localized production of, 51, 59n48; satellite technology and capabilities, 230–31, 233

compensated gross tons (CGT) as measure of workload, 75, 77, 94, 99–101, 102, 106n1, 191, 211n5

components. See systems and components

computer-aided design/computer-aided manufacturing (CAD/CAM) technology, 145, 154–55, 160n5

container ships, 96, 101, 190–91, 193, 194, 197, 198, 201–2, 204, 211n5, 278–79

corvettes: ASW capabilities, 116, 121; budget and funding for, 107–8; export of, 209, 264; force strength and projected production of, xvi–xvii, 116, 124, 125, 128–29, 131, 269–70, 285; future requirements for, 121; Huangpu production of, 105, 125; Hudong production of, 125, 128–29, 209; Liaonan production of, 125; Wuhan production of, 124, 125

crankshafts, 135

Crimea, 320, 323

cruisers, 113

CSIC. See China Shipbuilding Industry Corporation (CSIC)

CSSC. See China State Shipbuilding Corporation (CSSC)

CSSC Offshore and Marine Engineering (Group) Company Limited (COMEC), 66–67, 68–69, 89, 90, 105, 151, 152–53, 155. See also Guangzhou Shipyard International (GSI)

cyberspace and cyberwarfare capabilities, 308–9, 316n50, 325, 326

Dalian, economic development in, 42

Dalian Huarui Heavy Industry Group Co., Ltd., 135

Dalian Shipyard: aircraft carrier production at, 4, 12, 104, 112, 137, 138, 252–53; capital market access and activities, 66; CSIC ownership of, 85, 88; expansion of facilities at, 4, 104; location of, xv; merchant and military ship production at, 104, 153; mergers, integrations, and internal consolidations at, 12, 90; modular construction process at, 138; New Dalian Shipyard, 84, 85, 86, 90, 104; productivity and output of, 84, 85, 86, 88, 104, 203–4; satellite imagery analysis of, 137–38; ship production at, 104, 114, 118, 125, 137–38; submarine production at, 122; throughput volume, 93, 95; white-listed shipyards, inclusion in, 151

Dalian Vessel Heavy Industry Group Company Limited, 179–80

defense and national security strategy: early warning technologies, 303–4; external factors that shaped, 22–23; information revolution and, 300–301; integrated security system for, 45; land-based threats, decrease in, 25, 44, 251, 277; land-based threats, focus on, 2, 20; local war preparations, 22; maritime focus of strategy, 275–77; missile-centric firepower strike and counterintervention operations, 254; near coast defense, 19, 20–21, 28, 32–33, 35, 36, 222; near seas active defense, 19, 21–23, 28, 33, 34–35, 222, 261–62, 266, 277, 300; nears seas defense, far seas operations, 19, 23–25, 28, 33–34, 36–38, 222–23, 230–31, 251–52, 256–57, 266, 277, 281–87, 290, 294n19, 294n23; New Historic Missions strategy, 23–24, 251–52; Soviet invasion threat, PLA strategy for, 20–21; total war preparations, 22

defense budget and funding, 22–23, 26, 64, 69, 107–8

defense industry: bidding and procurement system, 157–59, 164n68; electronics industrial base, 226–29; fractured nature of, 232–33; organization and composition of, 43, 57n5; reforms to increase RDA, 224–26

Defense White Paper (2004), 281–82

Defense White Paper (2008), 283, 294n23

Defense White Paper (2012), 275–76
Defense White Paper (2015), 2, 25, 221,
    276–77, 281, 282–83, 293n6
Deng Xiaoping, 22
deployment of ships: evolution of war and
    mission of PLAN and, 4, 19–20, 26–38,
    265–69; far seas operations, 266, 277,
    281–87, 290, 294n19, 294n23; goodwill
    deployments, 267; surge operations, 267
Desert Fox, Operation, 22
Desert Storm, Operation, 22
design and naval architecture: advances
    in and changes in naval warfare, 6;
    advances in design and production
    technologies, 9, 263; CAD/CAM technol-
    ogy use, 145, 154–55, 160n5; design cost
    relative to total ship cost, 184; diffusion
    from commercial to military sectors,
    145, 149–50, 153–55, 160n5; digital design
    tool use, 49; displacement/full load dis-
    placement, 26, 39n28; evolution of war
    and mission of PLAN and, 4, 9, 19–20,
    26–38, 265–69; ideal military platform,
    312; imitative innovation, cost and time
    savings through, 7, 9; indigenous designs,
    263; naval strategy and, 19–20; payload
    and weight classification system, 26–27;
    production model, 130, 132; size of ships,
    9, 27; time requirement to design a ship,
    184. See also standards
destroyers: AAW mission of, 113, 114; budget
    and funding for, 107–8; Dalian produc-
    tion of, 114, 125, 137–38; force strength
    and projected production of, xvi–xvii,
    3, 113–14, 125, 126–27, 263, 269–70, 285;
    foreign navies, comparison to, 288, 289;
    future requirements for, 121; Jiangnan
    production of, 104–5, 113–14, 125, 126–27,
    137; mission focus of, 284–85, 287
diesel/gas turbine engines, 239, 245
directed energy weapons, 130, 311
dock cycle time, 92, 198
Donghai-10 (DH-10) LACM, 28, 37
drillships, 191, 200, 203, 204
dumplings analogy, 1

East China Sea, 7, 21, 254, 268, 282
Eilat (Israel), 31
electric propulsion: advancements in, 130;
    all-electric propulsion U.S. submarines,
    243; integrated electric propulsion, 244,
    247–48n33, 255, 305

electromagnetic compatibility standards,
    169
electromagnetic maneuver warfare (EMW),
    325, 326
electromagnetic railguns, 310–11, 326
electronic countermeasure systems, 224
electronics: aircraft carrier applications, 256;
    classifications and standards for, 227; cost
    relative to total ship cost, 184; develop-
    ment and production of, 221–22, 226,
    232–33; foreign and indigenous technolo-
    gies, integration of, 229–30, 233; foreign
    components and supply chain for, 221,
    226, 229–30, 233, 236n15; frigate combat
    control system, 229–30; industrial base
    for, 226–29, 232–33; integration of equip-
    ment and systems, 45; modernization of
    PLAN and, 222–23; purpose and func-
    tions of, 223–24; reforms targeting indus-
    try, 224–26; standards for, 227, 234–35,
    236n20; weakness in technology for, 1,
    5–6, 10, 221, 232–33
energy-efficient ships, 45–46, 52, 56
Europe: naval shipbuilding in, 103–4; pro-
    duction techniques assistance from, 154;
    shipbuilding industry cycles, 190
Europe/European Union (EU): cross-
    subsidy between military and merchant
    shipbuilding, 103; shipbuilding produc-
    tion trends, 76–81
export of ships, 42, 51, 67–68, 105, 125, 127,
    129, 209, 264, 280–81

F-14 fighters (United States), 327
facilities and infrastructure: capacity of
    and PLAN growth, 135–36; consolida-
    tion, integration, and industrial layout
    updates, 5, 48–53, 99, 105–6, 152; diffusion
    from commercial to military sectors, 145,
    149–53, 160n4; evolution of, 4; expan-
    sion and modernization of, 48–53, 58n31;
    limits on investment in, 49; location of
    shipyards, xv; maintenance and support
    for in-service vessels, 8, 13; quality and
    capabilities of, 5; satellite imagery analy-
    sis of, 135–42
far seas defense and operations capabili-
    ties, 6, 7, 13, 19, 23–25, 28, 33–34, 36–38,
    222–23, 230–31, 251–52, 256–57, 266, 277,
    281–87, 290, 294n19, 294n23
fast attack craft, 12, 116, 129

financial resources: bankruptcy and closure
  threats, 10, 98–99, 105–6, 147, 153, 278;
  bonds, 47, 65–66, 69; capital market
  access and activities, 47, 62, 63, 64–67,
  68–69, 89; challenges facing shipbuilders, 98–99, 105–6; decline in shipping
  demand and orders after financial
  crisis, 43, 56, 147–48, 193–94; defense
  budget and funding, 22–23, 26, 64, 69,
  107–8; expansion of financial channels,
  47; heavy tail financing schemes, 194;
  sources of information about, 192–93; for
  state-owned shipyards, 4, 10, 26, 56–57,
  264; white-listed shipyards, 10, 49–50, 99,
  145, 150–53, 161n26
Five-Year Plans/Guidelines, 56, 225–26,
  243, 262
France: helicopter purchases from, 33;
  nuclear industry in, 241; nuclear submarine technology capabilities of, 243;
  PLAN forces, comparison to, 13, 287, 288;
  TAVITAC system from, 229–30; turbojets
  purchases from, 30
frigates: AAW mission of, 114; budget and
  funding for, 107–8; export of, 67–68, 105,
  129, 264; force strength and projected
  production of, xvi–xvii, 3, 115–16, 125,
  128–29, 131, 263, 269–70; foreign navies,
  comparison to, 288, 289; future requirements for, 121; Guangzhou production
  of, 141; helicopter operations from, 33;
  Huangpu production of, 105, 115–16,
  125; Hudong production of, 105, 115–16,
  125, 128–29; Liaonan production of, 125;
  Wuhan production of, 141

General Armament Department, 9, 169–70,
  175n7
General Specifications for Naval Ships (GJB
  4000-2000), 9, 26, 169, 170–71, 174, 175n7,
  232
Ghana, 127
goodwill deployments, 267
Greece, 103
green shipbuilding, 51
Guangzhou Longxue Shipbuilding, xv, 88,
  90, 95, 105, 151, 152–53, 155
Guangzhou Shipyard International (GSI):
  capital market access and activities,
  66–67, 89; CSSC ownership of, 88, 89;
  expansion of facilities at, 105; Huangpu

Wenchong purchase by, 66–67; location of, xv; merchant and military ship
  production at, 105, 152; mergers, integrations, and internal consolidations at, 90,
  152; productivity and output of, 86, 88,
  89; renaming of, 66, 89; ship production at, 118–19, 141; throughput volume,
  95; white-listed shipyards, inclusion in,
  151. See also CSSC Offshore and Marine
  Engineering (Group) Company Limited
  (COMEC)
Guojia Junyong Biaozhun (GJB), 159, 167,
  168–72, 173–74, 175–76nn1–2, 175n7, 227,
  232, 234–35, 236n20

H-6G bombers, 30
Haijing 2901/Haijing 3901 offshore patrol
  vessels, 137, 143n7
Haiying HY-1/HY-1J/HY-3 missiles, 29
Hantong Ship Heavy Industry, 88, 89, 91, 95
Harpers Ferry-class amphibious ships
  (United States), 54
helicopters: ASW operations use of, 33;
  far seas defense operations with, 284;
  France, purchases from, 33; operations
  from corvettes, 116; Russia, purchases
  from, 33
hiding versus finding, 6, 302–6, 314n29
hitting versus intercepting, 6, 309–11
HJB standards, 167, 168, 171–72, 175n10
Hongqi-class missiles: HQ-1 SAMs, 31;
  HQ-7 SAMs, 31; HQ-9/HQ-9A/HHQ-9
  SAMs, 23, 32, 136; HQ-10/HHQ-10
  SAMs, 31, 114, 116; HQ-16/HHQ-16
  SAMs, 23, 32; HQ-61 SAMs, 31
hovercraft, 54, 60n71, 286
Hu Jintao, 23–24, 25, 144, 251–52, 258n10, 275
Hu Wenming, 51, 68–69, 147, 149, 279
Huanghai Shipbuilding, 88, 90, 91, 95
Huangpu (Guangzhou) shipyard: CCG
  cutter production at, 68; location of, xv;
  merchant and military ship production
  at, 153; productivity and output of, 64;
  ship production at, 105, 115–16, 125, 127,
  131; white-listed shipyards, inclusion in,
  151
Huangpu Wenchong Shipbuilding, 66–67,
  68–69, 86, 105, 151, 152
Hudong Shipbuilding Heavy Industry
  Company, 154

Hudong Zhonghua shipyard (Shanghai): bottlenecks in production at, 55; capital market access and activities, 67; CSSC ownership of, 87, 88; export of ships built by, 68, 105, 209; location of, xv; merchant and military ship production at, 152, 153; mergers, integrations, and internal consolidations at, 87, 90; productivity and output of, 64, 86, 87, 88; ship production at, 55, 105, 115–16, 117, 118–19, 125, 127, 128–29, 141, 202, 209; specialization and reputation building at, 55; throughput volume, 95; welding skills at, 55, 202; white-listed shipyards, inclusion in, 151

Huludao Shipyard: expansion of facilities at, 4, 138–41; location of, xv; merchant and military ship production at, 153; nuclear-powered vessel/submarine production at, 4, 109, 122–23, 132n8, 138–41; satellite imagery analysis of, 138–41

H/ZBJ-1 combat control system, 229–30

imitative innovation, 7, 9

India, 255; Indo-American relations and cooperation, 291–92; PLAN forces, comparison to, 13, 287, 288; Sino-Indian relations and Indian Ocean patrols, 291–92

Indian Ocean: Malaysian airliner search operations, 267; patrol operations in, 255, 285, 291–92; PLAN facilities in as places, not bases approach, 292; protection of sea lanes in, 283; submarine patrols in, 36, 239, 284, 286

Industry and Information Technology, Ministry of, 10, 49, 150

information technology: advanced information warfare, 254; C4ISR infrastructure, 221, 222–23; communications systems, 51; computing power growth, 298, 313n3; connectivity and, 299; datafication and information transparency, 298–99, 302; disruptive technology advances and naval warfare, 6, 296–98, 301–11; information revolution, 298–99; integration of equipment and systems, 45; intelligent machines and advanced computing, 299; naval warfare and the information revolution, 300–301; unmanned system operations and advanced computing power, 298; upgrades in shipyards, 50

Integrated Command Platform (ICP), 309

integrated electric propulsion (IEP), 244, 247–48n33, 255, 305

integrated innovation concept, 5, 177, 178, 179–80, 185

intelligence, surveillance, and reconnaissance (ISR) capabilities, 302, 303–6

International Seapower Symposium, Twenty-First, 14

introduction, digestion, absorption, and re-innovation (IDAR) strategy, 155–58, 178–79, 229–30

J-15 aircraft, 253, 284

J-31 aircraft, 253

Japan: domestic and international orders, 194–95; efficiency in SBI in, 184; goal to challenge SBI status of, 278; market changes, response to, 45; as model for SBI development, 42, 45; performance, productivity, and profitability in SBI, 195–204; PLAN forces, comparison to, 13, 185–86, 287, 288, 291; production techniques assistance from, 154; quality of ship construction, 210; SBI in, strength of, 5, 10, 11–12, 189, 206; shipbuilding industry cycles, 190–91; shipbuilding production trends, 76–81; throughput volumes, 93, 94, 198

Jiang Zemin, 22–23, 251

Jiangnan Shipyard (Shanghai/Changxing Island): bottlenecks in production at, 136; capital market access and activities, 67; Changxing Island move of, 85, 90, 104–5, 125; CSSC ownership of, 85, 88; expansion of facilities at, 4, 104–5; facilities at, 85; location of, xv; merchant and military ship production at, 104–5, 152; mergers, integrations, and internal consolidations at, 90; modular construction process at, 137, 138; productivity and output of, 64, 84, 85, 86, 88; satellite imagery analysis of, 137; ship production at, 113–14, 118, 125–27, 137, 143n7, 152; submarine production at, 110; throughput volume, 95; white-listed shipyards, inclusion in, 151

Jiangyang Shipyard, 86

Jingjiang Shipyard, 89

Jinhai Heavy Industry Company (Zhoushan Jinhaiwan Shipyard), 87, 88, 90, 95

Jinling Shipyard, 86, 88, 89, 95

John F. Kennedy (United States), 297

Joint Concept for Access and Maneuver in the Global Commons (JAM-GC), 323

Julang JL-1/JL-2 SLBMs, 28, 36–37, 109, 141, 286

Kanhai survey vessel, 120

Kilo-class (Project 877/636) submarines (Russia), 22, 35, 110, 111, 243, 329n9

KJ-200 airborne warning and control systems, 304

KJ-500 airborne warning and control systems, 304

KJ-2000 airborne warning and control systems, 304

labor efficiency, repeats required to double, 10

Lada-class (Project 677) submarines (Russia), 111

land-attack cruise missiles (LACMs), 13, 37, 284–85

landing craft air cushion (LCAC) vessels, 60n71, 117, 137, 141, 286

landing helicopter dock (LHD), 117, 122, 125, 127, 129

laser technology, 310–11

lean production methods, 48–53, 55, 59n43

Liaonan shipyard, xv, 125, 127

Liaoning, 37, 112, 125, 137, 138, 230, 244, 249, 252–55, 256–57, 284

Liaoning Bohai shipyard, 86, 87, 137

Liaoning scale mockup, 141

liquefied natural gas (LNG) carriers, 152, 190–91, 194, 202, 204, 211n5, 211n7, 278–79

lithium-ion (Li-ion) batteries, 10, 239–40, 245

littoral combat ships (LCSs) (United States), 319, 320, 325

Liu Chunlin, 243–44

Liu Huaqing, 21–22, 251

Liuhou-Xijiang shipyard, xv

Lloyd's Register, 172, 175n15, 209

Long-Range Antiship Missile (LRASM), 13

LPDs. *See* amphibious ships (LSTs and LPDs)

LSTs. *See* amphibious ships (LSTs and LPDs)

Luzhou Yard, 50

Machine Building, Sixth Ministry of, 42

Major Categories Relevant to Shipboard Electronics (GJB 832-1990), 234–35

Mao Zedong, 36, 144, 251

Marine Corps, U.S., 13–14

maritime power. *See* sea power/sea control

maritime security equipment, 51

Mawei shipyard, 86

Mediterranean Sea operations, 231, 267, 283, 285, 291–92

Melbourne (Australia), 251

merchant ships. *See* commercial/merchant ships

military operations other than war (MOOTW), 254, 283

military shipbuilding industry: bottlenecks in, 130, 135–36; capabilities and capacity of, 262–65; challenges in subcomponents, 10, 135–36; China Dream, shipbuilding for, 6, 261–70; coproduction of military and commercial vessels, 104–5, 145, 149–53, 160n4; demand signal, 265–69, 275–76; efficiency in and longer production runs of fewer ship series, 10; European shipbuilders, 103–4; integration of commercial and naval shipbuilding processes, 11, 279–80; merchant shipbuilding compared to, 101, 103–5, 185, 189, 264; merchant shipbuilding revenue earned by, 145, 146, 149, 160n7; preferential treatment and support for, 10, 62–63, 185, 264, 280–81; pricing of military ships, 160n7; production model, 130, 132; production techniques, 264–65; projected production of vessels, xvi–xvii, 4, 274–75; quality of ship construction, 203–4, 209–10, 280–81; satellite imagery analysis of infrastructure and production, 135–42; workforce quality and proficiency, 62, 185, 263, 264, 271n11

military-civilian fusion (MCF), 144. *See also* civil-military integration (CMI)

mine countermeasure vessels (MCMVs), 118, 124, 126, 269–70

missile patrol craft, xvi–xvii, 269–70

missiles: defense systems against, 309–11; missile-based air defense system, 31; missile-centric firepower strike and counterintervention operations, 254; naval strategy evolution and capabilities for operations with, 27–31; "paper missiles," 13; quantity available for deployment, 13; range of, 13; Russian/Soviet systems purchases, 23, 29, 30, 32; ship-defense systems, development of, 23; testing facility for, 141; U.S. capabilities for countering, 318–19; U.S. Navy systems, 13, 325–26; vertical launching systems, 13, 37, 109, 113, 114, 115, 242, 284–85, 312. *See also specific types of missiles*

modular designs and construction: advantages of, 136, 154, 155, 312; CAD/CAM technology use and, 154–55; expansion in use of, 9, 136, 153, 263; infrastructure for, 155; limitations of, 312; process for, 136, 153–54; production efficiency with, 9, 153–54; propulsion designs, 243; satellite imagery analysis of use of, 136–37, 138; submarine designs, 243

Myanmar, 129

Nantong China Ocean Shipping Company (COSCO) KHI Ship Engineering, 86, 87, 88, 95

Nantong Rongsheng Shipbuilding, 87, 88, 90, 95, 147–48, 195–96

naval architecture. *See* design and naval architecture

Naval Armament Research Institute, 9

Naval Command College, Nanjing, 14

Naval Intelligence, U.S. Office of (ONI): future naval vessel requirements, 120; military modernization in China, report on, 2–3, 263; SSBN patrol operation information, 241–42; worldwide maritime challenges, report on, 318, 328n2

Naval Research Institute, 9

Naval Research Institute (PLA), 25

Naval Strike Missile, 13

Naval War College (NWC): China Maritime Studies Institute, 2, 3; exchange program with Chinese naval officers and visit to, 14; International Seapower Symposium at, 14

navigation and control systems: electronics and capabilities for, 224; localized production of, 51, 59n48

Navy, U.S.: aircraft carrier strike warfare mission focus, 37; aircraft carriers and carrier-based aircraft, 318, 327; amphibi-ous fleet, 54; budget and spending, strategy, and programs debates, 321–23; C4ISR model for China, 222–23; capabilities of and PLAN modernization, 6–7, 12–14, 186, 270, 317–20; component availability and production bottlenecks, 136; cooperation and competition with PLAN, 14, 291; displacement/full load displacement, 39n28; distributed lethality concept, 324; exchange program with naval officers, 14; force architecture/structure, 323–24; force strength of, 186, 292, 324; high-end warfare capabilities, 7, 319–20, 324–26, 327–28; ideal military platform, 312; maritime strategy of, 13–14; mission focus of, 319–20, 329n11; PLAN capabilities to contest U.S. sea control, 7–8, 12, 13; PLAN forces, comparison to, 6, 7, 13, 185–86, 287–90, 295n39, 312; PLAN vulnerabilities to carrier aviation operations by, 31–32; submarine fleet, 325; surface combatants capabilities, 325–26; technology from, emulation of, 256; weight classification system, 26–27

near coast defense strategy, 19, 20–21, 28, 32–33, 35, 36, 222

near seas active defense strategy, 19, 21–23, 28, 33, 34–35, 222, 261–62, 266, 277, 300

near seas defense, far seas operations strategy, 19, 23–25, 28, 33–34, 36–38, 222–23, 230–31, 251–52, 256–57, 266, 277, 281–87, 290, 294n19, 294n23

networking and network warfare systems: capabilities for, 308–9, 316n50; integration of equipment and systems, 45; network resilience versus degradation, 6, 307–9, 316n50; reconnaissance-strike networks, 301; reconnaissance-strike swarms, 301–2

New Century Group, 87, 88, 89, 90

New Century Shipbuilding, 86, 87, 89

New Times Shipbuilding, 87, 88, 89, 90, 95

New Yangzijiang Shipbuilding, 87, 88, 90, 93, 94, 95

Nigeria, 127

nuclear propulsion and power: acoustic quieting, 10; advancements in and development priorities, 10, 241, 242–43, 245; advantages and challenges of, 240–41; aircraft carrier applications, 244, 255;

blue-water navy and use of, 241; civilian industry and naval competence, 241; core life and economic and operational efficiency, 240–41; current state of in China, 241–42; limitations on, 238; modular designs, 243; natural circulation reactors, 243; noise from, 35–36; nuclear deterrent role of SSBNs, 241–42; potential for, 238; power density, 10, 240–41; reactor design and development, 242–44; Russian assistance in development of, 10, 241, 242–43, 247n20; secrecy surrounding technologies for, 245; submarine applications, 240–44; U.S. designs and quietness of U.S. submarines, 243

Offshore Control strategy, 323
One Belt, One Road (OBOR) economic corridors, 231, 267
order of battle, xvi–xvii, 4, 7
over-the-horizon backscatter (OTH-B) radar, 304

Pakistan, 55, 127, 129, 239, 286, 292
patrol craft (PC), 121–22, 127
patrol/missile craft (PGG), 121–22
Pentagon Papers, 299
People's Liberation Army (PLA): budget and funding for, 22–23; land-based threats and strategy of, 2, 20, 25, 44; MOOTW doctrine, 254; network-centric warfare with Chinese characteristics, 22; private, nonmilitary enterprises of, 22–23; SBI role and requirements of, 4, 41, 55–56; Soviet invasion threat, strategy for, 20–21
People's Liberation Army Air Force (PLAAF), 21, 281, 282
People's Liberation Army Navy (PLAN): budget and funding for naval construction projects, 26, 64, 69, 107–8; capabilities of, expansion of, 6, 7, 253–54; cooperation and competition with U.S. Navy, 14, 291; exchange program with naval officers, 14; expansion and modernization of fleet, 3, 6–7, 12–14, 63–64, 127, 186, 251–52, 261–70, 317–20; fleet development knowledge gap, 130, 132, 274–75, 290–91; foreign navies, comparison to, 13, 185–86, 287, 288, 291; future vessel requirements for, 120–22; growth

of, SBI capacity to support, 6; mission areas and ship design, development, and deployment, 4, 9, 20, 26–38, 265–69; order of battle, xvi–xvii, 4, 7; power and strength of, 5; power projection by, 2–3, 7–8, 12, 13, 250, 254, 256–57; quality of force, 263; responsibilities of, expansion of, 23–25, 44–45, 222–23, 251–52, 256–57; at-sea training program, 291; second most powerful navy, growth projection to become, 6, 7, 13, 287; U.S. naval forces, comparison to, 6, 7, 13, 185–86, 287–90, 295n139, 312
People's Liberation Army Rocket Force (PLARF), 281, 282
Philippine Sea, 291
Phoenix air-to-air missiles (United States), 327
piracy and antipiracy patrols, 265, 267, 287, 290–91
Pomornik/Zubr-class LCACs, 60n71, 117
private shipyards: bankruptcy and closure threats to, 10, 98–99, 105–6, 147, 153, 278; capacity and resources of, 8–9, 10, 98–99, 264; challenges facing, 98–99; commercial peak ship construction, 8, 77, 81; commercial ship orders, decline in, 10, 135, 264; efficiency and innovation at, barriers to, 8–9, 11; naval contracts interests of, 4, 10, 264; overcapacity at, 62, 195–96; productivity and output of, 43, 57n6; size, stability, and competency of, 43, 206–7; weakness of compared to Korean and Japanese shipyards, 5, 10, 11–12; worker quality at, 10, 264
propeller design, 247–48n33
propulsion and power: advancements in, 6, 130, 245; aircraft carrier technologies, 6, 244, 249, 255; all-electric propulsion U.S. submarines, 243; conventional, 10, 238–40, 245; crankshaft production, 135; engine power control and monitoring systems, 224; foreign and indigenous technologies, integration of, 245; importance of, 245; localized production of, 51, 59n48; modular designs, 243; range of ships and, 6, 238; Russian assistance in technology development, 6, 10; self-developed engine technology, 200–201; speed of ships and, 6, 238; water density, power, and speed, 238; weakness in

technology for, 1, 6, 10, 238, 245. *See also* nuclear propulsion and power

Qingdao Beihai Shipbuilding Heavy Industries, 12
Qingdao Wuchuan Heavy Industry, 12
Qinshan shipyard, 86
Qiuxin shipyard, 86, 90, 118, 154
Quadrennial Defense Review (QDR), 318, 322

radar, 223, 284–85, 304
reconnaissance-strike networks, 301
reconnaissance-strike swarms, 301–2
regional hegemon, prevention of emergence of, 320–21
research, development, and acquisition (RDA): budget and funding for, 26; deficiencies in, 184–85; foreign and indigenous technologies, integration of, 5, 145, 155–57, 178–79, 185–86, 245, 256; IDAR strategy, 155–58, 178–79, 229–30; imitative innovation, cost and time savings through, 7, 9; indigenous innovation, 178–80, 185–86; integrated innovation concept, 5, 177, 178, 179–80, 185; integration of facilities and research-production activities, 49–51; publications and studies on technology development, 129–30; reforms to increase, 224–26; system for, 5, 180–84; technology development barriers, 177–78; technology transfer, 178
research institutes: 14 RI, 227; 20 RI, 227; 32 RI, 227; 38 RI, 227; 54 RI, 227; 61 RI, 309; 701 RI, 182, 183, 208; 704 RI, 228; 709 RI, 228, 230; 711 RI, 110, 306; 712 RI, 157; 713 RI, 182; 716 RI, 228, 230; 719 RI, 182, 183, 242–44, 247n20; 722 RI, 228, 230; 723 RI, 229, 230; 724 RI, 228, 230; CSIC institutes, 67; interaction/cooperation with enterprises by, 51, 184; research and design activities at, 154, 182, 183; reverse engineering by, 195; secrecy surrounding, 192; standards development role of, 170, 172; workforce at, 154, 204, 206
Russia/Soviet Union: access to technology, systems, and expertise from, 22; aircraft carrier capabilities and mission focus, 37; aircraft carrier technology purchases from, 112, 137, 252, 254, 256;

assistance from on propulsion technology development, 6, 10; assistance from on submarine development, 111; Crimea annexation by, 320, 323; helicopter purchases from, 33; maintenance and support for in-service vessels, 8; military capabilities of, 319–20; missile system purchases from, 23, 29, 30, 31, 32; nuclear industry in, 241; nuclear propulsion assistance from, 10, 241, 242–43, 247n20; nuclear propulsion, secrecy surrounding technologies for, 245; PLAN forces, comparison to, 287, 288; sonar systems purchases from, 32–33; threat of invasion by, 20–21, 22

S-300PMU (SA-10B Grumble) systems (Russia), 23, 32
salami-slicing tactics, 327–28
satellite imagery: analysis of and intelligence procedures, 134–35, 142; limitations of use of, 135; shipbuilding infrastructure and production analysis with, 135–42
satellite technology and capabilities, 230–31, 233
sea power/sea control: aircraft carrier capabilities and, 250, 254, 256–57; anti-access/area denial (A2/AD), 13, 281–82, 284, 294n19, 319–20, 323–27; C4ISR infrastructure and, 221, 222–23; capabilities to oppose U.S. Navy operations, 2–3, 7–8, 12, 13, 257; far seas defense and operations capabilities, 6, 7, 13, 19, 23–25, 28, 33–34, 36–38, 222–23, 230–31, 251–52, 256–57, 266, 277, 281–87, 290, 294n19, 294n23; future naval vessel requirements for, 120–22; goals for global and credible sea-based presence, 6, 12–13, 204–5, 250, 261–70, 275–77, 291–92, 320–21; second most powerful navy, growth projection for PLAN to become, 6, 7, 13, 287; ship design and building to contest control in western Pacific, 12, 257; space-based communications infrastructure and, 230–31; U.S. sea control, 319–20
sensors: advancements in and development of, 130; development and production of, 51; weakness in technology for, 10
Shanghai, economic development in, 42
Shanghai Edward Shipyard, 86, 87, 90

Shanghai Shipyard: CSSC ownership of, 88, 90; location of, xv; productivity and output of, 86, 88, 90; throughput volume, 95

Shangyou SY-1/SY-1A missiles, 29

Shanhaiguan Shipbuilding Industry, 12

Shenzhen, economic development in, 42

shipbuilding industry (SBI): advances in design and production technologies, 9; capacity and industry development, 81, 84–91, 98–99, 193–96; capacity of and PLAN growth, 6, 135–36; capacity utilization rate, 48, 94, 145, 147, 151, 152, 153, 195, 196; challenges and issues facing, 41, 42, 55–56, 61n79, 204–10; competition in, reorganization of to introduce, 42–43; complexity and size of ships, 10, 44–46, 54–55, 191–92, 211nn5–7, 278–79, 280–81; consolidation, integration, mergers, and downsizing in, 12, 26, 46–53, 55–56, 57–58n20, 90, 99, 105–6, 146–47, 152, 207–8, 225, 226–27, 278–79; construction time, 59n43; corporatization of, 42; culture of secrecy in, 158; decline in shipping demand and orders after financial crisis, 43, 56, 147–48, 193–94; diversification beyond building hulls, 51; domestic and international orders, 194–95; efficiency in, reorganization of to introduce, 42–43; expectations, role, and requirements assigned to, 4, 8, 41, 42, 44–46, 55–56; foreign assistance in advanced production techniques, 154; future policies for, 56; global shipping cycle, 189–93; government plan to aid, 147–49, 279; great-power status of China, role of SBI in development of, 8, 41, 204–10, 261–62, 291; growth of and expansion of capabilities, 1, 7, 13–14, 26, 42–43, 277–78; historical background of, 42–43; institutional culture in, 8–9, 11; integration of commercial and naval shipbuilding processes, 11, 279–80; knowledge gap about production and capacity, 130, 132, 274–75, 290–91; location of, 42, 57n4; mandated reduction in commercial shipyards, 11; market changes, response to, 45–46, 57–58n20; models for development of, 42, 45–46; number of shipyards and shipbuilding enterprises, 43, 48, 58n29, 81, 84, 99; orders for ships, 43; overcapacity in, 26, 46, 47, 56, 62, 135, 136, 140, 152,

193–96, 197, 205–6, 279; performance, productivity, and profitability in, 91–98, 105–6, 190, 196–204; political and strategic importance of, 44–46, 55, 56; present situation in, 44–46; pricing of ships, 127, 129, 280–81; production techniques, 145, 149–50, 153–55, 264–65; productivity and output of, 42, 43, 57n6, 84, 193–96, 211n13, 287, 290; quality of ship construction, 1, 7, 43, 51, 127, 129–30, 203–4, 209–10, 278–79; reform of by state to improve China shipbuilding brand, 41, 45–53, 55–56, 57–58n20, 58n31, 59n43, 224–26; scope of shipbuilding activities, 2; state guidance and policy directives, 41, 42, 55–56; success in, characteristics that influence, 97–98; technological challenges to, 5–6, 10, 44–46; vertical integration in, 45–46, 51, 58n21; white-listed shipyards, 10, 49–50, 99, 145, 150–53, 161n26; workforce quality and proficiency, 10, 43, 52–53, 198–200, 206, 263, 264, 271n11. See also design and naval architecture; facilities and infrastructure; military shipbuilding industry

Shipbuilding Industry Specification Requirements (2013), 49–50, 51–52

ships/warships: budget and funding for, 64, 69, 107–8; decommissioned ships, transfer of, 67–68, 129; dual-use civilian vessels, 53–54, 60n62, 208–9; force strength and projected production of, xvi–xvii, 1, 3, 7–8, 107–8, 132n1, 186, 263–65, 269–70; future vessel requirements, 120–22; maintenance and support for in-service vessels, 8, 13; modernization and replacement of, 262–65; operational lifespans of, 297; physical embodiment of maritime strategy, 4, 19; program for development of, 22; purchase price and maintenance costs for, 8, 13; quality of, 1, 7, 127, 129–30, 203–4, 209–10

Shtil (SA-N-7A Gadfly) systems (Russia), 23, 32

Silk Road/Maritime Silk Road, 267, 283

Sinopacific Group, 88, 89, 91, 95

Snowden, Edward, 299

sonar systems: active and passive towed array systems, 33–34, 35, 36, 121; electronics and capabilities for, 223; naval strategy evolution and capabilities for operations with, 20, 28, 32–34; Russian/Soviet systems purchases, 32–33; U.S. systems, 34; variable depth sonar, 28, 33–34

South China Sea, 7, 21, 251, 254, 257, 268, 282

South Korean shipbuilding: capacity and industry development in, 81, 84; consolidation and vertical integration in, 45–46, 58n21; domestic and international orders, 194–95; efficiency in, 184; goal to challenge status of, 278; industry cycles in, 190–91; market changes, response to, 45–46, 58n21; as model for SBI development, 42, 45–46; performance, productivity, and profitability in, 196–204; production in, 75, 84; production techniques assistance from, 154; production trends, 76–81; quality of ship construction, 210; shipbuilding power status of, 46; strength of, 5, 10, 11–12, 189, 206; throughput volumes, 93, 94, 198

Southeast Asia shipbuilding throughput volumes, 93, 94

Sovremenny-class (Project 956) guided-missile destroyers (Russia), 22, 23, 32, 33, 113, 114

space industry, 11

space-based communications infrastructure, 230–31, 233

Spain, 103

standards: access to, 174; assimilation of foreign standards, 9, 169, 173–74; basis for and focus of, 9; categories and types of, 167, 175n1; CB standards, 167, 172, 174; China Classification Society, 12, 167, 172–74; commercial ship construction requirements to support military mobilization, 12; cultural barriers to standardization and regulation, 11–12; development of, 167, 168–70; development of, responsibility for, 12; dual-use standards and barrier to CMI, 159; electronics classifications and standards, 227; evolution of, 173–74; foreign warship classification rules, 172–73, 175n15; GJB national standards, 159, 167, 168–72, 173–74, 175–76nn1–2, 175n7, 227, 232, 234–35, 236n20; HJB standards, 167, 168, 171–72, 175n10; international standards, adherence to, 51, 52; merchant shipbuilding standards use in naval shipbuilding,

104; national, military, and industrial standards for warships, 5; national and military standards for construction, 7; payload and weight classification system, 26–27; purpose of, 167

State Administration for Science, Technology, and Industry for National Defense (SASTIND), 45–46, 57–58nn20–21, 65, 75, 157, 182, 184

state-owned shipyards, 206; capacity and resources of, 8–9, 10; consolidation, integration, mergers, and downsizing in, 99, 105–6, 146–47, 152, 225, 226–27, 278–79; efficiency and innovation at, barriers to, 8–9, 11; financial resources for, 4, 10, 26, 56–57, 264; job and skills development program through, 8; mandated reduction in commercial shipyards, 11; maritime strategic-industrial transformation role of, 5; preferential treatment and support for, 10, 205–6; white-listed shipyards, 10, 49–50, 99, 145, 150–53

steel, 200

strategy/naval strategy: China Dream and blue-water navy, 6, 261–70; evolution of, 19–25, 37–38, 222–23; information revolution and, 300–301; missile-centric firepower strike and counterintervention operations, 254; national interests and goals and, 19–20; near coast defense, 19, 20–21, 28, 32–33, 35, 36, 222; near seas active defense, 19, 21–23, 28, 33, 34–35, 222, 261–62, 266, 277, 300; nears seas defense, far seas operations, 19, 23–25, 28, 33–34, 36–38, 222–23, 230–31, 251–52, 256–57, 266, 277, 281–87, 290, 294n19, 294n23; offensive-enabling capabilities, 300–301; salami-slicing tactics, 327–28; scientific nature of, 19; ship design, development, construction, and employment and, 19–20; ships as physical embodiment of, 4, 19; U.S. maritime strategy, 13–14; warfare areas and, 20, 26–38; warfare areas competencies and naval strategy evolution timeline, 27, 28, 39n30

strike warfare: aircraft carrier capabilities, 37; missile-centric firepower strike and counterintervention operations, 254; naval strategy and competency in, 20, 28, 36–37; precision strike capabilities, 25, 37;

precision strike systems, integration of within vessels, 45; submarine capabilities, 36–37; surface ship capabilities, 37

STX Dalian China Shipbuilding, 84, 85, 91; productivity and output of, 88; through-put volume, 95

subcomponents. *See* systems and components

submarine warfare, naval strategy and competency in, 28, 34–36

submarine-launched ballistic missile (SLBM) patrols, 268–69, 270

submarine-launched ballistic missiles (SLBMs), 28, 36–37, 109, 111, 141, 241–42, 286

submarines: AIP systems, 10, 35–36, 107, 111, 239, 245, 284, 305; budget and funding for, 107–8; Dalian production of, 122; force strength and projected production of, xvi–xvii, 3, 34–36, 108–12, 122–25, 132n8, 186, 269–70, 286, 329n9; future requirements for, 120–21; Huludao production of, 108–10, 122–23, 138–41; importance and value of, 34; largest force of, 34; missile deployment from, 35, 109; mission focus of, 34–36, 282, 284, 286, 305–6; modular designs, 243; noise from, 35–36, 305–6; nuclear propulsion advancements, 10; production time for, 140; program for development of, 22; propulsion methods and advancements, 10, 239–40, 305–6; Russian assistance in development of, 111; U.S. fleet, 325; U.S. submarines stationed in Pacific, 318; Wuhan production of, 110, 111, 124–25, 141

submarines, ballistic missile (SSBNs): force strength and projected production of, xvi–xvii, 3, 108–9, 122–23, 269–70, 286, 329n9; foreign navies, comparison to, 288, 289; future requirements for, 120–21; Huludao production of, 122–23, 138–41; mission focus of, 35, 36–37, 286; national pride and development and production of, 36; nuclear deterrent role of, 241–42; patrol operations with, 37, 241–42, 268–69; sea trials and weapons integration or loading of, 141

submarines, conventionally powered attack (SSKs and SSPs): budget and funding for, 107–8; force strength and projected

production of, 110–11, 124–25, 126, 286; Jiangnan production of, 126; mission focus of, 286; Wuhan production of, 124–25, 141

submarines, cruise missile (SSG), 124, 126

submarines, diesel attack (SSs): export of, 264; force strength and projected production of, xvi–xvii; mission focus of, 35

submarines, guided-missile attack (SSGN), 110

submarines, nuclear-powered attack (SSNs): advancements in and development priorities, 242; budget and funding for, 107–8; capabilities and operational missions of, 241–42; force strength and projected production of, xvi–xvii, 109–10, 122–23, 269–70, 329n9; foreign navies, comparison to, 288, 289; future requirements for, 120–21; Huludao production of, 122–23, 138–41; mission focus of, 34, 35–36, 284; national pride and development and production of, 35–36; noise from, 35; production of, 12, 63, 242. *See also* nuclear propulsion and power

Supply-class ships (United States), 119

Surface Warfare Officers School, 14

surface-to-air missiles (SAMs): availability and potential shortages of, 136; far seas defense operations with, 284–85; quantity available for deployment, 13; Russian/Soviet systems purchases, 23, 31, 32. *See also* Hongqi-class missiles

surge operations, 267

systems and components: aircraft carrier technologies, 256; availability of and production bottlenecks, 5, 135–36, 155; challenges in subcomponents, 10; cost of, 200–201; defense bidding and procurement system, 157–59, 164n68; diffusion from commercial to military sectors, 145, 149–50, 155–59; foreign and indigenous technologies, integration of, 5, 145, 155–57, 178–79, 185–86, 245, 256; integration of components for system-of-systems, 5, 45, 245, 256; integration of equipment and systems, 45, 145, 149–50, 155–59; localized production of, 50–51, 59n48, 156, 157–59, 200–201, 225; subcomponent design and production, 145, 149–50, 155–59, 160n4; technological level of shipboard systems, increase in, 50–51

Taiwan: amphibious ships for potential invasion of, 53–55, 60n62, 268, 285–86; carrier capabilities and operations against, 251, 254; independence of, prevention of, 30; Nationalist Party (Kuomintang, KMT) threat to China, 20; offensive capabilities in conflict with, 301; reunification with, 21; separatist activities and territorial claims in, 22, 251; Taiwan Strait crisis, 21, 23, 30, 31–32, 304; U.S. aid to, prevention of, 266

TAVITAC system, 229–30

tax money and policies, 47, 58n31, 205

technology: advancements in, 296–98; barriers to development of, 177–78; challenges to SBI, 5–6, 10, 44–46; digitization/virtual manufacturing and development of, 45, 50, 253, 265; failed next-generation programs, 297; foreign and indigenous technologies, integration of, 5, 178–79, 185–86, 245, 256; hybrid approach to, 5; indigenous development of, 5, 263; integration of equipment and systems, 45; political and military relationships and export of, 51, 59n52; publications and studies on development of, 129–30; raising technological level of shipboard systems, 50–51; steady-state incremental innovation, 297; training and expertise of workforce for development of, 263, 271n11. *See also* information technology

Thailand, 55, 118, 125, 127, 129

three-dimensional (3-D) printing, 265

Tianjin Xingang Shipbuilding, 12

torpedoes, 28, 33, 34, 35, 112, 179, 309

Treasure Boat Factory Ruins, 14

Tsuneishi Zhoushan Shipbuilding, 88, 89, 91, 95

turbojets, 30

Type 07 III LST, 124

Type 021 *Huangfeng/Osa*-class missile craft, 29, 121

Type 022 *Houbei*-class PTG catamarans, 63, 116, 121

Type 031 *Golf*-class submarine, 111

Type 032 *Qing* submarine, 111–12, 124, 141

Type 033/Project 633 *Romeo*-class submarines (China/Soviet Union), 29, 34, 110

Type 035 *Ming*-class submarines, 34–35, 110

Type 037 *Hainan*-class patrol craft, 121

Type 037-1G *Houxin*-class patrol/missile craft, 121

Type 037-I *Haiqing*-class patrol craft, 121

Type 037-II *Houjian*-class patrol/missile craft, 121

Type 039A/B *Yuan*-class submarines, 30, 35–36, 110, 111, 124, 126, 137, 239, 286, 305–6

Type 039G *Song*-class submarines, 30, 35, 110, 243, 286

Type 046 corvettes, 328

Type 051 *Luda*-class destroyers, 22, 29, 33, 114

Type 051B *Luhai*-class destroyers, 113

Type 051C *Luzhou*-class destroyers, 32, 113

Type 052/052A *Luhu*-class destroyers, 33, 34, 113, 230

Type 052C *Luyang II*-class destroyers, 30, 32, 33, 104–5, 113, 125, 126, 137, 284–85

Type 052D *Luyang III*-class destroyers, 27, 30, 32, 34, 37, 63, 105, 114, 125, 126, 136, 137–38, 262, 265, 284–85, 287

Type 053 *Jianghu*-class frigates, 29, 115, 116

Type 053H1/2 *Jianghu II/III*-class frigates, 33, 129

Type 054 *Jiangkai I* frigate, 115–16, 141

Type 054A *Jiangkai II* frigate: cost and pricing of, 63, 280–81; design and production of, 115–16; electronics suite for, 5–6, 229–30, 233; export of, 280–81; Huangpu production of, 105, 131; Hudong production of, 128; mission focus of, 32, 33, 34, 285

Type 054B *Jiangkai III* frigate, 115–16, 285

Type 055/055D cruiser, 27, 113, 114, 141, 152

Type 056/056A *Jiangdao*-class corvettes, 34, 63, 105, 116, 121, 124, 125, 128, 131, 141, 285, 328

Type 062-I *Shanghai II/III*-class patrol craft, 121

Type 071 *Yanha*-class icebreakers, 120

Type 071 *Yuzhao*-class LPDs, 54–55, 117, 125, 128, 141, 268, 286

Type 072 II *Yuting*-class LSTs, 122

Type 072A *Yuting II*-class LSTs, 60n69, 122

Type 072/-IIG *Yukan*-class LSTs, 60n69, 122

Type 073A *Yunshu*-class LSMs, 60n70, 122

Type 073-II *Yudeng*-class LSMs, 60n70

Type 074 *Yuhai*-class LSMs, 60n70, 122

Type 074A *Yubei*-class landing craft utility, 122

Type 079 *Yuliang*-class LSMs, 122

Type 081/081A *Wochi*-class mine counter-
measure vessels, 118, 124, 126
Type 082B *Wozang*-class mine countermea-
sure vessels, 118
Type 085 aircraft carrier, 112
Type 089 aircraft carrier, 112
Type 091 *Han*-class submarines, 22, 35–36,
241
Type 092 *Xia*-class submarines, 36
Type 093/093A *Shang*-class submarines, 30,
34, 35–36, 108, 109–10, 123, 132n8, 140,
241, 242, 243, 244, 286
Type 094 *Jin*-class submarines, 35, 36–37,
108–9, 123, 140, 141, 241–42, 244, 268–69
Type 095 SSN, 36, 37, 110, 123, 140, 242, 286
Type 096 SSBN, 109, 123, 140, 141
Type 272 *Yanrao*-class icebreakers, 120
Type 726 *Yuyis*-class LCACs, 60n71, 137
Type 815/815A *Dongdiao*-class auxiliary
general intelligence, 119
Type 901 *Fuyu*-class supply ships, 119, 121
Type 903/903A *Fuchi*-class auxiliary oiler
and replenishment (AOR) tankers,
118–19, 121, 128, 285
Type 904 *Danyao I-II*-class combat stores
ships, 119
Type 909 *Dahua*-class auxiliary general
experimental, 119, 128
Type 926 *Dalao*-class submarine rescue
vessels, 120
Type 6610/T 43 mine countermeasure ves-
sels, 118

Ukraine, 30, 104, 117, 138, 239, 323
understanding versus confusion, 6, 306–7
United Kingdom: Lloyd's Register, 172,
175n15, 209; nuclear industry in, 241;
PLAN forces, comparison to, 13, 287, 288;
shipbuilding industry cycles, 190
United States (U.S.): defense budget and
spending, strategy, and programs
debates, 321–23; Indo-American relations and cooperation, 291–92; maritime
strategy of, 13–14; military as most
technologically advanced, 297; nuclear
industry in, 241; nuclear propulsion,
secrecy surrounding technologies for,
245; nuclear submarine technology capabilities of, 243; quality of ship construction, 209–10; security and foreign policy
vis-à-vis grand strategy and geopolitics,

320–21; shipbuilding industry cycles, 190;
warfare capabilities of and PLA/PLAN
strategy, 22
unmanned systems: capabilities of and
advanced computing power, 298; development and production of, 12, 301;
publications on operations, principles,
and technologies, 130; unmanned aerial
vehicle development, 304–5, 314n29;
unmanned underwater vehicle development, 306

variable depth sonar (VDS), 28, 33–34
Varyag (Russia), 112, 137, 252. See also
Liaoning
vertical launching systems (VLSs), 13, 37,
109, 113, 114, 115, 242, 284–85, 312
Virginia-class submarines (United States),
243

Waigaoqiao Shipyard, 84, 85, 88, 90, 93, 94,
95, 151, 198
war/naval warfare: changes in, 297–98;
disruptive technology advances and
changes in, 6, 296–98, 301–11; evolution
of and PLAN ship design, development,
and deployment, 4, 9, 19–20, 26–38; far
seas mission for PLAN, 282–83; hiding versus finding, 6, 302–6, 314n29;
high-end warfare capabilities, 7, 319–20,
324–26, 327–28; hitting versus intercepting, 6, 309–11; information revolution
and, 300–301; naval strategy evolution
and warfare areas competencies, 20,
26–38; naval strategy evolution and warfare areas competencies timeline, 27, 28,
39n30; network resilience versus degradation, 6, 307–9, 316n50; network-centric
warfare with Chinese characteristics, 22;
pace of change in, 298; predictions about
change in, 311–12; understanding versus
confusion, 6, 306–7
Weapons and Armament Development
Strategy, 9
weapons systems: advanced asymmetric
systems, production of, 22; advancements in and new technology, 296–97,
309–11; development and production
of, 51; directed energy weapons, 130,
311; distributed lethality concept, 324;
guided/smart munitions, 130; kill chains

of, breaking, 324; mission areas of PLAN and design and development of, 9; power for operation of, 238; precision-guided systems, 302–4; reconnaissance-strike networks, 301; reconnaissance-strike swarms, 301–2; ship-defense systems, development of, 23; weakness in technology for, 10

welding skills and techniques, 49, 50, 55, 190, 199, 202, 203–4, 264

white-listed shipyards, 10, 49–50, 99, 145, 150–53, 161n26

Winglong/Pterodactyl 1 UAVs, 304

Wonang-class minesweepers, 118

Wu Shengli, 14, 300

Wuchang Shipbuilding (Wuhan): capital market access and activities, 66; CCG cutter production at, 68; export of ships built by, 68; location of, xv; productivity and output of, 64; ship production at, 110, 111, 118, 124–25, 127, 141; white-listed shipyards, inclusion in, 151

Wuhan lakeside complex, 141

Wuhu shipyard, xv, 86

Wuzhou-Guijiang shipyard, xv

Xi Jinping, 12, 44, 48, 144, 261–62, 267, 275–76

Xiaopingdao, 141

Xingang shipyard, 86

Y-8Q maritime patrol aircraft, 34

Yangfan Group, 87, 88, 95

Yangzhou Dayang Shipbuilding, 88, 89, 95

Yangzi River, 57n4

Yangzijiang Shipyard, 85, 86, 87, 90, 147

Yellow Sea, 7, 21

Yianjin shipyard, xv

Yin Zhou, 249, 252–53

Yingji-class missiles: YJ-1 ASCMs, 29; YJ-8/8A ASCMs, 29–30, 35; YJ-12 ASCMs, 30; YJ-18 ASCMs, 30, 35, 109, 114; YJ-62 ASCMs, 30; YJ-82 ASCMs, 35; YJ-83 ASCMs, 30, 116

Zhang Guangqin, 45, 56, 61n79

Zhang Shiping, 250

Zhangjiang shipyard, xv

Zheng He, 14, 286, 295n34

Zheng He Memorial Shipyard, 14

Zhonghua shipyard, xv, 86, 87, 90. *See also* Hudong Zhonghua shipyard (Shanghai)

Zhoushan, 33

Zhoushan Jinhaiwan Shipyard, 87

ZKJ-1 combat control system, 230

ZKJ-3 combat control system, 230

ZKJ-4 combat control system, 230

ZKJ-5 combat control system, 229–30

Zubr-class (Project 1232.2) LCACs, 60n71, 141

Zumwalt-class (DDG-1000) destroyers (United States), 244, 311, 318, 329n6